新时代商务英语专业系列教材
New Era Business English Series

总主编 / 翁凤翔　郭桂杭

International
Business
Negotiation

国际商务谈判

主　编 / 朱丹亚
副主编 / 余　静　谭　亮

重庆大学出版社

内 容 提 要

本书是面向商务专业本科学生的商务谈判教材,体现了国际商务谈判理论和商务谈判实践相结合,针对性和实用性相结合,真实性与通用性相结合的特点。全书共八章,系统地介绍了国际商务谈判的概念、特点、原则、过程步骤、谈判策略和技巧以及各国谈判风格等,并附有大量的案例和习题,适合商务英语专业的学生和从事相关工作的企事业人员使用。

图书在版编目(CIP)数据

国际商务谈判/朱丹亚主编.—重庆:重
庆大学出版社,2017.1(2021.8 重印)
商务英语专业系列教材
ISBN 978-7-5689-0384-4

Ⅰ.①国… Ⅱ.①朱… Ⅲ.①国际商务—商务谈判—
高等学校—教材—英文 Ⅳ.①F740.41

中国版本图书馆 CIP 数据核字(2017)第 006859 号

国际商务谈判
GUOJI SHANGWU TANPAN
主 编 朱丹亚

责任编辑:牟 妮 张晓琴 版式设计:张晓琴
责任校对:邬小梅   责任印制:赵 晟

*

重庆大学出版社出版发行
出版人:饶帮华
社址:重庆市沙坪坝区大学城西路 21 号
邮编:401331
电话:(023)88617190 88617185(中小学)
传真:(023)88617186 88617166
网址:http://www.cqup.com.cn
邮箱:fxk@ cqup.com.cn(营销中心)
全国新华书店经销
重庆市正前方彩色印刷有限公司印刷

*

开本:787mm×1092mm 1/16 印张:20.5 字数:489 千
2017 年 2 月第 1 版 2021 年 8 月第 3 次印刷
ISBN 978-7-5689-0384-4 定价:59.50 元

总　序

　　商务英语作为本科专业获得教育部批准进入我国大学本科教育基本目录已经好些年了。商务英语本科专业的身份与地位获得了我国官方和外语界的认可。迄今为止，据不完全统计，有300所左右的大学开设了商务英语本科专业。各种商务英语学术活动也开始活跃。商务英语专业与英语语言文学专业、翻译专业成为我国英语教学的"三驾马车"。商务英语教学在全国已经形成较大规模，正呈良性发展态势，越来越多的大学正在积极准备申报商务英语本科专业。可以预计，将来在我国，除了研究性大学外的大部分普通本科院校的外语学院都可能开设商务英语本科专业。这是大势所趋，因为随着我国改革开放和经济全球化、世界经济一体化进程的加快，各个融入经济一体化的国家和地区急需有扎实英语功底的，熟悉国际商务基本知识的，具备国际商务领域操作技能的跨文化商务交际复合型、应用型商务英语人才。

　　高校商务英语专业教育首先必须有充足的合格师资；其次，需要有合适的教材。目前，虽然市面上有很多商务英语教材，但是，完整的四年商务英语本科专业教材并不多。重庆大学出版社出版的商务英语本科专业系列教材一定程度上能满足当前商务英语本科专业的教学需要。

　　本套系列教材能基本满足商务英语本科专业1—4年级通常开设课程的需要。商务英语专业不是商务专业而是语言专业。所以，基础年级的教材仍然是英语语言学习教材。但是，与传统的英语语言文学专业教材不同的是：商务英语专业学生所学习的英语具有显著的国际商务特色。所以，本套教材特别注重商务英语本科专业教育的特点，在基础阶段的英语技能教材中融入了商务英语元素，让学生在学习普通英语的同时，接触一些基础的商务英语语汇，通过听、说、读、写、译等技能训练，熟悉掌握商务英语专业四级和八级考试词汇，熟悉基础的商务英语篇章，了解国际商务常识。

　　根据我国《高等学校商务英语本科专业教学质量国家标准》（以下简称《标准》），本套教材不仅包含一、二年级的基础教材，还包含高年级的继续夯实商务英语语言知识的教材，如《高级商务英语教程》1—3册等。此外，还包括英语语言文学专业学生所没有的突出商务英语本科专业特色的国际商务知识类教材，如《国际商务概论》《国际贸易实务》《国际贸易法》《市场营销》等。本套教材的总主编都是教育部商务英语专业教学协作组成员，参与了该《标准》的起草与制定，熟悉《标准》的要求，这为本套教材的质量提供了基本保障。此外，参与编写本套教材的主编及编者都是多年从事商务英语教学与研究的有经验的教师，因而，在教材的内容、体例、知识、练习以及辅助教材等方面，都充分考虑到了教材使用者的需求。教材的编写宗旨是：力求传授实用的商务英语知识和国际商务有关领域的知识，提高学生的商务英语综合素质和跨文化商务交际能力以及思辨创新能力。

教材编写考虑到了以后推出的全国商务英语本科专业四级和专业八级的考试要求。在教材的选材、练习、词汇等方面都尽可能与商务英语本科专业四级、八级考试对接。

本套教材特别适合培养复合型、应用型的商务英语人才的商务英语本科专业的学生使用，也可作为商务英语爱好者学习商务英语的教材。教材中若存在不当和疏漏之处，敬请专家、学者及教材使用者批评指正，以便我们不断修订完善。

翁凤翔

2016 年 3 月

Contents

Chapter V   Ways of Breaking an Impasse in Negotiation

Chapter VI   Communication Skills in International Business Negotiation

Chapter VII   Styles of International Business Negotiation

Chapter VIII   The Principles of Negotiation ················ **300**

Chapter I Basics of International Business Negotiation

learning Objectives

After studying this chapter, you will be able to:

- Define international business negotiation.

- Identify the principles of international business negotiation.

- Describe the characteristics of international business negotiation.

- Exemplify influences of cultural differences in international business negotiation.

1 Introduction to Negotiation and Culture

Case 1

The Race between Ford and GM
The Inside Track, or So It Seemed

The pole position, the inside track, sitting in the driver's seat, all described Jim Paulsen's circumstances in January 1995. In March 1994, he had been appointed the first-ever president of Ford of China, and job one was negotiating a joint venture with Shanghai Automotive Industry Corporation. Unfortunately, Paulsen and his Ford Taurus didn't get the Chinese checkered flag. Meanwhile, GM Buicks have hit Beijing boulevards first makes for a great story, filled with international relations machinations and corporate miscalculations.

Cultural differences were the key. Let us explain.

Ford Motor Company has always been one of the most famous global firms on earth. Everyone recognizes the blue oval logo. Indeed, Henry Ford was hawking his wares in urban China about the same time that **Pearl Sydenstricker Buck** was writing about feet-binding in rural China in her 1930s classic, The Good Earth. Henry Ford II was one of the first American executives to meet with Deng Xiaoping after China reopened its economic doors in 1978. Moreover, Ford had moved into the local area faster than GM. At the start of the race Ford already had three parts-related joint ventures in China with a fourth in the works. Although American Motors/Chrysler had been producing Jeeps in Beijing for some 10 years, the Shanghai Automotive deal was really the first major production venture open to American firms. Shanghai Auto was the largest and most profitable of all Chinese automakers, already producing Audis in a joint venture with Volkswagen. The Shanghai plant was targeted for production of about 100,000 **sedans** sand 200,000 **vans** per year—a $2 billion capital investment.

Ford had been talking with the Shanghai folks in secret for some time. But events in Washington, D.C. put the negotiations on the front pages in both countries. On February 6, 1995, the Clinton administration announced the imposition of trade sanctions on China for its continuous violations of intellectual property agreements, slapping 100 percent tariffs on $1.08 billion cellular phones, sporting goods, and plastic articles coming from the Middle Kingdom.

The Beijing response was twofold. First, **retaliatory** tariffs placed on CDs, video games, films, cigarettes, and alcoholic beverages coming from the United States to China. Second, the threat was made that all talks with American automakers about joint ventures would be suspended. Both Washington and Beijing put a February 26 deadline on discussions after which sanctions would go into effect.

On February 14, Lu Jian, President of Shanghai Auto, announced that both Ford and GM had been instructed to submit their final bids by the end of the month. "Previous to the 14th the identity of the Chinese company negotiating with Ford had been confidential. Moreover, Shanghai

Auto had been talking with Japanese firms as well." In an interview with the Wall Street Journal Mr. Lu stated, "Toyota was just *tooting* its horn because of the threat of a trade war with the United States... I told them frankly that, while we hope at some point to have cooperation with them, we will continue now to negotiate with the Americans. Toyota is at the back of the line."

It really didn't matter whether it was Toyota's demonstrated reluctance to share technology with the Chinese or the latter's obvious need to *bolster* the credibility of their counter threats regarding the auto talks with the Americans. In fact, both circumstances probably worked together to push Ford and GM to the front of the line. But, please note Mr. Lu's further comments in the Journal: "Everything is on track except for the possibility of a trade war. If a trade war breaks out, then everything is delayed, maybe canceled. If there is no trade war, then I can tell you that we will choose Ford or GM." Finally, we doubt that Mr. Lu spoke of the two American firms with consideration to alphabetical order.

Jim Paulsen in the Driver's Seat

So, as of mid-February, Ford was in the lead. And, Jim Paulsen was at the wheel. After visits to the U.S. Trade Representative and the Commerce and State Departments in Washington, D.C., Paulsen and his wife stopped over in southern California for a couple of weeks of cross-cultural training at the University of California Merage School of Business. "That's where we first met." Jim told us that he was appalled by the lack of knowledge about China displayed by all the Clinton appointees he had talked with. We had been recommended to Jim by the folks at the Ford Executive Development Center in Detroit. We had provided advice and training to executives there for a number of years regarding their Japanese business associations. About 2,000 of their executives had been through a three-day program of our design on negotiating with the Japanese. However, now the topic was China, a very different cup of tea! Jim and his wife spent most of the two weeks at the university working with Katherine Xin, a Beijing native who is now the Michelin Chair in Leadership and Human Resource Management at the China Europe International Business School (CEIBS) in Shanghai. Better cross-cultural training for a leadership role in China was available nowhere else. Jim Paulsen is a very bright and an affable Midwesterner. An engineer by training and a career-long Ford man, he had worked on plant-related issues in several foreign countries including Mexico, the Czech Republic, Poland, and France. However, he had had no previous experience living overseas.

Jim had spent the previous 18 months traveling back and forth to China working on the Shanghai Auto deal and others. Ford "put the *pedal* to the metal" with the announcement by CEO Alex Trotman that the company was sponsoring a research program for developing environmentally friendly auto engines with the Chinese Academy of Science. On February 16 he handed Song Jian, the Science and Technology Minister of China, a set of keys to a shiny new Ford Taurus, fitted with an engine that ran on a mixture of gasoline and methanol.

Meanwhile the trade row *fizzled*. As one *pundit* put it, threatening trade sanctions made sense for both sides in the piracy dispute, but actually implementing them made no sense at all. That is, talking tough served to consolidate domestic political power—both China and the United States, but neither country could totally afford the costs of a trade war. So the issue was settled by the end of February, of course only to arise again the following year.

However, the duel between the American carmakers was still.

GM followed Ford almost immediately with its own announcements about technology transfers to Chinese institutes. In March the firm contributed 1 million yuan (about $120,000 at the time) to establish the Delphi Automotive Systems Technology Institute at the prestigious Tsinghua University in Beijing. Oh, by the way, Tsinghua also happens to be the *alma mater* of many of China'ssenior leaders. In China, alma mater matters. It matters more than most westerners can imagine, and the arrangement at Tsinghua was just the first of several planned as components of the larger GM-China Technology Institute involving GM's technical centers and research labs.

Jim Paulsen was particularly good at managing the negotiations with the Ford home office. Jacques Nasser, then product development vice president in Detroit, had *nixed* a key product adaptation for the Chinese market. Because the Tauruses would mostly be driven by chauffeurs in China, leg room had to be maximized in the back seat—not a cheap change. Paulsen knew the Detroit organization well enough to risk going over Nasser's head directly to Alex Trotman. He won that battle, but the war waged on over the summer.

Enter Shirley Young

The key event in the race was GM's introduction of Shirley Young into its pit crew. Yes, women can and often do make a difference in international business negotiations. Ms. Young not only brought a marketing imagination to the GM team, but she also brought great gaunxi (connections). Young had joined GM in 1988 as vice president of Consumer Market Development. She had been a consultant to GM since 1983 and had worked for a variety of communications and marketing strategy firms, including a stint as president of Grey Strategic Marketing. She served on the boards of the Promus Companies, Bell Atlantic, and the Bombay Company. She was a vice chair of the nominating committee of the New York Stock Exchange and was a member of the Business Advisory Council for the U.S. State Department Agency for International Development. Ms. Young was also chair of the Committee of 100, a national Chinese-American leadership group, and on the board of the Shanghai Symphony Orchestra (the last after a $125,000 donation made by GM). In the educational community Ms. Young was a trustee of Wellesley College, Philips Academy Andover, and the Interlochen Center for the Arts, and on the board of directors of the Associates of the Harvard Business School. Her numerous awards included Woman of the Year separately for the American Advertising Federation and the Chinese American Planning Council. Yes, very well connected in the United States.

And, she gets a load of her China credentials. Ms. Young was born in Shanghai, and she still has relatives there. She speaks Mandarin fluently. Her father, Clarence Kuangson Young, is a hero in both China and Taiwan, having been killed by the Japanese when he was China's consul general to the Philippines during World War II. As a Tsinghua alum, he is memorialized on the campus in Beijing. Also, her stepfather was at one time the Chinese ambassador to the United States, the United Kingdom, and France. Yes, great guanxi. GM appointed Young as an advisor to Rudolph Schlais, the GM vice president in charge of China operations. Schlais himself had negotiated three joint-venture agreements in China before. But, GM also had her maintain a reporting relationship to a marketing vice president in Detroit. Thus, her role was more than an underling to Schlais. Her job was to promote technology transfer and to impart marketing expertise in China. Perhaps even more important than her professional brilliance, her connections, and her resume was the way she managed the negotiations. From the spring into the late summer the negotiations involved great numbers of Chinese executives and dignitaries who descended on Detroit to study their potential partners. Young organized GM's 1,000 plus Chinese-American employees to meet and greet the visitors and formed a committee to advise the company on relations with China. She was likewise successful in delivering the top American executives to Shanghai. For example, GM CEO John Smith made three trips to Shanghai during the negotiations. Five of GM's top seven executives also did the Shanghai *shuffle* during September and October. Such a dedication of executive resources was unprecedented in the history of the firm's international alliance efforts. Shanghai Auto executives were also treated to a trip to Brazil to see up close GM's new high-tech operations there. Rio is nice during the summer!

Shirley Young well understood that there is no such thing as international business. Nations don't talk to one another. Nor do companies talk to one another. Only people do. There is only interpersonal business. Particularly for the Chinese, face-to-face meetings and relationships between people at all levels are the essential elements of successful negotiations.

The Last Lap

On August 25 Vaughn Koshkarian replaced Jim Paulsen as president of Ford of China. Koshkarian's *biography* included a Northwestern MBA and 33 years at Ford, mostly in the finance chain of command. During the 1980s he worked in both Japan and Europe. Yes, he brought more international experience to the job than Jim Paulsen, but he still had no specific experience in China and no Chinese language skills. Jim Paulsen had served just 19 months in Beijing before retiring. According to him, it was actually more like seven months in Beijing, six months in Shanghai, and six months in airplanes flying between the two. Changing drivers was Ford's admission that it had fallen behind in the race.

The Post-Race Analysis

GM and Shanghai Auto inked their deal on October 31 in Detroit. Plans were to produce 100,000 midsized Buick Regals by 1997 in a new billion-dollar assembly plant in Shanghai. Eventually *minivans* would be produced as well.

Both Ford and GM had invested and/or committed millions of dollars in establishing technology institutes and component pans manufacturing facilities during the negotiations. At the time a Ford spokesperson in Beijing blamed the lost contract on the Taurus sedan—it was "too modern" despite the engineering changes Jim Paulsen had forced through the Dearborn bureaucracy.

Alternatively, GM explained that beyond its car capabilities it offered up technology from both its Hughes Electronics Corp. and Electronic Data Systems units. Ford couldn't match those broad computer technologies.

Jim Paulsen later **reminisced** in TIME Magazine, "We tried to find out more about how they were arriving at their decisions, but we didn't have enough Chinese-speaking people to establish close contact with the officials in Shanghai. We were playing catch-up and with fewer resources." In the same article Wayne Booker, president of Ford's Asia Pacific operations and Jim Paulsen's boss, added, "You can't understand a foreign market unless you have capable, experienced nationals on staff."

"Experienced nationals" need to be at or near the top of American foreign ventures, particularly in China. Jim Paulsen had been a very successful executive at Ford, but he simply did not have the resume for success in China. Training can go only so far. Even two weeks of the best possible cross-cultural training cannot make up for a lack of foreign living experience in an international manager's credentials. In a very real sense Jim Paulsen was not shanghaied by either Shanghai Auto or GM. Jim Paulsen was actually shanghaied ("put by trickery into an undesirable position") in Detroit by Ford itself.

Finally, as a postscript, we are happy to report that in January 1998 Ford finally did **wise up** and appoint an ethnic Chinese executive to a senior position in Beijing. MeiWeicheng has now replaced Vaughn Koshkarian as chairman and CEO of Ford of China (Koshkarian was bumped up to CEO, and later to president of Ford Asia Pacific). Cheng was a vice president and regional executive for General Electric's appliance businesses based in Hong Kong. And, at long last, in April 2001 Ford completed a 50-50 joint venture agreement with Chongqing Changan Automobile Company, China's third largest automaker, to produce 50,000 small cars in Sichuan province in the southwest. But Ford has still not recovered from being shamed in Shanghai. In 2005 GM took over market leadership from Volkswagen affiliated brands, and it still outsells Ford-produced cars in China by a three-to-one ratio (665,000 to 220,000 units).

(*Excerpts from* China Now *by N. Mark Lam & John L. Graham*)

Questions for Case-analysis:

1. What was the national and international environment for the negotiation between GM and Shanghai Auto?

2. What is the role played by Shirley Young? Is her role successful?

3. What differences in Chinese and American cultures can be summarized from Shirley Young's role in the negotiation?

4. How did Ford realize they were behind in the race? What were the steps they took to make up?

5. What was the attitude from Shanghai in the race in your mind even it was not mentioned in the case?

The above case illustrates some of the difficulties of international business negotiations. When negotiators are from different cultures, each may make different assumptions about social interaction, economic interests, legal requirements and political realities. These assumptions affect negotiators' decisions, like when and how to negotiate, their interests and priorities, and their strategies: the way they go about negotiating.

Today, international negotiation is much harder than ever before because international business itself is changing. The business world is increasingly globalized and diversified. More firms are doing business across borders. In early 2006, Luxembourg-based steelmaker Arcelor, which had successfully lured Canada's Dofasco away from Germany's ThyssenKrupp the previous year, became itself the acquisition target of Mittal Steel, an Indian-controlled firm headquartered in the Netherlands. During the same period, U.S.-owned Boeing sold 27,787-Dreamliners to Air India and finalized a supply contract with Japan's Toray for the carbon fiber needed to produce the aircraft. In China, Google Inc. (U.S.) negotiated with government authorities over regulatory conditions for operation of their Internet search engine. More competition means that executives need negotiating skills and the ability to forge co-operative agreements as never before if firms are to survive, let alone to remain competitive in the international marketplace.

Such being the case, in today's global environment, negotiators who understand cultural differences and negotiation fundamentals have a decided advantage at the bargaining table.

⇨ 1.1   Negotiation

1.1.1   Definition of Negotiation

People negotiate every day. In every ordinary day, we may negotiate with

- Our boss, regarding an unexpected work assignment
- Colleagues, deciding whether to stay late at work to finish a project
- Subordinates, regarding unexpected overtime
- Professors, getting an extension on our unfinished assignments
- A supplier, about a problem with raw materials inventory management
- A contractor, decorating a new kitchen at our home
- A banker, over the terms of a business loan
- A partner, deciding where and how to invest your joint capital
- A government official, regarding compliance with environmental regulations
- A recruiter, discussing the salary and benefits we feel we deserve
- A real estate agent, over the lease on a new warehouse
- A travel agency, arranging a trip abroad

- Our spouse, over who will walk the dog
- Someone we love, regarding making up, or rebuilding a relationship
- Our child, over when to go to bed
- A friend, regarding borrowing a musical instrument
- A car dealer, bidding for a used car

In short, negotiation is a common, everyday activity that most people use to influence others and to achieve personal objectives.

"Negotiation" derives from the Latin word "Negotiari", which means "to do business". Now in a broader sense, Negotiation refers to the process in which at least two conflicting, independent parties attempt (through the communication process) to reach a mutually satisfying agreement.

The world we are living now is full of conflicts. Conflict is inevitable and no culture is immune to conflict. Whenever one individual's needs, wants and desires conflict with another's, we have the potential for negotiation. For most of us, 90 percent of the resources we need to do our jobs and live our lives are owned by someone else. Therefore, negotiation is a survival skill. People use, or should use, negotiation skill for resolving disputes and reaching decisions in teams and other multi-party environment. In business, disputes often arise when deals do not work out quite the way all parties have envisioned. That's where negotiations come in.

Christopher W. Moore and Peter J. Woodrow (Moore and Woodrow, 2010) point out that negotiations take place in a wide range of contexts, from simple market bargaining to complex processes to end wars within or between nations. They provide a schematic range of situations in which people from different cultures often engage in negotiations (table 1.1).

The examples in the table represent both simple and complex situations and one that involve less or more conflicts. They note that situations of a relatively little conflict can easily become continuous and move toward the right side of the table. Therefore, trade negotiations are usually held in it in an atmosphere in which both sides are looking for mutual gain.

Table 1.1　Range of Negotiation Contexts

Less complex				More complex	
Market bargaining	Contract negotiation	Negotiation of international norms	Negotiation of bilateral or multi-lateral assistance (development, humanitarian assistance, military aid)	Social conflict	International conflict

continued

Less complex					More complex
Sales agreement (house, car, products, resources)	Trade agreement	Labor-management negotiations		Gang violence	Border dispute
		Environmental standards		Civil war secession	Dispute over a shared resource Invasion or takeover
				Ethnic conflict	Survival
Less conflict					More conflict

(*Adapted from* Handbook of Global and Multicultural Negotiation *by Christopher W. Moore and Peter J. Woodrow*)

1.1.2 Characteristics of Negotiation

Negotiation is a complex process which has the following characteristics:

1) Negotiation is a process.

It is a sequence of activities, perhaps with an underlying pattern. It is not a single event. During the negotiation process, choices are made, which will affect how agreement is achieved and what the agreement will be.

2) One negotiation needs at least two parties.

Having more than two parties does not alter the fundamental duality of the process. But when constituencies or other parties have an interest in the outcome of the negotiation, the negotiation becomes more complex.

3) Divergence in interests, goals for participants in a negotiation.

If there are no differences, there is no need to negotiate. The difference in interests, goals and ways of doing business is the source of conflict and competition in a negotiation. Then negotiation is a must for mutual satisfaction.

4) The incentive for both parties to resolve their disputes.

It is the incentive to reach agreement and expand business that generates cooperation between the parties. The need to settle their differences also helps negotiators understand their power.

5) Negotiations involve trying to reach agreement.

It suggests that negotiators might not always succeed and also that reaching a good agreement takes some effort. If a negotiation is reached easily then it is probably not a good negotiation, it is likely that some value has been left on the negotiation table.

6) Negotiations result in an agreement, which might be an agreement to walk away.

The notion of "agreement" sounds positive but nothing about negotiation guarantees that an agreement is a positive outcome. The parties might agree but only reluctantly. While the focus of a negotiation is on reaching agreement the most important aspect of any negotiation is not the agreement itself, but how it is implemented. The agreement is only a part of the outcome to any negotiation.

1.1.3 *Negotiation Stages*

Case 2

In 1982, GM and Toyota began their negotiations. Both appreciated the *tremendous* advantages of pursuing the *joint venture*: GM was motivated by the fact that the venture would produce a competitive, profitable compact car, designed entirely by Toyota to enhance its line. The final product, which was to be sold through Chevrolet dealers throughout the USA would give GM the opportunity of winning back its share of the small-car market. Finally, GM's management and workers would have the opportunity of observing Japanese manufacturing and management methods at first hand, and learn from this experience.

From the point-of-view of Toyota, the Joint venture was equally attractive because it would give them an *avenue* through which to establish their presence in the American market, at a time when public attitudes towards imported cars had been dampening. Two of Toyota's competitors, Nissan and Honda had already established their own plants in the USA; it was only logical for Toyota to *follow suit* to maintain its competitiveness. Unlike its competitors, though, Toyota didn't take as many risks since its affiliation with GM eliminated the need to invest additional capital in a plant.

However, at this initial stage, the problems and issues faced by GM-Toyota were tremendous. The primary negotiating parties involved were the GM-Toyota group vs. the American workers, formerly hired by GM at the Fremont plant. Other secondary negotiating parties with which the GM-Toyota group had to content were the Federal Trade Commission (FTC), other American motor-car industrial giants like Chrysler and the American public in general.

First, the joint venture needed the approval of the **FTC**, a major regulatory agency. Chrysler, one of GM's major competitors in the American motor-car industry, was *lobbying* strongly against the approval of the venture and filed a lawsuit, claiming that it violated the country's *antitrust* laws. Toyota hired a large Washington law firm to work on getting FTC approval. Eventually, the FTC ruled that since the joint venture was to be undertaken within a limited time period, it was legally permissible.

Secondly, the joint venture was affected by the actions of GM concerning its workforce at the

Fremont plant. GM shut down the plant in early 1982 but was still under contractual obligation to rehire the laid-off workers, should the joint venture with Toyota occur. Horror stories about the workers at the Fremont plant had been circulating for years. The Japanese were especially aware that the workers were notorious for drug use, *sabotage*, violence and high *grievance* rates. The plant, one of GM's worst, had a very poo history of labor management relations. They didn't want that to happen again, and so they were quite *adamant* about not hiring any of the former workers for the joint venture. On top of that, the Japanese had very basic doubts about the ability of even an adequate American workforce to deliver the same quality of performance and devotion they were accustomed to seeing in Japan. Toyota strongly demanded complete freedom in running the Fremont plant; and GM responded to it positively by guaranteeing them a totally free hand. Meanwhile the Fremont workers who were members of the United Auto Workers (UAW) Local 1364 were pushing for 100 per cent rehiring and the recognition of the UAW as their bargaining agent.

Thirdly, there were many communication problems between the Japanese and Americans because the US team didn't know the Japanese language, and the Japanese weren't proficient in English and needed more time to grasp the fundamental concepts of American labor law. Cross-cultural "noise" resulting from cultural differences had to be managed in discussions between the Japanese and the Americans.

Finally, in early 1983, GM and Toyota invited former US Secretary of Labor, William J. Usery, Jr, to act as the chief negotiator between their team and the parties they had to deal with. Usery was well aware of the opposing interests involved, and he was prudent enough to first clarify his position before he began his work. When he was interviewed by Toyota, Usery said he didn't want to be called "chief negotiator", because this implied he worked solely for Toyota and GM. He appreciated the need for him to be perceived as neutral, particularly by the UAW, in order to gain their trust and confidence. So he called himself facilitator, catalyst, mediator and consultant to improve his standing with the UAW and give him more credibility. By using those terms, he thought he would leave the impression that he was above the interests of all parties involved and would act *impartially*, even though he was in fact employed by GM and Toyota.

Usery knew that the timing of the negotiations for the *joint venture* was favorable. In 1983 the American motor-car industry was at a low point—thousands of workers had been laid off, and jobs were highly sought after. (Stage 1) (Stevens, 1988; Riemer, 1988; Sesit, 1988)

Before he started his mediation work, Usery knew that in order to be fully effective, he first had to be accepted by the **UAW**. So he met with the then UAW President, Douglas Fraser, and incoming President, Owen Bieber. He told them he had been retained by GM and Toyota as facilitator between them and the UAW. Fraser expressed support for the joint venture, but Bieber was *noncommittal*. They discussed the UAW convention that was coming up in May 1983; the UAW might condemn the joint venture at the meeting or, at least, refuse to take part in it until all Fremont workers were rehired. To prevent such resolutions from being passed, Usery suggested having a press conference before the convention to give the UAW members a clear understanding of the joint venture's intentions regarding the rehiring issue.

Here, Usery was faced with the ultimate difficulty of designing an initial presentation that would win UAW support, knowing fully well that Toyota was strongly against rehiring the Fremont workers. He knew too that Fraser's initial support for the joint venture was based on the **premise** that the UAW would eventually be recognized as the workers' official bargaining agent when the Fremont workers were rehired.

Before leaving for Japan, Usery met with GM executives to sound them out on how the UAW should be dealt with. Under American labor law, a firm may not bargain with a union until that union has been officially recognized. But a union cannot exist without its first having a workforce. That was precisely where the problem lay: negotiations with the UAW could not begin without having a workforce for the joint venture. GM's lawyers advised Usery to take the position of not recognizing the UAW until a full workforce had been hired. In the meantime the GM-Toyota group would take a neutral stand. It would recognize the UAW in the future and bargain with it when the UAW had the support of the majority of the workers hired by GM and Toyota for their Fremont plant. Usery anticipated that a neutral stance would be unacceptable to the UAW.

While caught in this dilemma, Usery left for Japan, where he began a series of intense educational sessions with Toyota executives. Thus he **rehashed** the fundamentals of American labor law and emphasized the crucial importance of recognizing the UAW and rehiring the Fremont workforce. Although the Japanese didn't **budge** from their initial position, Usery wasn't fazed and persisted in his campaign. He explained that refusing to hire a person on the basis of his or her previous association with the Fremont plant was illegal in the USA because it was regarded as discrimination. By refusing to hire the old Fremont workers, "atmosphere of harmony", so important to the Japanese, would be hard to establish. He remembered that the Japanese had publicly announced they were seeking "an atmosphere of harmony" in this joint venture. Toyota's hard line would only estrange the heavily unionized and liberal San Francisco Bay Area, where Fremont was located.

While Usery was in Japan talking with Toyota, GM announced it would have no responsibility for the venture's labor relations structure and that Toyota would be fully responsible for this task. Thus more pressure was placed on Usery to get Toyota to see things his way.

Usery finally succeeded in obtaining a **concession** from the Japanese by getting them to agree to use the old Fremont workforce as a "primary source" for recruitment. Long hours were spent simply getting the Japanese to understand the concept behind the words "primary source". Usery intended the phrase to mean that the joint venture would first hire from the old Fremont workers, but it would not be restricted from seeking workers from other sources as well.

Usery announced the intentions of GM-Toyota to use the Fremont workforce as a "primary source" of workers in a press conference held a few days before the UAW convention. This clarified their official position to UAW members, and there were no more serious objections to the joint venture by the UAW. Usery succeeded in maintaining goodwill with the UAW. (Stage 2)

(Solomon, 1987; Heard, 1987; Tully, 1988)

Usery scheduled several informal meetings with the UAWs new President Bieber after the May 1983 convention to try to move towards a greater degree of agreement with the union. Usery was disappointed that Bieber was not as enthusiastic about the joint venture as was the previous President, Fraser. For instance, Fraser had previously agreed that old seniority rights in GM need not be observed under the joint venture, which would be considered an entirely new *entity*. Bieber, new in his role as UAW President, needed to prove himself, and so he went back to the old extreme demands, namely recognition of the UAW and the rehiring of all the old workers.

Although Usery wanted to establish better interpersonal relationships with Bieber after the convention, his new "bottom line" demands got in the way. Even though there was no progress towards an agreement, at least Usery had a better idea of how deeply Bieber was committed to the stronger demands. (Stage 3) (Heard, 1987; Rossant, 1987)

To emphasize their claims to the full recognition, the UAW maintained that Roger Smith, GM's Chairman, had once implied he would guarantee such recognition. In addition, they demanded to deal with Smith in future meetings. Any binding obligation as a result of Smith's *alleged* guarantees was quickly denied by GM's representatives. Toyota's legal counsel responded to this situation by drafting a letter of intent. It stated that the joint venture intended to begin, intended to hire a workforce and intended to maintain a neutral position in the matter of recognizing the UAW. Bieber quickly rejected this letter of intent. He knew it was not legally binding.

Usery realized that the next time he went to Japan, he had to be more persistent and creative in handling the Toyota executives. He needed to reformulate their side's strategy to salvage the rapidly deteriorating relationship they had with Bieber and the UAW. Once again, it is important to recall that one of the main problems of the joint venture was that it could not bargain with the UAW since GM and Toyota officials could not legally recognize it as the official bargaining agent of the plant workers until the latter were hired and had held an election. The election's result would either be a union (probably the UAW) or no union. The UAW knew it was overstepping its bounds—it couldn't legally function on behalf of a workforce that wasn't there yet.

But after talking with his side's lawyers, Usery found it was possible for the joint venture officials to start bargaining even before a workforce was hired, if one of two things happened: (1) if it could be shown that the joint venture had bargaining obligations as a "successor employer", but NUMMI (New United Motor Manufacturing Inc., the joint venture of GM and Toyota) was a new entity and couldn't claim to be a successor to GM in Fremont; or the only other way successorship obligations could be assumed would be (2) that NUMMI agree to hire at least 50 per cent of the new workers from the old workforce. (Heard, 1987)

So, armed with this knowledge on his next trip to Japan, Usery jumped at the chance to reformulate his side's strategy by renewing his campaign to persuade Toyota to agree to hire at least a majority of the old workforces. (Stage 4)

When Usery met with the UAW again. His reformulated offer—NUMMI as a "successor employer" would hire at least 50 percent of the old workforce—was rejected by the UAW, who demanded that all members of the old workforce be rehired. Subsequent proposals sent to the UAW which reiterated joint venture demands were also summarily rejected. Each meeting that followed ended in **deadlock**.

Usery didn't give up, though. He continued to search for a solution or some loopholes that would satisfy both sides. When everybody else was giving up on the possibility of coming to an agreement, Usery finally realized that time had been wasted pursuing something that simply should not have been sought for in the first place: NUMMJ did not really need a collective bargaining agreement with the UAW. All that both sides really needed was to come to some kind of understanding that they were willing to work together on a cooperative basis and that labor relations would be handled with trust. When he realized this, Usery tried to convince both sides to sign a letter of intent, spelling out the areas of agreement between the joint venture and the UAW. The letter would schedule collective bargaining at some time in the future. Usery succeeded in convincing the UAW to sign the letter in principle. Then, after obtaining still another extension, Usery worked on getting both sides to agree on the contents of the letter. At this point, only minor matters of language had to be resolved in the drafting of the letter. Both sides were relieved that they didn't have to deal with the pressures of concluding a collective bargaining session with so little time left. And the UAW even made a gesture of good faith by disbanding the former Fremont local and revoking its charter. (Stage 5) (Tully, 1988)

A new problem cropped up after the UAW's gesture of good faith. Local 1364, the Fremont chapter of the UAW filed a lawsuit against the national union, charging that the national union violated its own constitution and by-laws. It also asked for an injunction to prevent NUMMI and the UAW from signing an agreement. The UAW responded that since the Fremont plant no longer existed, it acted within its rights to the charter. Eventually the case against the UAW was dismissed, both NUMMI and the UAW agreed on the language used in the letter of intent and it was signed.

At this point, Usery had other parties to worry about. He still had to get the FTC's approval of the joint venture. In effect, his job was to act as a public relations spokesperson for the joint venture to win the approval of the American public as a whole. Lee Iacocca, President of Chrysler, was most vocal in his objections to the joint venture. He said this was an underhanded way for GM and Toyota to gain an unfair advantage in the motor-car industry. Chrysler filed a lawsuit charging that the joint venture violated the country's antitrust laws, but later withdrew its suit when it formed its own similar joint venture with Mitsubishi. After GM and Toyota signed a consent decree giving the FTC the power to monitor its activities, the FTC approved the joint venture on 11 April 1984, about two years after GM and Toyota started their original talks.

Before the first Novas rolled off the Fremont assembly line, NUMMI set up an interim labor relations structure at the Fremont plant. It hired a large consulting firm to create the initial wage and benefits package for the first employees. The package was modified after the plant became unionized, and the new local and NUMMI conducted its first collective bargaining sessions. (Stage 6)

(*Adapted from* Trends in Multinational Business and Global Environments: A perspective *by William A.Dymsza*)

The GM-Toyota negotiation illustrates how the six stages apply to a typical negotiation.

Usually, a typical negotiation has the six main stages:

Stage 1: Pre-negotiation

A period of determining objectives in relation to the opportunities and problems involved in the scenario.

At this stage, determine your objective in relation to the opportunities presented by the environment and the difficulties posed by situational factors. List the relevant issues that affect your opportunities and constraints. Prepare a tentative list both outlining your interests and those of the other side (TOS) with an accompanying list of acceptable trade-offs. Establish the level of your best first offer. Anticipate TOS's reactions. What are your contingency plans for each possible reaction? You'll have to assemble your negotiation team at this stage. (Dymsza, 1984; Daniels and Radebaugh, 1986)

Stage 2: Entry

The formal sales presentation to TOS is made at this time.

This is when you make your first formal presentation to TOS. It should be a strong selling proposal.

Stage 3: Establishing effective relationships with TOS

This is the time for establishing trust and rapport and earning the right to learn the needs and objectives of TOS.

At this point, both you and TOS have to get to know one another better. International sensitivities are varied, and different cultures perceive this need differently. For instance, Americans and West Germans don't attach too much importance to personal matters. Their "bottom line" is the efficiency of carrying out the transaction itself, and they are impatient to get down to business immediately. Other people, such as South Americans, Mexicans, Filipinos, Chinese, Singaporeans, Malaysians and Japanese, attach great importance to this phase because long-term relationships are valued and nurtured in these cultures. In those nations the efficiency of the business transaction is subordinated to the interest of maintaining smooth interpersonal relationships.

At this stage, you'll need to earn the right to learn the needs and objectives of TOS. We say in our seminars that you can't even begin to negotiate until you learn these—and they are hard to find out. Remember that your initial presentation at the entry stage has been mostly based on your perception of their needs and objectives. This is the lime for you to refine your definition of their needs by winning the trust and confidence necessary to get past the level of pleasant civility to a deeper level of exchange of mutual information and interests. It is usually during the meetings at this stage that you are first able to discover the true feelings and thoughts of TOS about the issues. The "truth" often slips out in casual encounters because we tend to let our guards down then.

Stage 4: Learning more about TOS and reformulation of your early strategies

Mistaken and inaccurate assumptions are corrected at this time to arrive at better proposals to meet the need of TOS.

From the casual meetings that you use to establish a more comfortable level of interpersonal rapport, your focus shifts to finding out much more information about the needs and desires of TOS and about the situation. Since the "ice has been broken", it should be easier to obtain this information. This will help you correct your initial (incorrect) assumptions in formulating both the negotiating strategies that you have used earlier and those you plan to use.

Stage 5: Bargaining and concession-making

This is the dynamic part of the negotiation when parties involved take turns giving and taking, ideally, in defense of their "bottom line".

This is the critical part of the negotiating process. We recommend you follow four steps during this stage. It's an excellent way to conduct yourself. The four steps are: (1) separate people from the problem; (2) focus on interests, not positions; (3) invent options for mutual gain; and (4) insist on using objective criteria. We will explore each step in Chapter three.

Stage 6: Reaching agreement

After a period of exchanging *concessions*, the final round is reached when terms agreeable to both parties are made to constitute the elements of their written or verbal contracts.

At this stage, basic agreement over terms has been reached, and both sides get very close to finalizing their agreement. In most developed countries the written contract is the standard way to express the agreement. Some developed countries like Japan place a higher value on trust and honor which have been embodied in a personal relationship that has been nurtured and protected over a long time period. In fact drafting an extremely complicated contract in the presence of lawyers can even be insulting to people from Japan (and from countries similar to Japan). It is important for you to study the local practices, so that you will know the appropriate way to express your agreement.

⇨ 1.2　Culture

1.2.1　Definition of Culture

The foundation of who we are as individuals and as members of a group is initiated at birth and continues to be developed throughout our lives. This foundation is our culture. It guides how we think, what we believe, how we behave, and how we react. It is one of the main ingredients in our development as a member of our local as well as the global society.

When we think of culture, we often think exclusively in terms of national cultures that are often reported in the media. However, we find cultural differences at many levels. For instance, women and men constitute the two largest cultural groups in the world (Gilligan, 1982). We also encounter subcultures in the beliefs, attitudes, and behaviors of ethnic groups, regional groups, social classes, tribes, clans, neighborhoods, and families (Kahane, 2003; Sunshine, 1990). Governments and their agencies, corporations and private firms, universities and schools, civil society and nongovernmental organizations have their own specific cultures and ways of doing things, often called organizational culture (Deal and Kennedy, 1982; Schein, 2004). Culture is also rooted in religious beliefs, ideological persuasions, professions, and professional training and in the levels and types of education (Smith, 1989; Sunshine, 1990). Finally, families have cultures that are a blend or combination of the cultures of their adult members or of their extended families (McGoldrick, Giordano, and Garcia-Preto, 1982, 2002).

According to Samovar and Porter, "Culture is the cumulative result of experience, beliefs, values, knowledge, social organizations, perceptions of time, spatial relations, material objects and possessions, and concepts of the universe acquired or created by groups of people over the course of generations. It is socially constructed through individual and group effort and interactions. Culture manifests itself in patterns of language, behavior, activities, procedures, roles, and social structures and provides models and norms for acceptable day-to-day communication, social interaction, and achievement of desired affective and objective goals in a wide range of activities and arenas. Culture enables people to live together in a society within a given geographical environment, at a given state of technical development, and at a particular moment in time. (Samovar and Porter, 1988).

A useful metaphor for describing culture is an iceberg. Just like with an iceberg there is more to culture below the surface than above, and just like an iceberg, culture is not static, it drifts and shifts. The picture below illustrates the cultural iceberg. Visible above the squiggly "waterline" of the cultural iceberg are behaviors and institutions. Below the waterline is deeper, psychological level.

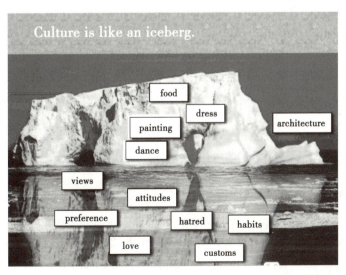

Culture is like an iceberg.

food
dress
painting   architecture
dance
views
attitudes
preference   hatred   habits
love   customs

(*Adapted from* Beyond Culture (1976) *by Edward T. Hall*)

1.2.2 Two Important Cultural Values for Negotiations

A value is a judgment of what is important in social interaction. A cultural value is a judgment shared by a group. National cultures differ in terms of shared values (Hofstede, 1980; Schwartz, 1994). Two such differences seem particularly important for negotiations: individualism versus collectivism and hierarchy versus egalitarianism. (However, other value continuums—such as a focus on traditional ways versus openness to change—may account for national cultural differences in particular negotiations.) (Kirkman, Lowe and Gibson, 2006; Brett and Crotty, forthcoming)

Individualism versus Collectivism. The continuum individualism versus collectivism distinguishes between cultures that generally place individuals'interests above those of the collective and cultures that generally place collective needs above those of individuals. In individualist cultures social, economic, and legal institutions promote the autonomy of individuals, reward individual accomplishment and protect individual rights. In collective cultures institutions promote interdependency of individuals with the others in their families, work establishments, and communities by emphasizing social obligations. Individual accomplishment reflects back on others with whom the individual is interdependent. Legal institutions support collective interests above individual interests.

Research generally categorizes nations in North America (excluding Mexico) and Western Europe as individualist cultures and pretty much the rest of the world as more or less collective, especially East Asia and Latin America. No one has studied Africa. (Hofstede, 1980)

Hierarchy versus Egalitarianism. The continuum hierarchy versus egalitarianism distinguishes between cultures that are differentiated into closed and inflexible social ranks and cultures in which social structure is relatively fiat, open, and malleable. In hierarchical cultures, social status determines social power, and social power generally transfers across situations. In egalitarian cultures, social boundaries are more permeable, and social status may be both short-lived and variable across situations.

Western cultures, especially Northern European nations, tend to be egalitarian. As you move south in Europe and on to Africa and south from North America to Central and South America, culture tends to be more hierarchical. Asian cultures are usually classified as hierarchical. (Schwartz, 1984)

1.2.3 Key Cultural Variables that Influence Negotiations

Case 3

It was Jason Wright's first important international business negotiation, and he knew he had to make a good impression and bring home a deal. He had prepared well, studied the markets, worked with his legal team to develop viable proposals, and learned a few phrases in the local language. He thought he was ready for his first meeting with Mr. Mota, the representative for

Shansu, the local company with which he was to make a deal.

Jason arrived at Shansu headquarters along with one of his legal advisors. He was ushered into a well-appointed room with comfortable easy chairs and offered something to drink. Soon Mr. Mota arrived, alone. Jason introduced himself and his colleague, and they all sat down. Mr. Mota looked at Jason with an *enigmatic* smile and said, "I see."

"But I haven't said anything yet," said Jason.

"Ah, you have said many things."

"Really? Please explain."

"Yes, I see that you have not been 'hearing'me—at least not yet."

"Now I am truly confused."

Taking pity on the young man, Mr. Mota explained, "Your company has sent a young man under thirty years old to negotiate an important commercial contract while I am old enough to be your father. I am here alone, yet you have brought your lawyer—and I see that he has a large document that looks like a proposal to me, although I could be wrong. I can see that you are eager to start talking about this deal we are to make. On the other hand, while I think I understand a bit about you, I don't know you—and you don't know me."

"I see," said Jason, beginning to sweat, and to fear that he would never get a decent bargain with this start.

"In any case," said Mr. Mota, "let us chat a bit, talk about your trip and what you have already learned about my country. Later you can have a rest, and then you and I can go to dinner together to visit some more. I will ask one of my legal team to accompany your colleague. We will have a pleasant time—and any talk of business will come at the right moment."

(*Adapted from* Lafarge Negotiations in China *by S.Fewer, D. Krohm and S.Yang*)

Questions for Case-analysis:

1. What does Jason expect to fulfill in the negotiation?

2. What is the preparation Jason has made? Is it enough? If not, make a list of preparations you think Jason has to follow before he walks into Mr. Mota's office.

3. Can you guess the cultural background of Jason and Mr. Mota? Is there any major difference between these cultures? How do these differences shape the negation?

Cultures do influence negotiations, especially international business negotiation. If negotiators fail to understand cultural differences due to different cultural backgrounds, they are more likely to encounter unnecessary misunderstandings, which may even endanger the normal negotiation. For example, during a negotiation between a class of Indian managers and American mangers, one of the American managers startled by the Indian managers'side-to-side head movements. Side-to-side head movements in U.S. culture mean no, no, no! The American manager thought negotiations were not going well, and he was really upset when many in the class continued this behavior during his debriefing. He asked his host professor, "What went wrong, they hated the class, how can we fix it for tomorrow?" He replied, "Why do you think that?" the manager said, "They shook their heads no, no, no all afternoon." "Oh," he said, "That means 'I'm listening.'"

It is normal to interpret those behaviors through the lens of one's own culture, and that such interpretation is frequently erroneous and may affect negotiation relationships and ultimately outcomes. An experienced business person must know how to circumvent the cultural barriers, try to find out common interests to get along, and deal with these differences with tolerance.

There are several important cultural variables that deeply influence negotiations: indirect dealing and direct dealing, high context and low context, relationship oriented and task oriented, and contractual and holistic cultures.

Direct Dealing versus Indirect Dealing.

People in some cultures feel quite comfortable dealing directly with another party in negotiation or in conflict resolution. They prefer meeting face-to-face with the people most directly concerned in order to try to reach agreements. Such people usually discuss a wide variety of issues quite openly, freely express emotions, and engage in arguments over important points. Most people from majority cultures in northern Europe, the United States, Canada, Australia, and New Zealand, and from India and Pakistan exhibit direct-dealing behavior.

In contrast, people from indirect-dealing cultures, especially in situations where there is actual or potential friction in their relationships, frequently prefer to carry on communications through a formal or informal intermediary. From their perspective, indirect communication allows face saving (honor or self-respect) for themselves or their counterpart, preserves smooth interpersonal or intergroup relationships, prevents direct confrontation, and can avoid uncomfortable interactions among people of different status or rank. Members of these cultures often find it embarrassing and needlessly disruptive to talk openly about conflicts, feelings, or competing interests, preferring to keep discussions general, noncontroversial, calm, and unemotional. People from many indigenous cultures around the world and some cultures from southern Europe, the Middle East, South America, and much of Asia prefer indirect communications.

The choice of direct dealing or indirect dealing is somewhat determined by the issues under discussion and the degree of tension that exists around them, the comparative rank or power of the two parties, and the risks if direct communications occur. In some cultures, business or government matters may be handled quite directly, while personal, family, or disputes over issue of honor might be addressed only indirectly. Relatively equal parties may engage in direct negotiations, while people of different ranks may be required to deal through others or feel more comfortable taking that approach.

High Context versus Low Context (Explicit Communication or Implicit Communication).

Often closely related to the direct versus indirect factor, cultures display a preference for explicit or implicit communication. Anthropologists Edward and Mildred Hall (Edward and Hall, 1990)developed a framework for understanding cultures along a continuum from high context to low context.

In high-context cultures, communication and much of the rest of human interaction is highly contextualized—in other words, the ways that people talk and deal with each other are culturally coded and dependent on prescribed patterns of relationships that in many cases are obscure to the outsider. Insiders follow unwritten rules—often quite elaborate ones—that they learn from childhood. The very meaning of words depends on the context: who says what to whom, the issues involved, and the degree of tension or controversy, for example, Communications among people in high-context settings are often imprecise, nuanced, and oriented toward saving face, preserving relationships, and allowing tactical flexibility.

High-context cultures are usually fairly homogeneous and maintain highly stratified social structures. Examples include many indigenous or tribal groups worldwide and the cultures of Japan and parts of China and Indonesia. Many of the countries of the Mediterranean and the Middle East are also high context. In addition, every county has subcultures that are high context, including extended family systems, some organizational cultures, and religious and other closely knit communities.

People in low-context cultures are much more explicit in speech and action. Discussions are more overt, detailed, specific, and clear, leaving little room for misinterpretation. The rules and expectations of interaction are often written down or even posted publicly. In a negotiation, people from a low-context culture might present a set of written proposals or demands, leaving little room for interpretation and, incidentally, often locking the parties into positions. Low-context cultures are often found in countries that have diverse populations due to immigration, such as Canada, Australia, South Africa, and the United States, where people from diverse backgrounds have become more explicit in their communications in order to work and live with each other; amalgamated countries in which diverse groups have been unified into a common nation-state, such as Germany, Russia (and the former Soviet Union), India, and Pakistan; or countries that have been colonized by any of these nations. In addition, countries with relatively egalitarian traditions and or laws, such as the United Kingdom, the Netherlands, and the Scandinavian countries, also generally use very low-context communications.

In a study, Salacuse (Salacuse, 1998a) inquired of 310 business executives. Lawyers, military personnel, diplomats, other professionals, and graduate students from North America, Latin America, and Europe about their communication styles, and whether they had either direct and explicit orientations or preferred more indirect and implicit patterns of talk during negotiations. His results show the percentage favoring indirect communications:

Table 1.2

Country	Percent
Japan	27
France	20
China	18
United Kingdom	12
Brazil	11
India	11
Germany	9
United States	5
Argentina	4
Spain	0
Mexico	0
Nigeria	0

Japanese, French, and Chinese respondents indicated that they had a stronger orientation toward indirect and implicit communications. When Salacuse controlled for gender, he found that 90 percent of the males and females responded to this question identically, with only 10 percent claiming an indirect style. It should be noted, however, that these were self-reports of a limited sample, not observed behaviors.

Relationship-oriented versus Task-oriented (Relationship Focus or Task Focus).

People view negotiations as having either an instrumental/task or relational/relationship focus (Wilson and Putnam, 1989).

People in some cultures when engaging in negotiations focus primarily on the substantive tasks at hand: the business to be accomplished, the work to be done or the contract to be agreed on. For example, "For most business executives and lawyers, particularly in North America, the goal of a business negotiation, first and foremost is achieving a signed contract between the parties. For them the contract is the definitive set of rights and duties that strictly bands the two sides, controls their behavior in the future, and determines who does what, when, where and how. According to this view, the parties' deal is their contract" (Salacuse, 1998b). Such individuals and groups often establish only enough of a personal relationship to get the job done, and no more. In fact, in many instances, it would seem that the sole purpose of developing a personal connection is to expedite the business; relationships are at the service of the task.

In other cultures, the people engaged in negotiations appear to take significant pleasure in meeting people, establishing close personal connections, and engaging in social activities—and view doing business as almost secondary or incidental. They would never consider making a business deal or negotiating an agreement with someone they do not know in some depth. They view establishing a personal connection as a necessary precursor to accomplishing tasks. This approach, often seen in Asia, considers "the purpose of negotiation as creating a business relationship. This view recognizes that, just as a map is not a country but only a very imperfect sketch thereof, a contract is not a business relationship. Although the contract that results from negotiations may describe the relationship, the essence of the deal between the parties is their relationship, not their contract" (Salacuse, 1998b). Thus, the major focus of parties with this orientation is on creating, building, and negotiating the terms of the relationship. They often take extended time prior to and at the beginning of talks to establish and build interpersonal connections. They take a long-term view toward relationships, see negotiations as happening throughout participants' lives (rather than being a one-time event), and are open to using third parties to assist them in resolving any interpersonal or intergroup issues and substantive problems that arise (Salacuse, 1998a).

Contractual versus Holistic (Boundaries: Holistic or Compartmentalized).

Some cultures divide life into neat compartments in which work focus or business life (diplomatic, commercial, manager—subordinate relations, and so forth) is separated from family or social networks. Such views might be reinforced by laws, regulations, or explicit ethical frameworks to prevent conflicts of interest, nepotism, and favoritism. People in many other cultures do not compartmentalize relationships, view all of life as connected, and observe only fuzzy boundaries at best between different kinds of relationships. For members of these cultures, business, friendships, family, and social networks intersect in endlessly fascinating and overlapping ways. For instance, in such cultures, it would be considered perfectly normal, even expected, for a businessperson to hire or give contracts to relatives or close friends—after all, they are known entities—while these actions in more compartmentalized cultures would be considered corrupt.

Table 1.3   A Brief Summary of the Key Cultural Variables

Members of indirect-dealing cultures are seldom explicit in exchanges and often prefer to communicate through intermediaries. They avoid strong expressions of feelings or any hint of disharmony. The meanings of yes and no are not obvious.	Members of direct-dealing cultures tell you what they think, directly and in person. They do not mind expressing feelings and will even shout and argue. For them, a yes is a yes and a no is a no. While harmony is a nice deal, "you can't make an omelet without breaking a few eggs."

Continued

High-context cultures understand meaning in context-based on who you are, your relationship with others, and norms that are universally understood by any member of the culture. Much is implicit unexpressed because it does not need to be pointed out; everyone (except outsiders) understands already.	Low-context cultures create meaning through explicit expressions: clear and direct speech, unambiguous messages, detailed documents, rules, regulations, and written norms and expectations, and so forth. Relationships are constantly formed, reformed and defined in the moment as needed and, depending on the context, through direct discussion. An outsider coming into a low-context setting might even be given a manual explaining exactly what is expected.
Relationship-oriented cultures depend on a series of affiliations to function in life. These may be based on long-term connections—family ties, friendships, ethnic groups membership, school or university associations, business relationships or other affective bonds. The primary task in any kind of negotiation is to establish or improve a relationship, which will serve as the basis for any future agreement or deal. In some cases, the relationship may be more important than any substantive elements of a settlement, as it will endure over time and provide the context of for resolving any misunderstandings or conflicts.	Task-oriented (or substantively oriented) cultures focus on the substantive matters at hand and the issues that have brought negotiators together, whether a business deal or a deep conflict. While members of these cultures may spend some time building a relationship, this is normally a means to the real end: the substantive Deal. In the extreme, task-oriented negotiators will sacrifice a relationship for a more advantageous settlement.
Holistic cultures do not separate relationships, feelings, context, specific compartmentalized people, relationships, joint activities, and substantive issues: they see them as integrally connected. They would rarely compartmentalize different elements of life: business relationships, work, home, social life. In these cultures, unwritten or verbal agreements are strongly valued, and in some cases, they may be seen as more valuable than written commitments or contracts.	Contractually-oriented cultures tend to issues, and diverse activities. They separate specific kinds of relationships (business, family, social) and are likely to make explicit agreements in each. An old joke illustrate the extreme: "He would sue his mother if he thought it get him a better deal." Written contracts are the last word.

(*Adapted from* Handbook of Global and Multicultural Negotiation (2010) *by Christopher W. Moore and Peter J. Woodrow*)

2 Concept and Characteristics of International Business Negotiation

⇨ 2.1 Concept of International Business Negotiation

Case 4

Lafarge, a French company, is the world leader in building materials, holding top positions in each of four areas: cement, aggregates and concrete, roofing, and gypsum. Lafarge attempts to establish a foothold as a major cement manufacturer in Yunnan province in China. Lafarge's planning *gaffe* involved a failure to understand the Chinese government's interests. Lafarge wanted to enter the Yunnan market profitably and quickly by taking full ownership of two state-owned cement manufacturers. Lafarge assumed the government would be willing to sell, if the price was right. But Lafarge was wrong. The government's interests were less in money than in access to Lafarge's state of the art cement-manufacturing processes. In 2004, the time of this negotiation, the Chinese government had plenty of foreign capital; what it needed was a means of upgrading its inefficient construction manufacturing industry, while maintaining jobs and ensuring a steady supply of construction materials. The government also knew that transferring state-owned entities to local interests would be viewed more favorably from a public relations perspective than would a direct sale to a foreign company.

Lafarge's strategic gaffe involved the choice of whom to send to Yunnan to negotiate. Lafarge initially sent two fairly junior members of their investment team to talk to the heads of the two Yunnan cement companies. Although Lafarge may have thought that they were simply engaging in some *due diligence* research—were these two the right companies to buy—the Chinese were *miffed* that a potential business partner would send analysts to talk to business directors. According to Sanjeev Krishna (investment officer for emerging markets at Health Sciences, International Finance Corporation—World Bank) the due diligence process in China is far different than in the West. In China, he advises, one needs to develop a solid relationship before embarking on the due diligence process. In the West, typically a lot of due diligence is conducted prior to an *entity* even deciding to develop a relationship.

The end of this story is that Lafarge is in Yunnan province and technical know-how is being transferred to the Chinese cement companies, but the ultimate deal was not quite what Lafarge had envisioned. Lafarge formed a joint venture with a Hong Kong company to purchase 80 percent of the Yunnan cement business. As a result, Lafarge's ultimate share was only half of that 40 percent, not the 100 percent it initially sought.

(*Excerpts from* Lafarge Negotiations in China *by S. Fewer, D. Krohm and S. Yang*)

The above case, the typical international business negotiation shows how culture affects negotiation. Sometimes even experience within a culture does not guarantee future negotiating success. Lafarge started doing business in China in 1994. Ten years later, when Lafarge opened negotiations in Yunnan province it already had cement operations in Sichuan province. To adequately integrate cultural knowledge into negotiation strategy requires more than experience; it requires an understanding of how and why culture affects negotiations.

International business negotiation (IBN) refers to the business negotiation that takes place between the interest groups from different nations or regions. It is a process in which both sides from different countries confer with each other about terms or conditions by information exchange.

As far as languages, social conventions, values, legal environments and political factors are concerned, international business negotiation involve more elements and tend to be more complex than domestic ones. It is more difficult to conduct as well. Additionally, culture variables add complexity to it. The failure to take culture into account is the real negotiation breaker.

➪ 2.2　Characteristics of International Business Negotiation

2.2.1　Language Barrier

One of the first obstacles encountered in international business negotiation is language barrier. In the globalized world, when we are conducting international business negotiations, there is an increasing need to interpret or translate from one language to another unless your counterpart also speaks your native language. English is most commonly-used language in international trade and business activities. If the other party is not from the English-speaking countries, other languages, such as French, German, Spanish, Russian and Arabic may be used in negotiation. People with multi-lingual skills are viewed as a mastery key to international business negotiation. However, learning a second language can be very difficult, for it demands considerable time and effort, but the rewards of knowing another language are immense. A person who often participates in international business negotiation must at least master one foreign language—for example, English. Learning a second language can provide greater insight into the emotions and values of another culture, and thus will increase your intercultural negotiation skills and competence. Almost every formal and important international business negotiations involve one or more individuals who are using a second language.

2.2.2　Cultural Difference

The link between culture and negotiation is complex. Anticipating cultural differences at the negotiation table helps negotiators make sense of those differences when they appear and adjust their own behaviors to reinforce or to block the other party's strategy. Negotiators from each culture come to the negotiating table with interests and priorities that are culturally based. In the negotiation between the Chinese government and Lafarge, the Chinese government had three interests: local control, updating technology, and uninterrupted delivery of cement. These interests and the high priority placed on them compared with simply attracting more foreign investment illustrate how culture affects interests. Despite rapid economic growth and membership in the World Trade Organization, China remains a planned economy; in the case of Lafarge, economic planning took precedence over foreign investment. Lafarge had two interests entering the Yunnan market: speed and profitability. These interests, too, were cultural. Lafarge is a for-profit enterprise. Its investments in China are motivated by its desire to make money for its shareholders. Lafarge was interested in bringing new cement technology to these plants in Yunnan province not because it is altruistic but because with new technology production would be more profitable. Note that neither the Chinese government nor Lafarge's interests required that Lafarge own 100 percent of the cement plants, even though Lafarge set out to do so. The fit between negotiators' priorities and interests is what generates potential.

Culture also may affect negotiators' strategic behavior: their confrontational style, their social motivation, and their strategic approach to negotiation. We know a little about strategic behavior in the Lafarge negotiation. Lafarge's initial confrontational strategy was direct, motivated by its goal to accumulate economic capital. It sent financial analysts to Yunnan Province to do due diligence, collecting information that would allow Lafarge to develop a target price that would ensure profitability. In contrast, leadership of the Chinese cement companies no doubt preferred a less direct strategy that engaged first in relationship building with high-level peers from Lafarge. They probably were concerned for their jobs. Financial analysts could not provide the relationship assurances they were likely seeking.

On the other hand, the diverse religious beliefs and social ideologies also have a great importance on the international business negotiation.

Case 5

The Chinese Company Adapting to the Islamic Culture and Customs

Company H is a large company and its products are among the best of the same line in China. They have already extended their business into several regions overseas. However, the Middle East remains blank, as they have no experience in doing business with Arabs.

One day, a delegation from Dubai—the most populous city and emirate in the United Arab Emirates (UAE) —visited company H. Mr. L, the chief representative of the company, received them. As the delegation was interested in the Company's products, both sides sat down for a negotiation on the products.

As the negotiation went on, Mr. L felt confused and bored because the Arabs asked for a break every hour. Then they went to the toilet to wash their hands and faces. When they came back, they knelt down to pray. As there was no towel in the toilet, the Arabs prayed with wet hands and faces. Mr. L found himself in a dilemma, because he did not know whether he should withdraw from the scene or not.

When it was time for lunch, the Arabs were treated to a rich dinner. When everyone was seated, the waitress started introducing the different dishes in English to the Arabic visitors. They all looked surprised and pleased at the variety. But this did not last long. When the waitress mentioned some specially cooked pork, the smiles disappeared from all those visitors'faces and all of them looked blue—no one said a word. Quickly they stood up and left the dinner table without bidding farewell to anyone, though there were some important Chinese local guests present. The same day, this Dubai delegation left the city without notifying Company H.

A few days later, the bad news reached Mr. L—his Dubai delegation had signed a contract with their competitor—Company C, and the contract was the very one which was being negotiated between Company H and that Dubai delegation. Mr. L got a strong blame from his boss for losing the opportunity to their rival's hand.

Three days later, Mr. L took the following actions:

1) Start a training program for all waitresses and persons involved in communicating with Middle East business people, and invite some professors to give lectures on the Islamic culture and customs.

2) Invite some Arabic teachers to teach the waitresses simple Arabic to communicate with the Arabic.

3) Set up a separate dining room with special set of dinner dishes for the Arabic.

4) Set up a special room close to the meeting room. This room would be used only for praying by those Middle Eastern business persons. In addition, he also put some compass and small carpets in the room.

5) Prepare some small towels in the toilet for the Arabs to dry their hands on before praying.

Half a year later, Company H had five customers in Middle East. All of them had visited Company H and were impressed by their understanding and respect for the Islamic culture and habits. Company H has been expanding their market share in the Middle East ever since.

(*Adapted from* Cultural Conflicts in International Business Negotiation)

Questions for Case-analysis:

1. What was the reason Company H didn't get the contract from the Dubai Delegation?

2. What actions did company H take following the failure of the negotiation? Were they effective?

3. Make a list of cultural differences involved in the case and the according way to deal with it in a negotiation.

2.2.3   Legal Environment

International businesspersons must have a thorough understanding of the complexity of the international legal environment. An international company is obligated to operate within the boundaries of the law.

The final outcome of an international business negotiation is the cross-border transfer of the object and the payment, involving not only domestic laws, but also related international business laws and international practices concerning international trade, international payment settlement/ international transportation and international insurance. A sensitive international business negotiator should be well informed of the new regulations and laws imposed home or abroad, with regard to the negotiation contents, so as to adjust the negotiating strategies accordingly.

Case 6

The EU Grounds the GE-Honeywell merger

Political and legal differences around the world can hit home and restrict strategic alliances even between two domestic companies because we are entering the era of the global reach of regulatory bodies. General Electric and Honeywell—two American corporations—had planned the $41 billion deal and gained approval from the Department of Justice in the United States. But the European Commission, the executive arm of the EU, has jurisdiction over mergers between firms with combined revenues of $4.2 billion, of which $212 million must be within Europe. The GE-Honeywell deal fell within these criteria. GE since the two companies, for example, employs 85,000 people in Europe and had $25 billion in revenue in 2000.

Whereas the U.S. antitrust regulation tends to focus on the potential harm to customers, EU's antitrust regulation focuses on the potential effects to business competition. Commissioner Mario Monti's decision to block the deal in June 2001 was based largely on a concern about potential "bundling". The concern was that GE would "use its *clout* to tie two corn products into a single package—jet engines and Honeywell *avionics*—and sell it at a price lower than European competitor could match." While the European Commission admitted that customers might benefit from lower prices in the short term, they were more worried about the long-term competitiveness of GE's rivals and the future of the aerospace industry. The EC wanted to remedy this potential scenario by selling off several businesses such as GE Capital Aviation Services ("Gecas"), an anti-aircraft and leasing business. Whereas GE had suggested various structural remedies to the concerns about Gacas, the Commission remained wary about the potential effects of vertical integrations. Noel Forgeard, CEO of Airbus Industry, the European plane maker that would have an interest in the competitive issues, said that he did not oppose the GE-Honeywell deal after discussing with Jack Welch how the deal would be structured.

Monti indicated that he would accept fewer *divestments* in other areas as long as he got the structural he wanted regarding Gecas. At that point, however, GE is now offering to sell businesses with $ 1 billion in revenues—half of its original offer—and has taken off the table most of Honeywell's avionics and aerospace products.

On June 14, 2001, Jack Welch, the highly successful chairman and CEO of GE, who postponed his retirement to see the deal with Honeywell to *fruition*, said, "We have always said there is a point at which we wouldn't do the deal. The Commission's extraordinary demands are far beyond that point. This shows you are never too old to get surprised."

Paul O'Neill, U.S. Treaty secretary, stated that the Commission's proposal to block the deal was "off the wall…They are the closest thing you can find to an autocratic organization that can successfully impose their will on thing that one would think are outside their scope of attention." However, Monti, obviously distributed by what he called attempts to bring about political intervention in the European antitrust case, later stated that the HE-Honeywell situation was a rare case of disagreement between the transatlantic competition authorities.

(*Adapted from* International Management *by Helen Deresky*)

Questions for Case-analysis:
1. What was the possible result?
2. Could there be better result? If so, Please explain your way of improving the negotiation result.

2.2.4 *International Political Factors*

International business negotiation is part of the political and economic relations between the countries and regions. When negotiations cross national boundaries, they enter a context of political and legal pluralism. This makes cross-national negotiations much more complex than same-culture negotiations. Failing to understand the political environment in which the negotiation is occurring can sabotage negotiations. Government provides the political and legal context for negotiations. Governments are frequently at or close to the table. Western and Eastern companies alike, regardless of their negotiation experience, too frequently stumble badly when they try to do business in a new cultural environment. A recent example is China National Offshore Oil Company's 2005 failed bid for Unocal, which was ultimately bought domestically by Chevron. CNOOC failed to take into account the risk that their acquisition could be blocked by the U.S. Congress. When Congressional approval appeared to be unlikely, CNOOC let Chevron outbid them for Unocal.

Another example is the Arcelor acquisition by Mittal. Arcelor S.A. was the world's largest steel producer in terms of turnover and the second largest in terms of steel output, with a turnover of €30.2 billion and shipments of 45 million metric tons of steel in 2004. The company was created by a merger of the former companies Aceralia (Spain), Usinor (France) and Arbed (Luxembourg) in 2002.Mittal Steel Company N.V. was one of the world's largest steel producers by volume, and also one of the largest in turnover.

The company was the target of a takeover bid by its rival Mittal Steel on 27 January 2006. However, the bid resulted in substantial increase in Arcelor's share value. Two members of the board of Arcelor, Guillermo Ulacia and Jacques Chabanier also resigned suddenly. On 26 May 2006 Arcelor announced its intention to merge with Severstal (OAO Severstal, Russian: Северсталь, "Northern Steel") is a Russian company mainly operating in the steel and mining industry, centered in the northern city of Cherepovets). Since then several economists, media and shareholders have questioned the intentions of Arcelor in announcing its merger with Severstal due to a perceived opacity in the transaction. But on 25 June 2006, the Arcelor board decided to go ahead with the merger with Mittal Steel and scrapped plans for Severstal merger. The new company is now called "ArcelorMittal". Arcelor also paid Severstal € 140 million as a "fine" for the fall-out of their failed talks. Arcelor's merger with Mittal created the worldwide leader in the steel industry, increasing its bargaining power with suppliers and consumers. Mittal Steel has agreed to pay 40.37 euros a share to Arcelor, almost double the amount offered by Mittal last time.

Arcelor shareholders preferred selling to Minal, a company registered in Rotterdam, incorporated within EU laws, and run by an Indian living in London, rather than selling to Severstal, a Russian company lead by a Russian oligarch, Alexsei Mordashov. Why? Mittal's EU-based political, legal, and economic environment apparently was viewed by shareholders much less risky than Severstal's. So negotiators engaged in international business negotiator must be highly sensitive to international politics. (Timmon and Kramer, 2006)

3   Principles of International Business Negotiation

Principles are fundamentals or guidelines, basic rules, beliefs or norms. In international business negotiations, every party is obliged to observe these principles. Understanding and implementing these principles help negotiators better apply negotiating strategies and skills and increase the effectiveness and efficiency of their negotiations.

➡ 3.1   Equality Principle

Case 7

Boeing Company in the United States was one of the largest airplane manufacturers in the world, with specialization in commercial jetliners and military aircraft.

Chengdu Aircraft Company was one of China's four major airplane producers. The latter was relatively small in size, focusing on producing military planes, and had never made any large civil jetliners. After China's opening to the outside world, McDonnell Douglas Corporation (MD Corp) entered into an agreement with Shanghai Aviation Industrial Corporation (SAIC) to co-produce MD-80 and MD-90 Jetliners in China, most of which were sold to Chinese airline companies. McDonnell Douglas' success in China motivated Boeing to initiate attempts to enter the Chinese market. For its part, China, after its successful cooperation with MD Corp, also intended to cooperate with the "Big Mac", the giant in the global aircraft manufacturing—Boeing. Therefore, the Chinese government decided to enlist Chengdu Aircraft Industrial Company to negotiate with Boeing about the technological introduction. Although there was a huge size difference between the Chinese and American companies, the two parties abided by the game principle of "equal and voluntary participation". After several rounds of negotiations, they finally settled an agreement for processing trade.

(Adapted from International Business Negotiation *by Dou Ran)*

Equality is the basic premise for international business negotiation. All parties, big or small, should be equal, no matter how great the gaps are in their economic power and organizational scales. All party has the same option for choosing the trade items and the terms. In the above case, The Chinese side intended to bring in a package of airliner production technology, but, after negotiation, China realized that apart from some minor technologies, most of the patented technologies would not be transferred by the American company. Even if some technologies could be transferred, they were limited to the rights of use, which were rather expensive. Meanwhile, the American company intended to sell planes directly to China, but China insisted that opening this market be timed to coincide with the technology transfer. In this situation, Boeing proposed that they could transfer the technology for assembling vertical fins. Though China realized that this was the least technical of all the plane production techniques, it represented an opportunity for an initial trial with Boeing.

Under this agreement, China did not need to pay for the patent with foreign currency. They would get the right to assemble the vertical fins of large jetliners and gain the assembling fee. On the other side, the Americans paved their way to possible large orders from China in the future at the lowest cost—by transferring only the least important technology and paying a minimal assembling fee.

Moreover, all party has the power to veto any clause under negotiation. In the above case, if China had refused to assembly only the vertical fins or the American had refused to allow assembling any part in China, then the negotiation would have broken down and ended in failure.

Additionally, all party should show respect regardless of their power and size. Although Boeing was powerful, it needed China's big orders for airliners, so it had to consider China's request for technology transfer.

Chengdu Aircraft Company itself was less powerful, but it had a China's big market behind it. Therefore, it did not need to be servile to the American Company. If any party abuses its power and bullies others, the negotiation will fail.

In international business negotiation, only under the principle of equality will no party be able to act against the other party's will and force his own will onto others.

⇨ 3.2　**Principle of Separating the People from the Problems**

Case 8

In 1990s, a dispute occurred between labor and management in an American investment company in Japan. The workers went on a strike because their demand for a pay rise and better working conditions couldn't be satisfied. Six weeks before, the Japanese workers had warned the American company's president in writing, but the management didn't take it seriously. Not until the day the strike took place and production stopped in the factory did the American president realize how serious the problem was. Then he designated management representatives to negotiate immediately with the workers. In the negotiation, the two sides, workers and management, reached an agreement about pay and working conditions. After the strike, the employees cleaned the demonstration site and cleared the ground of trash such as cigarette ends and paper cups, etc. During the following day, they worked overtime voluntarily (which was not a demand in the negotiation), finishing the production tasks delayed by the strike. The American president was confused, but one Japanese worker told him, "We went on strike because you didn't pay any attention to our legitimate demand. However, this is our company. Though we were dissatisfied with your behavior, we still like our company."

(*Adapted from* International Business negotiation *by Dou Ran*)

Roger Fisher and William Ury pointed out in their book *Getting to Yes*: *Negotiating Agreement Without Giving in* that "negotiators are people first". You will certainly encounter "people problems": such as problems in perception, emotion and communication when negotiating with others, and do not suppose that making small concessions will make these problems disappear. "People problems" are psychological problems, and as such they require psychological techniques (not business concessions) for their resolution.

It is feasible to deal with a substantive problem and maintain a good working relationship between negotiating parties. In order to deal with "people problems", three techniques are recommended for both parties to follow:

1) Develop empathy

　　A. We put ourselves in their shoes.

　　B. We avoid blaming them for our problems.

　　C. We help them participate in the process.

2）Manage emotions

    A. We allow them to let off steam.

    B. We do not overreact to emotional outbursts.

3）Communicate

    A. We listen and summarize what we hear.

    B. We avoid trying to score points and debating them as opponents.

    C. We do not berate them about what they are doing wrong.

The best time for handling "people problems" is before they become people problems. To do so, negotiators need to establish a working relationship with the other party. Be "partners", not "adversaries".

⇨ 3.3   Principle of Focusing on Interests, not Positions

Positions are particular courses of actions that limit the range of solutions available in a situation if you strictly adhere to them. Interests express our needs and desires which are satisfied by the positions we take up. Take the following example of sticking to a position. A woman walks into the cosmetic section of a department store. She sees on display a designer label Italian bag accompanying a makeup kit. She decides she wants the makeup kit only, not the bag. She approaches the sales person, points to the display and says, "Excuse me. I like the makeup set displayed with the bag somewhere up from there. I would like to buy just the makeup set. Is that possible?" Let's assume that an unprofessional and untrained sales assistant is taking this sale. What does this person do? The assistant merely says, "No, I'm sorry. You can't have the makeup kit. That item is sold as a set." How do you think the customer reacts? She walks out, naturally.

Now, let's change the characters and put in a well-trained sales assistant. What does this person do? After hearing the customer's request, he or she thinks carefully, "This lady wants the makeup kit, but I can't sell it apart from the bag. We're supposed to sell these in sets. I know she needs the makeup kit to improve her looks—but she doesn't need to do so at the fantastic price we're charging for this set on display. Hey, we have a makeup kit of the same brand in our pharmaceutical section. In fact, I think it's on sale! I should let her know that." So the customer's request is courteously responded to and she is informed about the availability of the same item in another department, while being told that she cannot buy the makeup kit apart from the bag. The result is a sure sale. With some insight, the well-trained salesperson persuaded the customer to abandon her position of wanting to buy the makeup kit from the cosmetic department apart from the bag. Knowing that the customer's interest was to get that particular makeup kit and nothing else, the sales assistant prudently redirected her away from her initial position of purchasing the item from the cosmetics department and buying it from the pharmaceutical department, where the same item was available at less cost. Not only did the sales person avert a possible loss of sale, but promoted the goodwill of the store as well.

Negotiations must be arranged around the central goal of gaining realistic interests: try hard to eliminate the discrepancies in commercial interests, while avoiding becoming entangled in positions. In doing this, we should:

1) Identify interests

A. We explore their interests which stand in our way.

B. We examine the different interests of different people on their sides.

C. We look at their human needs underlying their position.

2) Talk about interests

A. We summarize and accept their interests.

B. We describe our understanding or a problem before proposing solutions.

C. We try not to look backward and focus more on looking forward.

⇨ 3.4 Principle of Inventing Options for Mutual Gains

This principle is very much related to the third principle of separating interests from positions. The sales assistant in the above case could have presented other options to the customer, including telling the customer that a very similar brand of makeup kit was available from the cosmetic department for less money. Or that she could assemble the makeup items included in the kit on display simply by purchasing individual items of the same brand from the cosmetics department. This would cost her less money since she wouldn't have to pay for the bag too. This third step, inventing options, is the natural offshoot of separating interests from positions. By doing this, then, you can multiply the possibilities of coming to an agreement by thinking of more solutions that take into consideration the interests of the other side.

There are three factors hindering people from seeking for alternative solutions:

1) Distributive plan.

2) Seeking for only one solution.

3) Considering one's own options suiting one's own needs.

To get rid of these barriers, there are two steps to be taken:

1) Diagnose

A. We set aside the idea that their gains have to be at our expense.

B. We encourage each other to help solve problems.

C. We do not prematurely focus on an option before people are ready.

2) Invent creative options

A. We separate inventing options from evaluating them.

B. We develop several options before looking for a solution.

C. We look for common and complementary interests.

D. We look for options that would make the decision easier for them.

The ability to invent options is one of the most useful assets a negotiator can have. Negotiators should have creative thinking and develop multiple solution options.

⇨ 3.5　Principle of Insisting on Using Objective Criteria

Case 9

In an international conference of the Law of the Sea, India and America had a dispute over the issue of whether a marine mineral deposit demanded high-level technology, equipment, expert and management, only developed countries are usually have the abilities to engage in such business. Developing countries are restricted in many of these aspects and have to rely on developed countries to explore marine resources in their sea areas. Therefore, India, which represented developing countries, proposed that the ocean exploration company should pay 6,000 dollars as the initial fee to the host country for every area they explored. America, which represented developed countries, strongly opposed this proposal. The two parties had a fierce debate, but neither was able to persuade the other side. The meeting lasted a long time without any result due to this problem, and was forced to adjourn in mid-negotiation. At this moment, one representative said there was an economics essay about deep sea mining published by the Massachusetts Institute of Technology in America. In this essay, there was a model which was used to calculate the effects of various charges on the exploration profits. It was suggested that the negotiators consult this model. Having examined the model and the data, all the representatives thought that it was a model with objective criteria. The result they reached after their calculation based on this model showed what impact India's demand for an initial fee could have on the exploration company. If the exploration company should pay first when they wanted to explore, this expense might result in some difficulties in normal operation. But the initial fee would finally be added to the cost of the product, and then transferred to the price. Therefore, from the long term point of view, the exploration company would not be affected greatly. In the light of this information, Indian representatives reconsidered their suggestions, and decided to reduce the initial fee. The American representatives also realized that the initial fee was not unacceptable, so they no longer refused to pay such a fee.

(Adapted from International Business negotiation *by Dou Ran)*

When negotiators find themselves debating endlessly about one specific piece of data, they should consider bringing in an acceptable objective criterion. For instance, you are looking for exercise equipment. How would you go about your search? Would you simply take at face value the sales assistant's opinion at the sporting goods store? Wouldn't you suspect that the sales people are under some pressure from management to dispose of certain items? What then gives you bargaining leverage in negotiating with salespeople? In the USA one "objective criterion" you can consult is

Consumer Reports magazine which rates different products according to test standards; there are similar magazines in other countries. There are three points which should be considered to see whether a criterion is objective or not:

1) An objective criterion should be independent of wills of all parties and thus be free from sentimental influence of any one.

2) An objective criterion should be valid and realistic.

3) An objective criterion should be at least theoretically accepted by both sides.

Surely, different negotiation subjects and specific negotiation clauses involve different criteria and considerations. Experts' opinions, agreements between countries, routine international practices and legal practices of a country or an international organization, can all be viewed as objective criteria.

Pay attention: negotiators should focus on objective criteria firmly but flexibly.

Notes

1 **Pearl Sydenstricker Buck** (June 26, 1892—March 6, 1973), also known by her Chinese name **Sai Zhenzhu** (赛珍珠), was an American writer and novelist. As the daughter of missionaries, Buck spent most of her life before 1934 in China. Her novel ***The Good Earth*** was the best-selling fiction book in the U.S. in 1931 and 1932 and won the Pulitzer Prize in 1932. In 1938, she was awarded the Nobel Prize in Literature "for her rich and truly epic descriptions of peasant life in China and for her biographical masterpieces".

2 **sedan, van, minivan**

sedan/saloon (UK) —a car with seats for four or five people, two or four doors, and a separate area at the back for bags, boxes, and cases.

van—a medium-sized vehicle with windows all round, used for carrying more people than an ordinary car.

minivan—a large, high car that can carry more people than a normal car.

3 **FTC** (Federal Trade Commission)

The FTC is an independent agency of the United States government, established in 1914 by the Federal Trade Commission Act. Its principal mission is the promotion of consumer protection and the elimination and prevention of anticompetitive business practices, such as coercive monopoly.

4 **UAW**: International Union, United Automobile, Aerospace and Agricultural Implement Workers of America

The UAW is an American labor union that represents workers in the United States and Puerto Rico, and in the country of Canada. Headquartered in Detroit, Michigan, the union has about

390,000 active members and more than 600,000 retired members in 750 local unions, which negotiated 2,500 contracts with some 1,700 employers.

Vocabulary

adamant /ˈædəmənt/ *adj.* adamantly *adv.*

—impossible to persuade, or unwilling to change an opinion or a decision

e.g. I've told her she should stay at home and rest, but she's adamant that she's coming.

allege /əˈledʒ/ *v.*

—to state that someone has done something illegal or wrong without giving proof

e.g. It is alleged that he used his influential position to steal thousands of pounds of company profits.

alma mater /ˌælməˈmɑːtər/ *n.*

—(*formal*) the school, college, or university where you studied

antitrust/ˈæntitrʌst/ *adj.*

—relating to efforts to prevent companies from working together to control prices unfairly or to create a monopoly (a single company or small group of companies that is the only supplier of something)

e.g. Last month, it threw out an antitrust suit alleging collusion by the nation's largest phone company.

avenue/ˈævənjuː/ *n.* [C]

—a method or way of doing something

e.g. China and the United States are exploring avenues of financial cooperation.

biography/baɪˈɒɡrəfi/ *n.*

—the story of the life of a person written by someone else, or the area of literature relating to books that describe such stories

e.g. He wrote a biography of Lincoln.

bolster/ˈbəʊlstə/ *v.*

—to support or improve something or make it stronger

e.g. More money is needed to bolster the industry.

budge/bʌdʒ/ *v.*

—If something will not budge or you cannot budge it, it will not move.

e.g. I've tried moving the desk but it won't budge/I can't budge it.

clout/klaʊt/ *n.*

—power and influence over other people or events

e.g. The Queen may have privilege but she has no real political clout.

concession /kənˈseʃən/ *n.*

—something that you allow to do, or allow sb to have in order to end an argument or to make a situation less difficult

e.g. The firm will be forced to make concessions if it wants to avoid a strike.

deadlock /ˈdedlɔk/ *n.*

—a situation in which people can't agree and no progress can be made

e.g. The deadlock in the negotiations meant that the dispute was taken to arbitration.

due diligence

—the action that is considered reasonable for people to take in order to keep themselves or others and their property safe

e.g. People have to exercise due diligence and watch what's being bought on their credit cards.

—(*accounting*) the detailed examination of a company and its financial records, done before getting involved in a business arrangement with it, such as buying it or selling its shares to investors.

e.g. We had the opportunity to do due diligence on the books and we think $518 is a fair offer.

divestment /daɪˈvestmənt/ *n.* [C or U]

—(*finance*) the process of selling an asset, a business, or part of a business

e.g. The divestment of the US unit will remove a loss and help cut interest payable.

enigmatic/ˌenɪgˈmætɪk/ *adj.*

—mysterious and impossible to understand completely

e.g. He left an enigmatic message on my answering machine.

entity /ˈentɪti/ *n.*

—an organization or a business that has its own separate legal and financial existence

e.g. Nearly 90 entities, mainly private companies, mint gold in bars.

a commercial/corporate/legal entity

fizzle/ˈfɪzəl/ *v.*

—to finish slowly in a way that is disappointing or has become less interesting

e.g. Interest in the project fizzled after the funding was withdrawn.

follow suit

—to do the same thing

e.g. When one airline reduces its ticket prices, the rest usually follow suit.

fruition/fruˈɪʃən/ *n.* [U]

—(*formal*) an occasion when a plan or an idea begins to happen, exist, or be successful

e.g. None of his grand plans for a TV series ever came to fruition.

gaffe/gæf/ *n.* [C]

—a remark or an action that is a social mistake and not considered polite

e.g. I made a real gaffe——I called his new wife "Judy", which is the name of his ex-wife.

grievance/ˈgriːvəns/ *n.* [C or U]

—an official complaint by an employee that they have been treated unfairly

e.g. The aim of a grievance procedure is to encourage fairness in the handling of workpluce problems.

impartially/ɪmˈpɑːʃəli/*adv.*

—not supporting any of the sides involved in an argument

e.g. Administrative law enforcers shall enforce law impartially.

joint venture

—an arrangement between two or more companies to work together on a particular project

—a venture by a partnership or conglomerate designed to share risk or expertise

e.g. The two companies have entered into a joint venture agreement to develop a major casino hotel in Atlantic City.

lobby /ˈlɔbi/ *v.*

—to try to persuade an elected official to take a particular action or change a law

e.g. Council members have been lobbying colleagues on how to vote.

miffed /mift/ *adj.*

—slightly angry or upset

e.g. Some people get a little miffed by it.

noncommittal/ˌnɒnkəˈmɪtəl/ *adj.*

—not expressing an opinion or decision

e.g. The ambassador was typically noncommittal when asked whether further sanctions would be introduced.

nix /nɪks/ *v.*

—to stop, prevent, or refuse to accept something

e.g.The film studio nixed her plans to make a sequel.

pedal /ˈpedl/ *n.*

—a flat bar on a machine such as a bicycle, car, etc. that you push down with your foot in order to make parts of the machine move or work

e.g. I couldn't reach the pedlals on her bike.

premise /ˈpremɪs/*n.*

—an idea or theory on which a statement or action is based

e.g. They had started with the premise that all men are created equal.

pundit/ˈpʌndɪt/ *n.* [C]

—someone who is an expert on a subject and often speaks or writes about it

e.g. The collapse was not predicted by any of the financial pundits.

rehash /ˌriːˈhæʃ/ *v.*

—to arrange ideas, pieces of writing or film into a new form but without any great change or improvement

e.g. He just rehashes songs from the 60s.

reminisce/ˌremɪˈnɪs/ *v.*

—(*formal*)to talk or write about past experiences that you remember with pleasure e.g. My grandfather used to reminisce about his years in the navy.

retaliatory/rɪˈtæliətəri/ *adj.*

—used to describe an action that is intended to harm someone who has done something to harm you

e.g. The bill ends tax subsidies for US exporters that caused retaliatory action by Europe.

sabotage/ˈsæbətɑːʒ/ *n.*

—the act of doing damage or destroy something, for example, equipment or a system, that belongs to someone else, so that it cannot be used

e.g. Several acts of sabotage are committed against radio station.

shuffle /ˈʃʌf(ə)l/ *n.* [C]

—a shuffle is also a change in people or their positions in an organization.

e.g. The top-level shuffle brought Groncki into the White House.

—the act of moving things to different positions or into a different order

e.g. She gave her papers a quick shuffle.

tremendous /trɪˈmendəs/ *adj.*

—very great in amount or level, or extremely good

e.g. They were making the most tremendous amount of profit from their investment last year.

wise up

—to start to understand a situation or fact and believe what you hear it, even if it is difficult or unpleasant

e.g. It's about time employers wised up to the fact that staff who are happy work more efficiently.

Exercises

1 Multiple Choice

1) What is a pre-negotiation stage?

   A. A period of making a must list.

   B. A period of knowing the other party.

   C. A period of establishing relationship with the other party.

   D. A period of determining goals.

2) Which is a critical period of negation?

   A. Pre-negotiation.   B. Concession.   C. Bargaining.   D. Establishing relationship.

3) Which of the following is **NOT** one of the cultural variables that influence negotiation?

   A. Individualism   B. Task oriented vs. relationship oriented

   C. Holistic culture   D. Low context culture

4) What is **NOT** true of characteristics of negotiation?

   A. Negotiation is a process.

   B. One negotiation needs at least two parties.

C. Negotiation involves divergence in interests and goals for participants.

D. Negotiation will result in an agreement.

5) Which is **NOT** one of the six stages of negotiation?

A. Entry.   B. Establishing relationship.

C. Bargaining.   D. Reaching agreement.

6) What of the following is **NOT** one principle for international business negotiation?

A. Focusing on positions.   B. Mutual gains.

C. Equality.   D. Insisting on using objective criteria.

7) Which of the following is **TRUE** in international negotiation?

A. An objective criterion should be free from sentimental influence of any party in the negotiation.

B. An objective criterion should be realistic and possible be realized.

C. An objective criterion should be at least theoretically accepted by one side.

D. An objective criterion should be accepted by both sides.

8) What is **TRUE** of individualist culture?

A. Individualist culture rewards accomplishment.

B. Individualist culture encourages autonomy of individuals.

C. Individualist culture promotes interdependency of relationship between individuals.

D. Individualist culture focus on relationship between a person and his community.

9) What is **TRUE** of collective culture?

A. Collective cultures supports collective interests above individual interests.

B. Collective cultures does not promote individual accomplishment.

C. Collective cultures emphasizes on social obligations of an individual.

D. Collective cultures promotes interdependency of individuals with others.

10) What is **NOT** true of the following statements?

A. In low-context cultures, the rules and expectations of interaction are often written down or even posted publicly.

B. A negotiator should always be aware of the changes in international business laws and regulations.

C. The international business negotiation is often a process to deal with disputes arising from different practices in trade, payment, transportation and insurance.

D. In hierarchical cultures, social boundaries are more permeable, and social status may be both short-lived and variable across situations.

2 Interpretation of Terms

1) negotiation

_____

_____

2) international business negotiation

3) culture

4) hierarchical culture

5) egalitarian culture

6) high-context culture

7) low-context culture

3 True or False

___ 1) In hierarchical cultures, social power determines social status.

___ 2) Communications among people in high-context cultures are often precise with little flexibility.

___ 3) Negotiations take place in a wide range of contexts, from simple market bargaining to complex processes to end wars within or between nations.

___ 4) Negotiations will be determined by language barriers, different political situations and legal environments.

___ 5) Negotiation is a process involving two parties with different interest but incentives to resolve these differences and reach agreement.

4 Case Analysis

Case 1

A Chinese software company wanted to cooperate with an American software company, so they invited the American company to China to have a negotiation. The latter was very interested in this invitation because they all know that nowadays China is the would-be largest potential market in the world. Therefore, the American company sent three persons to China, of whom Mr. Green was the group leader. On the other hand, Mr. Wang, as the group leader of fifteen people, was in charge of this matter for this Chinese company.

When finally Mr. Wang saw Mr. Green at the airport, he smiled, "You must be very tired!"

Mr. Green was somewhat puzzled, but he did not pay much attention to that. Then, when they arrived at the hotel, Mr. Wang treated Mr. Green a big dinner. Mr. Green was at a loss when he saw that so much food was served. "That is impossible to eat out all that food," said Mr. Green. But Mr. Wang said, "I'm very sorry that we've just prepared some poor food. I hope you don't mind about it." Mr. Green was totally puzzled. "Who said that China is a developing country and Chinese are poor? If the poor live in this way, there must be no God!" He also considered Mr. Wang as an insincere guy apologizing for this big dinner.

Next day when Mr. Green suggested that they should begin the negotiation, Mr. Wang just laughed, "There is no need to hurry after all, and you three come to China for the first time, so just see around our city for several days. First enjoy yourselves, and then talk about business. Would that be all right?"

But Mr. Green was a little unpleasant, "If we don't begin our negotiation, what on earth did we come to China?"

"I know that our business is the negotiation, but we also hope that you can enjoy yourselves. We can start our negotiation several days later." said Mr. Wang.

"Business is business. We really appreciate your good will, but we came to China not for ourselves bur for the company," said Mr. Green.

Mr. Wang was a little embarrassed hearing this. But finally they began their negotiation. When they were all seated, Mr. Green felt very strange. He just couldn't understand why the Chinese company sent so many persons to this negotiation. After all, this was just a business negotiation, but not a big fight.

After Mr. Wang introduced all his members to Mr. Green, the latter finally found out that these people included sales manager, technician and some similar people. "I can't see why these people come." thought Mr. Green. Then he introduced his members to Mr. Wang, "This is my secretary, and this is the lawyer of our company." When hearing the word "lawyer", all Chinese people present felt somewhat disappointed and angry. Mr. Wang frowned and totally got no idea what to say. "Why lawyer? It's just like calculating family property in preparation for a divorce at a time when we are just beginning to fall in love." thought Mr. Wang.

During the negotiation, Mr. Green recommended several articles, but each time Mr. Wang would just say, "Oh, that's very good, but I have to talk with my boss." Mr. Green was very unpleasant, for he couldn't understand why the company sent Mr. Wang if he couldn't make any decision. What's worse, sometimes Mr. Wang would give some puzzling answers, like "I can fully understand this, but I am afraid there are many problems about this. It's very complex."

"Then what are the problems?" asked Mr. Green. This made Mr. Wang embarrassed and he just kept silent.

At last, Mr. Green couldn't help losing his temper any more, "I don't think that your company really wanted to cooperate with our company!"

Mr. Wang also felt angry, but he just said, 'Take it east. In fact, we do want to cooperate with you, but you can see that things are complex."

Mr. Green was so angry to these cloudy words that he accidentally fell back onto the seat. All the Chinese people present laughed asked, "Are you OK?' Mr. Green said nothing and left the room for he thought he was not respected.

The next day, he left China with his members.

Questions for Case-analysis:

1. Why did Mr. Green feel puzzled when he heard Mr. Wang say "you must be very tired" at the airport?

2. Why did Chinese serve their foreign counterparts such a big dinner? What did Mr. Green think of it?

3. When Mr. Green introduced his lawyer at the negotiation table, why did Chinese feel very uncomfortable?

4. Why did Mr. Green think that the Chinese company was unwilling to cooperate with his company?

Case 2

A famous male Brazilian footballer signed a one-million-pound-per-year contract with Manchester United Club in the UK. By the end of the year, he requested Manchester United to honor the agreement and pay the money, but the Club was short of money and asked him to wait for a few days. Strict interpretation of the law leaves no doubt that Manchester United Club obviously violated the contract. However, the Brazilian player found that the club did have problems with their cash flow, and the club did not intentionally delay payment to its players. If the player had not taken the club's interests into consideration as well as his relationship with the club and had resorted to the law, the two parties would have been in an adversarial situation.

So the player decided to negotiate with Manchester United Club. He proposed to revise the contract for their mutual benefits. The deadline of the annual payment of one hundred million pounds stipulated in the existing contract would be altered so that the payment would be made four times within two years at a rate of 25 million pounds at a time. In this way, the Brazilian player had 25 million pounds per half year, so he need not worry about his living, and Manchester United Club alleviated their difficulty in capital turnover.

Questions for Case-analysis:

1. Why did not the Brazilian football player press charges against Manchester United Club for not paying his salary according to the contract?

2. What could be the most possible consequence if he did so?

3. What principle of negotiations best describes the situation in the case?

4. Can you think of any other examples where you can apply this principle?

Case 3

Rod Zemanek, the principal negotiator, designer and Project Manager of an Australian chemical engineering consultancy, sent the Chinese a questionnaire, asking for information about specifications, resources, brewery capacity, products they planned to produce, budget, and business plans. The response he received convinced him to head to China to discuss a potential deal to build Guangdong province's largest brewery—a $20 million project. But, having heard from others about their China experiences, he decided to pitch only for the business in which his company had special technology to offer. "One of the first things you need to understand about China is that you can't compete against cheap, local rivals," he advises. "The Chinese only want foreigners involved if we can offer special technology they can't get at home. We knew if the Chinese could have got locally what we offered, they would not have approached us."

In the lead up to the negotiations, Rod Zemanek knew his business could provide strengths the Chinese business lacked. He had access to technology that could increase the capacity of the planned brewery while also reducing waste. He specialized in understanding and predicting market trends and had access to sophisticated, international market data the Chinese company lacked.

The Chinese party had no experience in designing breweries whereas, since 1983, Rod Zemanek had built or redesigned all Australia's major breweries and most of its boutique breweries. Before starting negotiations, he did extensive research on the Chinese market, including its beer industry and the Guangzhou company. He found that, despite the company's listing on the Shanghai Stock Exchange, it had direct links to the Chinese government.

When Rod Zemanek arrived in China, he discovered that the Chinese were also talking to German, French, and Belgian companies, and that the Chinese company's plans for the brewery were not as well defined as had initially appeared. "I decided my job was to be the expert, and I knew I should tell them what they needed, rather than let them tell me. It was clear they knew nothing about designing breweries."

Rod Zemanek also understood the sensitivities in pointing out the shortcomings of the Chinese plans. He had spoken with Chinese Australians (including two on his staff who had become the key members of his team in China) and read widely on Chinese culture, so he recognized the risk of causing the Chinese to lose face. To avoid doing so, he offered to work with the Chinese on developing the competitive brief using the latest technology.

This would allow him to begin building relationships with the Chinese before the tendering process had begun. It would also give the Chinese lead negotiator face with his bosses (and the Chinese government officials), as he would be able to develop a better business brief using foreign technology. It also gave Rod Zemanek's business a head start in the tender competition.

To ensure he was not misunderstanding the negotiations, which were being conducted through an interpreter with the Chinese team, Rod Zemanek had brought from Australia two of his China-born staff—a chemical engineer and an accountant. "I decided I needed to use my two Chinese team members as my interpreters, because the Chinese language is often not explicit: The meaning of what they were saying was often only implied. It was the best decision I made, because I got the chance to log onto real feedback."

Rod Zemanek also began to see the language barrier as an advantage. "Not knowing the language gave me carte blanche to completely change my mind on things I already had said, because I could use the excuse that I had not properly understood. They kept changing the negotiations on me, so it gave me the chance to do the same back and get away with it."

Rod Zemanek had great respect for his competitors. They were professional managers, corporate people. But they also had superior attitudes toward the Chinese, and indeed also toward Rod Zemanek and Australia. They refused to believe that a world-class brewery designer could be found in Australia.

After several weeks, the French and Belgian businesses pulled out, frustrated at the drawn-out negotiating process. They had offered their best price when first challenged and had left themselves no room to maneuver. Between them, the French and Belgian negotiators had two other problems. First, they were both professional managers involved in a number of projects, so it was easy for them to give up and go home to take up other projects waiting on their desks. Second, no one on the French team liked Chinese cuisine, so returning home looked very attractive to them.

Rod Zemanek, however, was a specialist chemical engineer who owned his own business, had already invested $350,000 in preparation, and was not inclined to walk away. "Chinese culture is so different that you need that local Chinese input. You can never have intuitive understanding of everything that influences and drives them—that would take fifty lifetimes. The next best thing is to have local contacts to guide you."

With the negotiations down to just two companies, Rod Zemanek tried a new tactic. He pitched the environmental benefits of his brewery design, explaining how his technology could make the Chinese brewery a world leader in waste management. His technological solution would diminish environmental waste while ensuring maximum capacity and building up the Chinese company's reputation as a world leader.

Finally, Rod Zemanek won the job to design the Guangdong brewery, and he also was exclusively commissioned to design a $5 million winery in Xinjiang province. This demonstrated how trusted he had become in China.

Questions for Case-analysis:

1. Did Rod do any pre-negotiation preparations? What were they and did they work? Why?
2. How does Rod's understanding of Chinese culture help him compete with the French and Belgian companies?
3. Can you summarize the tactics that Rod Zemanek used to win the Guangdong brewery project and explain how each one worked in different stages?

Reference

1. Brett, J. M. and Crotty, S. "Culture and Negotiation" in P. B. Smith, M. F Peterson, &D.C. Thomas (ed.), Handbook of Cross-cultural Management Research, Thousand Oaks, CA: Sage, 1998.

2. Daniels, John D. and Radebaugh, Lee H. International Business: Environments and Operations. Calif: Addison-Wesley, p. 15, 16, 826, 829, 1986.

3. Deal, T. & Kenney, A. Corporate Cultures: The Rites and Rituals of Corporate Life. Reading, Massachusetts: Addison-Wesley, 1982.

4. Deresky, Helen, International Management, 4th ed. N. J: Prentice Hall, 2002.

5. Dymsza, William A. "Trends in Multinational Business and Global Environments: A perspective", Journal of International Business Studies, p. 27, 28, 37. 1984.

6. Fewer, S., Krohm, D., and Yang, S. Lafarge Negotiations in China, Northwestern University, Kellogg School of Management, Evanston, Illinois, 2005.

7. Gilligan, C. In a Different Voice: Psychological Theory and Women's Development. Cambridge, MA: Harvard University Press, 1982.

8. Hall, Edward T., Beyond Culture. Garden City, N.Y.: Anchor. Press / Doubleday, 1976.

9. Hall, E. T.& Hall, M. R., Understanding Cultural Differences, Yarmouth, ME: Intercultural Press, 1990.

10. Heard, Joyce. "How Business is Creating Europe Inc.", Business week. 7 September 1987. p. 40.

11. Hofstede, Geert, Culture's Consequences: International Differences in Work-Related Values, Thousand Oaks. Calif.: Sage, 1980.

12. Kahane, D. "Dispute Resolution and the Politics of Generalization." Negotiation Journal, 2003, 19(1), 5-28.

13. Kirkman, B. L., Lowe, K. B. and Gibson, C. B. A Quarter Century of Culture's Consequences: A Review of Empirical Research Incorporating Hofstede's Cultural Values Framework, Journal of International Business Studies, 2006, 37(3), 285-320.

14. Lam, N. Mark & Graham, John L. China Now: Doing Business in the World's Most Dynamic Market, McGraw-Hill, 2007.

15. McGoldrick, M. (ed.). Re-visioning Family Therapy. New York: Guilford Press, 2002.

16. McGoldrick, M., Giordano, J., and Garcia-Preto, N. (ed.). Ethnicity and Family Therapy. New York: Guilford Press, 1982.

17. Moore, Christopher W. and Woodrow, Peter J., Handbook of Global and Multicultural Negotiation. San Francisco, CA: Jossey Bass, 2010.

18. Ohmae, Kenichi. Triad Powers: The Coming Shape of Global Competition (New York: The Free Press. 1985). pp. 64.68.69. 81. 118. 119.

19. Putnam, Linda L. and Wilson Steven R. Argumentation and Bargaining Strategies as

Discriminators of Integrative Outcomes, in Managing Conflict: An Interdisciplinary Approach (M. AfzalurRhim ed., Praeger 1989); Linda L, Putnam, et al., The Evolution of Case Arguments in Teachers' Bargaining, 23 Journal of the American Forensic Association 63-81, 1986.

20. Ran, Dou, International Business Negotiation. Shanghai: Fu Dan University Press, 2006.

21. Riemer, "Europe: taking the sting out of the plunging dollar", in B. Riemer and F.J. Comes, European Companies Exporting from U.S. Subsidiaries, Business Week, p. 72. 73.

22. Riemer, Blanca. "A cash-rich Europe finds the US ripe for picking", Businessweek. 25 January 1988. pp. 48, 49.

23. Rossant, John. "Can France's great sell-off sell Chira as president?" Businessweek. 25 May 1987, p. 76.

24. Rudd, Jill E. and Lawson, Diana R. Communicating in Global Business Negotiation: A Geocentric Approach, Thousand Oaks, Cali: Sage Publications Inc., 2006.

25. Salacuse, J. "Ten Ways That Culture Affects Negotiating Style: Some Survey Results." Negotiation Journal, 1998a, 14(3), 221-240.

26. Salacuse, J. "So, What Is the Deal Anyway? Contracts and Relationships as Negotiating Goals." Negotiation Journal, 1998b, 14(1), 5-12.

27. Samovar, L., and Porter, R. Intercultural Communication: A Reader. Belmont, Calif.: Wadsworth, 1988.

28. Schein, E. Organizational Culture and Leadership. San Francisco: Jossey-Bass, 1985.

29. Sesit, Michael R., "Japanese acquisitions in US jumped to $5.9 billion in'87; strong yen cited", Wall Street Journal. 21 January 1988, p. 14.

30. Smith, Peter B., Peterson, Mark F., and Thomas David C. The Handbook of Cross-Cultural Management Research, Thousand Oaks, Calif.: Sage, 2008.

31. Smith, R. Negotiating with the Soviets. Bloomington: Indiana University Press, 1989.

32. Solomon, Steven. "Europe's quiet revolution", Forbes. 14 December 1987. p. 52.

33. Schwartz, Shalom S. Beyond Individualism/Collectivism: New Cultural Dimensions of Values. in H. C. Triandis, U. Kim, and U. Yoon (eds.), Individualism and Collectivism, Individualism and collectivism: Theory, method, and applications. Cross-cultural research and methodology series, Vol. 18., pp. 85-117 London: Sage, 1994.

34. Stevens, Charles W. "Multinational firm still expect dollar to fall further", Wall Street Journal. II January 1988, p. 6.

35. Sunshine, R. Negotiating for International Development: A Practitioner's Handbook. Dordrecht: Martins Nijhoff, 1990.

36. Timmon, H. and Kramer, A. E. "Russophobia'Gers Blame for the Death of Severstal Deal," International Herald Tribune, June 27, 2006, p. 11.

37. Tully, Shawn. "Europe gets ready for 1992", Fortune. I February 1988, p. 81, 82, 84.

Chapter II Planning the Negotiation

learning Objectives

After studying this chapter, you should be able to

- Form negotiation team.

- Create information base.

- Draft negotiation plan.

- Make physical preparations.

Case 1

The negotiation teams from Eurol and the country of Saharaland are meeting to finalize an agreement that includes long-term leases for oil exploration, extraction, and transport. The Eurol team is headed by the vice president for exploration, joined by technical and legal advisors. The team has been working on strategies for weeks, developing a series of scenarios, predicting the likely demands of the Saharaland government, calculating costs and revenues under multiple scenarios, and estimating their bottom line, their dream deal, and the most likely settlement. They are armed with tables and figures, multiple scenarios and associated budgets, as well as legal opinions from the Company's legal experts, one of whom is on the team. They have also determined their likely strategy if the negotiations fail and the risks inherent in working in a country as unstable as Saharaland. The full team, including the vice president for exploration, participated in a strategy retreat in which they even conducted role-plays of negotiation scenarios, based on their research regarding the likely negotiation styles of the Saharaland team.

The Saharaland team is headed by the national vice president, who is joined by the minister for natural resources and several members of the oil resource unit within the ministry. The vice president has met with the president and received instructions to reach the best deal possible for the country; they have few other sources of revenue, other than foreign assistance and humanitarian aid, *in the wake of* twenty years of civil war. The president will review and approve any tentative agreement before completing the contract. The oil resource unit consists of two men with undergraduate engineering degrees who have done their best to estimate the kinds of revenues they might expect from the deal with Eurol. They met briefly with their minister, who merely asked if they were ready, and they assured him that they were. They have not met with the vice president, although he is a distant cousin of one of the engineers. The vice president is also aware that the Eurol vice president for exploration met with the president at a high-level summit on untapped oil reserves the previous year.

Here we can see two organizational cultures and two national cultures at work as the two teams get ready to negotiate an important commercial deal. One team feels obliged to prepare thoroughly and in considerable detail, while the other focuses mainly on the decision-making authority of the negotiation team and relationship dynamics. While some of the variations in preparation can be attributed to the differences in available financial and human resources, much of it relates to the cultural orientations of the two teams.

(*Excerpts from* Handbook of Global and Multicultural Negotiation *by Christopher W. Moore and Peter J. Woodrow*)

Questions for Case-analysis:

1. What do you think of the two negotiating teams?

2. What pre-negotiation preparations, in your opinion, will prepare you for the success in a negotiation?

There is an old adage "If you fail to prepare, then prepare to fail." In negotiating this is particularly true. The research evidence is clear: successful negotiator spend more time planning than average negotiators, and spend more time considering the negotiation from the other party's perspective rather than their own.

Preparing for a negotiation is not just reading up on the situation—it is knowing your business, understanding your motivations, knowing your skills, developing strategies and tactics, considering physical and emotional issues that might arise, knowing your limits, knowing your stakeholders' needs, knowing what is important and not important (and being able to differentiate between importance and urgency)—in short, knowing as much as it is possible to know before venturing into the negotiating arena. And the most important preparation is to know all of these things, and more, about your opposite party in the negotiation; which means doing research in all of those areas where you have no immediate information, so that when the negotiation starts, you are in the best possible position.

Research evidence from successful negotiators finds that they spend more time than average negotiators in the preparation phase, and more of that time thinking and preparing from the other party's viewpoint.

Pre-negotiation planning involves four preparatory stages: forming a negotiating team; creating information base; drafting the negotiating plan and physical preparations.

1 Forming Negotiation Team

Negotiation is a team sport, requiring all the specialized skills, communication ability, team spirit, and gamesmanship found in any professional sporting event. Structured properly and deployed in an effective and timely manner, a negotiating team can play a critical role in achieving victory at the bargaining table.

⇨ 1.1 The Size of a Negotiation Team

Rarely is international negotiation composed of two individual negotiators sitting across the table from one another. Most often, companies are represented by several individuals with different expertise needed to negotiate a specific contract. Teams vary in terms of size, composition, and authority. These variations enhance the complexity of reaching a settlement. Members of some cultures wish to deal with individuals or groups of equivalent rank in terms of organizational position, social status, or political influence. Teams of people with significant differences in rank would be disturbing or even unacceptable to them. Other cultures are less conscious of status and more tolerant of differences between negotiating teams, but in general, parties expect to work with counterparts of more-or-less equivalent position, status, and authority.

For example, in 2006, representatives of the Government of Sri Lanka (GoSL) and the Liberation Tigers of Tamil Eelam (LTTE) agreed to meet in Geneva to restart stalled peace talks. The GoSL sent representatives that it felt were of appropriate status and position to address the issues on the proposed agenda and represent the government's views. The LTTE sent representatives to the talks from higher-level positions in its structure than those of their GoSL counterparts. They believed that high-level talks required representatives from the highest levels. When the parties reached Geneva, the LTTE accused the GoSL of not sending equivalent counterparts with authority to reach agreements and refused to engage in negotiations. This dynamic was one factor that caused the talks to collapse.

Size of the team can often be construed as overpowering the other side. For example, China's negotiation team is typically twice as large as U.S. negotiation teams (Zhao, 2000). Given that China generally requires consensus in their decision making, it is not surprising that they would want to have representation of all interested parties at the table to hear the issues discussed. Compare that to the United States, where the decision maker is generally one person who receives advice from key people who are often part of the negotiation team.

Although we discuss international business negotiations as bilateral, often they are multiparty negotiations (Graham, Minhu, & Rodgers, 1994). For instance, two companies may be involved in the actual exchange of goods or services but key governmental agents or regulatory advisors may also be required parties in some cultures.

Who is really making the decision to accept or reject the agreement? It depends on the culture, the organizational culture, and the role of the negotiator. One of the difficulties some international negotiators face is determining if they are meeting with the final decision maker. For example, China typically sends the technical staff to the negotiation table to do the initial data gathering. It is not until the end of the negotiation that the CEO appears to accept or reject the agreement.

⇨ 1.2 Personal Qualities

Eight Qualities of the Best International Business Negotiators

It is desirable that a negotiator have the following qualities to achieve satisfactory negotiation results:

1) Understanding and working effectively with the decision-making processes peculiar to the countries they're dealing with.

Ideal negotiators mesh well with the wide variety of institutional norms and practices found in different countries. They can shift their strategies radically whether they're dealing with people from developing countries, which tend to have more centralized structures, or from developed countries, where decentralized decision-making is typical. Although most Western countries' decision-making patterns tend to be more similar than dissimilar, procedural differences are still present. West Germans usually process their decisions through committees composed mainly of technical people. The French emphasize the long-range view of their objectives and give low priority to short-term decisions, which they use for unimportant goals. Also, unlike most other developed countries, the French seem to adopt a more centralized decision-making structure, and this means it takes more time for their decisions to be processed. The French don't mind introducing conflict—in fact they are comfortable dealing with a lot of conflict during their negotiation sessions. Most nationalities, such as the Americans and Japanese, are usually unnerved by the stumbling-blocks introduced by conflict. Unlike the Americans and Germans, the French don't attach much importance to factual information in their negotiations.

Normally Third World countries have radically different decision-making practices. In Mexico, for instance, decision-making is centralized, and the personality whoever holds the position of authority largely influences the kind of decisions that are made. In fact authority tends to reside more in the person than in the position itself. People from cultures which are more used to having a certain degree of authority accompany a position are usually at a loss when they're in Mexico. Although the times of the caudillos (or "macho" men on horseback) are over, their influence on styles of decision-making in Mexico still persists.

Dealing often with the host government is necessary for multinational corporations (MNCs) which are interested in setting up projects in developing countries. When negotiating with the host country's government, the MNC usually emphasizes the multiplier-effect of the project's economic benefits, such as offering constructive competition, improving working conditions, developing local resources, and providing managerial and entrepreneurial skills. While the host government will be concerned about ensuring a rate of return that is high enough to satisfy the MNC, it will try to siphon off as much as it can above the rate of return in the form of taxes, shared profits or exchange controls to keep excess money in the country. Bilateral bargaining based on such economic considerations is the usual arrangement through which host governments and MNCs negotiate.

Uninformed MNCs make weak presentations about the positive political effect of their projects. This is unfortunate because host governments are normally concerned about achieving attractive economic benefits without inviting unnecessary political attacks from rival politicians and pressure groups. In one case, an Asian government persuaded an MNC to accept no more than 49 percent ownership along with a management contract allowing exclusive management control by the MNC. This way, the host government would not be criticized for allowing unreasonable foreign equity participation and, at the same time, the MNC would appreciate having total control over the project, even if it didn't have majority equity participation.

Quite a number of decision-makers in developing countries have been educated in the West or in Western-style universities in other parts of the world. Naturally, representatives of MNCs from developed countries prefer to deal with them, hoping they are more familiar with modern business practices and thus more predictable. Although this is partly true, Western educated negotiators in developed and less developed nations alike are still largely influenced by the institutional pressures of their cultures. Japanese educated in Canada or Australia will still have to deal with group norms in making decisions when they return to Japan.

Delays are another area of conflict. For instance, it is generally known that it takes longer to negotiate business deals in Europe and Asia than in the USA. Negotiators from "hurry-up" nations easily mistake delays as a *sinister* ploy on the part of TOS (The other side). They don't realize that, especially in highly centralized countries, decisions often have to pass through many layers of the bureaucracy.

Another area of difficulty is the lack of technical expertise on the part of negotiators from less developed countries. And it is not unusual either to find that negotiators from developed countries have only the vaguest idea about the social cost-benefit analysis that the government of the underdeveloped nation has made when studying their proposal. Ideal international negotiators gather information about how the host government evaluates proposals before they even begin their negotiations, and they spend a lot of time briefing the government about the technical content of the project.

2) Ideal international negotiators are flexible enough to handle effectively even the most delicate issues, such as bribery, and manage these issues within the context of the local culture.

Gift-giving or handing out payoffs has always been a contentious issue for negotiators whose cultures deem bribery unethical, while other cultures look at the same practices in a somewhat different context. The position of Western negotiators, particularly of North American negotiators, is to stick to the "bottom line", playing strictly by market rules and competing in terms of quality, price and service. To them, gifts and payoffs have no place in the impersonal market system. Often the laws of their countries prohibit payoffs. Many negotiators with these attitudes will walk out of negotiations, particularly in less developed countries where various forms of what they may consider as bribery form part of accepted business practices.

Three linked traditions provide the background that will explain to readers the cultural significance of payoffs. The first tradition is that of the "inner circle". The more communal cultures seem to have a greater need to divide society into those who belong to the "inner circle", or those with whom they have active business dealings, and those who belong to the "outer circle" of strangers and aliens. Preferring to deal only with those they know, such communities restrict their social and commercial dealings to members only of the "inner circle". A member of the "inner circle", for instance, may be asked to hire workers only from a particular clan in exchange for dependable labor.

The second tradition is that of preserving a system of future favors: members of the "inner circle" enliven their relationships through an exchange of favors. In Japan this concept translates as giri or "inner duty"; in Kenya it is uthoni or "inner relationship"; and in the Philippines it is utang na loob or "inner debt". In this system it is assumed that any person who is under obligation to another person or group has the duty to repay the favor at some time in the future. In the process of repaying the debt, of course, the person paid for the favor now becomes the debtor. A lifelong cycle of obligatory relationships has thus been formed.

The third tradition is that of gift exchange. People from nonwestern nations often value long-term personal relationships in business more than the material exchange itself. They use gifts therefore to express both their affection and willingness to maintain the business relationship indefinitely. Their logic runs thus: gifts seem to be an appropriate way of creating social ties and obligations with impersonal Westerners who generally in gatherings talk only about business. It is therefore necessary, if trust is to be cultivated in the relationship, to instill in the Westerner a sense of obligation.

International negotiators who understand how these three traditions relate work better within the "inner circle" of nonwestern business colleagues and participate actively in the exchange of favors and gifts. As a result, their companies are usually given preferential treatment in the market, and they gain access to an otherwise clandestine network of business contracts and intermediaries. At the same time, they become more trusted by the members of the local culture as they reinforce their contractual obligations.

3) Ideal international negotiators possess a keen intuitive sensitivity in an intercultural situation: they are able to empathize with their local counterparts, anticipate and respond appropriately to emotional and social needs that their local hosts may have a hard time expressing.

Here there are special sensitivities to be dealt with, for example, in negotiating with Asians, who place great importance on preserving smooth interpersonal relations and the appearance of harmony. They observe society's standards of what is right and wrong, acceptable and unacceptable, rather than their own internalized system of values. In that society making the appearance of conforming to society's standards is very much the basis of their personal worth. Asians, then, invest a lot more personally in preserving acceptable appearances than do Westerners. In addition, they judge persons more on the basis of their actions rather than their words.

International negotiators who understand these sensitivities behave appropriately in negotiations. For instance, when the American negotiators are in Asia, they never criticize their Asian hosts in public or try to force an answer out of them when the time isn't "right". Western negotiators avoid making scenes in public, especially if they're angry, knowing full well that Asians have the stereotype of them as rude and arrogant. During negotiations they allow extra time for their business meetings and avoid giving the impression that they're in a hurry. Rushing around leaves the impression that the Asian host is unimportant to the visitor. They also give their local hosts extra time to arrive at business decisions. **Astute** international negotiators also use the concept of "saving face" as a negotiating tactic in Asian countries, where this concept is most fully understood. For instance, they will say that they hesitate to make certain concessions which will result in their losing face. During negotiations they let the other side take the lead in determining procedures not only to give them a sense of importance, but also to understand and conform to the local ways of doing things.

Ideal international negotiators are able to attune to the sensitivities of whatever country they are in. For instance, when the American negotiators are in Latin America, they will open business meetings by discussing family matters important to the hosts before getting down to "shop talk". When negotiating with Europeans, they avoid using data that emphasize how the productivity of Europeans is lagging behind that of their own country. They know too that the West Germans, British and French are extremely sensitive about being compared with one another so they avoid so doing.

4) Ideal international negotiators can communicate and relate effectively with their local counter parts; they are keen observers of the subtle communication clues in the verbal and non-verbal behavior of their hosts.

International negotiators who are also effective communicators manage both the verbal and non-verbal content of the messages that flow between them and their counterparts. One of their verbal skills is the ability to use suitable language to summarize and test their understanding of what the other side has said, for example: "Correct me if I'm wrong, but as I understand it right now, your company is requiring us to offer a skills training program for both the local executives and technical personnel who will be involved in our joint venture. Is this correct?"

They also understand that when more than one foreign language is involved in the negotiations, there are greater chances of misunderstanding. The pitch and tone of voice alone, not to mention the words, can introduce communication "noise". The flat tones of the English make us think they're bored or sarcastic. Of course, this may not be true. When Arabs speak English, they sound as if they're shouting. The truth of the matter is over-assertion and exaggeration is the natural way they express themselves, or else, they fear, they might convey the opposite meaning instead. The Japanese concern for preserving face and harmony compels them to say hi or "yes" when they really mean "no". Effective communicators watch for these things. And for their part, they see to it that they use the appropriate pitch, loudness, tone, speed and rhythm associated with their intended meaning. If they're communicating in a foreign language they don't know too well, they will make sure they're assisted by an expert interpreter.

Greater sensitivity and sharp powers of observation are required in handling non-verbal communication. International negotiators who understand "body language" have a great advantage over those who don't. Why? Because non-verbal behavior is the most natural way we have of expressing our spontaneous and true reactions. Non-verbal behavior acts as a safety valve through which we release our pent-up emotions and feelings, especially in stressful and threatening situations. Negotiators express their frustration with frowns, groans and grunts when they perceive the other side to be unjustly demanding, unreasonably resistant to alternative solutions presented, or just plain difficult. Research studies also show that people tend to believe non-verbal behavior more than the verbal content of a message.

Ideal international negotiators who understand non-verbal behavior when abroad have first understood the cues of their own culture. From this understanding they find it much easier to appreciate the nuances of the behavior of foreigners. Take physical distance during conversations for example. They will notice that Mexicans and Italians tend to stand closer when conversing than the Dutch or Japanese do. They also know the differences in business protocol. For instance, Americans are more informal in conducting their business meetings. They believe that creating and sustaining a relaxed atmosphere is more ***conducive*** to effective communication, so they ***slouch***, put their hands behind their heads in a "flying elbows" position and sometimes even rest their feet on top of their desks. When exposed to this behavior, Asians and northern Europeans may quickly dismiss the Americans as rude and unpolished.

Effective international negotiators are flexible and able to complement the non-verbal behavior they observe. They recognize their responsibility of changing their behavior if the other side prefers to stick to their own way of behaving. In Mexico, for instance, the actions of Mexican soften strongly suggest an authoritarian mode and machismo, which they perceive to be necessary in maintaining their public image. The appropriate response of the international negotiator is to accord the Mexican the respect, deference and social distance the latter is obviously seeking.

5) Ideal international negotiators have personal stability, a sense of inner security and the ability to handle stress on-the-job.

Negotiating with foreigners abroad, or in your own country, introduces unusual stresses above the normal pressures associated with a negotiation with one's own countrymen. Ideal international negotiators are secure enough within themselves that they don't have a great need to be liked. Wanting to be liked makes you want to give away the store, just to see the other party smile! In dealing with strangers from another country, you may have a strong tendency to be solicitous at times, to earn goodwill. In some countries negotiators may try to take advantage of this. For example, American negotiators have reported that in their negotiation with the Chinese, the latter have tried to exert pressure on American negotiators by creating guilt feelings by reminding them of past American policies that promoted the "mistreatment" of mainland China.

International negotiators should be resilient enough to roll with the punches, especially when they are targets of the prejudice and negative behavior of others. For instance, some British business executives have seemed at times to consider themselves "superior" to their Australian counterparts, while the Australians who, naturally, resent this attitude have sometimes referred to the British as "Pommy bastards". Many French people are preoccupied with the perceived superiority of their language and culture; they think they hold a special position in the international arena on account of their culture and history. Some of them tend to ignore and lose respect for foreigners who don't speak their language.

6) Ideal international negotiators use humor, with good taste and discrimination to "break the ice" and enhance the pleasant ambience of the business negotiations.

In a country as seemingly socially forbidding and stolid as Japan, one British visitor succeeded in making his business hosts laugh. During their meeting the discussions moved on to economic issues and someone pointed out to the group that the new trade agreement offered by the Americans was "like a gift on a silver platter". No sooner had this been said than the British businessman realized an opportunity for light-heartedness. He quickly reached for a small item in the shopping-bag he had nearby, and said smilingly: "I myself have no silver platter for you today, gentlemen, but I hope you will accept this present instead." The Japanese gentlemen in the meeting broke out in laughter, and the incident etched this foreigner's graciousness on their memory for some time to come.

From the point of view of a Westerner, there was nothing particularly funny about the gesture. Nevertheless, the British executive captivated the Japanese, and he was pleasantly surprised at the response to his spontaneous attempts at levity. It is a rare pleasure indeed to be able to indulge in humor with one's foreign counterparts, considering the complexity of the cultural differences involved. Japanese humor, for example, which is based on word plays and "twittings" at tradition, is not easily appreciated by foreigners. On the other hand, the Japanese do not find Western humor based on irony particularly funny either. Some business executives have learned that when attempting humor in Japan, they should preface their statements with appropriate warnings like "A jokes coming! Here it is!" simply to help out their audience. Others have suggested trying jokes without words through antics like card or magic tricks.

7) Ideal international negotiators can tolerate ambiguity and are patient with their counterparts, even under situations of great pressure.

Westerners have the stereotype of the "inscrutability" of Orientals, and undoubtedly there is some basis for this. Part of the challenge of dealing with Asians is their unexplored potential for verbalizing and expressing thoughts and feelings. Societal constraints, such as the rules governing "saving face" and the authoritarian tenor of some cultures like China's Confucian tradition, have held them back. And so the forthright and direct Australians, who always seem to be honest about what they have in mind, say that they often have to do a lot of digging to find out what the Asian really wants to say.

The negotiating situation with the Chinese presents its own unique hurdles too. American negotiators have reported that the mainland Chinese hold their cards close to their chest and refuse to reveal their own needs and objectives, even after a lot of time has been spent breaking the ice. Without any guidelines about what the Chinese really need, foreign negotiators are really navigating in the dark and are less effective in their proposals.

If you are an ideal international negotiator, you will persist through ambiguous situations and wait for TOS until they are willing to share vital information, or until they are convinced that you have earned the right to know their real needs. You will also exercise deliberate patience, especially as you await final decisions by the different parties involved in the negotiations. You are also prudent enough to build a good deal of extra time into your schedule, to allow for bureaucratic delays, procrastination and extra-thorough deliberations by TOS.

8）Ideal international negotiators get involved with TOS's organization, actively seeking allies and extending their network of influence throughout TOS's company.

One observer of international negotiations remarked that negotiators dealing with foreigners miss a lot of other business opportunities because they fail to reach out, extend and cement their initial relationships. They erroneously believe that the momentum obtained from the signed contract would carry them through to winning future contracts. Take the case of an American engineering firm that succeeded in obtaining a one year operation and maintenance contract in Asia. Since the technology they introduced was so superior, they thought their technical efficiency alone was enough to build a foundation for a long-term relationship. The locals who worked for the Asian company were highly dissatisfied with what they perceived as unfriendly, impersonal and arrogant behavior on the part of the Americans. They kept this to themselves, though, and without letting the Americans know it, they made overtures to other engineering firms about future contract work. Eventually the American firm lost out to another foreign bidder.

Effective international negotiators nurture their interpersonal relationships at all times; they take nothing for granted. They realize the value of spending additional time exchanging social pleasantries, feedback and loyalties. They study the power networks of the local community and create gestures of goodwill to penetrate these networks. They try hard to become part of the "inner circle" normally closed to unknown aliens or strangers. They pay the price of what it takes to be socially accepted and rewarded in the local community.

⇨ 1.3　The Criteria for Picking Negotiation Team Members

Whenever you select people to serve on your negotiation team, keep the following criteria in mind:

1）The particular skills you seek.

2）The personality of potential team members.

3）Any organizational considerations that affect selections.

4）Your overall negotiation strategy.

5）Any agreements you have on team size.

Let's examine each of these elements in detail.

1.3.1　The Particular Skills You Seek

The type of expertise needed for your negotiation team will be dictated by what it is that you're negotiating. However, many negotiations require skills in accounting, law, and the technical area that's the subject of a negotiation. In addition, subject matter experts may be needed on limited aspects of the negotiation. As a general guideline, limit the selection process to those functions that you consider to be primary for negotiation success. Whenever possible, select specialists to be included as "on call" participants when meetings take place. That way, the expertise is available if needed, without adding people with limited responsibilities as active members of the negotiation team.

1.3.2   The Personality of Potential Team Members

This is a subject that's regularly overlooked when picking members of a negotiation team. And even if someone is commonly recognized as having a "quirky" personality, that fact is usually overlooked because of the person's expertise. This ignores the reality that negotiating is a people-oriented endeavor and picking the wrong person can do a lot of damage.

Therefore, as a general rule, look for folks who are team players with a keen sense of when to talk and when to listen. By the same token avoid anyone with a big mouth, a big ego, or an ax to grind.

TIP: If you have someone whose expertise is needed that you don't want at negotiation sessions, get their counsel before, after, and during breaks in your meetings.

1.3.3   Any Organizational Considerations that Affect Selections

One aspect of team selection that can't be completely avoided is the question of organizational politics. This is particularly true in large organizations where individual departments have functional responsibilities that may in some way be affected by the outcome of negotiations. Naturally, departments with a direct interest in the results should be consulted, and may have one or more participants on the negotiation team.

However, other groups may also be interested in the negotiations so as to protect their real and/or imagined interests. Their actual cause may be nothing more significant than a turf battle, or resentment that their group is excluded from the negotiations. But this is sometimes a tricky subject to deal with. After all, executives in positions of power that give them the opportunity to throw roadblocks in your path are a force to be reckoned with.

On the other hand, you're planning a negotiation session—not a mass rally for dissidents. Therefore, to avoid problems in this area, bring as many people on board as is necessary during your planning sessions. However, don't add them to your negotiation team unless it's unavoidable.

1.3.4   Your Overall Negotiation Strategy

Picking a negotiation team is in part dictated by your negotiation plans. These considerations include not only what you're negotiating, but also whom you're dealing with. For instance, you may know that your opponent is easier to deal with on a one-on-one or small group basis. That being the case, it behooves you to limit your negotiation team.

The flip side of the coin is that you may have reason to believe that a large entourage will work in your favor. For example a good-sized group can convey a psychological sense of power to others. However, don't get too enthusiastic for this sort of maneuver, since your adversary may counterattack with his own army of experts.

Furthermore, the inherent problems of a large group can more than offset any possible psychological advantage.

Of even greater consequence than your opponent's attitude toward group size, are your own feelings. If you feel more comfortable with a smaller group, then that's the way to go—as long as this doesn't hurt your negotiation stance.

Finally, there are negotiations which by their very nature require secrecy. In these situations, you will want to limit your team to an absolute minimum.

1.3.5 *Any Agreement You Have on Team Size*

It's not uncommon for both parties to have a prior agreement as to the number of participants. In fact, it's advantageous to know who you will be facing across the negotiation table. That way, you can *factor* this knowledge in when you select your team. Apart from the desires of the negotiating parties, logistics alone can influence the number of participants. The facilities where negotiation sessions will be held must be taken into consideration. And, of course, if you're negotiating at a distant site, cost can also be a factor.

The suggestion is when you're going through the routine of selecting your negotiation team, you obviously want to limit its scope to the number necessary to do the job. However, negotiations are complex, and technical issues may be raised that weren't considered when you assembled your team. This may force you to halt negotiations, while you regroup and get the expert advice you need. You can minimize this problem by including experts in your internal planning sessions even though they won't participate in negotiations. By doing this, they are briefed on your strategy if you have to call on them. This approach can save a lot of time and confusion.

⇨ 1.4   **The Make-up of the Negotiation Team**

For most important business negotiations, the negotiation team should include members with primary responsibilities in each of the following areas: financial, legal, operations or production (technical and management, either together or separately), and general company management. In many procurement situations, various end users of the products or services involved should also be included on the negotiation team or, at least, made available as team resource individuals. Besides, if the negotiation takes place between two different countries, the interpreter is needed. But selecting an ideal negotiation team leader is of primary priority. The potential strengths provided to the team by various functional areas are outlined below.

1.4.1 *Leading Personnel*

This person should have all the attributes of any one thought to have leadership qualities. In addition, this individual should be exceptionally strong in traits that are **conducive** to success as a negotiator. These include:

- An ability to make sound decisions under extreme pressure.
- The tact to mold divergent viewpoints into a consensus.
- An even-handed temperament.
- The flexibility to adjust to changing conditions.
- A talent for projecting trust and confidence.
- A **knack** for sorting fact from fiction.

In addition, the designated team leader should be someone who has the complete confidence of any superior who has veto power over the negotiation results. Otherwise, this opens the door to widespread second-guessing, which can cause serious problems.

Furthermore, the person selected should be someone who supports the purpose of the negotiations. It doesn't make much sense to entrust negotiations to people who don't want to see them succeed unless that is the underlying agenda of the negotiations. For instance, diplomatic negotiation between countries occasionally conducted even though there is no intention of reaching an agreement. However, for the most part, negotiations are entered into with an ultimate agreement as the goal, and it helps to have a negotiator who will have that interest in mind.

Of course, it's also nice to be able to select someone with a personality that will interact well with the party they will be negotiating with. However, it's difficult enough to find someone who fills most of the bill, so how well your choice will interact with their counterpart is best left to conjecture. The only rare concern here is that you don't pick someone who has a personal **antagonism** against the other party.

POINTER: One of the most frustrating feelings for a negotiator is to suffer the fate of being second-guessed by others. Even more outrageous is the practice of senior executives short circuiting the negotiation team and dealing directly with their counterpart. This often results in haphazard agreements which both parties have to live with. The bottom line is that people entrusted with the authority to negotiate should be allowed to do their job. Otherwise, there's little incentive to put forth their best effort if they expect to be overruled. Furthermore, once other parties recognize that it's easy to succeed by going over a negotiator's head, then the negotiator's position is permanently weakened. Therefore, once negotiation leaders are appointed, they should be given full support by their superiors.

1.4.2   Financial Personnel

This person should be qualified accountant or other financial analyst if you want your negotiation team to be effective in accessing proposals and various business alternatives. To maximize objectivity, this individual ideally should not be an employee or officer of the division responsible for the procurement or other transaction. Many firms assign a member of their corporate accounting, financial planning or professional consulting department to the team for this purpose.

In some situations, an independent accountant may be used.

Regardless of the source, the financial member of your team should have the following features:

- Considerable experience in assessing alternative methods of consummating the transaction involved.

For example, in a procurement transaction, the financial representative should be qualified to analyze differing methods of acquiring and financing equipment. Where your firm is a public company or otherwise subject to various pronouncements of the accounting regulatory bodies, the financial team member must also appreciate the impact that alternative business decisions may have on your company's financial reporting obligations.

- Being capable of assessing, or at least communicating with experts concerning, the tax aspects of the transaction under consideration.

1.4.3   Legal Personnel

This person should be competent legal counsel especially in significant negotiations. To have any realistic opportunity to shape the contractual documents in an important business transaction, your lawyer must be:

- A full member of your negotiation team.

Participation on the negotiation team offers one of the best methods of permitting the attorney to gain critical background information, become thoroughly familiar with the transaction, and preserve the *leverage* necessary to engage in effective contractual bargaining.

- Having considerable experience in drafting and negotiating contracts in the specific area involved in the transaction.

Although lawyers who specialize in probate, real estate closings, and personal injury cases may be very successful in their respective areas, such individuals seldom have any meaningful experience in negotiating and handling complex business contracts. Given the increasingly specialized nature of the law today, you should select an attorney with proven contract drafting and negotiating experience.

1.4.4   Operations/Technical Personnel

Depending upon the business transaction involved, your operations division, or a comparable technical area, should ordinarily be well represented on your negotiation team. Usually two technical or operating representatives may be advisable. One of the team members should have:

- Considerable technical expertise in the subject under consideration (e.g., the products or services being acquired).

The other member should have:

- Departmental or divisional responsibilities.

This combination ensures that the team will be able to assess specific technical problems, and, at the same time, appreciate overall goals and problems in the applicable department or division. Where a negotiation team includes only a single operations representative, the risk is that the individual involved will either be technically deficient or unable to understand the broad management issues faced by the division.

Care should be taken to ensure that the team does not become top heavy with technical personnel. For your team to be effective, it must remain relatively small and manageable.

1.4.5 General Corporate Management

A member of upper-middle or senior management should always be included on your negotiation team, even if the person cannot take the time to attend all team meetings and negotiating sessions. This management representative is important for several reasons:

- First, the senior manager can ensure that the transaction under consideration will be consistent with overall company goals and objectives, both short and long-term.

- Second, the management member can provide input as the proposed transaction is structured. This advice may enable your team to shape the transaction in a manner that offers significant financial, business, or policy advantages to your company. Company management is generally in the best position to assess the impact that a proposed negotiating decision may (or should) have on the company's financial and operating goals and management policies.

- Third, it minimizes second guessing. Many business transactions are financial and political hot potatoes. By having a senior management official plugged in from the start, your negotiation team not only has the advantage of management input; it also has the advantage of prior management commitment. From a practical standpoint, your senior management will be far less likely to second guess the transaction at a later date if a management-level executive actually participates in the negotiation process. In this regard, a five-minute explanation of the transaction to management or the board of directors just before the contract is signed is no substitute for actual involvement from the beginning.

- Fourth, it reduces the likelihood that your negotiating opponent will attempt to go around your team to senior management if the negotiations deadlock or otherwise appear to be progressing inappropriately.

- Fifth, the management member of your team may provide a psychological advantage during the negotiation process. For example, the management member can implicitly remind the other members of your team that the company places considerable importance on the transaction involved and on the successful outcome of the negotiations.

- Sixth, the management member of the team can also add immediate strength to team decisions, particularly decisions to deadlock negotiations or reject a given proposal made by your negotiating opponent.

1.4.6 Interpreters

In a negotiation between two countries, interpreters are often at the core of the negotiation. A qualified interpreter should not only be a bilingual expert but also be able to judge correctly the intention of the speakers, and fill the gap of words omitted deliberately or habitually. He should also be able to convey the meaning and intention of the negotiating parties appropriately and faithfully.

Sharpness and quick understanding of the interpreter does not mean he can interpret speaker's words as he assumes. When the speaker's points are blurred and obscure, what he should do is to clarify the points again with the speaker. Another significant function of the interpreter is to iron ups and downs in the course of a negotiation when the tension is becoming high and some negotiators utter unfriendly words emotionally.

For the interests of the interpreter and smooth progress of the negotiation, it is suggested one interpreter be invited throughout the entire negotiation. The interpreter's quick and accurate understanding depends not only on his knowledge of language but also his knowledge of the background of the negotiation and its development, which means the more he is involved in the negotiation the better he functions.

Their translation skills will directly affect the effectiveness of communication and negotiation.

2 Creating Information Base

Case 2

In the 1960s, China began the exploration of the Daqing oil-field, and all the information about it was almost confidential. Apart from a few people who were involved in this project, others did not even know the specific address of it. However, the Japanese not only heard of that, but also got the accurate details. All the information collected has been achieved without any spies or agents. They did not bribe the authorities or the masses. Instead, what they depended on was just the public information issued by our government and their comprehensive analysis. In July, 1966, there was a photograph which had been signed out on the cover of the "China *Pictorial*", describing how diligently the workers pioneered the Daqing oil-field. They struggled for the exploration of the Daqing oil-field against the *fluffy* snow, wearing quilted jackets. It was this picture that enabled Japanese to make a judgment that the oil-field might be located in northeast part of China. Then, the Japanese noticed a report in the "People's Daily", saying that when he went to Majiayao, Wang Jinxi said loudly, "How huge the oil-field is! And we are supposed to throw the bad name of Backward Country in oil development into the Pacific." Therefore, the Japanese got the old map of Manchukuo period, and found that Majiayao was a village located in southeast part of Hailun County, Heilongjiang Province, which was about 10 kilometers eastern away from a small railway station of Zhaoan. Later, the Japanese version of "Chinese People" reported that the Chinese working class carried forward the spirit of fearing neither hardship nor death, and all the equipments had been carried by their shoulders to the site without any help of horses or carts. Accordingly, the Japanese considered it indicated that Daqing oil drilling was not very far from Majiayao, because these people could not bear so many equipments for that long distance. When the news that Wang Jinxi had been invited to attend the Third National People's Congress hit the papers in 1964, the Japanese certainly have concluded: the Daqing oil-field had yielded much oil; otherwise Wang Jinxi could not be the representative of NPC. After that, they made a further calculation, according to a photo of oil-field rigs in the "People's Daily", to identify the diameter of the oil wells. All the data resulted from the handles of the racks on the drilling platform. Meanwhile, they fully analyzed the statistics in the government work report issued by the State Council, and subtracted the amount of oil in the past from that of the national gross production on oil, estimating the average amount of oil production in the Daqing oil-field. Therefore, they designed proper equipments for exploration of that oil-field on the basis of surveys they had conduced. Thus, when the authority of Daqing oil-field announced that it would seek for the design of oil facilities from all over the world, Japanese had already prepared well for the plans of existing programs and equipments without being known by other countries. Eventually, they succeed greatly in the negotiations with the representatives of Daqing oil-field.

Once your negotiation team has been organized, the first and most basic step in preparing for a specific transaction is determining your firm's requirements. Whether viewed from a negotiating or technical perspective, this step essentially involves creating an information base. Before your negotiation team can move effectively to the bargaining table, your firm's goals must be thoroughly defined and understood by all personnel involved in the transaction. Moreover, before these goals can even be formulated, your negotiation team must have adequate background information concerning relevant business needs, problems, and potential solutions. In essence, your negotiation team must know what it is striving to achieve, and why, before it can develop and implement the negotiating strategies necessary to get there.

The creation of a solid base of relevant information is critical to the overall success or failure of your negotiating efforts because most business negotiations are won or lost on the basis of two elements:

(1) Which team has better information; and (2) which team is better able to apply and manipulate that information in the context of the specific negotiations?

The categories of information required for a particular transaction will vary depending upon a wide variety of factors. Some companies divide the information gathering process into the collection of internal and external information. Others categorize the process according to the technical or functional areas involved (for example, financial, legal, data processing and so on). Still other firms allocate the process into purchaser and supplier stages, subdividing each into more detailed technical areas. While all these approaches are perfectly valid, the following discussion describes the information collection process in terms of general information, market information, laws and regulation information and cultural information.

⇨ 2.1　Obtaining General Information

For most business firms, the information collection process should begin with a survey directed to a variety of representatives: operation management and technical staff, senior company officials, the ultimate end users or customers of any applicable company division, and representatives of the financial division. The goal should be to collect problems, objectives, priorities, and needs covering a wide range of technical, financial, legal, and managerial issues.

The information collection process varies from transaction to transaction and from company to company. Consequently, no firm description of mandatory steps can or should be formulated. Nevertheless, the following areas should generally be included, or at least considered, in creating the information base for most business transactions.

2.1.1　The Qualification and Credit Status of the Partner Company

The qualification and credit status consist of the history and status quo, economic and political power, corporate reputation (its liabilities), capital quantity, operating capability, bank credit and such of the partner company. Specifically, these are:

- The history and status quo of the partner company refers to the establishing time, registered office address, main business scope and the number of the employees, etc.
- Economic and political power refers to the annual turnover, financial or fiscal conditions, market share and position in its industry at home or abroad, of the partner company or organization; whether it has any political influences or what its political tendency is like.
- Corporate reputation refers to its status of assets and liabilities, brand popularity and word-of-mouth in the market.
- Capital quantity refers to total assets, fixed assets, current assets, cash flow, etc.
- Operating capability refers to status of operating profit and loss, contribution ratios of major products, the ability to develop new products, etc.
- Bank credit includes the names and numbers of contacting banks. Credit it enjoys and whether it has bad accounts in banks, etc.

2.1.2　Negotiation Representatives' Profiles

Information about the negotiating representatives from the other side mainly includes:

- The number of the negotiating representatives.

- The composition of the negotiation team.
- Limits of their authority.
- Their identity and status.

The number and composition of the negotiators refers to how many negotiators have been chosen to participate in the negotiation and how the team is formed or what people is it composed of? (For example, vice president, project manager, technician and interpreter and so on). Limits of the negotiators'authorities refer to whether the negotiation participants are the direct associates (manufacturer, importer and exporter, wholesaler, retailer) or their agents. If they are the former ones, do they have the authority to make decisions? If they are the latter, what are their limits and scope of authority as an agent? Identity of negotiators refers to their nationalities, birth places, diplomas, qualifications, family backgrounds, characters, hobbies, etc.

2.1.3　Existing Contract Files

One of the most frequently overlooked information collection sources is your own contract files. As part of the survey process, your staff should analyze all relevant previously executed agreements to determine what problems have arisen in similar transactions. This review should include all contract-related documents and materials, including side letters, counterpart proposals, presentation letters, marketing brochures, and test criteria and results. In each situation, the promise or the contractual commitment should be compared to the actual performance. Problems and solutions relating to prior transactions should be carefully reviewed.

2.1.4　Counterpart Relationship History

As an adjunct to the formal document review noted above, your staff should also prepare a narrative chronology of all past relationships involving the same counterparts or type of transaction that will be involved in the proposed negotiations. The discipline involved in this technique can be quite educational. The resulting historical perspective can refresh memories, educate new members of management, and pinpoint previous problems that might otherwise be overlooked in the future negotiations. The old adage that history repeats itself is as applicable to most business negotiations as it is to the world at large. Remarkably, firms that experienced serious problems with one counterpart only a few years ago walk into the same or a very similar problem with a new counterpart. Businesses seem particularly prone to forget past problems when they are in the process of changing back to a previous counterpart. Somehow, these firms only seem to recall the problems caused by their recent counterpart.

2.1.5　Other Companies

Once you begin to frame your corporate requirements, the information collection process should be expanded to include other firms that have had experience with the same counterpart, equipment, or transaction that will be involved in the upcoming negotiations. Many executives recognize that other companies can be extremely valuable sources of information and advice on such hard topics as equipment performance and operating expenses. However, these executives often fail to appreciate that other firms can be equally good sources of negotiating information. The key in seeking this type of information is to *zero in* on the past problems, financial concessions, and negotiating successes and failures experienced by the firms being surveyed. To be sure, many individuals are not too eager to discuss their errors, omissions, and failures.

Nevertheless, you can normally gather valuable insight and advice if you take a professional, low key approach of "We can all learn from common successes and failures". A workshop or training session environment, such as that found at conventions, meetings, and seminars, often offers the best setting for a candid information exchange.

2.1.6　Other External Sources

In addition to other businesses, several other external sources of information should be considered. Trade publications offer a wealth of information concerning industry developments, rumors, and opportunities. This information often can (and should) affect your negotiating strategies. Every member of your negotiation team should read or scan several of these publications. In addition to considering the more traditional industry publications, your information collection efforts should also include several specialized newsletters or similar services designed to supply current insight about business practices, pricing, and ploys. Even more than general industry periodicals, these publications are likely to supply advice or cautions that will directly affect your negotiating strategies.

⇨ 2.2　Obtaining Market Information

As the general information collection process outlined above is executed, your negotiation team should also assess the market factors that may be relevant to the proposed transaction.

Negotiators should make synthesis comparisons concerning:

- technological specifications
- uses
- purchasing costs
- quantity available
- freight charges
- domestic market prices
- international market prices
- product's life cycle and competitiveness
- patents
- necessary accessories

- after-services
- the like of the negotiation item

Case 3

In 1983, Shanghai government decided to build subway line 1 using foreign investment. France, Germany, Britain, USA, Japan, Italy and Canada expressed their intentions to extend co-operation and loans. And in particular, France proposed that it would like to provide more favorable government loans, which is characterized by the following features: no cash is provided, and instead the borrower has to purchase the equipment manufactured by loaning countries with the loans. However, Shanghai government decided to adopt international competition system by carrying out internationally adopted *"Net Present Value"* (NPV) evaluation, i.e. to make a synthesis evaluation on the capital, technology and prices proposed by the bidding companies and grade their systematic projects, capital conditions, technical plans and equipment prices respectively as A, B, C, D and E. Eventually, Germany got the bid for its advantage of 100% government soft loans (France offered 46% government loans and 54% commercial loans) at annual interest rate of 0.75% with a loan period of 40 years. Its quotation was 10% lower than France and 30% lower than Britain. The major of Shanghai made an immediate decision that they would make use of German loans, purchase German vehicles and equipment and send represen-tatives to Germany to make investigations, conduct negotiations and sign contracts.

(*Adapted from* Shenjiang Service Guide, Sep. 6, 2006)

Questions for Case-analysis:

1. Why did Shanghai government decide to adopt NPV evaluation?
2. What's the advantage of the evaluation?

⇨ 2.3   Obtaining Laws and Regulation Information

Laws and regulation information are also crucial to the proposed transaction. Before the negotiation, we need to know whether the transacted items will be regulated or restricted by the laws and regulations of our country or our partner's country, or by international laws.

Case 4

A Fish out of Water

Roger O'Leary, an Australian, was sent by his firm, a manufacturer of rubber products, to replace one of the *expatriate* managers in its Kuala Lumpur branch, Malaysia. Staffing the firm was the prime concern at present, and a comprehensive 45-day recruiting program had been launched to obtain the best local talent available to hire to the firm. Roger was assigned to head this recruiting project and briefed about the local laws concerning hiring Bumiputras (Malays, or "sons of the soil"), Chinese and members of other ethnic groups. Roger participated in all phases of the hiring process, particularly at the interviews; at night he ***pored over*** many application forms. After a month, Roger had a good picture of the quality of people available and keenly eyed certain candidates for specific positions. He had a problem in staffing the new products department: he wanted to hire a Chinese male, who was a highly skilled and experienced chemical engineer; no one else could match his qualifications. He talked to the Head of Personnel to try to find ways around the government requirement to hire a Bumiputra for that position. Roger was disappointed that the rule could not be changed. Before coming to Malaysia, he thought the laws would be simple to follow there. He had not realized how strongly ***ingrained*** his bias towards ***egalitarianism*** was until now. He didn't like the prospect of having to contend with these restrictions in the future. So he asked his head office for a transfer.

Actually, the law did strike a sensitive emotional chord in Roger. It is true that Roger was trying to bend the rules to suit his views, but he wasn't really trying to reform company policies. The rationale for the law very clearly favors Bumiputra participation in the Malaysian economy. This was plain to see, and Roger understood. Roger didn't really expect himself to react negatively to the government's employment guidelines. In fact, Roger had been briefed about these hiring conditions in Malaysia before he arrived. He thought it would be easy to comply with the rules after he was on the job. Until he took this post, he didn't realize how much he valued equality and fair treatment. The hiring situation clearly created a clash of values. Finally, Roger's sense of rationality was violated by a law that prevented him from hiring the best-qualified person.

(*Excerpts from* World-Class Negotiating: Dealmaking in the Global Marketplace *by Donald W. Hendon and Rebecca Angeles Hendon*)

Questions for Case-analysis:

1. How would you explain the way Roger reacted, asking for a transfer?
2. What's your choice if you are assigned to the position?

⇨ 2.4 Obtaining Cultural Information

In an increasingly globalized world, we interact with people from other cultures in many contexts. Cultures do affect business negotiations. Anticipating cultural differences at the negotiation table helps negotiators make sense of those differences when they appear and adjust their own behaviors to reinforce or to block the other party's strategy. So collecting cultural information will help negotiators to adjust their use of negotiation strategy to achieve their interests.

Third World "Cronyism"

Henri Deneuve, a Frenchman, has owned for the past three years a medium-sized firm in Indonesia which manufactures consumer products; it has been profitable throughout that period. The plant there imports all its plastic components. One day, the government announced that a state trading firm would handle all importations of plastic. The government said that this would indicate for the first time the volume of imported plastic; it also said that it would save local manufacturers money because it would bargain for lower prices from international suppliers. Six months later, Henri thinks the new system has only made plastic much more expensive to purchase, and the delays in delivery are much longer than before. His trade association wrote him and the rest of its members the following letter: "We will *petition* the government to get rid of the state trading company. The fees it charges have made imports much more expensive, and their inefficiency causes delivery delays. Many manufacturers who rely on imported plastic raw materials have had to shut down due to the dramatic increase in production costs." The trade association also said that the head of the state trading company is a nephew of one of the top government officials. Even so, it would still go ahead with its lobbying efforts. That night, Henri looked at his financial statements and was alarmed by the trend of increasing expenses. He felt frustrated about the local political setup and started to think about transferring his operations to another nation in south-east Asia. How would you view the situation?

Are Henri and the trade association correct in thinking that the local business environment is dominated by special interests protected by political backers?

Yes. Instead of saving the local business executives money, the state trading company has been making money out of each transaction. Processing of imports has taken longer because of the artificial bureaucratic procedures that were imposed. The dominance of the extended family in the political elite in Indonesia is a well-known phenomenon—not only in that country, but also in other developing countries, such as the Philippines. This kind of "cronyism" is a reality Henri will have to learn to accept and live with if he is to continue working in Indonesia.

(*Excerpts from* World-Class Negotiating: Dealmaking in the Global Marketplace *by Donald W. Hendon and Rebecca Angeles Hendon*)

3   Drafting Negotiation Plan

The negotiation plan is one of the most important preparation activities. A well-prepared intercultural negotiator will find it valuable to implement preparation strategies prior to meeting his or her counterpart because they can contribute significantly to the probability of successful talks and outcomes. Drafting the plan has the following steps:

⇨ 3.1　**Perform a Context Analysis**

A context analysis permits a broad understanding of the situation in which negotiations will occur. Potential elements of a context analysis include the following:

A. Identify and understand the people and parties who will be involved in negotiations.

- Who will participate in negotiation sessions—from your side and from the counterpart's side? What are the cultural implications and norms determining inclusion or exclusion of individuals from talks? What is the structure of the two or more sides: a single individual, a team, or several sub-teams?
- What kind of authority to negotiate do you and your counterpart have?
- Who are the primary and secondary parties to the conflict or business transaction? What party or parties have been left out of the negotiation, and why?
- What do you know about your counterpart as a group or organization and the individuals involved? What are their backgrounds and personal histories? Are they likely to adhere to traditional norms for their culture or work according to international business, diplomatic, or organizational norms?

B. Understand the situation in which negotiations will occur and the general purpose of the negotiations:

- What are the general purposes and desired outcomes of the negotiation process? From your perspective? From the perspective of your counterparts? Are these in alignment?
- Is the focus of talks on building a relationship, completing a transaction, or resolving a conflict? Is this a one-time process or part of a long-term relationship?
- What is the history behind the negotiations? For specific individuals involved? For the groups, organizations, or nations? How might history influence the negotiation dynamics?

C. Identify positive preconditions for negotiations and develop strategies to mitigate negative ones. Typically, some (though rarely all) of the following preconditions for negotiations must be met for successful talks:

- Parties have been identified who are willing and ready to participate.
- The parties depend on each other to get their interests or needs met (interdependence).
- The parties agree on at least some issues and interests.
- The parties have the necessary resources, time, and energy to negotiate.
- The parties have effective means of leverage or influence.
- The outcome is unpredictable. (If the outcome were known or predictable, there would be no need to negotiate.)
- There is a sense of urgency and deadline (pressure to reach agreement).
- The parties have no major psychological barriers to participation or settlement.
- The issues are negotiable.

- The parties have the authority to decide.
- One or more parties lack a better alternative to reaching a negotiated agreement (Fisher and Ury, 1981, regarding the concept—of the best alternative to a negotiated agreement, or BATNA).
- If necessary, the parties are willing to compromise.
- The parties believe that it is possible to reach an agreement and are willing to settle.
- External factors exert a positive influence or do not present barriers (for example, views of associates, political climate, economic conditions, and security situations).

⇨ 3.2   Complete an Issue, Interest and Power Analysis

In addition to analyzing the people, parties, situation, and preconditions, a negotiator needs develop an understanding of the issues involved as the parties see them, the interests held by the various stakeholders, and the kinds of power they enjoy.

A. Explore the potential framing of issues:
- How do you frame the issues to be discussed?
- How does your counterpart frame them?
- Do you both see issues in approximately the same way, or are there stark differences?

B. Identify the potential interests of you and your counterpart:
- What are your interests in relation to the issues at hand? In the ideal, what do you hope to accomplish through the negotiation process? What would you settle for?
- What do you guess to be the interests of your counterparts—and their ideal and bottom line?

C. Assess the emotional charge of the negotiations, and develop potential strategies for handling it:
- Are the issues to be discussed fairly neutral for you and your counterpart, or is there a strong emotional connection for one or all? (Note that if the context is conflict resolution, there will almost always be an emotional component.)
- If there is an emotional charge for one or more parties, what are the potential strategies for handling those dynamics?

D. Evaluate the parties' willingness to talk and reach agreements and develop strategies for promoting effective talks or alternative means to get interests and needs met.

E. Assess the parties' means of influence and power:
- What are your sources of power and influence? What are the sources for your counterpart?
- How might you mobilize your own sources of power—and what strategies will your counterpart likely use to mobilize his or her power and influence?

➡ 3.3 Complete a Process Design

The list of procedural issues presented in 2.1 covers almost all of the issues that typically arise regarding the procedures for a negotiation. In a simple negotiation process, many of these would be irrelevant or handled informally. In higher-stakes or more formal negotiations or those conducted under tension or conflict, these issues may become quite important. In fact, they may become the focus of a whole series of pre-negotiations simply to bring the parties to agreement about how negotiations will take place. Typically, two or three meetings are required just to work out procedural issues before the parties are ready to address matters of substance.

3.3.1 Who Will Be Involved

1. Which parties (primary, secondary and so on) will be involved—and how?
2. What will be the size and composition of negotiation teams? Any provision for substitutes or alternates?
3. Will the participation of observers be permitted?
4. Will legal counsel or other advisors participate, and if so, how?

3.3.2 Organization with and among Teams

1. Role assignments within teams: spokesperson, topic or issue leaders, researcher, writer or editor and so on;
2. Designation of working groups, technical teams, or sub-committees by topic or issue.

3.3.3 Basic Rules and Organization of Sessions

1. Will negotiation sessions be closed or open?
2. What is the agreed venue and physical setup of negotiation sessions?
3. What are the agreed behavioral guidelines among parties? Acceptable and unacceptable behaviors (i.e. respect for values, no personal attacks, no attribution of motivation, limits on emotional displays and so on)?
4. What are the recognition and protection of legal rights and administrative mandates?
5. How will agendas be developed?
6. How will meetings be chaired or facilitated?
7. Is there need for a third-party neutral (mediator, facilitator...), and if used, what is the role or function of the third party?
8. What is the schedule of meetings, beginning and ending times?
9. How will basic rules be enforced?

3.3.4   *External Relationship and Communication*

1. How will the parties relate with their constituencies and decision-making authorities?
2. How will the parties interact with the media (press releases, briefings, and so on)—if at all?

3.3.5   *Organization of Sessions*

1. How will agendas be developed?
2. How will information be collected and shared among parties (especially if the negotiations call for gathering and analysis of new data through a negotiated process)?
3. Who will make initial opening statements and in what order?

3.3.6   *Reaching, Recording and Implementing Agreements*

1. How will parties know that they have reached an agreement?
2. How will the meetings be recorded and how will agreements be written?
3. What will the process or final approval of agreements (including those directly involved in the negotiation sessions, and if needed, other people not involved)?

4   Physical Preparations

The time and place of negotiations can have a material impact on the outcome of a particular bargaining session. Unfortunately, few business negotiators seriously attempt to control the negotiating environment to their advantage. Some individuals fail to appreciate the importance that environment can play. Others appreciate the effect of the negotiating environment, but refuse to alter the setting because they do not want to engage in artificial or manipulative actions.

To be an effective negotiator, you must recognize the importance of environment and appreciate that, if you do not seek to control the negotiating environment, your opponent may well do so. The following paragraph explores a number of relevant environmental factors, and indicates the methods that can be used to gain maximum negotiating advantage from altering the applicable environment.

⇨ 4.1   **Plotting the Location**

The best place to negotiate is wherever you can optimize your control of the bargaining process. Every experienced negotiator recognizes the physical negotiating environment that seems to reinforce his or her ability to achieve negotiating success. For some negotiators, the golf course, the hood of a car, or a luncheon table at the club offers the best environment. For others, a formal conference room in their own or their client's offices provides the only secure location. For still others, the offices of the opponent maximize the negotiator's opportunity for success. The key point to remember is that to waive the right to pick the negotiating site, or to exercise that right carelessly, is an unforgiveable error.

At the outset of any business transaction, you should assess the relative advantages and disadvantages of negotiating at your office, at your opponent's location, or at a neutral third site. Because the pros and cons of a particular location may vary depending upon the stage of the negotiations at the time of a given bargaining session, you may need to reassess this matter from time to time as the negotiation process continues to progress.

4.1.1 Home Court Negotiating

For many individuals, negotiating on their home court provides substantial benefits.

1) Advantages

Negotiating is a team sport and, in a simplistic sense, the home team advantage can be just as applicable in business bargaining sessions as it is in football or baseball contests. Negotiating on your home ground:

- improves your ability to control such critical factors as travel, food, fatigue, and physical surroundings.
- permits your team to avoid many of the psychological and physical problems associated with adapting to a new and temporary physical environment.
- maximizes your team's access to your firm's other resources, including staff support, personnel, files, and final decision makers.
- permits one or more of your senior executives to set the tone and lay down the ground rules for the negotiations, both at the outset and as discussions continue.

2) Disadvantages

Despite these advantages, home court negotiating also offers potential problems. For example, unless your negotiation team exercises substantial discipline, the press of ongoing business at your site may be difficult to channel or otherwise control. Because of this fact, home office negotiations:

- are often plagued by persistent interruptions and pressures that cause distractions and morale problems for the home team.
- makes it more difficult for you to implement certain limited authority and deadlock tactics. If the negotiations are being held at your headquarters, you may be less able to assert that you cannot gain management approval on a particular matter until a later date or time. Moreover, as a general principle, it is easier to walk out, or threaten to do so, than it is to throw someone out. Thus, while your negotiators have numerous methods of packing up to leave at your opponent's site or at neutral location, this flexibility is not present when the negotiations are held at your own offices.

- enhances your opponent's ability to pull an end run and attempt to influence or undermine your negotiating authority, simply because of your opponent's proximity to your firm's senior executives.

4.1.2　*Guest Court Negotiating*

Because of these disadvantages of home court negotiating, some experienced negotiators prefer to bargain at their opponent's offices, at least during certain stages of the negotiation process.

1) Advantages

This approach can be particularly effective for a purchaser negotiating for the acquisition of products or services to be supplied by a *vendor*. When properly orchestrated, negotiations at the vendor's site:

- ensure that the proposed transaction will have high visibility within the vendor organization.

This visibility provides two benefits to the purchaser. First, it gives the purchaser's negotiators an opportunity to meet with senior management or marketing representatives within the vendor organization, thereby increasing the purchaser's ability to affect a substantive compromise on important issues. Second, this visibility places the spotlight on the vendor's negotiators, exposing them to substantial pressure and criticism if, for example, the purchaser's negotiators walk out. (One experienced purchaser negotiator always schedules this type of actual threatened walkout just before a scheduled lunch with a vendor executive vice president.)

- makes it more difficult for the vendor to implement various limited authority ploys.

For example, the vendor's negotiators are less able to complain about needing to go to corporate, being unable to make a given decision, or being unable to locate particular informational or human resource.

- improves the purchaser's focus and reduce the fatigue associated with marathon bargaining sessions particularly where the purchaser's negotiators are experienced business travelers, bargaining at the vendor's site.

As noted above, lengthy negotiations at the purchaser's site often create time pressures and interruptions for the purchaser's negotiators.

- eliminates many of the purchaser's negotiators' day-to-day interruptions and devote their full attention to achieving an optimum transaction.

Because the negotiators are out of town for a stated duration, they can avoid some of the morale problems that can and do arise from the cancelled meetings, unreturned telephone calls, and late night sessions (where family dinners are either delayed or abandoned) that plague home site negotiating sessions.

2) Disadvantages

Nevertheless, negotiating at your opponent's site can create serious problems. Inexperienced purchaser representatives are particularly likely to face disadvantages when negotiating at a regional or headquarters location of the vendor. In this situation, inexperienced purchaser negotiators:

- may be overwhelmed by the vendor's attention, interest, and apparent dedication, as the vendor puts on its finest game of show and tell, factory tours, and management luncheons.

This danger is particularly great: (1) early in the negotiation process, when an appropriately impressed purchaser may decide that the vendor is so experienced and committed that formal negations are not necessary; and (2) when the purchaser's negotiators are inexperienced, again raising the risk that they will determine not to proceed with proper negotiating principles.

- Negotiating at the vendor's site may also cause problems relating to travel, fatigue, and inability to control the physical environment.

4.1.3   Third Place Negotiating

Negotiating at a neutral third site has many of the advantages and disadvantages discussed above. The problems and benefits of traveling to a site away from distractions are present. Both sides are still able to execute limited authority ploys. Both parties face the disadvantage of being unable to access resource people, files, and management. Neither party has the immediate ability to control the physical advantage, although the party making the reservations and meeting arrangements may seize this opportunity. (Even at a neutral location, the host may have an inherent advantage in setting the tone for the negotiations.)

In some situations, the idea of a neutral site is more apparent than real. Some negotiators volunteer to use an apparently neutral site, but actually select a location with which they are both comfortable and experienced. Their opponents frequently agree to the suggestion, without considering the possibility that the neutral site may actually be a carefully selected, favorable location.

⇨ 4.2   Designing the Physical Surroundings

The physical environment of the negotiating arena can be as important as the city in which the negotiations are held. Factors such as decor, temperature, seating, lighting, and convenience to business and personal amenities can have a significant impact on the physical negotiating environment. By understanding the interrelationships among these factors, you can gain a far better understanding of negotiating dynamics. By manipulating these factors—before your opponent manipulates them against you—you may be able to achieve subtle but important advantage at the negotiating table.

In considering this area, you should appreciate that some environmental factors tend to encourage agreement, while others tend to cause disagreement. By understanding these factors, and using them to your advantage, you can create a physical environment that increases the likelihood that you and your opponent will reach agreement at a given session. On the other hand, you can employ these factors in a manner that will reinforce your desired negotiating message that agreement at this time is not possible.

4.2.1   *Decor*

Where the negotiations will be held at your own facilities, or neutral offices selected by you, the appointments should generally be reasonably rich in order to instill self-confidence in your negotiators and convey a sense of strength and control to your opponent. However, exceptions to this general rule exist. For example, if you are negotiating with a much smaller company, the possibility exists that rich surroundings will overwhelm your negotiating opponent and create a defensive atmosphere. On the other hand, times may exist when you wish to create an attitude of particular richness and good taste.

Many small businesses elect to negotiate at private conference facilities (perhaps at a private club, hotel, or law firm) in order to avoid bringing their negotiating opponents to their own spartan location. Still other firms turn this approach around, emphasizing that financial concessions are an impossibility, as the surroundings of the firm's own offices will support.

The element of decor can also be carried down to considerable detail. Some of the best business negotiators carefully select the books, paperweights, and mementos that will be placed in their offices or on their desks for a given negotiating session. One of the more effective techniques in this regard is to leave an autographed copy of a particularly good "how to" book on a nearby coffee table where your negotiating opponent is likely to pick the book up and recognize that you may have retained the author—or, worse, may have a continuing friendship with that individual. Some business executives go so far as to change certain of the photographs on their office walls, particularly where the pictures involved have political significance. For example, a photograph of you and a well-known politician may do you a great deal of good.

Case 6

The manager of a button enterprise in Yiwu, Zhejiang province encountered the representative of a world-famous fashion company at the Fashion Festival in Paris and intended to establish business relationship with the well-known company in order to export their buttons and accessories to it. After looking at the button samples brought by the manager from Yiwu, the French company invited him to have a face-to-face talk a week late. Seated in the modern and stylish meeting hall, the manager from Yiwu got to feel a little inferior.

As a matter of fact, this was just a negotiation strategy of the French company: on the one hand, through the comparison between the worldly well known big company and the Chinese small enterprise, and the comparison between the magnificent and stylish hall and the small humble workshop, the French company wanted to impose a psychological pressure on the manager from Yiwu; on the other hand, the French company intended to force the Chinese part to reduce the expected value so as to make great concessions on the quotation of buttons and accessories because they knew that the Chinese part was anxious about the high cost of staying in France, hoping to close the deal as soon as possible.

Since the French Company had studied the button samples brought by the manager from Yiwu, when they decorated the negotiation hall by putting some fashionable clothes with the similar buttons and several fashions with buttons of unusual styles, they meant to imply that their company had already received the new samples you just brought then and your production skills were too far away from the techniques of the unusual buttons! But it seemed that the manager from Yiwu was not shocked. After having a close look at all the buttons on the fashionable clothes, he pointed out the differences between his products and other similar products as well as the advantages of his products in style, color and production complexity. Then he said calmly, "In the same or superior level of quality, the prices of our products are only 1/3 as much as the Italian buttons. As for those these kinds of unusual buttons, there is no difficulty in skills for us, we can post the counter samples by express mail to you after I am back in China and I can promise our buttons would be more beautiful than these but at only half the price of Italian buttons. How do you like my idea?"

(Excerpts from International Business Negotiation *by Dou Ran)*

The French Fashion company chose the magnificent guests meeting hall of their own headquarters as their negotiating site rather than the hotel where the guest from Wenzhou lived with the hope of forcing the manager from China to feel humble or inferior in the elegant and graceful environment so as to cut the prices at their will.

4.2.2 Business and Personal Amenities

The relative availability of business and personal amenities can also have an impact on the negotiating environment. For example, in most lengthy negotiating sessions, room must be provided for breaks and team *caucuses*. If you wish to facilitate agreement and a feeling of cooperation, you should go out of your way to ensure that both sides have access to approximately equal facilities. On the other hand, if you wish to create a feeling of relative hostility and disagreement, you can provide minimal or no facilities for caucuses by your negotiating opponents. In between, you can assign pleasant but somewhat substandard caucus rooms to your opponents, while permitting your own team to caucus in the main conference room or in a first-class nearby location. Internet and telephone facilities for contact with the home office or outside advisors can be handled in a similar manner, and with similar results. If you wish to create pressure on your negotiating opponents, you can limit access to outside internet and telephone facilities or permit opposing representatives to use internet and telephones in public offices, at secretarial desks, or similar locations. On the other hand, if you wish to provide a professional atmosphere stressing cooperation, you can provide a separate conference room for the internet and telephone calls desired by your opponents.

Access to such personal amenities as restrooms, coffee, soft drinks, and food can be manipulated with the same results. For example, if you wish to create a feeling of impatience and reinforce the idea that only a short meeting will be permitted on a given subject, you can avoid providing easy access to coffee, other beverages, and food. On the other hand, if you wish to create the impression that you are prepared to negotiate full-time until agreement is reached, you can stress the availability of beverages, food, and other personal amenities as may be required. Although the idea of manipulating something as basic as restroom facilities may seem abhorrent, some business executives have been known to do so. This manipulation can be as subtle as always sending your negotiating opponent to the locked public facilities "down the hall," where a key must be obtained each time from a receptionist or other party. (In the meantime, of course, your own negotiators use facilities within your executive offices, or, at least, produce their own keys to the public facilities.) Some negotiators go considerably farther in order to emphasize a particular point. One of the best stories involves the senior negotiator who exclaimed, just as his negotiating opponent was excusing himself for a short trip to the restroom, that, "You can darn well stay where you are until we get this issue resolved. As far as I'm concerned, if anybody leaves this room until we get this issue taken care of, the deal is off." Whether this attitude is right or wrong, it can certainly have an impact on the negotiating environment.

4.2.3 *Temperature and Lighting*

Temperature and lighting also have an impact on the negotiating environment. The manipulation of these factors (to the extent permissible within environmental guidelines) can facilitate agreement or disagreement, as desired. Although various individuals have different reactions to temperature levels, you will generally facilitate agreement (say, all negotiators will enjoy maximum mental sharpness) if the temperature of all meeting rooms is cool to cold. On the other hand, you will ordinarily reduce the likelihood of agreement if the meeting rooms are warm and stuffy.

Agreement will also be facilitated by good lighting. Your own negotiators will avoid suffering any disadvantage if the lighting is the same type (for example, cool ray fluorescent) that they are used to working under. Dim or uneven lighting can be a serious annoyance, and reduce the chances that agreement will be achieved. At the other extreme, glare can have a similar impact. An office or meeting room with bright sunlight may be a pleasant meeting place, but if the seating arrangements and window coverings are placed in a fashion that creates glare for one side or the other, or that precludes one negotiator from clearly seeing into the eyes of his or her opponent, tension will be created, and the individuals without the glare problems will enjoy superior negotiating control.

4.2.4 *Seating*

Seating arrangements in the meeting location should also be considered. The likelihood of achieving agreement will be enhanced if all negotiators have relatively similar seating arrangements, with no individual sitting at a higher level or in more comfortable seating than his or her opponents. On the other hand, seating can be used to increase the likelihood of disagreement, shorten the meeting session, or create a feeling of control in one party or the other. For example, by placing your opponents in extremely uncomfortable chairs, you will be likely to reduce the length of the bargaining session, or, at a minimum, create tension. By seating your opponents in chairs that are lower than those used by you and your colleagues, you will increase your relative control and power in the negotiations. (When placed in this situation yourself, you can overcome part of the disadvantage by frequently standing, thereby gaining your own level advantage over your still seated opponent.)

The impact of seating can also be combined with other environmental factors, such as lighting. For example, if the meeting room contains windows (whether curtained or not), your negotiating opponents can be seated facing the glare and distractions of the outside world. Your own negotiators can be seated with their backs to the window, thereby eliminating this adversity from their standpoint. Some experienced negotiators carefully select the location of the conference room or other meeting facility to ensure that the desired seating arrangements can be achieved.

The shape of the table must also be assessed, as different table designs create, or assist in creating, different negotiating environments. (Perhaps the best example of the importance of the size and shape of the negotiating table can be found in peace negotiations among opposing governments. Soldiers may continue to die on the battlefield for many months while government negotiators bargain over the shape of the table and the number of sides, if any, that it will have.)

1) Setting of Round Tables

A round negotiating table generally conveys a collegial feeling because it has no obvious head or sides. Such a table can reduce tension and infer that all seated at the table are colleagues and approximate equals.

Although many fine negotiators suggest that a round meeting table and other pro-agreement environmental factors should be the standard setting for any bargaining session, the blind application of this approach is seldom advisable where your team suffers from a lack of negotiating leverage. This *caveat* is particularly applicable in sales negotiations where the supplier relies heavily upon a warm relationship and subtle marketing ploys to lull the purchaser into a sense of happiness, wonderment, and security. In this situation, a round negotiating table or an informal office seating area only reinforces the supplier's efforts to let relationship overshadow reality. In this circumstance, a more formal seating arrangement may better serve the purchaser's interests, by emphasizing its relative negotiating strength, position, and equality. Once this critical positioning has been achieved, the purchaser's negotiators can more safely employ alternative seating arrangements and other environmental factors to signal concession and agreement at the appropriate time.

2) Setting of Rectangular Tables

On the other hand, a rectangular table usually has a clearly defined head. As a result, those seated around it ordinarily **gravitate** toward their respective sides and (especially at larger tables such as those found in board rooms) the seats acceptable to their position in the relative pecking order.

3) The Arrangement of Opposing Negotiators at the Table

Regardless of the table shape selected, the arrangement of opposing negotiators at the table can also affect the negotiating environment. For example, where the table has an obvious head, many lead negotiators prefer to seize that seat in order to optimize their control of the meeting. (The head of even a rectangular table varies depending upon the room layout, seating order, and local practice. In some situations, the functional head of a rectangular or free-form table may be in the middle of one side, rather than at either end.) Other lead negotiators, generally those with strong experience and confidence levels, prefer to select a position in the middle of the table, forcing one of his or her negotiating opponents to sit in what soon becomes a hot seat at the traditional bead of the table. These negotiators use their superior negotiating abilities to develop and impose dominance from an unexpected location in a successful effort to keep their negotiating opponent on the defensive.

Where a rectangular table is involved, the feeling of tension will generally be heightened if each party's negotiators sit on one side of the table. In contrast, a more collegial feeling can be gained by informally mingling the negotiators around the table without seizing sides. However, if pushed to an extreme, this approach can actually create further tension; for example, by having one party's negotiators choose alternate seats around the entire table, forcing all opposing negotiators to be separated from one another. Such an extreme approach is seldom recommended, but where it is employed it is likely to have substantial impact.

4) Physical Surroundings of the Negotiation Room

Physical surroundings should also be considered where the negotiations are held in an executive's office rather than in a conference or meeting room. For example, in an office, a couch or chair grouping around an end or coffee table conveys informality, warm business relationship, and likely agreement. In contrast, seating which places the executive in his or her desk chair, across a broad desk from the visitor sitting in a relatively straight-backed chair facing the desk, creates a formal and slightly strained position that enhances the superiority and control of the executive. As suggested above, this feeling of superiority can be enhanced if the guest chairs at the desk are relatively soft and low, thereby giving the executive a height advantage even while all parties are seated.

5) Conference Facilities

Ideally, the executive or conference facilities used by you and your negotiating team should include enough meeting rooms and arrangements to permit you to select and control alternate environments as needed. Because of the important negotiating advantages that can be achieved from selecting among alternative negotiating environments, office facilities should never be designed or remodeled without appropriate consideration of the resulting negotiating environment. To achieve appropriate flexibility, facilities used for negotiations should contain at least two small meeting rooms, one with a round table and one with a rectangular table. A larger, more dramatic room should also be available to upgrade important sessions. This room is often most effective when it has an unusually shaped table, such as an octagon or free-form design. Tables such as these usually permit alternative seating arrangements that can be made more or less collegial, as required.

The conference area should also include private offices where smaller (often preliminary) meetings or brief follow-up sessions can be held. Ideally, these offices should include both formal "across the desk" seating arrangements and informal conversation groupings. One particularly effective arrangement for an executive office involves four chairs around a small round or square meeting table—much the same layout found in many residential breakfast areas. Where this approach is used, the desk layout in the office might include a setting in which the executive sits with his or her back to a window, thereby placing the traditional two guests chairs facing the window. Blinds or drapes can then be used to create glare or visual comfort for the executive's visitors.

All of these physical environments have only one goal: to give you and your negotiators the best possible tools in your efforts to optimize your bargaining position. By selecting and controlling these environments, you can create a meeting that maximizes the opportunity for business relationship and agreement or that stresses differences and suggests the need for continuing efforts to bring the parties closer together.

⇨ 4.3 Fighting the Fatigue Factor

4.3.1 The Harm of Fatigue

1) Fatigue obviously affects a negotiator's mental sharpness and ability to recognize and defuse an opponent's ploys and tactics.

2) Fatigue reduces the negotiator's ability to employ his or her own tactics.

3) In many individuals, fatigue reduces patience and increases the potential for uncontrolled anger.

4) Fatigue may also signal an actual or potential lack of preparation when it is related to overwork.

5) Fatigue can affect ongoing negotiations such as accuracy and judgment.

Even when carefully trained, the members of a negotiating team can lose their sharp edge when exposed to the grinding pace of a round-the-clock negotiation. Accuracy is likely to be sacrificed, thereby opening the way for errors in such basic matters as product lists and proofreading. Perhaps more importantly, judgment may also be impaired. For example, an attorney may not understand the full business or legal impact of a provision proposed by an opposing marketing representative or lawyer. A financial expert may not appreciate the interest expense of adding relatively inexpensive programming and education service into a lengthy equipment lease.

6) The fatigue resulting from long-term bargaining may also slowly take some of the fight out of a negotiating team.

As the hours draw on, dinners are missed, families are not seen, other work piles up on the desk, and the members of the negotiating team begin to wonder whether the entire transaction is worth all this effort. As a consequence, they may not pursue a given point with the vigor required to achieve their negotiating goals and objectives. Although the impact is generally more subconscious than conscious, compromises may be affected far sooner than during the earlier stages of the negotiations.

The adverse consequences of fatigue are frequently heightened by various sense-of-urgency ploys. A negotiator suffering from the effects of fatigue is particularly susceptible to rationalizing that completing the negotiations or consummating the transaction as soon as possible is in the best interest of his or her firm.

Because of these and other negatives, you should avoid scheduling negotiating sessions when you or your colleagues are suffering from fatigue.

4.3.2   Steps to Minimize the Adverse Effect of Fatigue

Several steps can be taken to minimize the adverse effect of fatigue. Although these solutions can be employed to minimize the impact of fatigue at any stage of the negotiating process, they are particularly helpful during the critical last few hours of lengthy bargaining.

1) You and your colleagues must recognize the problem—and its complexity.

You must appreciate that fatigue can and will occur, and that it will adversely affect your performance and that of your colleagues. Although a high aspiration level and sense of drive can be extremely important in helping you survive marathon negotiating sessions, a substantial difference exists between this type of drive and a naive unwillingness to admit that fatigue can reduce the effectiveness of your performance. In recognizing the effects of fatigue, you should also appreciate the interrelationship between fatigue and a sense of urgency. When manipulated together, the two factors can be particularly effective weapons for your negotiating opponent.

2) You should determine at the outset to minimize the effect of any false sense of urgency.

This can be done in a number of ways, but one of the most effective methods is to recognize that the proposed transaction is almost always as important to your negotiating opponent as it is to you. A second method of minimizing the sense of urgency is to place the transaction in a proper perspective from your standpoint. In this regard, the easiest rule is to remember that, with rare exceptions, neither your company nor the country is likely to fail if the agreement being sought is not consummated by the date demanded (or threatened) by your negotiating opponent.

3) You should be alert to efforts by your opponent to divert negotiating priorities from critical

issues to insubstantial subjects.

Particularly where only a limited time period is available for the negotiation, these actions by your opponent may signal an effort to delay critical negotiating issues until the end of the bargaining session—when your negotiating team may be particularly tired or vulnerable to urgency ploys.

4) You should strive to control the effects of fatigue, using the environmental factors suggested in this chapter.

One of the best methods of controlling the fatigue of your negotiating team as a whole, and often increasing the fatigue level of your opponent, is to bring in someone fresh. The interjection of an alert, impeccably dressed "varsity squad" replacement at a mature stage of the bargaining session can help your team maintain or regain control, permit the newcomer to address tired issues with more clarity of mind and better results, and extract meaningful concessions from your opponent.

5) You should adopt an affirmative tactic to turn the fatigue factor against your opponent.

By turning the effects of fatigue against the opposing negotiators, you generally gain two advantages. First, the fatigue and confusion faced by your opponent will increase your relative bargaining position and weaken your opponent's ability to use fatigue to its own advantage. Second, by causing you and your colleagues to focus on the fatigue factor, the approach will keep your team members constantly alert, and more immune, to any efforts by your opponent to use fatigue and a sense of urgency as affirmative negotiating tactics. Although the idea of turning fatigue against your opponent may seem manipulative, immoral, or socially unacceptable, you may find that you really have little choice. In serious, lengthy bargaining, fatigue will be a relevant factor: you can either have it used against you, or you can seek to use it to your own advantage. The possibility that fatigue will not be a factor, or that it will be a neutral one, is most unlikely.

Several techniques can be used to maximize the effects of fatigue to your own advantage. These techniques should be employed in varying degrees, with due respect for your negotiating opponent—both in terms of his or her own well-being and the possibility that your opponent may apply the same tactic against you in a future bargaining session.

As suggested above, one of the more indirect methods of maximizing the effects of fatigue is to save critical points until late in the negotiating session you're your opponent will suffer from a low level of resistance and a high susceptibility to urgency ploys. This approach can be particularly effective where your opponent has suggested that you review the entire document and negotiate each important point along the way. By spending considerable time discussing points that are actually quite minor from your standpoint, you can often lure your opponent into spending substantial time and energy arguing these less critical issues. When the important points are finally reached, your opponent may well be too tired, from a physical and mental standpoint, to achieve optimization of the important contractual provisions.

Subtle comments can also be used to manipulate the fatigue factor. Carefully placed observation concerning your opponent's missed dinners, late hours, and the volume of other work that must be piling up, all will drive home the impact of fatigue. Some negotiators begin these observations by making apparently innocent inquiries about the wife and kids. These discussions slowly shift to inquiries about hobbies, vacation plans, and other activities that are rather clearly not being pursued due to the lengthy bargaining session. As suggested above, ploys based upon a sense of urgency can be particularly effective methods of capitalizing upon the effects of fatigue.

The effects of fatigue can also be manipulated by controlling the time and method of discussing various issues. For example, this approach can permit you to rotate your own negotiating team members in and out of the negotiations over a period of days or hours, while forcing your opponent to keep his or her entire negotiating team at the front at all times. In a long bargaining session, the ability to give your own negotiators a chance to catch a bit of rest, a shower, or simply some quiet time, can give you a significant advantage at the negotiating table—particularly if your opponent's team members do not enjoy similar opportunities.

⇨ 4.4   Planning Travel Schedules

Travel often results in temporary fatigue, even where the distance is relatively short and the negotiator has made many business trips previously. When negotiations must be linked with travel, you and your colleagues should strive to allow adequate rest and adjustment time before the actual conference. Although the ability of different individuals to bounce back after traveling obviously varies, one of the best general methods of reducing the potential adverse effects of negotiating trips is to travel during the afternoon and early evening of one day and schedule the negotiations for a primary period on the following day. For most negotiators, one of the worst schedules involves travel late into the night on the day before an early morning bargaining session.

Time and rest are not the only important factors associated with travel. The quality of travel can also be a critical element. Particularly during times of economic decline, many companies insist that all employees travel tourist class and not exceed stated per diem amounts for room and board. Although these budgetary constraints should not be dismissed lightly, they also should not be applied indiscriminately, particularly when the travel is directly linked to negotiating a multimillion dollar transaction. When viewed in the proper perspective, first-class travel costs very little. Yet the value of that travel can be substantial in a negotiating context.

The best rule is a very simple one: all members of your negotiating team should travel first-class on all key trips. Regardless of whether the additional amenities or service are worth the higher cost when viewed in terms of slightly wider seats or somewhat better food, first class travel reduces fatigue and the potential for outside annoyance.

In addition, first-class travel has a subtle but important psychological advantage. Very simply, it makes the negotiator feel that his or her company is willing to spend a little more money to ensure his or her comfort and convenience. First-class travel tells the employee, "You're important to this company and you're on an important assignment where we want you to be at your best so you can do your best." This subtle pat on the back can do a great deal to give a negotiator that extra drive and edge necessary to gain and keep a high aspiration level and a strong psychological negotiating advantage.

⇨ 4.5　Following the Negotiator's Diet

A negotiator's diet can have a significant effect on his or her effectiveness at the bargaining table. At its most basic level, food affect metabolism. Lack of food—particularly at normal mealtimes—can distract attention and bring on increased fatigue. Consequently, any negotiating schedule should make proper allowance for meals.

However, assuring adequate intake is not the only metabolic problem. For most individuals, food temporarily dulls the senses as digestion ensues. Although some negotiators conduct their best performances over a lengthy dinner, most individual perform relatively poorly for about an hour after a medium-to-heavy lunch or dinner. To minimize this problem, you should avoid scheduling key negotiating sessions immediately after lunch or dinner. Where meals must be scheduled during lengthy negotiations, the schedule should provide for a caucus session or other noncompetitive period immediately after a meal. If the intensity of the negotiations does not permit this luxury, you and your colleagues should exercise basic dietary restraint.

4.5.1　Rules for Negotiators' Diet

The rules are relatively simple, and can be put to good use at formal dinners or conference table box lunches.

A. Eat lightly.

By reducing intake, you will minimize the lethargic or full and sleepy feeling that so often follows more extensively meals.

B. Avoid rich foods.

Light, easily digest meats like chicken or fish will generally have less impact on sharpness than fatty red meats or rich casserole dishes and desserts.

C. Avoid alcohol (including beer and wine).

Regardless of one's personal views toward drinking, the fact remains that alcoholic beverages dull the senses and dull senses have no place in the negotiating arena. Although exceptions certainly must be made from time to time, ideally you should not consume any alcoholic beverage within two to three hours before a negotiating session. Where practicable, you should have an alcoholic drink only at the end of the day's bargaining and debriefing sessions. Even then, moderation must be exercised if negotiations will resume early the following day.

4.5.2 *Methods of Manipulating the Food Factor to Your Advantage*

In considering the effects of food on the negotiating environment, you should appreciate that certain of your negotiating opponents may attempt to manipulate the food factor to their advantage. Indeed, depending upon your own approach to this issue, you may elect to do the same. Several methods are available to achieve this result—some defensive and some offensive.

1) If you and your negotiating opponent have different "normal" mealtimes, you should always strive to dine on your own schedule.

This approach will minimize the disruption faced by you and, depending upon the difference in schedules, may create a physical and psychological disadvantage for your opponent. Some negotiators actually heighten the impact of such a move by intermittently asking their opponent if he or she would like to get something to eat—and then carefully delaying the meal until some time later.

2) If you have a favorite restaurant, eating habit, or type of food, always pursue it in order to reinforce your own negotiating environment.

Some negotiators carefully manipulate this effort to their advantage. These individuals are able to combine the food factor with the physical location factor in order to achieve optimum negotiating advantage. This is especially true when the negotiation is held in home court.

When the negotiation is held in guest court or a third place, you may try to follow the rules for negotiators' diet and eliminate the influence of the foreign food.

⇨ 4.6 **Dominating the Psychological Environment**

In addition to controlling the physical negotiating environment, you should also strive to control the psychological environment.

Strategies to Control the Psychological Environment

A number of subtle strategies are available for this purpose, all of which are designed to increase your sense of control, confidence, and dominance at the relative expense of your negotiating opponent. Although these strategies are employed more easily when you are negotiating on your own ground, most can be implemented at any location.

A. Keep your negotiators feeling fresh and relaxed.

Particularly in drawn-out bargaining sessions, you should use every effort to keep your negotiators feeling fresh. Adequate sleep is desirable, of course, but not always possible. Where sleep is restricted and the bargaining sessions are long, you should attempt to rotate the members of your team in and out of the negotiating conferences. Members that are rotated out should relax and take a legitimate break from the pressure of the negotiating arena. A good shower, a fresh change of clothes, and a few minutes of feet-up rest can substantially rejuvenate an experienced negotiator. The ability of a negotiator to achieve this relaxation may depend upon both location and commitment. For example, if the negotiations are being held at your offices, and the negotiator lives nearby, a quick trip home for dinner and some time with his or her spouse and children can be highly affective. On the other hand, this type of break can actually contribute to increased tension. Valuable relaxation may result if the negotiator and his or her spouse preplan the dinner and make a mutual commitment toward creating a short, but enjoyable, break. Further tension will result if the negotiator is experiencing family problems or if the spouse and family use the short period of "relaxation" to barrage the negotiator with problems of the home front or questions about whether the negotiations will ever be concluded.

Where the negotiator lives too far away from the negotiating site to go home for a break, relaxation may still be possible at a company cafeteria, lounge, or athletic facility. In important marathon negotiations where relaxation would otherwise be difficult, some experienced negotiators rent nearby hotel rooms, either to be shared for temporary rest and relaxation or to be checked into for living accommodations for the duration of the negotiations. Where the negotiations are held at a location other than your own city, a similar approach should be employed. In such out-of-town negotiations, your hotel accommodations should always be close enough to the bargaining site to permit your negotiators to rotate back to the hotel for brief periods of rest and relaxation.

B. Minimize the rest and relaxation available to your negotiating opponents.

Maximizing the amount of rest and relaxation available to your own negotiators is only one side of the coin. Some negotiators attempt to achieve further control of the psychological environment by minimizing the rest and relaxation available to their negotiating opponents. Several methods are available to implement this strategy.

- Prepare a lengthy or involved question to an opposing negotiator prior to a planned break for dinner or rest.

Some negotiators make certain that opposing team members always have some reason to be present at the conference table or at a private caucus. Where this approach is used, a lengthy or involved question may be directed to an opposing negotiator just prior to a planned break for dinner or rest. The question is accompanied by a plea that the opposing negotiator use the planned break to call headquarters or research the matter, as may be required for clarification. This approach can also be used effectively to isolate or wear down a particular member of an opposing negotiating team. For example, an overaggressive attorney may be positioned into staying up all night to draft a particularly complex provision, even though it is most unlikely that the provision will ever be used. If the attorney believes that his or her complex approach will be accepted, the lawyer may spend considerable personal resources in an effort to come up with the necessary provision. The drafting effort itself causes considerable fatigue; however, the really adverse psychological factor occurs when the provision is ultimately rejected rather than accepted.

- Wear down your negotiating opponents through apparent courtesy and kindness.

Other negotiators wear down their negotiating opponents through apparent courtesy and kindness. This approach is most effective where the opposing negotiators are visitors in your city. To implement this approach, you simply have other executives in your firm entertain your visiting opponents while you and the members of your negotiating team go directly home for a good night's sleep. When carefully orchestrated against negotiators with relatively little experience in such matters, this approach can have a devastating effect—particularly over a period of several days.

- Manipulate various physical elements.

The psychological negotiating environment can also be affected by manipulating various physical elements, such as those discussed in the preceding section. For example, when the negotiations are being held at your offices or those of your attorneys, you should maintain a bright and cheery environment for as long into the night as negotiations continue to progress at a satisfactory level. Particularly if your negotiating opponent seriously hopes to execute an agreement that evening or by some other early deadline, you can contribute a (sometimes deliberately false) sense of hope by keeping secretarial staff available for typing last minute changes. However, if negotiations fail to progress, you can drastically alter this apparently favorable environment to evidence your displeasure. Such a change in the psychological negotiating environment might be effected by sending all secretarial personnel home, cutting back on lighting, and shutting down copiers and other office equipment. These actions can have almost the same psychological impact as deadlocking the negotiations, while at the same time permitting the conference to continue at a somewhat strained level. As suggested above, similar changes in the psychological environment can be implemented by altering or delaying mealtimes, the availability of coffee and other beverages, and the timing of rest room breaks.

⇨ 4.7   Resolving to Alter the Environment

Regardless of the techniques employed, you should recognize the importance of controlling your negotiating environment and take appropriate steps to ensure that control throughout the negotiating process. Although the affirmative use (or manipulation) of environmental factors may at first seem unprofessional or even unethical, you should carefully consider all relevant sides of this issue before relegating environment to chance. Several points support the suggestion that the recognition and employment of environmental factors, within reasonable limitations, is an acceptable and advisable negotiating tactic.

- First, environmental factors such as those discussed in this chapter can have a significant impact on negotiating leverage.

  If you fail to appreciate the impact that these factors can have, the input to your selection of tactics and other negotiating judgments will be incomplete.

- Second, experienced negotiators are well aware of the advantages of controlling the negotiating environment.

In many instances, if you do not attempt to control environmental factors in your favor, your opponent will strive to turn those same factors against you.

- Third, recognizing and controlling the environment does not require you to engage in unethical or inappropriate business tactics.

You can and should limit your control of environmental factors to those deemed reasonable and appropriate by you. Quite justifiably, you may not determine to starve your negotiating opponent or lock all of the restrooms. On the other hand, you can and should appreciate the impact that food and meals have on the negotiation process, and ensure that any judgments made by you reinforce your position rather than that of your opponent. Indeed, if you consider yourself to be a true purist, you must have a sound knowledge of environmental factors in order to ensure that your judgments do not permit either side to gain advantage or disadvantage from the employment of those factors under actual bargaining conditions.

Vocabulary

antagonism /æn'tægənɪzəm/ n. [U or C]

—hate, extreme unfriendliness, or active opposition to someone

e.g. There's a history of antagonism between the two teams.

astute/ə'stuːt/ adj. astutely adv. astuteness n.

—able to understand a situation quickly and see how to take advantage of it

e.g. an astute investor/business woman

his astute handling of the situation

an astute observer of human behavior

caveat/'kæviæt/ n. [C]

—a warning to consider something before doing anything more

e.g. One caveat: while the plans can offer an opportunity to accumulate significant wealth over time, they cannot guarantee the safety of employee contributions.

—a statement that limits a more general statement

e.g. Behind every set of statistics there's always a caveat.

conducive/kən'duːsɪv/ adj.

—providing the right conditions for something good to happen or exist

e.g. Such a noisy environment was not conducive to a good night's sleep.

egalitarianism /ɪgælɪ'teəriənɪzəm/ adj.

—the belief in and actions taken according to egalitarian principles

egalitarian /ɪgælɪ'teəriən/ adj.

—believing that all people are equally important and should have the same rights and opportunities in life.

e.g. an egalitarian society

The party's principles are basically egalitarian.

expatriate /ek'spætrieit/ *n.*

—someone who does not live in his or her own country

e.g. A large community of expatriates has settled there.

factor /'fæktə/ *v. n.*

factor in /into

—to include as an essential element, especially in forecasting or planning

e.g. You must factor insurance payment into the cost of maintaining a car.

fluffy /'flʌfi/ *adj.*

—soft and like wool or like fur

e.g. fluffy toys

  a fluffy cake

—light and full of air

e.g. Beat the eggs and sugar together until they are fluffy.

gravitate/'græviteit/ *v.*

gravitate towards/to sth/sb

—to be attracted by or to move in the direction of something or someone

e.g. Susie always gravitates towards the older children in her play group.

ingrain /in'grein/ *v.*

—to establish something such as a belief so firmly that it is not likely to change

e.g. We want to ingrain good financial habits in people.

inscrutability /in,skruːtɪ'bɪlɪti/ *n.* inscrutable *adj.*

—not showing emotions or thoughts and therefore very difficult to understand or get to know

e.g. It is when you ask about China's ambitions for its place in the world that inscrutability sets in.

knack /næk/ *n.*

—a skill or an ability to do something easily and well

e.g. She has the knack of making people feel comfortable.

  There's a knack to using this corkscrew.

Net Present Value

—the present value of an investment's future net cash flow (= difference between the money coming in and going out) after the cost of the original investment has been subtracted

e.g. Countries that have received help so far have seen the net present value of their debt burden fall by an average of 40%.

pictorial /pik'tɔːriəl/ *adj.*

—shown in the form of a picture or photograph

e.g. The exhibition is a pictorial history/record of the town in the 19th century.

petition /pə'tɪʃən/ *v.*

—to make a formal request to sb in anthority, especially by sending them a petition e.g. The group intends to petition Parliament for reform of the law.

pore over

—to look at and study something, usually a book or document, carefully

e.g. She spends her evenings poring over textbooks.

He pored over the letter searching for clues about the writer.

slouch /slaʊtʃ/ *v.*

—to stand, sit or walk with the shoulders hanging forward and the head bent slightly over so that you look tired and bored

e.g. Straighten your back - try not to slouch.

A couple of boys were slouched over the table reading magazines.

A group of teenagers were slouching around outside the building.

in the wake of

—close behind and in the same path of travel

e.g. missionaries arrived in the wake of conquistadors and soldiers

—as a result of; as a consequence of

e.g. power vacuums left in the wake of the second world war

sinister /ˈsɪnɪstər/ *adj.*

—making you feel that something bad or evil might happen

e.g. The ruined house had a sinister appearance.

A sinister-looking man sat in the corner of the room.

zero in

—to direct all your attention towards a particular person or thing

e.g. We must decide on our target market and zero in on it.

Social media allows you to zero in on consumers who'll be receptive to your messages.

vendor /ˈvendə(r)/ *n.* [C]

—(*commerce*) a company or person that sells a particular product

e.g. They are the nation's leading vendor of organic dairy products.

Street vendors sell hot dogs outside the museum.

—(*law*, *property*) someone who is selling something, especially property

e.g. The purchaser and vendor need to agree the details of the contract.

caucus /ˈkɔːkəs/ *n.* [C]

—(*politics*) a group of people with influence or an interest in something who meet to consider a particular issue or problem

e.g. He added that his caucus would fight to restore the governor's health care plan.

—(*meetings*) in the US, a meeting held to decide which person a political party will support in an election

e.g. party/Democratic/Republican caucus

The amendment would have eliminated the party caucus system for choosing candidates.

Exercises

1 Multiple Choice

1) What makes an ideal team leader of the international business negotiation?

  A. Having a good temperament.

  B. Being confident and reliable.

  C. Being able to make decisions under pressure.

  D. Having flexibility.

2) What should be designed as in physical surroundings?

  A. Lighting

  B. Décor

  C. Seating

  D. Personal facilities

3) What is the ideal financial personnel in a negotiation team?

  A. Having considerable experience.

  B. Making concessions under pressure.

  C. Being able to bargain about the price of the negotiating goods.

  D. Being able to make assessments on tax issues of the transaction.

4) Which of the following is **NOT** one of the advantages of Home Court Negotiating?

  A. Permit your team to avoid problems.

  B. Improves your ability to control important factors.

  C. Maximize your team's access to your firm's resources.

  D. Set the tone and lay down the ground rules for the negotiations.

5) What is **NOT** considered as the general information in preparation?

  A. Operation management and technical staff of the TOS.

  B. The objectives of the TOS.

  C. The priorities of TOS.

  D. The possible legal issues concerning the transaction.

6) Which is **NOT** one of the management profile of TOS in an international business negotiation?

  A. The number of the negotiating representatives.

  B. The make-up of the negotiation team.

  C. The education background of the negotiating team.

  D. The limits of the representatives'authority.

7) What of the following is **TRUE** of guest court negotiation?

  A. It will ensure the proposed transaction to have high visibility.

  B. It will reduce the fatigue in the bargaining sessions.

  C. It will cause the overwhelming attention from TOS.

  D. It can eliminate the interruptions from the other side.

8）What is **NOT** ture of including one management personnel in the negotiation team?

A. To increase the communication from top to the bottom.

B. To ensure that the transaction will be consistent with overall company goals and objectives.

C. To provide constructive advice as the proposed transaction is structured.

D. To eliminate guessing outside the team.

9）What is **TRUE** of preparing for a negotiation?

A. It is not just about reading up on the situation.

B. It is knowing all about your business and understanding your motivations.

C. It is knowing strategies and tactics.

D. It is divided into physical and emotional preparation.

10）What is **NOT** true of the following statements?

A. The physical surroundings of a negotiation, like the décor, lighting and amenities will be essential to the negotiation process.

B. Home court negotiation will make it more difficult for you to implement certain limited authority and deadlock tactics.

C. Designing the proper diet for negotiation team will avoid wine and rich food and increase diet diversity.

D. The composition of a negotiation team will always include technical, financial and legal personnel as well as management.

2 Interpretation of Terms

1）qualities of the international business negotiator

2）market information

3）power analysis

4）context analysis

5）physical preparation

6) process design

_____

_____

7) pre-negotiation preparation

_____

_____

8) home court negotiating

_____

_____

9) guest court negotiating

_____

_____

10) third place negotiating

_____

_____

3 True or False

___ 1) In a negotiation where multiple languages are spoken, it is much more likely to have misunderstandings about the goals and attitudes of the other side.

___ 2) The best negotiation team is formed by several individuals with different expertise and rankings in a company.

___ 3) In selecting a right team member for a negotiation, expertise is more important than the personalities.

___ 4) A member of upper-middle or senior management should always be included on your negotiating team.

___ 5) The management member of your team will always provide a physical advantage during the negotiation process.

Reference

1. Birnbaum, Phyllis. "Humoring the Japanese". Across The Board. October 1986. p. II.

2. Burt, David N. "The nuances of negotiating overseas". Journal of Purchasing and Materials Management, Winder 1984. 5. 6.

3. Business International Corporation. Business Strategies for the People's Republic of China. (New York: Business International Corporation. November 1980). p. 310.

4. Caleroand, Henry H., Oskam, Bob. Negotiate The Deal You Want, New York: Dodd & Mead.

1983. pp .108-9.

5. Copeland, Lennie and Griggs, Lewis. Going International: How to Make Friends and Deal Effectilely in the Global Marketplace (New York: Random House. 1985). p. 112.

6. Fadiman, Jeffrey A. "Special report: a traveler's guide to gifts and bribes". Harvard Business Review July-August 1986.4. 124. 125. 126, 130.

7. Fayerweather, John, Kapoor, Ashok. Strategy and Negotiation for the International Corporation: Guidelines and Cases. Cambridge Mass.: Ballinger. 1976. p. 38.

8. Fisher, Glen. International Negotiation: A Cross-Cultural Perspective, Chicago: Intercultural Press, 1980. pp. 28-30.

9. Heiba, Farouk I. "International business negotiations: a strategic planning model". International Marketing Review. Autumn-Winter 1984.9.

10. Hendon, Donald W., Hendon, Rebecca Angeles. World-Class Negotiating: Dealmaking in the Global Marketplace.

11. Kapoor, Ashok. "MNC negotiations: characteristics and planning implications". Columbia Journal of World Business, Winter 1974, 125.

12. Lamont, Douglas. "International bribery: cases involving Pacific rim nations and recommended actions", paper presented at Academy of International Business Conference. Southeast Region, New Orleans, Louisiana. USA. 4-7 November 1987: "How to speak basic baksheesh: a palm-greasing primer". Trips. Spring 1988. I. 53-6.

13. McCall and Warrington. Marketing by Agreement. op. cit.. pp.42-5. 47.48.

14. McCaffrey, James A., Hafner, Craig R. "When two cultures collide: doing business overseas". Training and Development Journal. October 1985. 39(10).28.

15. Mehrabian, Albert. "Communication without words". Psychology Today. September 1968. 2. 53-5.

16. Moore, Christopher W. and Woodrow, Peter J., Handbook of Global and Multicultural Negotiation. San Francisco, CA: Jossey Bass, 2010.

17. Pye, Lucian W. "The China trade: making the deal". Harvard Business Review. July-August 1986. 4. 77.

18. Pye, Lucian W. Chinese Commercial Negolialing Slyle, Cambridge. Mass.: Oelgeschlager, Gunn. And Hain. 1982. p .35.

19. Ran, Dou. International Business Negotiation. Shanghai: Fu Dan University Press, 2007.

20. Searls, M. W Jr. "Business negotiations with the People's Republic of China". American Chamber of Commerce. Doing Business in China (Hong Kong: South China Morning Post. 1980).pp. 138-40.

21. Sheth, Jagdish N. "Cross-cultural influences on the buyer-seller interaction negotiation process". Asia Pacific Journal of Management, September 1983, 51.

22. Solomon, Richard H.. Chinese Political Negotiating Behavior: A Briefing Analysis (Santa Monica. Calif.: Rand Corporation. December 1985). pp. vi. 2. 5. 8.

23. Wells, Louis T. Jr. "Negotiating with Third World governments", Harvard Business Review. January-February 1977.55(1).73. 79.

24. Shenjiang Service Guide, Sept. 6, 2006.

Chapter III   Executing the Negotiation

Learning Objectives

After studying this chapter, you should be able to:

- Define the opening, bargaining and closing phase.

- Describe each step in these phases.

- Identify the common mistakes made in each phase of a negotiation.

1   The Opening Phase

The opening stage is for laying out arguments. You use the information you have gathered to construct the most persuasive argument you can for what you want, why you want it, and why the other side should give it to you. Here is where it is important to be clear about your goals, to be able to argue well for what you want, and to be able to listen to what the other wants so that you can present counterargument.

You also listen to the other side's presentation. You take notes on what they say and listen clearly for what you think is most important to them. This is also a critical time to ask questions and learn as much as you can about what they want.

In the opening stage, much of the tenor and tone of the negotiation is established. There are three key actions: build the climate, agree ground rules and do activities for first meetings.

⇨ 1.1   Building the Climate

The international business climate refers to the atmosphere and surroundings that one or both parties create before the negotiation gets a start, which can reflect the frankness, national characteristics, cultural attributes, style choice and psychological implications of one party or both parties.

Climate issues may include:

- Location: Will you meet at your place or theirs?
- Seating arrangements: Will members sit across table or at each end? Will there be team seating?
- Access to technology and communication: Is there a phone, fax, computer, Internet, or calculator?
- People: Who is there and who is not?
- Time frame: How much time is allocated for this meeting?
- Refreshments: Will there be any? If so, what kind?

The first thing to point out here is that you start to build the climate long before you sit down together in the negotiating arena. Every interaction and lack of interaction that takes place prior to the negotiation begins to create the climate for the discussion. If you ignore someone in the office, whether intentional or not, and then sit in a negotiation with them the next day, they will already have developed a negative impression of you. However small that is, it is a hurdle that you must overcome in order to build a positive climate for the negotiation.

In the opening stage, every behavior communicates. If the other side intends to have a collaborative, win-win type negotiation, they will work to establish a positive climate. Many unskilled negotiators are so quick to get down to business that they ignore this critical juncture in the process. During the Paris peace talks to end the Vietnam War, there was a climate issue about the "shape of the table." At first, it is thought to be a euphemism for shaping the agenda. However, this issue had to do with the literal shape of the negotiating table and the seating arrangements. The parties had to negotiate this issue before any substantive progress could be made. Another example is: In a negotiation with one of the company's clients, the company's negotiators arrived on time, but were kept waiting, and later were faced with three additional people at the meeting, one of whom turned out to be very confrontational. Whether they intended to or not, the opposing side's behavior set an adversarial tone.

Different negotiation climates have different impacts on the negotiation.

1.1.1 Positive and Friendly Atmosphere

Case 1

February 1972, President Nixon visited China, and the two sides launched an international negotiation of great historical significance. In order to create a harmonious environment and atmosphere of negotiations, the Chinese side, under the leadership of Premier Zhou Enlai personally, with careful preparation and organization in the negotiation process, and even carefully selected folk music of both countries to be played in the banquet.

At the welcome banquet, President Nixon was simply listening stayed when the military band played skillfully "Beautiful America" selected personally by Premier Zhou. He absolutely did not expect to hear his familiar music in Beijing of China, because this is the favorite of his life, and also the specified music played in his inauguration.

While toasting, he specially went to thank the band, and the state banquet reached a climax at this time, and a harmonious and warm atmosphere also infected with the American guests meanwhile. A little orchestra won the harmonious atmosphere of negotiations, which cannot be denied being a *superb* art of negotiation.

Japanese Prime Minister Tanaka of the last century 70s arrived in Beijing to restore the normalization of Sino-Japanese diplomatic relations. He rested at the guest house with tense mood, waiting highest summit between China and Japan. The temperature in Guest House is so comfortable that Tanaka was very relaxed and talking and laughing with his escort. His secretary Shigezo looked at the thermometer carefully; it is "17.8 degrees". That "17.8 degree" was Tanaka used, not only making him feel happy but also creating conditions to smooth progress of the negotiations.

(*Excerpts from* International Business Negotiation *by Huang Wei and Qian Li*)

The signals we are sending to opposing negotiators when our negotiation becomes increasingly important in international negotiations where business protocols are strange or unknown. Do we intentionally work to put them at ease or at a disadvantage? Many negotiators negotiating in different cultures ignore the significance of building a relationship as part of setting a positive climate.

Members of cultures often differ as to when they believe that negotiations actually begin. Cultures with a high task orientation and a need to reach concrete and tangible agreements rapidly often believe that negotiations begin only when parties start to discuss substantive issues. Everything before that is merely a preamble to the main task at hand, that is, conducting a content-focused discussion and achieving a deal.

Cultures that place greater emphasis on the development of affective relationships and building trust frequently see negotiations as involving a wider range of interpersonal or intergroup interactions, many of which must take place before substantive discussions can be held. Members of these cultures consider that negotiations begin as soon as the negotiators start communicating with each other, directly or indirectly, or meet face-to-face. For example, in Chinese commerce, "Negotiation sessions are preceded and punctuated by banquets and often karaoke sessions. These are used to strengthen relationships among the Chinese, to build trust, flatter associates and provide an ambience in which to talk about the negotiation in a relaxed way" (Blackman, 1998).

This discrepancy of views regarding when negotiations begin can cause intercultural problems. One party keeps wondering why the other wants take time for all this small talk or social interaction and his counterpart wonders why the other is so brash as to keep pushing to talk about substantive issues when a positive relationship has not yet been firmly established.

Depending on the situation and culture, the first face-to-face contacts between a negotiator and her counterpart may take place before formal negotiations and at a different site. This might be a greeting at an airport or a social occasion. Because of different cultural expectations regarding when negotiations actually begin, it is important to develop a strategy for this first face-to-face encounter. Regardless of when members of cultures believe that negotiations begin, it is safe to assume that each party will be sizing the other up and making initial judgments about their counterpart before substantive discussions start. These initial meetings, no matter how brief, are often critical in shaping how counterparts view each other, and they can affect later negotiations (Gladwell, 2005).

Negotiators from task-oriented cultures, where socialization with counterparts prior to discussions is not common, often see this social time as unnecessary, merely going through formalities, or a waste of time. However, negotiators from relationship-oriented cultures view such social occasions as a valuable investment in a trusting relationship, which they consider to be critical for later substantive talks. Even at the level of simple trade, Sanger notes that shop-keepers in a number of cultures and countries go out of their way to welcome potential customers into their shops and build relationships before beginning substantive transactional talks: They often offer something to drink, typically tea. If it is a slow day, they will even sit down and drink tea with a customer themselves. I have encountered merchants who insisted on giving me a tour of their houses (which are often adjacent to their shops) before we began negotiations. One took me up on his roof to show me the view. One insisted we play a friendly game of backgammon before setting about negotiating over the price of the backgammon set. Others have introduced me to their children. Another even had me meet the animals the family owned including a cow, and several chickens. (Sanger, 2002)

In some cultures, carefully organized socializing may take hours or even days, and it may be initiated by one or more of the parties for a variety of reasons. They may be conducted so that counterparts can get to know each other personally and develop personal trust. They can also be designed to encourage participants to be more at ease with each other, and possibly let down their guard and disclose important information. Informal interactions may be used to conduct informal sounding about views on upcoming negotiation issues. Finally, they may allow the hosting party to demonstrate respect for the visitor. In some cases, this may establish expectations for future reciprocity due to the social exchanges that have been made or the care for creature comforts that have been provided. Many travelers have noted this dynamic among carpet sellers from Turkey to Afghanistan. Drinking tea, meeting the family, spending lots of time, and unrolling many carpets for the customer to peruse set up expectations that the visitor will buy, the merchant will make a sale, and each will gain "a new friend". Similar dynamics can occur in more complex negotiations as well.

The context, venue, and timing for socializing can be quite varied, depending on the cultural norms for pre-negotiation activities and the kinds of talks that are to be conducted. Opportunities for socializing may include informal meetings over coffee, tea, or alcoholic drinks; having a meal together at a fine restaurant, a banquet hall, or the host's home; going on a historical or cultural tour or field trip, often to impress the visiting negotiator about the importance, longevity, and strength of the culture of the counterpart; attending a traditional cultural performance or engaging in a sporting event; or engaging in a pre-negotiation cultural ritual common in the host's culture.

An example of a pre-negotiation ritual can be seen in the culture of the Maori peoples of New Zealand. There negotiations traditionally begin either when Maoris are negotiating with each other or pakiha, non-Maoris, with the parties engaging in elaborate greeting rituals, especially when talks are to be held in a marae, the traditional Maori meeting house. The hosting party generally meets the visiting party outside the marae and verbally challenges the visitors to state their intentions. Once an explanation has been shared and demonstrated by respectfully picking up an object that has been thrown down on the ground by the hosting party as a test of sincerity, each party briefly begins to tell the story of their historic relationships with each other, often describing both positive and negative interconnections. If positive connections are recognized, parties may rub noses and "share breath," and then enter the marae, where stories and discussion of connections continue. After a period of time, one of the parties may raise a substantive issue of concern and the groups will begin to discuss it. Talks may be extensive, and a meal may be served and consumed in the course of deliberations. (Tauroa and Tauroa, 1986).

Suggested Strategies for Coordinating First Direct Contacts

If you are the host

- Identify your norms and those of your counterpart regarding first face-to-face contacts and where and how such meetings might take place.

- As the host, examine your own cultural norms for first contacts, and try to determine how they will be received by your counterpart. If they are likely to be understood and well received, proceed to adhere to your common practices.

- Consider activities and times for socializing that will be comfortable and pleasurable for your counterpart, as well as provide opportunities for you to achieve other relationship-oriented goals.

- If you are the host and determine that adherence to your cultural norms may have an adverse impact on your counterparts or their views toward you, your organization, or your culture, consider how your practices for first contacts might need to be modified to achieve a more positive impact on the visiting negotiator.

If you are the visiting negotiator

- Consider whether you will try to avoid complying with norms for first meetings that you are not comfortable with, adhere to your own cultural norms, adapt or adopt those of your counterpart, or introduce new behaviors or activities for the first contacts.

- If you are from a task-oriented culture and your host is from a relationship-oriented culture, be prepared to engage in extensive social activities prior to formal negotiations. Delay initiation of substantive discussions until your host indicates that it is time to shift to this focus.

- In relationship-oriented cultures, substantive discussions may begin to happen very informally and in the context of socializing. When substantive sounding does begin, take this as an indication that your counterpart is beginning to feel more comfortable about his relationship with you and has started to informally probe your views on the potential for and content of upcoming substantive talks.

- If you are from a relationship-oriented culture and your host is from a task-oriented culture, you may be asked to engage in substantive discussions before you feel ready, that is, before relationship-building activities have taken place. Consider whether you want to propose some form of interaction to meet your needs for getting to know one another, even if such interactions are very brief from your point of view.

1.1.2 *Brief and Straightforward*

This climate refers to state views or ideas without cover to the negotiating partner, so as to start the ball rolling. It is more suitable for the two negotiating sides with long-term business cooperation, and both sides are relatively satisfied with the cooperation of the past, so they can better understand each other without too much civility, and reduce a lot of diplomatic language. Both sides save time, and put forward its side views or requirements directly and openly, on the contrary, which can generate trust. For example, in the bilateral negotiation of China's entry into WTO, New Zealand and China have few conflicts and are complementary to each other, both parties found the solution in the related competitive fields. Meanwhile, China hoped the round of negotiation would create a beneficial situation for the following bilateral negotiations, so we had finished the bilateral negotiation in quite a short time.

1.1.3　Tense and Contradictory

This is an atmosphere opposite to the friendly and positive style. It occurs if negotiation parties fail to cooperate in a pleasant way, or one party makes requests which are hard for the other party to accept before the opening. In this case, the atmosphere may turn to be so tense and contradictory that it may lead the negotiation to the verge of crisis.

Case 2

It's a **blistering** hot day outside, but in the conference room, the air-conditioning is on high and so is the chill in relations between your team and the representatives of the other company in these joint venture contract talks. In spite of the chill, you can feel **trickle** of sweat under your shirt as you watch the other side's reaction to the new cost-sharing proposal from your side.

"It seems to me," their senior negotiator says slowly, laying the paper down and eyeing each of you in **rum**, "that this represents a serious shift in your position." He pauses so long you almost jump in with an explanation, but then at the last possible moment, he continues, as if you weren't even in the room, "A violation of our previous verbal understandings." Another pause, but he clearly has the floor and nobody interrupts. "I'm not sure where this leaves us." Then he sits back, as if withdrawing from the discussion and the room falls silent.

You take a breath and tell yourself not to get **rattled** and make any unplanned concessions. Then you catch your boss's eye and try to communicate nonverbally that he shouldn't say anything rash either.

But it's too late. Leaning forward anxiously, your boss begins a lengthy explanation, his hands gesturing more and more wildly as he talks, as if they could somehow compel the other party to understand. "It's really, really, not intended as a deal breaker," he says. (You wince at the term; the other party had't actually threatened to break the deal yet. He is overreacting. He always overreacts.)

"We thought it was, honestly, a very minor thing, and that you'd understand since our situation has changed since we last talked, right?"

Oh, no! You think, trying not to roll your eyes in front of the other side. Now he's asking rhetorical questions, which of course they won't answer, leaving him fumbling for an awkward way to continue.

"Well, um, anyway, as I was saying," he stumbles ahead, "our cost structure has changed significantly since then what with the rising fuel prices, and to tell you the truth, we're having a little trouble with our efforts to roll our labor contract over without having to renegotiate the benefits package. Now don't get upset about that or anything; I'm sure it will all be settled by the time we close our deal, but it does change our view of the cost structure somewhat. I mean, it just makes sense for us to be cautious, and if we index the cost contributions, like, like in the written plan we, um, proposed today, we, um, we won't be quite as exposed to long-term uncertainty, which is a good thing."

He finally sits back, exhausted, and wipes his brow. You make a mental note to sit nearer him at the next meeting (if there is one) so you can reach out and grab him before he starts up again.

Their senior negotiator is still sitting quietly, looking at the lot of you as if you were insects that needed stepping on. He doesn't blink or make any movement. Clearly he has no intention of answering. After a long pause in which your boss shuffles papers nervously, one of their more junior people clears her throat and says icily, "So, let's just get this clear. In addition to going back on your initial proposal about cost sharing, you are also telling us that you have a labor dispute and that your energy costs are out of control?" She sits back again, glancing briefly at her boss and asking with her eyes, "Why are we even dealing with these bozos?"

You look at your boss again and realize that this situation is about to erupt like tossing a lit match into a fireworks stand. He's beginning to smoke already, and the only thing keeping him from jumping in with an even more unguarded response is that he doesn't seem to know which part of her statement to tackle first. Something has to be done, now, to get this negotiation back under control.

You glance at your handheld e-mail receiver (it's off, but the other side doesn't know that), push back your chair, stand, and walk around to your boss's chair. Leaning over to whisper in his ear, you say, "Sorry to interrupt, but something very important has just come up that requires your urgent attention. You'll have to ask for a fifteen-minute break. Now."

As you hustle your boss out of the room, you marvel at the skills of the other side. They read your boss beautifully: a guy who runs his business well but negotiates very badly because he thinks his view—and only his view—is the *legitimate* one. So he gets flustered if everyone isn't pleased with his proposals and remarks, They jumped on a minor issue—probably not the one they intend to negotiate hardest today—and used it to soften your side up and put you on the defensive early in the talks. And they clearly have the emotional control to make the most of the situation. The way their senior guy used pauses and managed to drop his bomb in a few short sentences and then sit back and watch the chaos unfold without saying anything further: that's mastery of competitive negotiating! His assistant is no slouch either. She knew just when to step in and twist the knife. If you hadn't pulled your boss out of the meeting, he would have either started yelling and driven them out of the room or uttered some major concession that nobody would have been able to take off the table.

(*Excerpt from Mastering Business Negotiation by Roy J. Lewicki and Alexander Hiam*, *Published by Jossey-Bass*)

1.1.4 Sedate and Reserved

Though one party acts enthusiastically and positive, the other party—especially the host party creates a rigid, and serious atmosphere out of the consideration of cultural customs and negotiation strategies so as to direct the negotiation towards the direction and result they hope for.

Case 3

An American company was selling a production assembly line of advanced technology. Each sent a strong large-scaled negotiation group to Tokyo for the formal negotiation. The American party was quite confident out of the trust in its own technology with the hope to win.

In the opening of the negotiation, the American party demonstrated how advanced their technology was, how reasonable their price was and how perfect their after-sale service were. But the Japanese representatives appeared to be a little bit stiff and kept keeping notes and silent. The American representative had finished the speech, only to find the puzzle look on the faces of the Japanese representatives. They asked the Japanese whether they had any questions. But surprisingly, the Japanese said they could not understand it at all. The American representatives had to restate their presentation time and time again, and their previous excitement died away. The negotiation atmosphere had turned from an enthusiastic and warm one dominated by the Americans to a depressing and rigid or reserved state coming along with the Japanese attitudes. The Japanese party saw that it was time to actions, so they seriously pointed out a succession of technological defects and price issue, which made the Americans very embarrassed and greatly agitated.

Eventually, the Japanese company pressed the price of the production assembly line to the lowest level acceptable to the American party.

(*Excerpts from* International Business Negotiation *by Dou Ran*)

In fact, the Japanese understood every issue that American party had presented. But in the enthusiastic atmosphere created by the American party, the proposal of the Japanese party could hardly be accepted by the Americans. So the Japanese side adopted the tiresome strategy by turning the warm and friendly atmosphere into a cold and stiff one, leaving the Americans weakened and demoralized. Thus, the Japanese changed the original disadvantageous situation into an advantageous one, and changed his inactive and passive role into an active and dominant role in the negotiation, and finally, achieved their target of introducing the most advanced technology at the lowest cost.

As a matter of fact, the climate of international business negotiation is not limited to the types listed above. In most cases, we should create an advantageous climate before or in the opening of the negotiation so as to direct the negotiation and manipulate the other negotiation rivals. If a harmonious climate is set up in the very opening of the negotiation, both parties will have easygoing communication and discussion; if in the very beginning, one of both parties let off steam and blame each other, it will cast a shadow on the negotiation.

⇨ 1.2   Agreeing on Ground Rules

This action focuses on agreeing on the issue that you want to discuss, and clarifying any requirements from either side regarding the agenda, timetable, form of agreement, etc. so that you can contently progress into the negotiation in a spirit of cooperation. Once again the primary communication styles are people (sharing and listening) and ideas (connecting and envisioning).

1.2.1   Agenda

Negotiation agenda refers to the arrangement for the timing and site choice of the negotiation, and issues discussed. It includes the order of the issues to negotiate and its main negotiation methods like what to negotiate first, what others to negotiate later and what is the final goal to attain, etc.

An agenda for the negotiation is important, especially when there are a number of issues to be discussed. Often these issues will be interrelated and sometimes dependent on each other, so it is important to make sure that you approach them in the right sequence. Sequencing agenda items can be accomplished by a number of methods.

A. Ad Hoc Discussions

In this approach, a party proposes an agenda item for discussion. If the other party concurs, they discuss it until an agreement is reached. After the issue is successfully settled, parties select another issue for discussion. This one-at-a-time approach, with little regard for the total sequencing of issues, proceeds until all issues have been discussed. This process offers significant flexibility, and parties can often build trust as each issue is sequentially settled. However, manipulation is also possible if a party consciously selects an issue for the agenda at an opportune moment that may later influence another party's power or ability to make trades on future issues.

B. Group Conversation

In this approach, parties just begin talking about issues in general and ultimately begin to focus on one. A solution may or may not emerge as a result of general conversation, and without a structure, discussions may meander and become unfocused and time-consuming. Members of cultures who feel comfortable with many activities happening at once often favor this approach to issue sequencing. This style is also common in informal interpersonal negotiations, or in tribal or communal societies that have relatively unstructured decision-making processes and less-focused group dialogues. In each of these settings, the participants desire more holistic solutions that consider many variables and the input and interests of the whole group.

C. Alternating Choices of Items

In this approach, parties alternately select issues to place on the agenda for discussion. This process usually works initially, but often breaks down if one negotiator refuses to agree to the order or placement of an issue raised by another party. Like the ad hoc and simple agenda approaches, this approach may also create problems when issues of linkage and trading are required to reach agreements.

D. Creating a Simple Agenda

In this approach, one party proposes a complete agenda that contains all the issues to be discussed. The issues are then discussed and resolved one at a time, in the order the initiator proposed them. This process works well for meetings, conferences, or negotiations where there are no significant disagreements about the issues or no interrelated or linked issues or where significant individual advantage cannot be gained through sequencing. However, this approach to agenda formation may not be acceptable for complex topics, where issues must be linked in order to create solutions, or where conflict is high. (Gulliver, 1979) notes that the simple agenda approach often tends to subvert the ordering of items almost immediately in serious conflict situations. If parties feel locked into a simple agenda by premature procedural agreements, they may use manipulative stalling tactics to gain leverage on items later in the agenda.

E. Ranking according to Importance

Parties jointly select and place the most important issues at the top of the agenda. The process is often connected with a bargaining theory that assumes that if parties can initially agree on key issues, discussions about sub-issues will fall into place. However, parties often do not have the same assessments regarding the importance or priorities of issues. If this is the case, this approach to agenda formation may break down. Gulliver (1979) notes that this method generally works best when parties have no claims or counterclaims against each other, no previous offense has been alleged, or negotiators are trying to establish a new relationship.

F. Working from General Agreements to Details

In this approach, parties focus on identification and discussion of key principles or concepts that will serve to guide future discussion of individual issues. Such principles provide a framework that can both shape future solutions to specific issues and provide standards and criteria to which solutions should conform or comply.

G. Placing Less Difficult Items First

This approach has often been referred to as gradualism (Weiss, 2003): one or more parties sequence issues to be discussed from easier and less complex to harder and more complex, so as to facilitate a gradual sequence of agreements. Parties identify, individually or together, several important issues they believe will not take too much time to discuss, be it too difficult to resolve, or be complex. Issues are often small, self-contained (not linked with others), less emotionally laden, and not symbolic of more conflicted issues. These issues are placed at the beginning of the agenda, and parties discuss them before tackling more complex issues.

"The logic behind the approach is that trust is low, and parties therefore need to take small steps to create initial trust and or foster a positive atmosphere, so that subsequent vital issues may be broached" (Weiss, 2003). In addition, by discussing less-volatile issues first, parties experience decision-making success early on and create foundational agreements that they may risk losing if they do not continue the negotiations. This provides an incentive for approaching more difficult issues. For this process to work, the items placed at the beginning of the agenda have to be perceived as important and significant for formulating a settlement agreement.

H. Addressing the Boulder in the Road

Often in negotiations, one or more major issues are stumbling blocks for agreement on the remaining others. Unless progress is made on one of these barrier issues, the parties will become bogged down. The logic for this approach for agenda development and issue sequencing is that "it proposes to address the more complex issues first, thereby moving the 'boulder' or greatest obstacle; this enables easier resolution of the remaining issues" (Weiss, 2003).

I. Grouping

Parties identify issues that have components in common and sequence topics according to similarity. Grouped items may be resolved individually or as part of packages that address a specific area of inquiry.

J. Trade-Offs or Packaging

Negotiators identify issues that are potentially related and link them together to facilitate the development of trades or package agreements. Linking is a common way to handle issues that cannot be settled independently or require concessions on one to reach agreement on another. The linkage, package, and trade-off processes for agenda formation are common when:

- Information and possible settlement options on all issues need to be identified and discussed before an agreement can be reached on any single one.
- One or more negotiators fear they will lose leverage for the favorable resolution of later issues if they reach an agreement on specific key issues early in negotiations.
- One or more parties believe that issues on which agreement has been reached and are considered to be closed may need to be reopened based on the settlement of later issues.
- A total package is the only way to reach an agreement because a package's total gains and losses on all issues are shared in such a way that they are mutually acceptable to all parties.

A common sequencing process for issues that must be included in a package agreement is for negotiators to reach a series of conditional agreements that can be modified and later combined into a total and comprehensive final settlement. Since the agreement for anyone issue is conditional and each agreement may be modified before approval of a final package, the order in which they are discussed is less important.

Another sequencing process for packages is referred to by Zartman and Berman (1982) as the "leap-to-agreement" approach. In this variation, negotiators discuss all issues fully but reach very few, if any, agreements along the way. Toward the end of negotiations or as a deadline approaches, the parties individually or jointly assemble a total package that contains gains and losses for all sides and meets all or most of the parties' basic interests. Often a party proposes that a counterpart accept a proposed package as is or with minimal modifications, or the package will be withdrawn.

If a negotiator proposing a package understands the issues and interests of all parties and has taken significant steps to address and meet them in a "yes-able" proposal that the other party cannot refuse (Fisher and Ury, 1981), there is often a high probability that the proposal will be accepted in totality or with minor revisions by a counterpart. Package proposals are often positively received because they indicate a willingness of one party to recognize the interests of the other, demonstrate models for trade-offs, and do some of the hard work of putting together a proposal that the other party may not have the time or ability to do.

However, packages also are rejected because the recipients were expecting to make agreements throughout negotiations and resent the fact that a total package has been thrust on them, do not like the take-it-or-leave-it tone of the proposal, believe there are better ways to satisfy individual and joint interests, or prefer to be involved in the agreement and package development and have no procedural and psychological satisfaction.

K. Incremental or Alternating Discussion and Agreement

Parties initially discuss all of the issues, reaching agreements where they can and then moving on to other issues. Several more rounds of discussions are held, covering the same issues again in greater detail until agreements are reached on all issues. This method combines the grouping, group conversation, and package methods.

L. Assigning Smaller Issues to Subgroups

Often a large group will have difficulty adequately discussing all issues in the depth or detail necessary, especially if the topics are complex or the parties fraught with tensions. Frequently separating out specific issues (either simple or hard ones), fractionating topics into smaller parts, and assigning them to a subgroup of negotiators who work on them simultaneously are productive approaches to agenda development and discussion sequencing. Subgroups examine the issues, explore options, and develop recommendations or proposals that they bring back to the larger group for consideration and, everyone hopes, approval.

Agreeing an agenda is another opportunity to build a positive, collaborative working relationship with the other party. What do they want to see on the agenda? What issues would they like to discuss? What order do they want to tackle them? What are their timetable and deadlines? You can build an agenda together and that way signal your intention to collaborate and subtly indicate that you see power balanced between you. Once again, in more complex and difficult negotiations, agreeing an agenda is a negotiation in its own right.

1.2.2 Timetable

Making sure that there is an agreement on the timetable for discussions is another opportunity to set up the meeting for success by envisioning what would be achieved in that time, and what would then be achieved in further meetings, should they be required. It also means that there is transparency on each other's deadlines for an agreement. This may appear to give a potential advantage to the other side, who could exploit your deadline by delaying tactics, putting more pressure on you to agree to a deal that is not in your favor. But the credibility and trust that you build by being prepared to take this risk nearly always pays dividends.

1.2.3 Form of Agreement

The final ground rule that should be discussed is the form of agreement that both parties need, assuming the conclusion of a successful negotiation. Transparency and expectations are the key important elements again — unexpectedly bringing in a team of lawyers at the contracting stage of the agreement is not a good signal of trust. Similarly, insisting on having something in writing when the other party assumed a handshake would be enough risks losing the goodwill built during the discussions. Discussing the form of agreement is a great opportunity to share expectations and show reciprocation and concern to meet the other party's needs. It also has a more subtle effect in that it is stating a clear assumption that you expect to reach an agreement—another opportunity to envision success and foster collaboration.

Having created the climate and agreed the ground rules, you can then move on to the next phase of the doing activities for first meetings.

⇨ 1.3 Activities for First Meetings

First meetings may encompass a wide range of activities depending on the people, issues, and cultures involved—for example:

- Welcoming comments, greetings, or speeches
- Introductions of individuals, team members, or other participants
- Rituals that affirm both the occurrence of the meeting and the connections being established between the parties
- Non-task-oriented talk to build or enhance relationships or to test the strengths of the parties' bonds

- Exchanges of gifts that symbolize the start of negotiation or the desire to build good working relationships among negotiators
- Expressions of willingness to engage in future substantive discussions
- Discussion of procedures for future negotiation
- General introduction of substantive issues that will be discussed in more detail in future meetings
- Formal opening statements that detail the parties' intent to engage in talks, propose processes for discussion, share general or specific views on issues, or present concrete proposals regarding issues of individual or joint concern
- Partaking of refreshments or a meal
- Watching or participating in entertainment provided by the host negotiation team

1.3.1 Welcoming Comments, Greetings or Speeches

Most negotiations begin a welcome by one or more negotiators. The welcome may occur either before parties sit down to begin discussions or at the beginning of formal talks. There is quite a range of practice regarding welcoming speeches. In some cases, a senior person may attend only this initial meeting to provide his or her blessing, wishing the parties success in their efforts. In some cases, only the host will offer a welcome. In others, a spokesperson or team leader of each team will make a welcoming statement. In some settings, it is expected that each person will make a brief welcoming comment. Welcoming comments may be brief and to the point, or quite long in duration, lasting up to an hour or more.

In welcoming statements, different cultures emphasize the psychological and relationship, procedure or substantive issues to be addressed in future interactions.

A. Psychological and Relationship Welcomes

These statements include recognition of existing connections between the parties; affirmation of positive feelings between them; recognition of the importance, rank, or status of a counterpart; emphasis on the importance of current or future talks; and expressions of goodwill or hope. The example of the first meetings between Maori delegations to negotiations between Maoris and pakiha described earlier in this chapter illustrates this kind of psychological or relationship opening.

Negotiators from many West African nations often use elaborate psychological or relationship openings in interpersonal meetings, informal talks, and more formal negotiations, especially if a conflict is not at issue:

"The course and temperature of the first greeting are of the utmost significance to the ultimate fate of the relationship which is why people set much store by the way they salute each other: it is essential to exhibit from the very beginning, from the very first, second, enormous, primal joy and geniality. So for starters, one extends one's hand. But not in a formal manner, reticently, limply; just the opposite—a large, vigorous gesture, as if one's intention were not so much to offer one's hand, as to tear other's off. If, however, the other manages to keep his hand, whole and in its proper place, it is because, understanding the ritual roles of greeting, he has likewise executed the same broad, forceful gesture. Both of these extremities bursting with tremendous energy, now meet halfway and, with a terrifying impact of collision, cancel out the two opposing forces. Simultaneously, as the hands are rushing toward each other, the two individuals share a prolonged cascade of loud laughter. It is meant to signify that each is happy to be meeting and warmly disposed to the other.

There ensues a long list of questions and answers, such as "How are you? Are you feeling well? How is your family? Are they all healthy? And your grandfather? And your grandmother? And your aunt? And your uncle?"—and so forth and so on, for families here are large with many branches. Custom dictates that each positive answer be offered with yet another torrent of loud and vibrant laughter, which in turn should elicit a similar or perhaps even more Homeric cascade from the one posing the questions...

If the laughter dies down, then either the act of greeting has come to an end and they will now move on to the substance of the conversation, or, simply, the newly met have fallen silent to allow their tired vocal chords a moment's respite. (Kapuscisnski, 2002)

More formal meetings in these cultures often begin with the host or a specially designated person making a long and elaborate speech that recognizes the status of all parties involved. He or she may use multiple honorifics to describe the fine character of the participants, their past achievements, and the importance of their presence and involvement in current talks. In addition, the speaker may emphasize the value that he or she places on the meeting, the significance of the issues that will be discussed, and the importance to all concerned that the talks be successful. These greetings, while ostensibly focusing on the counterpart and future interactions with the counterpart, are also designed to bring honor to both those being welcomed and the speaker and his or her group.

A classic example of this greeting process occurred at the opening of the fiftieth anniversary conference of the African National Congress in South Africa. At this meeting, held to select the next executive committee, "a huge praise singer in tribal costume pranced into the hall, chanting extravagant compliments with long vowels which slowly expired like a siren. In the silence that followed, Mandela appeared in his yellow shirt, walking slowly to the platform. A row of interdenominational priests blessed the conference, including the veterans of the struggle" (Sampson, 1999).

Greetings in negotiations involving Chinese, especially those from mainland China, may also involve rituals that stress the importance of the relationship between the involved parties and the significance of the meeting. Chinese negotiators in their opening remarks often emphasize the importance of establishing bilateral friendships and enduring relationships characterized by trust and mutual respect. The opening is both a statement of the goal of future talks and a strong appeal for reciprocity from the counterpart—both to reciprocate with a similar verbal statement and to work toward achieving the Chinese definition of friendship.

Northern European and American negotiators generally make less elaborate welcoming statements that serve similar psychological and relationship purposes. They often stress similar points as those identified by Africans, but in a much abbreviated form and with fewer rhetorical flourishes.

B. Procedurally Focused Welcomes or Greetings

In contrast to the psychological and relationship openings, procedurally focused welcomes or greetings, while noting the importance of relationships and desired substantive outcomes, emphasize the need for discussion of procedures for the upcoming talks. This kind of welcome is characteristic of low-context cultures that are more explicit about negotiation processes or that place high value on transparency and procedural fairness. A negotiator using this approach for greeting a counterpart, after briefly welcoming the other team and introducing his or her own members, might proceed to say, "We truly welcome the opportunity to hold these upcoming talks and trust that they will be conducted in good faith by all involved. We expect that we will all engage in talks with open minds and that we will be forthcoming with data needed to make wise decisions. We trust that the process will show respect for all participants, enable us to explore each of our respective interests and provide space for generating solutions that will meet all interests to the greatest extent possible. In our future discussions, we will describe the procedures that we would like to use for negotiations and outline a sequence of steps that we believe will lead to successful problem solving."

C. Substantive Welcomes or Greetings

These openings spend time detailing the topics or issues that will be discussed in negotiations rather than focusing on relationship and psychological or procedural issues. In this approach, after a brief introduction and acknowledgment of the other participants, the speaker moves rapidly to an outline of substantive issues to be discussed or even concrete offers. This type of greeting might include the following topics:

- The history of the issues or problem to be discussed
- A listing of issues to be addressed
- The importance of the issues to one or all parties
- A description of the general or specific interests of one or more parties

(either independent of or in association with specific issues)

- An outline of principles that might guide selection of solutions
- Possible options for consideration for settlement of issues or resolution of a conflict
- Specific offers, proposals, or positions to address concerns or satisfy interests

While we have discussed psychological and relationship, procedural, and substantive focuses for welcomes and greetings separately, many cultures blend the three, placing more or less emphasis on each depending on the culture or the type of negotiations to be conducted. The mix is dependent on the cultural orientations of the involved negotiators and what they expect to achieve at this stage of the negotiation.

Regardless of the form that welcoming statements take, they usually have the most positive impact on counterparts if they are sincere, genuinely stress the importance of discussions and the issues of concern to all parties, indicate a willingness of the speaker and his or her party to engage in good-faith discussions, express an openness to hearing the views of all parties, and indicate a commitment to find mutually acceptable and workable solutions. Welcoming statements that emphasize differences between parties, which rank them one above another or exhibit one-upmanship, generally do not promote mutually productive talks.

D. Suggested Strategies for Coordinating Welcoming Statements

- Identify the cultural norms of your counterpart regarding the content and process for making welcoming or greeting statements.
- Determine whether you will adhere to your own cultural norms regarding welcomes, or modify your response in a way that will be more culturally acceptable to your counterpart.
- If an elaborate welcome is required, spend adequate time developing one, and take care to mention all of the important persons who will be in attendance.
- Make the welcoming statement as positive as is realistically possible, given the importance of the issues that will be discussed.
- Consider who is the most appropriate person to make the welcoming statement and from whom it will best be received by your counterpart: The spokesperson or team leader, an authoritative decision maker, the most senior member of the team, a man or a woman, and so forth.

E. Introduction of Individuals, Team Members or Other Participants

Either after or prior to welcoming comments or speeches, parties usually take time to introduce the participants in negotiations. Obviously introductions may be forgone if all of the parties know each other or have worked or negotiated with one another before.

What is included in introductions and how they are made is often culturally determined by the status and rank of the person making the introduction in their society or organization, what individual negotiators consider to be important to convey about themselves, and what they think a counterpart needs to know about them. For example, a number of years ago, one U.S. mediator team was working with the staff of the Sri Lankan Ministry of Justice to set up a new nationwide mediation system. At the first meeting between the Sri Lankan and U. S. team members, individuals were asked by the Americans to introduce themselves. The Americans first made brief introductions, about three minutes each, describing where they came from, their organization and a bit about their experience as mediators and setting up similar systems. The Sri Lankans introduced themselves by telling their family history, where they had attended university, what they had studied, the degrees they had received, a complete job history, and a description of the role they hoped to play in the new project. Each individual's introduction took more than twenty minutes! Similarly, Americans facilitated an interactive workshop with participants from all over the world. The Americans and Europeans generally introduced themselves in a minute or less, while the participants from South Asia and Africa were quite expansive, taking up to ten minutes each.

Depending on how they are seen by the person making them, what they want or do not want to convey to a counterpart, or what they are asked by a counterpart to communicate, introductions may serve a variety of purposes. They can:

- Provide a name to the face of a counterpart.
- Give a title that describes what the individual does or responsibilities in the organization they represent.
- Indicate the rank or status of the negotiator and how he or she fits into the team or organization participating in negotiations—as well as in relation to counterparts.
- Define the formal role that the person will play during negotiations, such as spokesperson, facilitative spokesperson, technical expert, or recorder.
- Indicate (possibly) the role the individual will play in team or organizational decision making.
- Provide information on the educational background and expertise of the individual.
- Present personal or family information about the individual (family background, parents, spouse, children and their ages, and so on).
- Give information about the groups to which the individual belongs or is affiliated with (family, kinship group, clan, tribe, honorific or secret societies, ethnic group, religious group, firm, organization, regional grouping, political party, country).

In some cultures and situations, only senior people who will be directly engaged in negotiations and will be speakers are introduced. It is not unusual in these situations for a team spokesperson to avoid introducing his or her team members, saying rather, "The rest of the people you see here are members of my team. They are from relevant departments concerned about the agreement or will be involved in its implementation."

On occasion, the real decision maker may be neither the spokesperson for the team nor directly identified as the team's superior. However, this person will be in the room and able to observe negotiations. This pattern has been observed in some negotiations between Chinese from mainland China and negotiators from the West, or in high-conflict situations where the party that perceives itself to be in the weaker position is unwilling to take the risk of identifying its real leader to its counterpart. Depending on the situation, counterparts will need to decide if it is important for them to know the names and roles of all of the people present or if they will accept the structuring of participation in negotiations proposed by their counterpart.

Since introductions are one of the early places where negotiators can begin coordination with each other, care should be taken when considering how to make them and what kinds of introductions will help promote the best results.

F. Suggested Strategies for Coordinating Introductions

- Conduct background research on how members of your counterpart's culture commonly make introductions-who makes them, in what order, what they think is important to say, what they want to hear, how long they usually take, and so forth.

- Decide how you and other members of your culture will make introductions and whether your norms are likely to be acceptable to your counterpart. Try to model similar levels of information and disclosure on that provided by your counterpart.

- Pay special attention to norms regarding rank and status when making introductions and whether senior people usually speak first or last.

- If the members of the culture that you are negotiating with are organized in a strong hierarchy, consider mirroring their sequence of introductions so that people on your team of corresponding rank and status are introduced in a similar way and sequence.

- Develop an opening statement that will be culturally acceptable to your counterpart and will provide this individual or the team with information that you think they would like to know.

- Avoid making introductions that your counterpart will dislike: bragging, exaggerating experiences, stating long lists of accomplishments, or putting significant emphasis on you as an individual over your group, unless these behaviors are culturally appropriate. In general, try to avoid one-upmanship when making introductions, because this behavior tends to create competition with other team members or with counterparts.

G. Building Working Relationships and Trust

In previous chapters, we explored a range of orientations toward creating and enhancing relationships between negotiators. At the beginning stage of negotiations, this process may only be getting started. Attitudes and behaviors exhibited by individual negotiators, team leaders, or members of teams at this stage of the process often have a disproportionate impact on future discussions. For this reason, great care must be taken to continue to build good working relationships. This may involve spending extensive time in social activities or engaging in relationship-building conversations. For example, in Islamic cultures, "one of the most important ways to build trust ... is to conduct a leisurely conversation prior to discussing the issues themselves. Such conversation fulfills yet another objective of the early stages of negotiation, which is information gathering. If the trust-building conversation is successful, the particular information needed may be made available in a rather short time" (Alon and Brett, 2007).

H. Suggested Strategies for Coordinating Relationship Building

- Demonstrate nonverbally—by culturally appropriate eye contact, nodding appreciatively, leaning forward toward the person who is speaking, sitting still and not fidgeting, and not engaging in activities that indicate inattention—that you are listening attentively to what is being said.

- Avoid facial expressions such as staring at the counterpart without periodic breaks in eye contact; scowling; frowning; looking at the ceiling or floor; closing your eyes (although Japanese counterparts may do this), which can be perceived through the counterpart's cultural lens as indicating lack of interest; immediate disagreement ; or hostility to what is being said or conveyed.

- Restate from time to time and in your own words what you have heard to show that the speaker has been heard and to give him or her an opportunity to confirm that you have understood accurately. However, avoid interrupting the speaker's presentation to do this.
- Ask occasional quest ions about what has been said, with the goal of increasing understanding and not challenging, demeaning, or objecting.
- Identify specific procedures that may be needed for future discussions, ask for procedural suggestions, or make proposals for alternative approaches that could be used.
- Avoid becoming positional about possible procedures that may be used or engaging in "process fights".

I. Initiating Discussions on Substantive, Procedural or Relationship Issues

Parties enter negotiations with varying understanding of the topics to be addressed and how they are expressed. They also have different levels of information about their specific issues, interests, and preferred solutions and those of other negotiators. In some situations, issues and outcome possibilities may be clear, and negotiators will have to spend little time exploring details. In other cases, parties may lack information on a number of dimensions. At the beginning of negotiations, a negotiator may be unclear about:

- The basic issuers at stake.
- The range of alternative choices or strategies available.
- The solutions that will best meet his or her interests or needs.
- The number and identity of people who should be involved in the negotiations (or whom they will affect).
- The way that other negotiators will make decisions.

The negotiating parties can gain a better grasp of these questions through early discussion of procedural or relationship-oriented issues.

J. Opening Statements

In formal negotiations, parties typically each make an opening statement. Opening statements provide the best and perhaps the only opportunity to present the full scope of your views and approach (thereafter, the discussion will shift to details, and the subsequent presentation of new concepts or conditions will not get the same attention that they received in the opening statements). This means spending far more time and thought in preparation of opening statements than you have done before: making it well planned, well researched, and well structured. An important underlying aim is to persuade the other side that your reasons for taking any position are sound and well-supported. If the other side presents new information that requires changes or additions to your opening statement, you should make them before going any further. The emphases of such statements vary tremendously in terms of their focus on substance, procedure, or relationships. We will examine each of these strategies below.

1) Opening Statements Focused on Substance

The most common, but not always the most effective, way to open negotiations is to focus immediately on substantive issues to be discussed. In this approach, the negotiator elaborates on one or more topics. Moore (2003) and Lincoln (1981) list the common components used by negotiators who open with a focus on substance, and we examine each of these:

- Focus on presentation of history, need for a change, and position.
- Focus on identification of issues and background facts.
- Focus on issues and merit for change.
- Focus on issues, priorities, preferences, and interests.
- Focus on issue and presentation of an offer or position.

2) Opening Statements Focused on Presentation of History, Need for a Change and Position

This combination is quite common in many situations and cultures. The negotiator first reviews the background of the problem or dispute, describes the status quo (and in disputes why it has caused damage), identifies why changes are needed or desirable, and then, optionally, proceeds to detail an opening position that he or she feels would address or solve the presenting problem. This type of opening frequently forces the parties into positional bargaining.

3) Opening Statements Focused on Identification of Issues and Background Facts

In some cases, a negotiator may dispense with a description of the history of the problem and proceed directly to identify the issues that he or she wants to discuss and provide some of the relevant data related to them that will lay the groundwork for further talks. Issues and relevant background information may be presented in several ways:

- Defined only generally or vaguely and ultimately left for each negotiator to flesh out in later discussion.
- Presented briefly in the form of a list of topics to be discussed with relatively little detail on each item.
- Presented in an exhaustive manner that provides significant information on each.

Vaguer or more general presentations of issues usually occur in cultures where it is not the norm to be direct or explicit, or in situations where a party wants to move more cautiously into substantive discussions. Many Asian, African, and indigenous cultures follow this pattern, as do cultures where there are significant power differences between parties or where honor or face saving is important.

Brief and explicit listing of topics is common in cultures that like to proceed to rapid and direct structured problem solving. U.S. negotiators often start with a listing of issues and provide lots of facts in a direct manner before beginning to explore positions, options, or possible solutions.

4) Opening Statements Focused on Issues and Merit for Change

The negotiator introduces a topic for discussion and then focuses on educating her counterpart about why a change is necessary. Often the presenter avoids any detailed clarification of interests or presentation of a position or proposed solution until she feels that the counterpart has been convinced that the status quo needs to change. The assumption behind this strategy is that if a party can make a convincing case that the current situation is intolerable and that change is needed, reaching later agreement on a particular solution will be easier.

5) Opening Statements Focused on Issues, Priorities, Preferences, and Interests

The negotiator identifies an issue or issues to be addressed and then details the substantive, procedural, or psychological or relationship interests that must be satisfied through negotiations. Focusing on interests instead of positions prepares the ground for possible interest-based negotiations and joint development of mutually acceptable solutions, although it does not guarantee this outcome.

6) Opening Statements Focused on Issue and Presentation of an Offer or Position

The negotiator may dispense with any discussion of the history, the merits for change, or a description of interests. Rather, the negotiator briefly states an issue and immediately presents a preferred solution or position to settle it. Such a position may or may not be negotiable. At times, the negotiator presents an extreme position to educate the counterpart about how important the topic is to the presenter or about important interests. However, this style of opening can lead to a stalemate or even a walkout if the opening position is seen as too extreme. It also provides little information about why a solution is being proposed and makes it harder to explore other options that might satisfy the interests in another way.

7) Influences on Substantive Openings

Several factors influence the focus and content of substantive openings whether (1) a negotiator is from a low or high context culture; (2) the focus of negotiations is transactional (business) or the resolution of a dispute; (3) the parties are dealing with a single or multiple topics; (4) the issues at stake and potential outcomes are perceived to be either distributive or integrative in nature; and (5) one or both parties have sufficient power and influence to advocate for their preferred solution.

In general, when negotiations are focused on resolving a dispute, at least initially only a few central issues will be in question. When potential outcomes are more likely to be distributive than integrative or one party has significant influence, both parties are more likely to emphasize substantive openings and present positions or offers early in the process. Proposals are put forward to make demands, educate a counterpart, or serve as reference points from which negotiators may later make modifications or offer concessions. However, when negotiations are more transactional in nature, multiple issues are under discussion, there is potential for integrative outcomes, or parties want to downplay the exercise of power or coercive means of influence, negotiators pursue a varied range of approaches for presenting substantive issues.

In a comparative study of U.S. and Japanese transactional negotiations and strategies, Adair, Weingart, and Brett (2007) found that American bargainers (from a low-context culture) reach agreements with higher joint gains when they focus early in negotiations on information exchange about their specific priorities and preferences and those of their counterparts, and defer taking positions or making offers until later in talks, when the parties are better informed about each other's interests. U.S. negotiators, like those from the United Kingdom, tend to move fairly rapidly to identify key issues and present detailed information about them.

In contrast, Japanese negotiators (from a high-context culture) ultimately reach settlements with greater joint gains when they present only tentative offers early in talks and then follow them up with a series of subsequent trial offers that are constantly modified based on information or comments provided by their counterpart. Japanese negotiators tend to use tentative proposal making as a way to share and gain information about their own priorities, preferences, and interests and those of their counterpart. They also use them to conduct informal testing regarding what options are acceptable. Interestingly, unlike many bargainers from low-context cultures, Japanese negotiators do not seem to become anchored inflexibly to their early offers or positions. They view presentation and discussion of offers as an important form of information exchange.

Let's examine the orientation of several other cultures toward substantive openings. Direct and rapid substantive openings in formal negotiations are common for French (Cogan, 2003), German (Smyser, 2003) and Russian negotiators (Schecter, 1998; Smith, 1989). Slower substantive openings are more common among Chinese (Solomon, 1999) and Japanese negotiators (Blaker, 1977a, 1977b), Hodgson, Graham, and Sana, 2000); and people from more traditional cultures.

French negotiators generally want to speak first and seize the initiative in talks. They believe that if they can frame the discussion and present concrete positions to address the issues, their approach will drive the agenda and give them additional leverage to achieve their goals (Cogan, 2003). The presentation itself is made in the form of a long speech that details their position on the issues. "The French mind-set is 'positional'; that is French negotiators come to the table with a clear idea of what is to be their final position" (Cogan, 2003). They generally present their position, the solution that they are advocating to meet French interests, in a forceful, logical and eloquent manner. They begin with an opening focused on principles, followed by a presentation of the facts, and a finally a summary in which they advocate what they see as the only logical conclusion: their position. Their logical approach is highly deductive, that is, they move from general principles to a final logical conclusion. They tend to save their most important point until the end of their speech. In the early stages of negotiations, French negotiators are often more interested in presenting their views than listening to and understanding the interests of their counterpart.

German negotiators generally consider their opening remarks to be the most important in the negotiation process. In a substantive opening, the first concept to be presented is the Gesamtkonzept, the governing principle that provides the logic for specific points advocated in their overall position, and it forms the framework for all subsequent discussions and negotiations. The Gesamtkonzept is presented in a manner that covers the most important issues to be discussed in negotiations, outlines the desirable outcomes, and demonstrates how it meets both the counterpart's interests and needs as well as German interests. The presentation of the Gesamtkonzept is almost always very detailed, because German negotiators want their counterpart to understand and accept the concept. Early mutual agreement on the governing concept is very important, because all following discussions about options flow from concurrence on this overarching principle:

When they present their positions, German negotiators do not normally play shadow games. Nor do they waste time. They state their views openly and plainly. They have no mysteries and do not try to keep their proposals opaque. What you see is what you get. They know what they want. They do not try to present one position in order to advance another. They do not normally use devious tactics, such as presenting false issues as a tactical ploy while planning to drop those issues at the first opportunity. They simply outline, sometimes at staggering length and in painstaking detail, what they believe they can legitimately claim on the basis of the concept they have presented (Smyser, 2003).

After the presentation and what Germans believe is a tentative agreement on the Gesamtkollzept, they may proceed with outlining subsequent issues and their initial positions. These too will be presented with similar thoroughness and detail as that used for the governing concept.

Russian negotiators commonly open negotiations with a focus on substance and an effort to seize the initiative, but their approach is different from the French. Russians often request that their counterpart provide an opening position and then proceed to counter it. In taking an opening stance, "Russian negotiators never open discussions with a position close to the final position. Russians rarely make an attempt to establish a mutual framework of agreement rather they wait for the other side to reveal its position, and then, relying on carefully prepared instructions, open with a maximal demand. They make a concerted effort to intimidate their negotiating partner and establish a position of dominance and superiority" (Schecter, 1998).

Chinese negotiators rarely open with a detailed focus on substance and, like Russians, often want their counterpart to make the first move or proposal. This cultural pattern is well illustrated by the beginning of negotiations between Chinese officials and Henry Kissinger in 1971. Zhou Enlai, the host, said to Kissinger, "According to our custom, we first invite our guest to speak. Besides you have already prepared a thick (briefing) book. Of course, later on we will give our opinions also" (Solomon, 1999).

8) Opening Statements Focused on Procedure

Another way of opening negotiations, which is not as common as direct substantive openings, is to focus on the negotiation procedures, which lay the groundwork for later substantive discussions. Moore (2003) and Lincoln (1981) identified a number of advantages to opening negotiations by engaging both or all negotiation teams in a joint discussion about the procedures to be used in the negotiation process. (Clearly this is applicable only if the negotiation process will be either a single quite extended session or multiple sessions. Time and energy spent on procedural questions is rarely needed for short and simple interactions.) A procedural opening:

- Provides a jointly developed sequence for the negotiation to which all parties are committed.
- Allows the parties to practice making decisions as a team.
- Provides information about the behavior, attitudes, and trustworthiness of the other parties.
- Allows parties to practice making agreements on problems that are neither substantively important nor as emotionally charged as the issues in dispute.
- Provides an opportunity to build habits of agreement.
- Demonstrates that agreement is possible and that the situation is not hopeless.

Procedural openings that address specific stages and tasks to be achieved during talks are common in many diplomatic negotiations, where parties need to lay an adequate framework before commencing substantive discussions. They are also common in cultures that are highly aware of process, deem explicitness about procedures to be important, and emphasize transparency or involvement in determining how issues will be tackled. For example, American, British and German negotiators (from low-context cultures) tend to place more emphasis on making process decisions explicit in negotiations than do their counterparts from high-context cultures, such as France, Japan, China, some Latin American countries, and indigenous communities. The low-context patterns of communication make the rules and assumptions about interactions more explicit. Members of the high-context cultures are also deeply concerned about process, but they have little or no need to engage in transparent discussion about it, as the rules and assumptions are "understood" in the context.

9) Opening Statements Focused on the Psychological Conditions or Relationships of Disputants

This approach aims to improve the relationship of the disputants either before or as a major element in discussions of substantive issues or procedures. Openings focused on relationships usually involve statements affirming the past or current relationships of the parties, expression of positive expectations for the future, and emphasizing the value of building productive working relationships as a means of achieving mutual benefits. Psychological and relationship openings are usually followed by a shift to substantive discussions using one of the approaches already described.

Indigenous cultures and those that rely extensively on good relationships to establish trust and long-term compliance with agreements that are reached often spend considerable time at the beginning of negotiations discussing relationship-oriented issues: reviewing past connections among the parties, affirming friendships, stating visions for future relationships, sharing common experiences (meals, drinks, entertainment), or performing rituals that affirm connections. Maori greeting rituals and Chinese or African speeches that affirm friendly relations are examples of these kinds of openings.

10）Selecting the Focus of an Opening Statement

The choice of whether to make an opening statement with a primary focus on substance, procedures, or relationship depends on:

- The relationship of the parties and level of trust among them when entering this phase of discussions.
- The type of issue, problem, or conflict to be addressed.
- The level of emotional intensity parties feel about each other or issues that will be discussed.
- The readiness or ability of the parties to focus on substantive issues at this stage in the negotiation.

The choice about an opening is made based on several considerations:

- If parties have established a degree of openness, tolerance, rapport, positive relation-ships, or respect prior to or during the previous stage of negotiations, consider proceeding with a substantive opening.
- If there is significant apprehension, tension, or mistrust between parties, consider making a psychological or relationship opening statement prior to focusing on substantive issues or agree to discuss procedures prior to discussing content.
- If the issue is highly tension ridden or parties are contentious, consider focusing on procedures, such as how best to discuss issues about which there is significant disagreement.
- If it appears that parties are ready and willing to discuss substantive issues, determine which kind of substantive opening will be most effective and result in further productive discussions and best help you meet your needs. Think about the potential impacts, both positive and negative, on your counterpart of each form of substantive opening.
- Assess whether your counterpart needs to hear your views on the history of issues or merits for change, and whether she wants a listing of issues for future discussion or an in-depth presentation on how you see an issue or issues.
- Determine whether it is better to focus on a presentation of your issues, some of the interests or needs that you want to have addressed and abstain at this time from putting forth proposals or positions, or whether you want to put forward a position.
- If you determine to put forth a position in your opening statement, decide whether it should be an extreme one or a maximum high demand as a tool to educate your counterparts about the importance of the issue or solution to you and encourage them to readjust their sights regarding what they will have to provide in order to reach an agreement. Alternatively, put forth a more reasonable position as an illustration of what might work for you, but indicate that if your needs or interests can be met in other ways, you are open to exploring other options.

1.3.2   *Suggested strategies for coordinating opening statements*

Opening statements cause problems when one party delivers one kind of opening and the other party delivers a different one. This is common between negotiators from cultures that are oriented toward tasks or substance and negotiators from other cultures that emphasize extended relationship building and indirect or gradual exploration of substantive issues. Ideas for coordinating these issues include these:

- Consider the kind of opening statement that your counterpart might use or expect, and deliver yours in a similar manner.

- Allow your counterpart to lead in making an opening statement and illustrate the kind of opening he prefers. Then decide if you want to adopt that approach, adapt yours to that approach, adhere to your own cultural norms, or explore the development of alternative ways to layout issues for discussion.

- Adhere to your own norms for making an opening statement, but be prepared to modify or correct it after hearing the opening of your counterpart. For example, if you make a substantive opening with an emphasis on positions and your counterpart makes an opening statement focused on relationships followed by an explanation of some of her interests, consider following up her comments with some relationship-oriented statements of your own, or reciprocating disclosure of interests by sharing some of your own.

An Example of a Rather "Standard" Opening Statement

Your opening statement is critical to a serious discussion of the issues. Although we have discussed the three different focuses of opening statements, there is still a rather "standard" opening statement that we may use in the opening stage of the negotiation, with which we may modify some parts of it according to the situation. The "standard" opening statement usually includes:

- the background to the present meeting including the history of your discussions so far
- your views on the industry, its past and probable future
- trends in direct and indirect competition
- supply and demand expectations
- the parameters and goals of investment and cooperation that you are seeking
- plausible projections or expectations of sales, etc.

It should not include any concrete offers from you, or any positions you are taking on price, delivery, equity, etc. concrete offers should not be made until all conceivable issues have been presented, and you know that their thinking is as well.

1.3.3 Example of an Opening Statement

The opening statement is delivered by Japan Moving Company to Tianjin Port Company, China.

"We, Japan Moving Company (JMC) from Tokyo, have been approached by you, Tianjin Port Company (TPC) here in North China, to form a transportation joint venture, to specialize in shipping personal effects and commercial cargoes.

Our research indicates that by the end of 2007, China's total length of expressways had reached 53,600 kilometers, and meanwhile, China has a total number of 31 provinces, autonomous regions and municipalities, each with more than 1,000 km of expressways. In 2007, the national cargo throughput of your port reached 5.28 million tons, rising 14.8% year on year. We understand that TPC is NOW one of the top five ports in China. The main business of Tianjin Port Company is the airport logistics industry; and you are striving to become a regional passenger transport hub and a super cargo gateway in North China, by taking Changi Airport in Singapore and Hong Kong Airport as your criteria. Except for the period 2005 to 2007, your company has maintained a high level of investment. Most of its investment is concentrated in North China, followed by Northwest China. In the future, we understand, non-aviation business will be the main source of growth.

Japan Moving Company (JMC) has recently started inbound shipping and moving services—that is, shipping services from other countries to Japan. Presently JMC is offering services from the USA, UK, France, Germany, Italy, Australia and New Zealand. We have been concentrating on shipping services from Japan to countries overseas. However, we receive many inquiries from people who moved overseas from Japan with us and also new potential customers about shipping to Japan. This led us to realize the need for this service.

JMC is an international shipping company operating out of Tokyo, Japan, offering economical shipping services to individuals and corporate. JMC was founded in Tokyo in 1995. With a reputation for premier services, competitive rates and expert knowledge on overseas shipping, we have quickly grown to be one of the most well-known international moving companies in Japan. Our goal is to provide "easy-to-use" shipping services at competitive charges, meeting or exceeding our customers' expectations when moving from Japan.

We are eager to establish China as an important new market for JMC. So we thought it was perfect timing when your Vice-President, Mr. Wang Guoai, approached us some months ago. By developing this new business venture with you as our partner, seems the perfect way to enter the Chinese market."

2   The Bargaining Phase

Case 4

The Macau Jockey Club in China was commissioned to negotiate with an Australian jockey club about introducing ten horses of fine breeding. The seller, the Australian jockey club, would sell the horses as long as the price was above 1 million Australian dollars per horse on the average; Macau Jockey Club, aimed to pay no more than 1.5 million Australian dollars per horse. The two sides did not know one another's bottom price (quoted above), but both of them would benefit if they could close a deal including 10 horses at a total price of 10~15 million Australian dollars.

The buyer requested the seller to quote a price first.

The information the seller had gathered, included the following: as the horse racing season was approaching in Macau, a number of local race horses had to retire because they were ill or overage. But pure-bred European horses were over a million or even several million Euros each, so, it would not pay for a small jockey club like Macau Jockey Club to buy them for their racing season. In contrast, Australian race horses, also thoroughbreds originating from Europe, were practically priced, and were the logical first choice for the Macau Club. Therefore, the seller estimated that the Macau Jockey Club would pay at least 12.5 million Australian dollars for these 10 horses, and may be they would pay as high as 17.5 million Australian dollars. Nevertheless, the Australian side had not planned to quote a price too high for fear that the buyer would perceive them as lacking sincerity, and would abandon the bargaining too soon and turn to New Zealand for the purchase. Thus, the Australian jockey club made an initial bid for a total price of 17 million Australian dollars for the 10 horses.

Though the Macau club had anticipated the seller's bottom line, this quotation was higher than they had expected. Anyway, the seller's first quoted price was 2 million Australian dollars higher than Macau's highest acceptable price (resistant point). However, judging from the quotation, the buyer estimated that the seller's expected price would be above 15 million Australian dollars. If this were the case, it would be difficult to reach an agreement. Hence, the buyer made a probing counter-bid at a total price of 12 million Australian dollars.

Because there was a big gap between the opening prices that the two sides quoted, their representatives had to haggle over them. The seller's counter-bid was a total of 15.5 Australian dollars and the buyer countered again with a bid of 13.5 million Australian dollars. Finally, the seller suggested that meet halfway and agree on a price at 14.5 million Australian dollars. The Macau club accepted that price, feeling pleased without showing it: they had saved 0.5 million Australian dollars for their club! They did not know that the seller got 4.5 million Australian dollars more than their original bottom line.

(*Excerpts from* International Business Negotiation *by Dou Ran*)

There are many obstacles to hurdle on the way to a negotiated agreement. Perhaps one of the most vexing that many folks face is defending price objections. Whenever you're selling anything, the other side always thinks the price is too high. And on the rare occasion when they don't, suspicions then center on whether or not there's something fishy because of a low price.

For many negotiations, price is the paramount issue. However, when price isn't a major factor—or even an element in your negotiations — it's still crucial to negotiate an agreement that has a high probability of satisfactory performance. Therefore, considerable care must be taken in negotiating each and every provision of proposed agreements.

The bargain phase in international business negotiation covers broad period of time from the end of the opening phase to the beginning of the closing phase. During this time, all negotiating parties confer about substantive issues and items. It constitutes the central and most difficult stage in the whole negotiation process.

Bargaining in international business negotiation involves three key aspects: quoting a price (offer), bargaining over the price, and making compromises.

⇨ 2.1 Offer

Offer means offering price, which includes not only products inquire, but includes a variety of conditions of the entire transaction (including the quantity of goods, quality, packaging, price, shipping, insurance, payment, inspection, claims, arbitration, etc.). The negotiator must decide whether he is going to make the first offer or let the other side make the first offer. This often can be a dance in itself, as each party encourages the other to lay his cards on the table first.

2.1.1 Significances of Making the First Offer

Making the first move is significant for at least three reasons.

A. It gives lots of information to the other side.

The others learn whether you intend to be more aggressive or friendly and get a chance to size up your offer against his own target and walk away. Right away, he begins to get a sense of whether the two of you are likely to come to an easy agreement or are looking forward to a long, exhausting deliberation.

B. Once the other knows your opening offer, he can adjust his own opening offer to be more or less extreme than planned.

Adjustment in private is much easier than adjustment in public. If you have already made a public opening offer and find it is too extreme, you will have to publicly back up and propose a more conservative opening, but you risk confusing or angering the other side. If you have not made an opening offer, nobody will know if you changed it at the last minute.

C. When the other party adjusts his opening offer, he is also likely to be adjusting where the parties are most likely to settle.

There is a subtle, unspoken but very important negotiation principle at stake here: once opening offers have been made, negotiators tend to believe that a likely settlement is in the middle of their two opening offers. If the buyer quotes $4,000 for the car and the seller counter offers at $3,400, both parties are likely to look at $3,700 as a reasonable settlement (assuming that number is not too far away from the earlier planned target). Often, many negotiations are no more than a 1-2-3 deal: (1) you make an offer, (2) I make a counter offer and (3) one of us says something like, "Let's just split the difference." The negotiation is over.

Thus, deciding who goes first may be a critical part of an opening move. In general, you should let the other side go first if:

- This is unfamiliar negotiating territory. You have never negotiated for this before.
- You don't know much about the expectations of those on the other side or what they will see as a fair opening or settlement.
- You are not sure whether your opening offer will look reasonable or extreme to the other.
- You want to be able to adjust your opening based on what the other side tells you.

In contrast, there may definitely be times when you should go first:

- You have done a lot of negotiating for these items before and know what a fair settlement would be.
- You know your opponent well and how he is likely to respond.
- You want to convey that you are strong, in charge, and know exactly what you want.

2.1.2 *Advantages in Having the Other Negotiating Party Make the Initial Offer*

A. It gives you an immediate idea of how far apart the respective positions are.

For example, if your opponent's initial offer differs substantially from what you consider to be reasonable, you have several options.

On the one hand, you can state that the offer isn't even in the ball park, and then proceed to a factual discussion aimed at undermining the offer. Your objective here is to get the other party to make another offer, without you having even given an inkling of what your position is. This isn't likely to be successful unless you're dealing with a novice negotiator, but it's certainly worth a try. The worst that can happen is that the other negotiator will avoid being lured into a detailed discussion of his offer until you, in turn, lay your cards on the table in the form of a counter-offer.

As an alternative, you can simply give the offer a broad brush rejection, and come back with a counter-offer which is equally farfetched. The purpose of this isn't to be spiteful, but rather to hedge your bets until the negotiations proceed far enough to establish the opposition's intentions. Obviously, if their initial offer is way out of line, they either haven't done their homework, or even more likely, are using an unreasonable offer as a negotiating ploy.

Consequently, if you respond with a reasonable offer that is very close to your negotiating limit, you are putting yourself in an unnecessary bind. That's because after a little back and forth discussion, the other side may suggest splitting the difference. Naturally, you have to refuse, since you will be splitting the difference between your reasonable offer and the excessive proposal made by the other side. This would place you in a difficult position to get the negotiation gap closed because you have little left to concede in exchange for the other side making movement from their initial offer.

Actually, whether or not you are successful in getting the other side to make the initial offer, or do so yourself, always make sure that your first offer gives you leeway to make concessions as negotiations proceed. Otherwise, you will be making it much harder to reach agreement. Most people aren't happy unless they can get some concessions from the other side. They assume that a first offer isn't going to be a favorable one, and therefore aren't satisfied unless they can negotiate more favorable terms than the opening offer.

B. Another advantage of having the other party make the first offer is the chance—however slight—that you may receive a better offer than what you would be willing to settle for.

If so, your negotiations may well turn out to be short and sweet. Surprisingly enough, considering the advantages, who makes the first move is often based on nothing more complicated than being the one to ask the other party for their offer.

A good way to do this is to pop the question as soon as the opening pleasantries of a negotiation session are concluded. As part and parcel of your request, it's also beneficial to set the stage for how you expect the negotiations to proceed. What you want to do is state that you intend to be reasonable in an attempt to reach a speedy agreement, and assume the other side is similarly disposed. A typical request for an offer could go like this:

"John, I want you to know that we intend to be reasonable in trying to reach an agreement, so why don't you give me an offer we can accept without a lot of back and forth nonsense."

If John makes an offer close to what is acceptable, a counter-offer that leaves a narrow gap could be made by saying something such as, "That's just a little more than I can buy John, but if you can raise your figure $20,000, we've got a deal." On the other hand, if John's offer is way out of line, indignation can be expressed in the form of, "I told you we would be reasonable, and you throw that kind of figure on the table. Let's go over the details of how you arrive at that." This approach immediately focuses the discussion on the opposition's offer, without you having made a counter-offer.

Of course, the details of how an offer is solicited will vary with the circumstances. What's of concern is to maneuver yourself into position to ask the other side for their offer at the start of negotiations.

NOTE: In many situations, an initial offer may have been requested and received before negotiations begin. This is standard practice in many business transactions where price is the predominant element. If you have received an offer prior to negotiations, attempt to start-off the session with facts showing the unreasonableness of the offer. This will force the other side into a defense of their offer, rather than allowing them to attack the soft spots in the facts and figures supporting your position.

⇨ 2.2　Making Offers and Having Them Stick

In limited situations, it may be appropriate to make an initial offer that is far in excess of your negotiation objective. However, for the most part your offer should be within the range of credibility, while making allowances for any concessions that are needed to reach agreement. In the first place, an initial offer that is credible, may be accepted outright by your opponent, or with just minor adjustments having to be made.

Even more important, the credibility of your initial offer sets the tone for the negotiations. For instance, if you make an offer that's so out-of-line it's not believable, your opponent will pay it little heed. Furthermore, it might encourage the other negotiator to be just as unreasonable. This will only serve to widen the gap in the respective positions, which is a forerunner of a long and difficult negotiating session.

Another pitfall of an unreasonable initial offer is that it will require a great deal of movement in the form of concessions to ultimately reach agreement. This, of course, means you have to raise your offer in relatively large chunks if you're the buyer, or conversely, lower it substantially if you're on the selling side of the table. As a result, when the other negotiator sees substantial movements in your position, it arouses suspicion as to just how much fat is built-in to your position. This can lead to an attitude of, "Hey, if this guy can change his position like that, let's see how far I can get him to go." Consequently, even when your opening offer has been whittled down to a reasonable figure, your opponent may still negotiate in the belief that you will go even further.

Along with establishing credibility by making an offer that's reasonable, you also have to be able to defend your offer if you want to make it stick. If you have done your pre-negotiation preparation, it shouldn't be hard to do this. Documentation supporting your offer, expert opinion and comparisons with similar deals, are all part and parcel of proving the validity of your offer. In other words, if you make a reasonable offer, and are able to defend it against attack, then you should be able to reach agreement somewhere within your range of acceptable terms.

Several Ways to Encourage Quick Acceptance of Your Offer

The longer negotiations drag on, the greater the odds that agreement may never be reached. So for this reason, as well as the time, money, and uncertainty involved with conducting extended negotiations, it's advantageous to encourage a quick acceptance of your offer. There are a number of techniques you can use to do this. They include:

A. Make Your Offer Conditional in Terms of Time.

For instance, "Mr. Adams, I'll make you a one-time offer good until 5:00 P.M. tomorrow."

Putting a time limit on an offer puts pressure on the other side to give it prompt consideration. However, they may assume you're just bluffing, and wait it out to see what happens. This is especially true if you don't offer a valid reason why a time deadline must be imposed. Therefore, make this technique more effective by establishing some necessity that justifies your deadline. It's particularly helpful if this reason is something that appears to be beyond your control. For example, "Jim, I'll make you one last offer of $5,000,000, but it must be accepted by Friday, since that's when my loan agreement expires."

B. Offer Incentives for Prompt Acceptance.

Adding value to an offer in exchange for early acceptance can be used to encourage a quick response. For instance, "If we can close this deal today, we'll absorb the shipping charges over the course of the contract." Here again this approach is made more convincing by using a sound basis to justify your offer. Otherwise, if agreement isn't reached within the deadline, and negotiations continue, the other side will have an expectation that your incentive will be included in the agreement when it's reached.

NOTE: Anytime you offer something of value, it's extremely difficult to backtrack and take it off the table—no matter what conditions you attach. Therefore, don't casually make conditional promises, since with or without the condition. You have signaled a willingness to make what you promise a part of any resultant agreement.

C. Establish an Imperative Deadline.

This can take many variations. It can be base on third party commitments, (" My subcontractor can't meet deliveries, unless we have an agreement this week."), higher authority ("The President has given us until Wednesday to finalize this, or the money is going for another research project."), or performance factors, ("The manufacturing capacity we need won't be available unless we can start within two weeks."). In essence, the basis for a deadline may be real, or only the result of your creativity. Whichever it is, the essential point is that it be believable.

D. Strategies for Your Opening Offer

1) Clear

Your opening offer should clearly state your interpretation of the issue, and your proposed solution: "I would like to make an offer for the supply of product to your organization. For the volume you are requesting, I can guarantee supply provided we have 40 days' notice and you can pick up from our warehouse. This would then allow us to offer a price of £ 150.00 per tonne."

2) Decisive

You can indicate the firmness of your offer by the use of language. The harder your language, and the stronger the tone of voice in which it is delivered, the firmer your offer will sound: for example, "we would like…", "we must have…", "I am happy to discuss different options…", "We cannot move from our bottom line, which is…" How firm or how flexible you should make your opening offer will depend on your negotiation strategy. If you use differing communication patterns during the negotiation, then you will confuse the other party with your intentions.

3) Specific

When you make a quotation, you should be explicit and straightforward. It is inadvisable to use ambiguous words like "about," "approximately", " probably". A specific offer allows the other party to know your expectations more precisely. It is easy to do so if you present your offer in writing. When you make an offer orally, you might as well put it down on paper or on a display board to let the other side see it clearly at a glance.

E. When to Withdraw Your Offer

Withdrawing an offer once it's made isn't easy, even without reaching agreement. If there's a lesson in this, it's not to make an offer on the assumption that it can just as easily be withdrawn. The truth is that once an offer is on the table, the other side views that offer as your current position, even after it's withdrawn. The circumstances are rare where you can make an offer, withdraw it, and then subsequently negotiate an agreement better than the withdrawn offer. Common sense says that if you offer \$100,000, withdraw it, and then offer \$90,000, you won't be taken seriously.

Nevertheless, there are valid grounds for withdrawing an offer that's currently on the table. These include:

1) When Circumstances Change

We live in an ever-changing world, and during the negotiation process events may occur which make your existing offer a bad one. The reasons may range from a sudden financial setback to a change in your competitive business climate. From a negotiation standpoint, it's useful to distinguish between offers that are withdrawn due to a reason that makes further negotiations useless, and those where it's justified to continue negotiations under the changed circumstances. In the first instance, other than breaking-off the discussions as amicably as possible, there's little else to do.

On the other hand, if you want to continue the negotiation process with the changed circumstances being taken into account, you have to make your case for withdrawing your offer. It becomes necessary to explain the specifics of why your offer is no longer valid. Obviously, if the cause is something beyond your control, there's a greater likelihood the other side will be reasonable about it. But if it's something such as an internal business problem, your opponent is likely to hold your feet to the fire if the changed conditions will mean a new offer less attractive than the one that was withdrawn.

2) Withdrawing an Offer

Withdrawing an offer is sometimes used as a negotiation tactic in the hopes of forcing the other side toward agreement. However, for the most part this is a silly maneuver, since it's seldom taken seriously when an offer is withdrawn and the discussions continue on. Therefore, if you are in a position where you attempt this tactic, be prepared to walk away from the table in the hope that the other side will contact you. If your ploy works, they should either agree to your terms, or at least make a better offer than they had previously proposed.

A better strategy than a sudden offer withdrawal is to make an offer conditional when it's first proposed. Say something such as, "I'll go to $90,000 if we can settle today." This is particularly effective if you can provide a factual basis as to why the offer will be withdrawn if it's not accepted. For instance, "I can offer you $524,000 if we settle this week. Otherwise, I'll have to withdraw my offer and recompute the figures, since new labor rates take effect next Monday." Obviously, the greater the credibility attached to your reasoning, the better the chances of convincing your adversary.

There comes a time in many a negotiation where little progress is being made, and the prospects for agreement become increasingly bleak. At these times, when you are ready to pack it in, you may have to choose between (1) ending negotiations with no intention of resuming them, (2) leaving your offer on the table. With an invitation to contact you if they decide to accept it at a later date, or (3) withdrawing your offer, with the understanding that it's being done because no progress is being made.

Naturally, ending negotiations without leaving the door open should only be done when, all things considered, that is the logical choice. As for choosing between leaving your offer on the table, or withdrawing it, to a large degree that will depend upon what stage negotiations were in when they ended. If you have made what is in fact your final offer, then you might as well just leave it opens with an offer to contact you if it's subsequently acceptable. However, even here, time constraints should be given for acceptance of the offer. For instance, say "My offer remains open if you choose to accept it within the next two weeks."

⇨ 2.3 **Bargaining**

Case 5

A Dutch company wanted to purchase a piece of capital equipment. The seller was a Scottish firm, a public company, and the quoted price of the equipment was $20 million. The buyer had decided that price was one of a number of issues that they intended to table. The Scottish company was undoubtedly state-of-art in the area of technology in which the buyer was interested. The problem was simply that they had never done business with the seller before. So, how could they know that they were getting value for money?

They wrote to the Scottish company and said: "Look, we are quite happy to accept your technological capability, but how do we know that your offer represents good value? Please send us the working drawings for this equipment so that we can see what we are getting for our money." The seller sent the drawing as requested. Once the buyer had the drawings, they went straight into their engineering drawing office. Using the drawings, the equipment that they planned to buy was broken down item by item and listed in a set of manuals. They then sought two quotes for each item to try to establish a complete material cost. Buyers should note that it is not necessary to know what an item is or does for the information to be of value to them. For example, to this day they have no idea what a "Regan riser handling tool" is, nor do they need to know. The importance of the analysis lies in the fact that a specific component has been identified and the quantity of such components that will be used is known.

They then obtained the seller's annual reports for the past five years. Material ratios, labor ratios, overheads and marketing costs were calculated, and built into a fiscal model. The average of the seller's profit for the past five years was also calculated and built in. The end result of the exercise was that their estimate differed from the quoted price by nearly $250,000, which gave them cause for concern. They buyer reworked the figures several times until they were confident that the model was correct. And at the right psychological point in the negotiation, they handed the seller the estimates and manuals, together with a summary sheet, and simply said: "That's what we make it, show us where we are wrong." The seller never could, and the buyer did not pay the $250,000.

(*Excerpts from* International Business Negotiation—Theory, Cases and Practices *by Bai Yuan*)

After one side gives an offer, the other side may follow it up with bargaining, which is the most active, dynamic and vital part of the whole business negotiation. At any rate, offer is simply a kind of exploration without commitment, in which the parties probe the possibility of reaching a contract, but the quoted terms and conditions are not firm and are subject to change without notice. The bargaining or a bargained exchange for consideration is the process in which the two sides show their genuine intention to close a deal with their real efforts directed toward reaching agreement on an actual closing price.

2.3.1　Counter-offer

In general practice, when an offeree has received an offer, he usually would not accept it immediately, instead he would try to amend or alter some terms of the offer. For instance, if the offeree finds the price too high or the shipment too late, he would try to change these terms. In doing so, he would make a counter-offer. Counter-offer is a reply to an offer that adds to, limits, or modifies materially the terms of the offer. It is a new offer made by the offeree. The original offer becomes null and void, and its original offeror is not bound by anymore.

The counter-offer indicates one's intention to agree upon a contract. For example, part A makes an offer of $800 per ton (makes an offer), which part B thinks is on the high side. Part B requests that Part A quote a more reasonable price; Again, Party A quotes a new price $780 and in response, Part B proposes an explicit price for closing the deal—$750 (makes a counter offer).

How to make a counter-offer?

The art of the deal is negotiating. The goal, when you're countering a seller's offer, is to get the lowest price and best terms possible. Once you reject the initial offer, you must decide how much to counter.

With regard to the price range, a counter-offer can either be a proportional one or one based on cost analysis:

- A proportional counter offer refers to a proposal in which one party asks the counterpart to adjust the quotation proportionally; to lower the total price by a certain percent.
- A cost-based counter offer is made on the basis of cost analysis of the items under negotiation, proposing an appropriate price for the counterpart's quotation.

When a manufacturer establishes a price for an item of merchandise, it begins by considering two basic cost functions. These are variable costs and fixed costs. Variable costs are usually associated with raw materials and labor, although other cost elements may be taken into account. Fixed costs are those costs that the supplier has to bear irrespective of whether it manufactures anything or not. If the company has a factory, then it has few options but to pay rent, rates and insurance. If it has staff on the payroll, then their wages and salaries have to be met, even in the absence of any business being undertaken.

It is the fixed cost elements that should attract the buyer's attention, because fixed costs can be divided into two further categories. These are planning and production expenses, and marketing and distribution costs. Planning and production costs relate to such things as expenditures on plant and equipment, and such administrative costs as salaries, insurance, depreciation and interest on overdrafts. The second set of expenditures provides for the cost of running the marketing operation (including the sales force), and will also include a provision for retailer support. Put simply, the equation looks like this:

$$
\begin{array}{ll}
 & \text{variable cost} \\
+ & \text{fixed cost} \\
\hline
= & \text{cost of product} \\
+ & \text{profit margin} \\
\hline
= & \text{selling price}
\end{array}
$$

To gain bargaining advantage, a buyer should examine the second category of fixed costs, i.e. the marketing and distribution component. Within this category, manufacturers dealing with the retail sector build in a sum of money explicitly for the purposes of retail support. It is important to recognize that this retailer support is built into the cost structure of the product before the profit component is added. From the accounting point of view, retailer support is regarded as s sunk cost. This is to say, the money is written off against forecast sales at the moment that the budget is struck.

This is an important point and needs to be clarified further. The money designated for retailer support is built into the seller's cost structure for the purpose of subsidizing the promotional activities of the retailer. It is built in to support not a single retailer, but every retailer that the supplier deals with. The money does not come from the supplier's profits; it is built into the cost structure of the merchandise before the profit component is added.

Once the buyer understands how a seller's cost structure is put together, then the tactics of how to gain a disproportionate share of the retailer support that is available become clear. If the buyer puts an agenda together based upon those issues that derive their cost base from the fixed cost component of the seller's cost structure, but taking a small bite at each he can effectively end up with a substantial proportion of the retailer support that is available.

If a buyer is involved in a once-off procurement (which could be an item of capital equipment) or is laying down long-term contracts for substantial quantities of raw materials that will be delivered over time, or is tending to place a large order of a product, then a careful analysis of the seller's cost structure should be considered.

With regard to the items connected in the counter-offer, there are three categories: bargain item by item, bargain by classification and bargain as a whole.

- Bargain item by item: In a counter offer, equipment of different types can be bargained for separately one by one, or different sets of equipment bargained for set by set. Alternatively, each factor in the negotiation, such as a design fee, material expenses and training fees and such components can be bargained one by one.
- Bargain by classification: The items under negotiation may be classified by such groups as models or price range. For example, they can be divided into three classes based on their prices: high priced, medium-priced and low-priced groups. Then, they can be bargained for one by one, with bargaining emphasis on the high-priced group.
- Bargain as a whole: A counter offer might be made to bargain over the negotiating subject as a single entity, indicating a total price at which the parties might close the deal.

The selection of bargaining methods depends on information about relevant prices and the customary practices in hand. If there is inadequate information for reference, a counter offer based on cost analysis is highly recommended.

Generally speaking, bargaining item by item favors the buyer. Bargaining by classifications is often acceptable to both sides. Bargaining as a whole appears to be more convenient and simple, but is more beneficial to the seller. Buyers do not like this method of bargaining, especially for complex transactions, such as the purchase of a large complete set of equipment. Bargaining as a whole should be avoided in the initial phase of negotiations. It is more appropriate for the final phase of bargaining.

2.3.2 Bargaining Tactics

In the bargaining process, you have to know when to say "No" during negotiations, how to respond to tactics used by your adversary, as well as figure out ways to hurdle seemingly insurmountable problems.

A. Techniques for Justifying and Getting a High Price

No matter how reasonable you think your price is, when negotiations begin, it's a foregone conclusion that the other side will challenge your price as being too high. There are two principal reasons for this:

- Everyone wants to get a good deal, and accepting what's initially offered runs counter to this sort of mindset. Simply put, people like bargains, and if they are deprived of the opportunity to reduce the price, then they aren't convinced that they're getting one.

- There's a natural assumption that your price is inflated. As the thinking goes, everyone wants to maximize their profits, so your initial price must be too high.

Because of this natural tendency to suspect that an initial price is a loaded figure, it's useful to have alternative positions prepared before you start to negotiate. If you do this, then you give yourself some built-in flexibility to reduce your price. Of course, if you don't have to make any significant reductions, then all the better.

Nevertheless, it's not always possible to reasonably inflate an initial offering price. For example, if you're selling a common item with a well-established market price, any price substantially above the norm won't be taken seriously—unless, of course, you can substantiate the reason for the difference. Consequently, if you're facing this sort of difficulty, you have to use other means to convince the buyer that your price is indeed fair. This is a dilemma commonly encountered by sellers with prices that are traditionally higher than the competition.

But take heart if you find yourself in this position, since salespeople consistently command and receive premium prices in competition with lower priced competitors. So whether you want to better your bargain, even though you have price flexibility, or are compelled to justify a high price which can't be lowered, you have to use techniques that justify the price.

B. How to Overcome Anyone's Price Objections

No one is in a worse position entering into negotiations than someone who thinks their price is too high. Yet, all too often, people sit and haggle over price at a bargaining table when they have little real conviction that their price is reasonable. Needless to say, this is a guarantee of failure.

Sure, everyone knows tales of someone who supposedly can sell anything to anyone at any price. And there's little question that if one looks long and hard enough, a fool can be found to throw money away. However, super sellers are few and far between, and although fools may be somewhat easier to find, they're by no means hiding under every rock. This means, that to be successful in justifying a high price, you need to be knowledgeable—not lucky.

The starting point for anyone trying to negotiate a high price starts long before they begin to bargain. The first thing you have to know is your pricing strategy. In essence, what is your price based upon? Are there solid reasons why your product costs more than the competition? Such factors as quality reliability, and customer service are obvious examples of areas where your product may be priced higher for substantive reasons.

On the other hand, the basis for a high price may be something more subtle, such as snob appeal or status. After all, sports cars that can reach speeds of 140 miles per hour aren't bought with that primary purpose in mind. Unless, of course, the buyer is seeking to establish a world record for speeding tickets.

The same philosophy applies to a wide range of luxury goods which aren't purchased based on any correlation between price and value. The old saw, "If you have to ask the price, then you can't afford it," rings true for many items sold on an emotional appeal. But more to the point of everyday reality, "a price is only too high if the buyer thinks it is." Which means, you can get most any price for anything, as long as you can prove its worth to the buyer.

At any rate, as a start in getting the price you want, you first must know what it's based on. After all, you're not very well-armed to defend a price if you don't know the basis for it. Therefore, if you are selling something tangible or intangible—sit down and figure out why it's worth what you want for it. These sales points might include any of the following elements:

- Sell benefits—Be able to show the buyer the benefits to be obtained by buying your product.
- Sell value—Show how even though your price appears higher, it actually is cheaper based on its performance.
- Sell competitive edge—Convince the buyer that what you're selling will enhance their business. For instance, "Joe, you'll help your own sales by buying from us. As you know, everyone in the industry knows our reputation for quality, so our quality helps sell your quality."
- Sell personal pride—"The location of this building will enhance the professional image and status of your firm."
- Sell uniqueness—The "It's one of a kind," argument has been used to justify high prices for an awful lot of pretty common items.
- Sell service—"We'll be there when you need us."

In fact, the number of ways you can substantiate a price during negotiations is as fertile as your imagination. But besides being able to overcome objections to your price, it's equally essential to recognize that price itself may not be what the buyer is objecting to. Often, price becomes a handy excuse for someone who doesn't want to make a deal for reasons other than price. The truth is that a "Your price is too high" statement by a buyer is the business equivalent of the seasoned criminal's "I didn't do it" when accused of a crime.

However, while the criminal is innocent until proven guilty, your price is too high until you prove otherwise. As a result, when you receive an initial price objection, find out why the other party thinks the price is too high. Keep probing until you can pinpoint the basis for their objections. For instance, is it (1) based on competitive prices, or (2) the category in general?

Get whatever information you can from the other party, and then proceed to resolve it. Then, and only then, you may discover that there's something else they object to. But until you overcome the price objection hurdle, you'll never get to the real reason.

TIP: If you have competition in what you're selling, the most valuable thing to know besides your own product is your competitor's. In fact, if it's feasible to do so, buy it, try it, and in general "kick the tires" to find out what makes it tick. After all, it's pretty difficult to differentiate your product from the competitors' if you don't know what they have to offer.

C. How to Cut a Big Price into Small Parts

One way to overcome the obstacle of a high price is to cut it down to size. What you have to do here is show the buyer that the price, is in fact, quite reasonable when it's analyzed in terms of its components. For example, if you're selling a product, you're also selling quality. Show the buyer the specifics that go into making your product one of better quality than competing products. Support your arguments with figures that prove the reliability of the item. A little bit of detailed data can be far more convincing than all of the rhetoric in the world. Figures add credibility to the argument that your price is indeed reasonable.

This type of approach can be useful in many types of negotiations. For instance, if you're selling a building, identify the many advantages that comprise the price other than the building itself. Location, traffic patterns, the building design, low property taxes, the demographics of the area, and a host of other factors all work toward showing the prospective buyer that your price is reasonable.

One of the biggest hang-ups folks face in justifying price is acting defensively about it. They end up countering price objections with, "Yea, but…" and then try to prove why their price isn't high. It's generally far better to be forthright about your price. Admit that it's higher right at the start, and then go on to show why it's really lower than anything the competition is offering. What you want to do is give the buyer valid reasons that justify your price.

If you think about it, people don't make objections to price alone, other than as a negotiating ploy, or to disguise some other reason for not making a commitment. Instead, they object to a price based on a product's perceived value as opposed to a similar product and/or service. Therefore, your job is to cure their lack of knowledge by showing them how and why the sum of the parts add up to a very reasonably priced whole.

D. Turning High Prices into Bargain Basement Buys

A savvy method for removing price as an issue at the bargaining table is to adopt the attitude that your price is, if anything, too low. Admittedly, this isn't easy to carry off, but it can be done in many circumstances. Remember, people salivate over bargains. An awful lot of cocktail party conversation centers around comparisons of who got a good deal on something. Therefore, if you can convince your counterparts that they're getting a bargain, you can remove price as an obstacle. To do this successfully, pitch angles that shout "bargain". One of the oldest ways in the book of doing this is to tout beating a price increase by buying now. It may seem hackneyed, but people are conditioned to rising prices. As a result, they are susceptible to buying at today's prices if they can be convinced that tomorrow's will be higher.

To be convincing in this regard, try to present evidence that supports your statements. Show that the cost of raw materials is increasing, or that a key supplier and/or the competition has recently raised prices. If nothing else, use general economic inflationary trends—assuming they support your argument. Frankly, it frequently isn't all that difficult to find support for a position that prices will be going up. The key is to present your argument with enough background data to convince the buyer that it's true, and not just a Ploy to support your price.

Another angle for justifying a price as a bargain is by using comparisons with competitive items that appear to be priced lower than yours. Buyers seldom look beyond a basic price when making comparisons. After all they're looking for the best buy they can get. However, a lower competitive price is often the result of comparing apples and oranges. The competitor's lower price may result from not offering the same value.

Therefore, always make sure, whenever a buyer touts a lower price elsewhere, to establish precisely what the buyer is talking about. Are the items actually comparable in all respects? If you take the time to dig into it, you'll often find that there are significant differences. It might be something as basic as a difference in quantities, delivery schedules, or payment terms. The fact is that with a little bit of effort, it's not all that hard to show that no matter what competitive prices are, your price is indeed the best buy.

E. Selling "Negative Net Cost" instead of Price

One alternative that can eliminate price hassles entirely is to concentrate on the "negative net cost" to the buyer. What you're doing here is pitching angles that show how much the buyer will increase revenues and/or decrease costs by buying your product and/or service. The key here is to show the buyer in specific terms how your product at your price will save money.

Whenever possible, make direct comparisons with other alternatives that may be available to the buyer. As an example, let's assume that you're selling a non-repairable item at a unit price of $100, while a competitive item is available for $80. The key difference is that your item has a service life of one year versus six months for the competitive product. The potential purchaser uses fifty of these a year, and they have to be replaced when they fail. Your product has a yearly cost of $5,000 (50 units × $100), while the competitive unit costs $8,000 on a yearly basis (100 units × $80).

Since your unit lasts twice as long as the competitor's, the cost to the buyer is $3,000 less on a yearly basis. Therefore, the buyer is saving $60 per unit on a yearly basis by buying your product. Obviously, this is a far less complex example than the realities of the real world that you may encounter. Yet, there are many opportunities that lend themselves to this sort of justification. They may not be as easy to compute, but if you can come up with the figures, you have with one stroke turned a high price into a bargain basement buy.

NOTE: One final point relative to price is to always make sure you get substantive concessions whenever you reduce your price during negotiations. If you drop your price without any reciprocal concession by the other side, you are in effect admitting that your price was inflated. This tends to make folks wonder just how inflated the price is, and consequently encourages them to seek further price reductions. Although everyone likes to see a price get reduced as evidence that they're getting a bargain, doing it too easily creates unnecessary suspicions. The harder you make a negotiator work for a price concession, the more convinced that person will be that it was their effort—not inflated prices—that accounted for the reduction.

F. Take It or Leave It Types: Finessing Them into Negotiating

Another approach you will face at the negotiation table is the "take it or leave it" offer. It pretty much boils down to, "This is what I'm offering. If you don't want the deal on that basis, then let's just forget about it." There are three basic moves you can make when confronted with this sort of dilemma.

- Keep talking and ignore the ultimatum. If the other side doesn't bolt, you will immediately know they aren't serious.
- Consider your alternatives. If they are better than the deal being offered say, "I'll leave it. Call me if you change your mind." This often induces the other party to become more receptive, and they may immediately say, "Wait a minute. Let's talk this over." But if they don't, walk out the door, and proceed with your alternative. If they subsequently contact you to reopen negotiations, then you're in the driver's seat.
- Invent a competitor. If it's feasible, invent a competitor who will give you a better deal. Admittedly, this bluff may be called, leaving you with little choice but to accept an unreasonable offer or break off negotiations. However, this approach can serve to establish how serious the other side is about their ultimatum.

Overcoming a "take it or leave it" offer often involves playing a game of brinkmanship. Of course, there are many more pleasant pastimes than playing a game of chicken when a business deal is on the line. However, a "take it or leave it" strategy can only succeed if you succumb to the temptation. And in the long run, avoiding a bad deal by walking away is preferable to staying and getting stuck. Furthermore, once you refuse to be bullied this way, it's less likely that anyone who hears about your taking a stand will try the same tactic on you in the future.

G. Splitting the Difference and Its Pitfalls

If you do a significant amount of negotiating, it's inevitable that you will cross paths with negotiators whose sole solution to bargaining hang-ups is splitting the difference. It doesn't matter whether the negotiation positions are poles apart or too similar to quibble about. A confirmed split-the-difference negotiator always wants to cut the dollar difference down the middle.

At first blush, this may seem like a pretty practical approach, and it is under certain circumstances. For example, if extended negotiations have narrowed the gap in positions to a point where the only disparity is a judgment call as to whether the final price should be "X" or "Y" then reaching agreement at a midpoint can be a practical resolution. On the other hand, splitting the difference is frequently used as a substitute for negotiating the merits of the relative positions of the negotiating parties. It's a tactic that is used by both inexperienced negotiators and seasoned bargainers. However, the end result can be quite different.

Skilled negotiators most often use this tactic to avoid discussing the details of negotiation differences when they know their position on the merits is weak. Conversely, novice negotiators use it as a substitute for railing to properly prepare their negotiation position. Simply put, they don't know what they're doing. So they make a ridiculous initial offer, go through the motions, and then suggest splitting the difference. So when you face a split-the-difference situation, the first thing to consider is whether it's being proposed by a pro or an amateur.

There are several pretty basic considerations that shouldn't be ignored whenever you're considering an offer to split the difference. These are:

- What baseline are you operating from? As a minimum, you should never split the difference if the result would exceed the highest price you're willing to pay as a buyer, or fall below the lowest price you can accept as a seller.

EXAMPLE: You're the buyer and your walk-away price (the most you would pay) is $1,300,000. Your last offer was $1,000,000, while the other side stood at $1,800,000. But the other negotiator, offers to split the $800,000 difference, which would result in a price of $1,400,000.

- Quite obviously, the more reasonable your offer. And the more unreasonable is that of your adversary, the worse off you're going to be. Therefore, never split the difference unless both positions are within a range that you consider fair.

EXAMPLE: A reasonable price for certain items is somewhere between $2,200,000 and $2,400,000. You, the seller are asking for $2,400,000. The buyer is offering only $1,800,000, which is below your cost to produce. He offers to split the $600,000 difference, which is an unacceptable price of $2,100,000. However, if his offer was $2,200,000 and you split the $200,000 difference, then the price of $2,300,000 would be acceptable.

- Who makes the initial offer during negotiations is important. If you make the first offer, which is a reasonable one, and the other side counters with a figure that's totally out of line, splitting the difference is out of the question until the gap in positions is narrowed.

EXAMPLE: Assume a fair price is about $1,500,000. You (the buyer) make an initial offer of $1,300,000, and the seller counters with a selling price of $2,500,000. Splitting the difference of $1,200,000 would have you paying a price of $1,900,000.

- Avoid the "even dollar" syndrome. When negotiations take place, there's a tendency to talk in round numbers. Millions, and tens of thousands, are the sums bandied back and forth. As a result, folks forget about the smaller amounts in between. Because of this, you can make money by using uneven amounts.

EXAMPLE: Let's say splitting the difference during a negotiation comes to a compromise amount of $2,400,000. You (the buyer) might want to respond by saying something such as, "That's pretty close. I'll agree if we can make it $2,379,500." Of course, try to give some justification for the reduction. What the reason isn't significant, as long as it has some ring of reality to it. The fact is that when folks have been thinking in terms of hundreds of thousands of dollars, smaller amounts ($21,500 in this example) tend to get treated as automatic give always.

- Reap other benefits from a split-the-difference approach. Negotiators who get hung up on splitting the difference concentrate so hard on selling that approach, so that they can tend to ignore non-dollar issues. Therefore, you may be able to negotiate a bundle of concessions in other areas that more than offset what you might lose by splitting the difference. So try to tie-in buying the other guy's dollar approach if he'll accept your other terms.

H. Coping with a "Best and Final" Offer You Don't Want

Often, with much fanfare, a negotiating adversary will announce that the offer he has just made, or is about to make, is his last offer. Naturally, the intent of doing this is to convince you that you are now in a "take it or leave it" position. Of course, if the offer happens to be acceptable to you, then by all, means accept it. However, more often than not, the offer isn't palatable. This supposedly leaves you in the position of accepting an unsatisfactory offer, or ending up with no deal at all.

The truth is that more often than not a "best and final" offer is neither the best that can be made, nor the last offer that will be forthcoming. What is really constitutes is an implied ultimatum that if you don't accept the offer, negotiations have ended. Consequently, when you face this sort of bluff, the proper move is to call it. This can be done by rejecting it outright and saying something such as, "That's not acceptable because…," meanwhile giving a recap of the reasons why you won't accept it. This method of refusing an alleged final offer bounces the ball right back into the other negotiator's court. He essentially then has to either break off negotiations, or continue the discussions. If it's the latter, then there is tacit acknowledgment that there is still room for an improved offer.

An alternative tactic is to just keep on talking as if the ultimatum hadn't been issued. If the other side continues to negotiate, then here again their threat to walk has been exposed as a bluff. What most folks worry about when they are presented with a "best and final" offer is that the other side will break off negotiations if it's not accepted.

However, on closer examination, the threat isn't as serious as it seems to be. So what if they do take a walk? There's nothing to prevent you from calling them in a day or two and either resuming negotiations, or accepting their last offer if you feel it meets your objectives. If they are getting a reasonable deal, they're not about to hang up the phone on you.

The bottom line is that this sort of a threat isn't as serious as it seems. The greatest hazard it creates is that someone will bite the bait and accept less than satisfactory terms solely because of a fear that otherwise there won't be any deal at all. And anytime the choice is between a bad deal, or no deal at all, the savvy negotiator will gladly let the other party take a hike.

CAUTION: If you are the one in a position to make a final offer, make certain that it is exactly that—at least as far as things stand at the present moment. In other words, if it isn't accepted, be prepared to get up and leave. Otherwise, if you continue to negotiate, your credibility is gone. As a result, when you get to where your last offer is in reality the best you can do, it isn't likely to be believed.

Of course, if you do bluff and it's called, that doesn't prevent you from changing your position if and when negotiations do resume. You can waltz around the fact you backed-off your position by citing some new information that came to your attention.

The general rule for "best and final" offers is to refuse them if you're on the receiving end, and walk away from the table if you make one that's not accepted. Of course, make sure that you don't arbitrarily reject a fair offer, just to see if you can squeeze a few more dollars out of the deal. In the long run, such tactics only serve to alienate people whom you may have to work with in the future.

I. Overcoming "Even Dollar" Negotiation Hang-ups

You may recall that in the discussion on splitting dollar differences in case 6. It was mentioned that negotiators generally use round numbers. It was pointed out that in splitting the difference, you could benefit by using odd figures. However, using uneven numbers have an even greater significance involving credibility.

An amount such as $124,542.76 appears more credible than $125,000. There's an aura of computational accuracy that implies it isn't just a random number thrown out for feelers. This is especially true in negotiations where offers and counter-offers are bandied back and forth. Negotiators naturally suspect that the figures tossed out aren't computed with any degree of precision. Therefore, if you deviate from this expectation by using odd dollars and cents, you can add an extra measure of believability to your numbers.

Using uneven numbers have other advantages, such as making it easier to move more slowly when dollar concessions are made. Because your figures appear to be computed down to the last cent, it's easier to argue that you've moved as far as you can. Let's look at a capsulated version of how this works.

Case 6

Background   Albert and Benjamin are in the final stages of negotiations, with only the final price still being discussed. Albert's last offer was $450,000, while Benjamin was at $521,376.54.

Discussion

Albert: Ben, I can go to $480,000, which is half of the difference. Let's close on that. (Of course, he didn't quite split the difference in half, but negotiators love to pick-up the extra buck.)

Benjamin: Let me look at the figures, and see what I can do. (Ben returns after a brief recess) I went over everything in detail with my number crunchers. Frankly, my first offer of $521,376.54 was rock bottom. However, in the interests of settling this thing, I'll go to $509,898.34. Let's wrap it up there.

Albert: (Looking and sounding peeved) Now wait a minute. I raised my offer $30,000.

And all you gave up was $11,000. We won't get anywhere at this rate.

Benjamin: In the first place, AI, it's more than $11.000. (Only $478.20 more) But that's not the point. I made an initial offer based on the minimum I could accept. To chop that $11,000, I had to go back and cut the labor I need to do the job. I've got the figures right here to support that. You agreed that the amount of labor I was using was reasonable, and now you come along and want me to cut it further. We're not playing a numbers game. I proposed what we need to do the job. I can't cut that just because you're looking for a bargain.

Albert: You can't tell me Ben that you don't have at least a 10% contingency factor built-in to your proposal. Taking 10% off of your $521,000 would put you around $470,000. I'm offering $480,000.

Benjamin: My $521,376.54 was my best estimate to do the job assuming everything went according to plan. If something goes wrong, I'll be eating the costs. It's as simple as that.

Albert: (Appearing disgusted) I'll go to $500,000 even, but not one penny more.

Benjamin: (After another twenty minutes of back and forth discussion) Let me take a final look. (He returns a half hour later, slumps down in his chair) I went over everything again, and frankly there's nowhere else 1 can cut. All I can do is take something off our hoped for profit and make a final offer of $506,375.20. That's it period. All you need to do to settle at that figure is move about one percent from your $500,000.

Albert: After a bit of a protest agrees with Ben's final figure of $506,375.20.

The important point here is to convey credibility when you present your numbers. This gives you a framework to sustain your arguments which doesn't exist when round numbers are tossed back and forth.

NOTE: Along with a failure to use precision in numbers, your choice of words can also have a bearing on the reception an offer receives. Never make the careless mistake of couching your offer in language that doesn't denote finality. Qualifiers such as "about $255,000", "approximately $2,000,000," Or "roughly $10,000,000" are to be avoided. They send a signal that your offer isn't final, whereas every offer you make—even if it's the tenth offer—should be presented as if it were your last.

J. Using the Shock Value of a "Quick Hit" Offer

Negotiations often get bogged down in hassling over minor details, which have little impact in terms of a final agreement. One way to move things off of dead center is to make a sudden offer at a totally unexpected moment. There are a couple of benefits to doing this.

In the first place, it immediately moves the course of the discussion away from the subject at hand. This is particularly useful if the other negotiator happens to be targeting one or more particularly weak points in your negotiation position. If nothing else, your sudden offer forces the other side to pause and consider it. Of even greater consequence, if the bargaining has been particularly difficult, your unexpected offer may have appeal as a way to break a deadlock.

Although, as previously mentioned, it's usually better to have the other side make the first offer, there are also circumstances where it may be preferable to make a "preemptive strike" initial offer geared toward securing quick agreement. The reasons for doing this will be closely related to the details of any individual negotiation. A few such instances are:

- If you face a deadline unknown to the opposition, putting an offer on the table can move things along.
- To feel out the opposition by making a high initial offer. Their reaction can be useful in gauging the future course of the negotiations.
- Certain facts not known to your adversary increase the value of what you're negotiating for. Therefore, you may want to make an attractive first offer to get the deal under wraps.
- If your negotiating position is strong enough to dictate terms. Under these conditions, the longer you negotiate, the more you signal a willingness to make concessions.
- If the value of the subject matter under negotiation is difficult to ascertain, making a first offer will let you set the base price for negotiations.
- If the circumstances are such that making the first offer will be seen as a sign of good will. This is particularly true where the other side is a more or less reluctant partner to the negotiations.

K. How to Parry Counter-offers Effectively

Rejecting counter-offers can be dealt with in a variety of ways. To some extent it depends upon how realistic the counter-offer is in relation to the offer you made. If it brings the respective positions relatively close to agreement, you may simply want to stand firm on your offer, and see if you can get the other negotiator to move a little bit more. As an alternative, you may suggest splitting the difference, to conclude the deal.

The more difficult problem arises when the counter-offer comes nowhere close to your offer. Let's look at various alternatives that can be used to respond when this happens.

- The most obvious rebuttal of a counter-offer is a straightforward rejection. However, unless the terms are outrageous enough to be laughable, a blunt, "No" isn't satisfactory. A flat rejection may well lead the other negotiator to believe that you're just stonewalling. This, of course, will only serve to harden the stance of the other side.

Therefore, whenever you reject an offer, give valid reasons for your rejection. This not only adds credibility to your rejection, but it also puts the other side back on the defensive in terms of refuting your reasoning. Incidentally, comparisons work especially well in justifying the rejection of a counter-offer. Hence, if it's at all possible, compare the proposed counter-offer—or any of its components—with similar projects, prices, or whatever else constitutes a comparison in the particular case.

EXAMPLE: Mr. Arnold, your offer is way out-of-line. Comparable leases in buildings within the business district are 30% lower than what you're proposing. I've got a list here which shows what others are paying for similar footage with terms comparable to what I offered you.

- When you receive a counter-offer on a project that is complicated and comprises many elements, take the time to analyze it in detail. It may well be that certain aspects of the counter-offer are satisfactory, while others are unreasonable. By looking at the components, you can then decide whether or not to reject the offer as a whole, or opt to attack it piece-by-piece. The latter method gives you the advantage of accepting the good points, and rejecting those that you don't agree with.

EXAMPLE: Carl, I've gone over your offer in detail with my cost accounting people. We can live with your material costs, as well as the overhead rates proposed. However, both your direct labor costs, and the hours proposed to do the job, aren't even in the ballpark. In order to get this thing resolved, let's concentrate on the labor. For one thing, you've proposed 3,800 hours of senior technician time...

NOTE: When you reject an offer in this manner, try to launch right into the problem area. Doing this shunts the discussion onto the issue you want to attack.

- On occasion, you may find it preferable to reject a counter-offer by simply downplaying its significance. Be lighthearted about it, without being insulting. This approach indicates that you don't take the proposal seriously, and are treating it as a counter-offer that's being thrown on the table for posturing purposes.

EXAMPLE: Adam, if I didn't know you better, I'd think you were blowing smoke in my ear. You can't be serious about a counter-offer that puts us two million bucks apart. Give me something more realistic, so we can get down to some serious negotiating.

- If the circumstances fit, you may just want to plead poverty. Adopting a position that you can't afford the deal based on what the other party is recommending does two things. First of all, it plants the idea that you may not be able to financially handle what's proposed. The bottom line is that the other side either has to consider giving you a better deal, or risk seeing you walk away from the table. Alternatively, your opponent may just think your objection is based upon the price being too high. This puts the other side back on the defensive in terms of justifying the value of what's being offered.

EXAMPLE: The bottom line on your counter-offer is that I'd go broke if I agreed to it. If I pay $2,300 a piece for your sub-assemblies, I'll end up losing $200 a unit on every machine I sell. It's that simple, so for us to do business, you'll have to do better than that.

- Another way to deal with a counter-offer is to come right back with your own counter-offer. However, be careful not to try and close the difference in the positions too quickly, or you'll find yourself giving up most of the cash. So just adjust your offer slightly from your original position. This sends a signal that you're not likely to move much from your original position, while at the same time it indicates your willingness to negotiate.

EXAMPLE：Your company offers a price of ＄5,495,000 to perform computer support services for the ZZZ Corp. They make a counter-offer of ＄4,900,000. You immediately respond with, "We can go down to ＄5,480,000, but that's about as close as we can cut it."

NOTE：The less you move from your initial position in one jump, the greater the possibility of convincing someone else that you don't have much room to maneuver. Conversely, when people make a substantial move from their initial offer, it signals that they have plenty of leeway to play with.

- If you want to bring matters to a head rather quickly, you can reject a counter-offer with a veiled threat to walk away from the table without making a deal. Perhaps this will force the other side to get serious in a hurry. However, it's prudent to have other alternatives in case they decide to stand pat and call your bluff.

EXAMPLE：Victor, if you can't do better than that, there doesn't seem to be any point in continuing the discussions.

NOTE：Remember, that if the other side keeps you negotiating further, without making a better counter-offer, they know you are only bluffing. So after a short while, if they don't give you a better proposal, you might want to emphasize your point by packing your papers and saying something such as, "Like I said, Vic, there's no point in going further, unless you are willing to move. So what do you want to do?" In other words, to make this work successfully, you have to be willing to head for the door. Otherwise, you will have lost your credibility, and will likely be in for a long and difficult negotiation.

L. Asking for the Moon to Get What You Want

As has been mentioned several times before, you should always leave a cushion in any initial offer to give yourself room to maneuver toward an agreement. Nevertheless, for the most part, your offer shouldn't be so extreme that it won't even be considered credible by your adversary. A completely unrealistic initial offer might cause a negotiation breakdown right at the start, resulting in the other party walking away before any bargaining has even begun. Alternatively, it might encourage an equally farfetched counter-offer, making it that much more difficult to reach a final agreement.

However, there are instances when you should at least consider starting-off negotiations with what could be viewed as pie-in-the-sky demands. These circumstances include：

- When the other side makes an initial offer that is unreasonable.

If this happens you have a choice of (a) refusing to negotiate until they give you a reasonable offer, (b) making a credible counter-offer, and negotiating hard to close the gap—which means they have to move a lot further than you do, or (c) responding with an offer that's equally out of touch with reality.

Simply refusing to negotiate has the potential for causing an immediate crisis, which could possibly break-up the bargaining before it has even begun in earnest. Alternatively, if you respond to an outrageous offer with a reasonable proposal, you may be putting yourself in unnecessary difficulty. This can happen if the other negotiator wants equivalent concessions made along the way to close the gap between his unrealistic offer, and your credible response. Naturally this is a negotiation nightmare, since you're trying to move the other position the proverbial mile, while the other side only has to move you a few yards. This can put you with your back to the wall in terms of an ability to make any further concessions. This isn't an insurmountable obstacle if the opposing offer was merely a negotiating ploy, but it may mean a long and arduous negotiating session. As a result of the inherent difficulties involved in choosing alternatives (a) or (b) as the method for responding to an outrageous offer, simple expediency dictates giving consideration to counterattacking by making an equally outrageous initial offer of your own.

- When you are making an initial offer where you are uncertain as to the real value of the item.

The subject matter under negotiation may be such that you aren't really sure of its reasonable worth. Although this isn't likely to happen in most business transactions, in some instances it's not beyond the realm of probability, especially if the topic of negotiation is some type of intangible. When you're faced with this kind of dilemma, it pays to make a ridiculously low offer initially, which you can later raise if circumstances justify it.

- When the other side doesn't perceive the true worth of the item being negotiated.

This can happen when the other party is ill-informed, merely naïve, or you have information—unknown to your opponent—that the true value is far different than surface appearances indicate.

- When your negotiating position is so strong that you're justified in asking for considerably more than would ordinarily be justified.

This can happen when a buyer has a unique need for something you're selling. Therefore, by virtue of being in the driver's seat, you may be able to ask for—and get a premium price. Conversely, if you're the buyer in a situation where the seller has an urgent need to make the sale, you may be successful in offering significantly less than would otherwise be reasonable.

CAUTION: Be prudent about making unrealistic offers and demands when the subject matter of the negotiation has a readily recognizable value. It's great to anticipate a windfall profit, and there is always a temptation to give yourself plenty of maneuvering room for making concessions. However, extreme demands can at best lead to a difficult negotiation, and at worst can lead the other party to walk away, leaving you with no deal at all. Furthermore, in agreements that require some form of continuing performance by the other party, if you stick it to them at the bargaining table, they may make life difficult for you during the period of performance. The most fruitful negotiations are generally those in which both parties are reasonably satisfied with the final agreement.

⇨ 2.4　Making Concessions

The heart of negotiation is the way both sides make concessions to get what they really want. A concession is a critical issue that may affect both the substance of a negotiation and the relationship between the parties.

2.4.1　Key Factors that Influence Concession-making

Several key factors may influence concessions.

A. Negotiators use concession-making behavior for different reasons.

Concessions can indicate a willingness to work with the other party. They can often be viewed as an offer of good will. United States negotiators are known for making concessions first before their Asian counterparts. However, because the U.S. negotiator makes concessions before the issues have fully been discussed, which is the Asian style, U.S. negotiators may suffer in the amount of gains compared to their Asian negotiation partners.

B. The rate at which concessions are made and who initiates the first concession.

Buyer-seller negotiation research indicates that first concessions and rate are often determined by the role of the negotiator. The rate and timing of concessions can aid the negotiation process or disrupt the process and limit the range of possible outcomes. That is, if you make concessions too early before a full discussion has occurred, you may find fewer options for bargaining later.

Furthermore, early concessions may create suspicion and distrust. Some cultures wait until the end of the negotiation to make concessions, whereas others tend to make them throughout the process. The difference in rate and timing of concession making can influence possible gains. In addition, there is a distinct difference among intercultural negotiators regarding the timing of concessions. For instance, U.S. negotiators tend to make small concessions often and expect concessions to be reciprocated, whereas Chinese and Japanese negotiators often wait until the end to make concessions and may make rather large ones if they are satisfied with the general principles of the agreement. A result of U.S.-Japanese negotiations is that Japanese negotiators often fare better in the agreement because the U.S. team has already conceded much of what they had available (Graham, 1985; Menger, 1999). This is also true for U.S.-Chinese business negotiations (Zhao, 2000).

In general, it is best to make small concessions at first and wait for reciprocal moves before offering another concession. Trade-offs are an important part of the concession process. Also, keep in mind that some concessions are likely to come late, so leave yourself room for movement in the final stages of the agreement. Deadlines will influence the rate of concession making. As one approaches a deadline for agreement, concession behavior may increase.

The use of logrolling often results in achieving a positive integrative outcome. Shapiro and Rognes (1996) found that integrative settlements were achieved for parties who "logrolled (i.e. conceded on issues of lesser importance in exchange for concessions on issues of greater importance)". By trading off issues based on priority, negotiators were able to avoid simply trading concessions, which often results in a compromise solution. Logrolling can allow for negotiators to obtain what is most important to them and successfully reach an agreement.

Always calculate your concessions. Rinehart and Page (1992) suggest to determine your concession level by "multiplying the importance of the issue by the degree of concession made on that issue and summing the products for all the issues that were negotiated". By calculating the concession levels of each party, negotiators can then assess the value of their agreement. However the perception of importance is subjective, and therefore misrepresentation could result. Having said this, calculating your concession level is an important tool to gauge the negotiation process.

C. Know that concessions are critical for the agreement and the long-term relationship.

If people feel beat up at the end of concession making, they are likely not to do business with you again. Short-term gains for giving little and getting lot at the expense of the relationship is short-sighted. Long-term partnerships in the international market are worth achieving, and concessions are necessary.

2.4.2　How to Concede—the Dos and Don'ts

The following are brief guidelines on how to concede:

- Give yourself enough room by starting off with a high offer if you're selling or with a low offer if you're buying.
- Get the other party to open up first while you keep your objectives, needs and demands hidden.
- Don't ever be first to concede on a major issue. It is OK to concede first on minor issues, though.
- Give "straw-man" concessions, or those that really give nothing away. But make the other party think that they're really valuable to you. (You need to be a good actor or actress here.)
- Make the other party work hard for every concession you make, so that they'll appreciate them more.
- Trade-off: get something for each concession you make. Remember that saying, "I'll consider it", is a concession, because it raises the other party's expectations. Say instead, "What will you give me if I consider it".
- Concede slowly—as far as possible; don't concede at all, if it can be avoided.
- Say "no" often (the trouble with "no", though, is that most people can't take a "no" very well, and you might lose momentum early in the negotiations, so you will have to time this negative response precisely so as not to turn the other party away completely).
- Don't be afraid to take concessions back, if you haven't signed the contract yet. Remember the pros of concession in pattern seven. (You'll need to be careful about using

this, however; taking back concessions could give the other party the impression that you're not dependable; you must choose the right situation to use it in—it might be OK to do so when the other party reneges on a promise, for instance).

- Keep a record of your concessions, and those of the other party, to see if there's a pattern. By studying them, you can respond to the other party's future moves more appropriately.
- Constantly keep the other party's expectations low by not giving in too often, too soon or too much.

2.4.3 Tactics of Making Concessions

Following are some suggestions for how to make concessions successfully. We consider success in concessions to be a personally satisfying outcome that also leaves the other party reasonably satisfied.

Here are the tactics:

- **Do your homework.** Know what you want. Be sure you have clear goals and objectives. You need to know what you want to fight for and what you are willing to give up. You need to be strongly committed to your objectives, or you may be forced into a position of giving away everything, or at least those things that you wanted most.
- **Prioritize your goals.** If you are going to compromise, you need to know what you must have, as opposed to what would be nice to have. The nice-to-haves may be given up for obtaining the must-haves. Remember that you need to be prepared to make significant concessions in order to compromise. Don't begin if you aren't flexible.
- **Know your walk-away and alternatives.** This can give you power in the negotiations, because at some point. You may be better off pursuing your alternative than settling for a suboptimal agreement. Know your walk-away point, so that if you need to, you can abandon the negotiation. This too can give you power.
- **Know which person will make the decision.** If the person you are negotiating with does not have the authority to make an agreement, you may be spending a lot of time waiting while he or she consults with the one who does. It may be better and more efficient for you to present the benefits of your proposal to the decision maker.
- **Show that you want to negotiate.** Say and do what is necessary to overcome the other party's reticence or distrust. Look at the other party's problems, and try to make sure that your proposal effectively resolves some of their key issues. This will give you an image of empathy and fairness, which is necessary for effective compromises.
- **Try not to be first side to make a major concession.** Since making concessions may be interpreted as a sign of weakness, the other party may take advantage of this and become aggressive, pushing you further than you wish to go. This will escalate the proceedings so that the more you give in, the more the other party will ask for. You will find yourself moved into an accommodating strategy, not a compromising one.

- **Do not wait until the deadline to offer a compromise.** Compromises should be offered from a position of strength, not as a last-ditch gesture, which would suggest to the other party that you are in a weaker position. If the deadline is close and you want to offer a compromise, offer it early enough that the other side can truly consider it. If you wait too long, the other party's deadline may have passed, and either he or she will be very upset or may have passed and either he or she will be very upset or may have lost all possibility of advantage and now may simply want to sabotage the negotiation process.

- **Start with small compromises.** A gradual or staged approach can help you to move toward more compromise. If you work in small steps, each party can move toward a reasonable solution. Moving too fast may escalate the other party's demands.

- **Use your concessions to your advantage.** When you make a concession, be sure that the other party gets the message that you are interested in a positive outcome and want to deal with him or her. Ask for a reciprocal concession in return.

- **Don't make unreciprocated concessions.** If you've made a concession and the other panty isn't responding, it can be tempting to make an additional concession. But this just conditions him or her to wait you out. You never want to give the impression that you're negotiating with yourself. Make him or her reciprocate before you move again.

- **Use your offers to communicate where you stand.** As you approach the end of your offers, they should be smaller and fewer to signal the other party that you are near the end. If the other party is alert, he or she will understand that you cannot be pushed to make further offers. The same is true for your side: watch the other party's offers, and be alert for signs of distress. When he or she has reached their limit, you should not push for more concessions. You risk breaking off negotiations entirely.

- **Do not push too hard.** Try to avoid the classic assumption of negotiation that you have to win everything you can. Pushing may result in negotiations coming to an abrupt halt, since it sends the message that you are competing instead of collaborating. Imagine you are interviewing a young manager who seems perfect for the job of leading a project team, a position that normally pays $85,000 per year. If the candidate says she's interested in the position and would be happy to do it for $150,000 per year, you may be put off by her pushy first offer and have second thoughts about continuing to negotiate with her. If another candidate asks for $90,000, you may think he's reasonable and easy to deal with and compromise on a salary of $87,000. Perhaps that was the target of the first candidate too, bur her pushy first offer destroyed her chances of landing the job.

- **Remember that the split does not have to be even.** In compromising, it may not be possible, or even desirable, to split it down the middle, although that is the most frequent way it is done. A compromise is often based on where the two parties currently stand, but that does not mean that they made equal concessions to get to that point. If one party has moved $2,000 from the starting point and the other party has moved $5,000 and they are still $4,000 apart. A split down the middle is a compromise, but it yields a deal that means one party had to concede only $4,000 while the other conceded $7,000. It's a good idea to remind the other party about how you got to where you are if you find yourself in danger of getting the short end of the stick in a situation like this. (If it's the other party's problem, then you have to decide whether you want to be strictly fair and ethical, or if you want to suggest that split down the middle and see if you can get away with a compromise that goes slightly in your side's favor. Think your ethics and values through in advance so you are clear on the extent to which you want to keep this compromise strictly symmetrical.)

- **Seek win-win compromises**. Ask the other party about his or her underlying interests and concerns. It may be that while your solution can't meet all his or her needs or interests, what you can do together is an improvement over the existing situation. The compromise looks distinctly better than no agreement.

- **Try not to close too quickly.** Although a scarcity of time is one of the primary compromise motivators of compromise strategy, it does not mean you have to do it with lightning speed. You may be eager to complete the transaction, but if a deal occurs too quickly, people frequently wonder whether they could have done better. If you are selling, make at least one counteroffer so the buyer will be confident of having obtained the best price. If you are buying, offer low at first and then move up. People like to feel that they have earned what they've won. Resist going for the 1-2-3 deal (offer, counteroffer, and then split it down the middle). It takes at least a few more rounds to be sure you've forged a decent compromise.

- **Promote the long-term benefits**. Point out that there can be an ongoing relationship between the parties (if this is true). One benefit of a successful compromise is that at best, the future is not put in jeopardy, and the possibility of future business together remains viable. In fact, a compromise now might lay the ground work for future collaboration. Looking at it from another angle, a negotiation that does not go well presents the potential of lost future business.

- **Stay focused on the issues.** The other side may use dirty tactics in trying to push for more concessions. Try to ignore these if possible, and stay with your established bottom line. In other words, be firm, particularly if the other party switches to a competitive style.

- **Be polite.** Avoid the hardball tactics of competition. Compromises should be civilized deals, marked by respect and good manners. As Miss Manners so ably puts it, "Everybody wants other people to be polite to them, but they want the freedom of not having to be polite to others."

3　The Closing Phase

In the final closing phase there are two key actions：

- Put a potential deal together
- Make an agreement

The key communication style for this phase is action, which has the outcome of a deal—the desired result of a negotiation.

⇨ 3.1　Putting a Potential Deal Together

At its most simple, this step is a summary of the preceding step in exploring which pulls together the accepted exchanges that form the bargain："So, if I can summarize the discussion. You have agreed to deliver the goods to our locations within 14 days from order, and in return we will pay you the price of £ ×× per tonne, 50 per cent with the order and 50 per cent on delivery. Is that your understanding?"

Of course, not all discussions will be that clear cut, but if the bargaining phase has been well managed, there will be some possibilities that would form the basis of a deal. If the options are not clear, then it is a signal that you may need to explore some more or be prepared to return to exploring if your potential deal proposal does not work："I think we might have the basis of a deal. I can see that if I did X and also added in Y, and you were able to reduce your price by £ Z, then that is something I could agree to. Do you see another potential deal?"

This approach offers some final trading to close the gap and broker the deal. If you take this trading route, the requests should be small on both sides and, ideally, not on areas of principle that have not already been discussed. An expectation of a large final trade is more likely to extend the negotiation than close it, and suggests that the bargaining phase was not completed effectively.

Another scenario in closing is that you or the other party, or both, need to consider the potential deal in more detail, get a final sign-off of the conditions, or seek authority to agree from another person in the organization. Here, you should get a clear understanding of the summary deal, the next step each party is making and a date for reconvening the discussion："So, the deal on the table is that you deliver the goods within 4 days from order, and in exchange we pay £ ×× per tonne, 50 per cent with the order and 50 per cent on delivery. We will adjourn the discussion so that we can confirm the details of the deal with our logistics and finance groups, and reconvene at 2pm on Wednesday to sign the agreement."

（Always fix a date and time and fix the conditions regarding who is doing what—don't leave it to chance or make an assumption that the other side sees things the same way.）

This is the step in the whole negotiating process that you have been leading up to, so, although you don't want to rush to get here and risk pushing for a deal too early, you equally don't want to put off closing the deal out. If the potential deal that you foresee doesn't fit, then it is quite likely that the other party is thinking about closure as well and has something in mind. It is important to ask for the deal. If it doesn't work, you can always retrace your steps into exploring. It is only a potential deal; all is not lost if it isn't immediately accepted. You just need to ask, "What else needs to be there for the deal to work for you?" This then gives you the opportunity to push for what the salespeople call a "presumptive close": "If I agree to this condition, then we have a deal?"

Any sign of reluctance to close by either party might suggest that there are some lingering concerns or unexpressed fears about the negotiation. If one party is feeling uncomfortable at the end of a negotiation, this must be dealt with for the agreement to be successfully implemented. If it is not dealt with satisfactorily, then there is—at worst—a possibility that you won't get an agreement, and at best, there will be difficulties in implementing the deal. So, even though you are in action style, which is not responsive in its nature, you need to stay alert to the feelings and reactions of the other party.

⇨ 3.2 Making an Agreement

This is the final action step, and should reflect the understanding of the form of contract that was understood when discussing ground rules in the opening phase. It sends the wrong message of win-win cooperation if you suddenly spring a condition of agreement on the other party at the last minute. Your own, and the other party's, organizations might have some standard requirements for agreement and terms and conditions of contract. These are also potential areas for negotiation in their own right in more complex deals.

The simple requirement here is that there is an understanding and clarity on both sides about the agreement that has been reached. Even if you only need a verbal agreement it is always good practice to get it in writing, just so that there is a clear understanding on what has been agreed. Time spent just summarizing the details will lead to much saved time in the future when managing implementation glitches.

⇨ 3.3 Common Problems in the Closing Phase

Unforeseen difficulties are quite common at the end of negotiations, but particular issues arise in intercultural negotiations. We list the most frequent dilemmas and offer possible strategies for responding to them:
- "We don't understand the agreement (or what we are agreeing to)." This dilemma takes place when the parties do not speak the same language, have different levels of language skills and sophistication when working in a foreign tongue, or have different conceptions of what the proposed agreement means or the terms being used to describe it. Some parties may also use purported misunderstanding as a tactic for encouraging a counterpart to reveal

more, a means to force a counterpart to be more specific, or to delay agreement. Strategies for addressing this problem include continuing to talk until mutually understood terms can be agreed to, asking what part of an agreement is unclear and then addressing this specific problem, or obtaining better language interpretation so that a party can work in their native tongue.

- "We do not understand the wording/interpretation/translation." Working across languages is not always easy. Even among people who share the same language and culture, differences in accents, wording, idioms, or colloquial expressions may cause barriers to understanding. When working across cultures where participants speak different languages, problems are magnified, because people may not be working in their native tongue or are using words for which there is no translation or commonly understood meaning (Moore, 2004). For example, "Arabic has no word for 'compromise' in the sense of reaching agreement through struggle and disagreement. But a much happier concept, taarradhin (tah-rah-deen), exists in Arabic. It implies a happy solution for everyone, an 'I win, you win.' It's a way of resolving a problem without anyone losing face" (Moore, 2004). In China, people get things done through guanxi. This concept entails building good relationships by giving gifts, sharing meals, granting favors, and developing a norm of reciprocity. In Japanese, the term yoko meshi is a combination of the words for "boiled rice" and "horizontal" and literally translates as "eating boiled rice horizontally." "This is the how the Japanese define the peculiar stress induced by speaking a foreign language: yoke is a humorous reference to the fact that Japanese is normally written vertically, whereas most foreign languages are written horizontally" (Moore, 2004). In Swahili, the language of much of East Africa, the word bado is used to say no, but exclusively when "it is theoretically possible that the action may occur in the future" (Moore, 2004). For example, a person who is asked whether it is possible to execute specific terms of agreement may answer bado, meaning "not at this time, but it might be possible in the future." Similarly, the Swahili term sa sa hapi translates literally as "right away", but immediate action for the speaker may not mean the same thing to the listener.

The use of language and particular wording is an important issue in intercultural negotiations. There are negotiations in which the parties engaged multiple interpreters and translators to good effect; often each interpreter has a different native tongue but is a professional translator in another language. For instance, in negotiations between Russian and American officials, each side brought an interpreter—the American a native English speaker who was expert in Russian and the Russian a native speaker of that language who was a professional translator of English. In these situations, the translators can discuss meanings, vocabulary, and word use in order to assist the negotiators. Before sessions, negotiators can also provide their interpreters with a list of terms they will be using in upcoming talks, and ask the interpreters to agree on the terms that will be used by all concerned to convey the same information and meaning.

Confusions over terms and their meanings, written translations, and interpretations of working documents or, especially, final agreements can be disastrous. A classic example is the different wordings in the English and Maori texts of the 1840 Treaty of Waitangi in New Zealand. The treaty signed between British colonists and a number of indigenous Maori clans, defined the legal relationships between settlers and local people. Unfortunately, there were significant differences in the English and Maori translations and understandings. The British colonists generally proceeded to expropriate Maori land, while the Maori understood the treaty as protecting their rights. The variations in wording and interpretations allowed British colonists to gain full control of the islands and the land. It was not until the mid-1970s that the different interpretations of the treaty and resultant impacts on the Maori began to be addressed through the establishment of the Waitangi Tribunal (Yenson, Hague and McCreanor, 1989; Treaty of Waitangi, 1840).

To overcome such translation and interpretation problems, all parties should use translators who are native speakers of their own languages and expert in that of the counterparts to draft and review all documents for consistency of meaning. Ideally, all drafts and final documents should be read, edited, corrected, and approved by multiple translators and readers to ensure accuracy and similar intent.

- "We need more time." or "We will have word from our superiors within the next week/ month/year." This request is common among negotiators from cultures that do not make decisions rapidly or where time and speed are not as critical. It is also typical of collectivist cultures, where approval or ratification of an agreement must be obtained from multiple individuals, groups, or levels in a bureaucracy before a decision is final. Negotiators working with counterparts from Native American tribes in the United States, First Nations in Canada, the bureaucracies in the People's Republic of China, India, Japan, and many Latin American countries have often reported this kind of request.

Note that the plea for more time can also be a tactic to avoid ratifying an agreement that is less than satisfactory or is displeasing to a negotiator's superiors, or it might be used to obtain time to see if a better deal can be obtained from a competitor. Some negotiators seek delays while internal organizational dynamics change or until external development allow a more favorable outcome. Delays have also been used as a way for a party to say, "No, no deal", without ever having to reject a proposal directly, clearly a preference of an indirect-dealing negotiator.

Negotiators facing a request for more time first have to figure out if the delay is valid and needed, a stalling tactic, or an indirect rejection of the settlement. Sometimes this can be determined through off-the-record informal talks with counterparts at various levels in an organization, discussions with third parties or more indirect sleuthing. If the added time is truly required to obtain approval for a final agreement, the negotiator must decide how long he or she is willing to wait for a response. If a settlement is time limited, competitive advantage is lost, or there are other options, a negotiator may not want to wait. However, if agreement seems likely with just a little more time, it may be desirable to agree to more time. Extensions can even be made with the negotiator's stipulation that if more time is allowed, the expectation is for a favorable decision.

- "What you did/said earlier offended us. We expect an apology/a new offer/a concession from you to make it right," This request may be valid or a ploy for gaining additional concessions. Before responding, the negotiator must consider the issue from the point of view of the counterpart (that is, not based on what would be difficult, uncomfortable, or offensive in your own culture). If the claim is valid (something said or done really was uncomfortable or offensive to the other party), he or she will need to decide what can be done to address the problem in a manner that is culturally, politically, and ethically appropriate for all parties. A third party might be able to help to sort this out.

If the claim of offense seems spurious or designed merely to gain advantage, the negotiator may want to adhere to his or her original view or position and avoid making any apology, offer, or concession. However, this strategy needs to be executed carefully, for even if the claim is a bluff, unless it is in the interest of the counterpart to settle, he or she may use its rejection as an excuse to terminate negotiations. Note that apologies can be quite effective and do not necessarily require any additional concession on a matter of substance.

- "By the way, we have one more issue. We need one additional thing from you in order for us to close the deal." This is one variation on the doorknob strategy: parties employ it when the end is in sight and the parties are literally about to walk out the door together, having reached an agreement. (This is slightly different from the next tactic.) Psychologically, the parties have come to substantial agreement, perhaps after a difficult series at exchanges, In this circumstance, one party uses the positive prospect of a deal to bring up one more issue in the belief that the lure of the almost completed deal will induce their counterpart to make additional concessions.

This kind of move can be interpreted in several ways: the party knew about this issue all along, and is just bringing it up now as a way of forcing the other party's hand on a relatively minor matter; the counterpart did not know about the issue, or it was raised by a superior in the process of obtaining approvals; or this was, in fact, one of the most important concerns in the negotiations, but the counterpart was unable to raise it earlier for whatever reasons—and at this point, you might start "real" negotiations on a core issue. Faced with one of these possibilities, the negotiator must decide if this is an important or minor issue for both parties. He or she must also determine if the other party is bringing this up now as a tactic for forcing a concession or for scuttling the negotiations, or if they have been bargaining in good faith, and this issue has really just emerged.

- "Well, we are not getting anywhere. I am leaving." This is the more classical doorknob strategy or doorknob close in which a party says, "We will walk out the door if you do not give us what we want." Parties exercise this threat of a total breakdown in negotiations unless they get their way, often when talks are not going well or they are not getting their way. (Note the contrast with the previous tactic, which specifically uses the fact that things are going well as a lever.) This is a common tactic among North American negotiators engaged in negotiating labor contracts, and in some negotiation sectors internationally.

The response should be governed by the perceived legitimacy of the move, the risk its use poses to the breakdown of negotiations, and the negotiator's willingness or capability to respond. If it appears to be a bluff, the negotiator may want refuse to give in. However, he or she must be willing to risk the entire settlement if the threat is genuine. If the threat appears to be real, he or she must decide how far to go to meet the concrete demands to salvage a deal.

- "Isn't there just a little bit more?" This is a common bargaining tactic in many intercultural negotiations for all levels of interactions between individuals, groups, businesses, or national governments. It is particularly common when the requester is from a lower-power or lower-status group than the counterpart. The tactic is often coupled with requests for fairness, righting of past wrongs, or claims that what the person is asking for is very little in comparison to the resources of the more powerful counterpart. Interestingly, the tactic works, especially if the party to whom the request is being made can be made to feel guilty or obligated in some way to the person making the request. We saw this tactic in practice in India. Whether it was the rickshaw driver or a businessperson, everyone seemed ready to ask for "just a little bit more." It has also been a common practice in negotiations with diplomats from the Peoples' Republic of China.

- "A sweetener for me/my boss/the organization would help get this approved in a timely manner." In some cultures, this would be called a bribe, but in others, it is common practice to promote agreements. In considering such requests, negotiators need to be clear that they are not violating ethical standards or laws. For example, when the American company negotiated with government officials to start an infrastructure initiative in a Middle Eastern country, one of the Americans was asked by a counterpart to give a small research contract to another government official who was not directly involved with the project. The counterpart suggested that the proposed recipient official could perhaps be "given a little money to do a token research project that might in some way be of assistance to the project"—which, by the way, would secure his support for the initiative. After assessing the request, finding that the proposed official did not have any of the research skills that would justify a research grant and that the request was really for an illegal bribe, the Americans rejected the request.

- "Don't you trust us?" This statement often relates to issues regarding compliance to an agreement and reflects resistance to clear compliance mechanisms. The question can be used to secure a concession based on real or claimed emotional bonds, without any tangible assurance of goodwill or mechanisms to ensure compliance by the counterpart. It can be used in both good faith and in bad and as a way to strengthen emotional commitments or gain advantage over a counterpart. Of course, even posing the question exposes a lack of trust in the relationship: if there is true trust, the question need not be asked; if there is a lack of trust, asking the question invites a false assurance or an acknowledgment that trust is missing.

Negotiators from relationship-oriented cultures are likely to rely on personal relationships to ensure commitments to agreement. Negotiators from contractually oriented cultures will probably want more tangible assurances. The dilemma is how to ask for clear procedures or mechanisms without damaging relationships. As was said in the 1990s in international negotiations between the United States and the Soviet Union over nuclear arms control, "Trust but verify."

- "I want my lawyer (or legal team) to review our agreement." While seeking legal assistance may be normal and acceptable in many cultures, it is not in others. The desire to involve lawyers may be perceived by negotiators from some cultures as an indication of mistrust, unnecessary adversarial behavior, or nit-picking.

- "This would be very difficult." or "No, it is not possible!" The first is common in indirect-dealing cultures where it is difficult to say no directly. The second is common in Central and Eastern Europe where, at least in the past, saying yes was riskier than saying no, because someone who said no could not be held responsible by superiors for a problematic decision.

When encountering a no in intercultural negotiations, negotiators must first determine what no means in the counterpart's culture. If a counterpart from Indonesia or Japan says that something is "very difficult," the negotiator will have to decide how hard to push the issue, and if the decision is to pursue it further, find a way to explore it indirectly. However, if the counterpart saying no is from a direct-dealing culture, the negotiator can ask why, probe the logic and rationale, and explore what it would take to change the no to yes (or from niet to da) (Richmond, 1992).

Vocabulary

superb/suːˈpɜːb/*adj.*

—of excellent quality; very great

e.g. The team's superb athleticism compensated for their lack of international experience.

　　She gave a superb performance as Lady Macbeth.

blistering/ˈblɪstərɪŋ/*adj.*

—(especially of sunlight, heat, etc.) very severe or intense

e.g We went out in the blistering heat.

trickle/ˈtrɪkl/*v.*

—to arrive or move somewhere slowly or gradually

trickle back

e.g. Foreign capital has been trickling back, as investors seek higher returns than they can find at home.

trickle in

e.g. Customers trickled in throughout the afternoon.

trickle out

e.g. Details have begun to trickle out since the deal was struck at Monday night.

rum /rʌm/ adj.

—unusual and strange

e.g. She's a rum girl.

rattled /rætld/ adj.

—worried or nervous

e.g. Walter got rattled when they didn't call.

Exercises

1 Multiple Choice

1) What is a climate or atmosphere we want to create at the beginning of a negotiation?

    A. Warm and polite.   B. Direct and frank.

    C. Tense and contradictory.   D. Positive and friendly.

2) Which is the critical period of a negation?

    A. Pre-negotiation.   B. Concession.

    C. Bargaining.   D. Establishing relationship.

3) Which is **TRUE** of a sedate and reserve negotiation atmosphere?

    A. It helps to create trust between the two sides.

    B. Japanese rather than Americans tend to create this kind of atmosphere.

    C. It will always cast a shadow on the negotiation.

    D. It's a very common atmosphere in an international negotiation.

4) What is **TRUE** of the first contact of the two parties in a negotiation?

    A. Identify norms and traditions.

    B. Communicating goals and objectives.

    C. Being patient with the cultural norms of TOS.

    D. Trying to know the strategies of TOS.

5) Which is **NOT** one of the ways to propose an agenda?

    A. Ad hoc discussions.   B. Finding an alternative.

    C. Group conversation.   D. Reaching a simple agenda.

6) Which of the following is **NOT** a form of an agreement both parties want to achieve in a negotiation?

A. Transparent.

B. Including visions of both parties.

C. Reciprocated.

D. Objective.

7) Which of the following is **NOT** true in the first meeting of an international negotiation?

A. Having non-task-oriented talk to build relationships.

B. Preparing welcoming comments or speeches.

C. Introducing substantive issues that will be discussed later.

D. Expressing the willingness to engage in the coming discussions.

8) What is **NOT** true about welcoming comments?

A. Including the comment of existing relationship.

B. Emphasizing the value of the meeting.

C. Going through the details of the negotiation.

D. Introducing the procedures of the coming talk.

9) What is **TRUE** of regarding the welcoming speech?

A. Determine whether you will adhere to your counterpart's cultural norms.

B. Identify the cultural norms of your counterpart.

C. Spend time to elaborate your appreciation of the coming of TOS.

D. Make the welcoming statement as positive as is realistically possible.

10) What is **NOT** true of the following statements?

A. In low-context cultures, only senior people who will be directly engaged in negotiations and will be speakers are introduced.

B. Try to adhere to the cultural norms of your own party and your counterpart when making a welcoming speech.

C. In the first meeting of a negotiation, one party had better avoid any exaggerated body movement to leave a reliable impression on TOS.

D. It is natural to assume that your counterpart's price is inflated.

2 Interpretation of Terms

1) The opening phase of a negotiation

2) The bargaining phase of a negotiation

3) The closing phase of a negotiation

4) Agenda

5) Opening statement

6) Building the climate

7) Offer

3 Case Analysis

Price Negotiations for the Technology Import of Five Color/Quinary-Color & Chromato-graphy Printing Machine Line Equipments

In mid November, 1992, Factory Director Zhou who worked in a printing factory in Shenyang came to Germany with his four colleagues to have an 11-day technical inspection and the price negotiation.

The supplier was a manufacturing enterprise of world class which was located in Heidelberg. Its technology had been widely renowned around the globe. Therefore, the Chinese company predicted that this would be a hard negotiation. Then the Chinese company began to prepare its strategy of psychological warfare.

The German company sent a vice technical director to accompany the Chinese guests. Since he was quite confident in their technical equipments and despised that of those foreign counterparts, the Chinese personnel never approved of nor appreciated the production methods, products or manufacturing skills of the German company during the inspection of several such enterprises in Germany, Spain and Belgium. They, on the contrary, raised many questions, making the director busy in introducing and explaining all the time. Thus, the Chinese company could have a better understanding of the function, characters, qualities as well as many other highly technical issues about the maintenance, including many defects that hadn't be successfully handled of this company's products.

On the other hand, the Chinese personnel intentionally inquired the technical level and market price of the similar products and equipments in other countries. Thus, the director might think that the Chinese company was also interested in the similar line equipments and technique of other countries who would further report to his company. Then the German company would not be quite confident in the business. In the meantime, the Chinese personnel had conducted a thorough inspection of its consumers in advance with the focus on knowing the defects as well as the outfit and consuming conditions of the spare parts. The Chinese company considerably increased its likelihood of success. For instance, when visiting one print factory called Mei Feier in Frankfurt, they noticed that the producing assembly line of the Five-Color & Chromatography Printing Machine was working. Via the managing staff's introduction, they knew that quality of the presswork was negatively affected because of instability of the cut-off knife plus desynchrony of the print wheels. The who production consequently needed to be readjusted which severely affect the efficiency. It was obvious that the world-class company was in effect not perfect.

The technical negotiation about equipments and technique which was held in the Heidelberg headquarter of the German company was completed within one day after the inspection. The head negotiator, Mr. Brawen, together with his four coworkers, firstly laid emphasis upon their 2.18 million dollars offer and fully stressed that their equipments were worldly renowned.

The Chinese party had predicted that. Hence they suggested a 1.7million offer based on information they obtained in advance which was far lower for the German to accept. The reason for this was that the Chinese company wanted to avoid an unacceptable offer by the German party. But such a low offer would inevitably arouse the German's rejection. As expected, Mr. Kedelis, the sales manager, immediately stood up, and almost shouted, "This is unbelievable!" He insisted his offer and did not want to make a concession. Then the Chinese refuted his remarks with the help of the inspection in Frankfurt, saying, "Your company's technique is not perfect and there still exist some problems", and asked the vice technical director to testify their refutation who did not deny, demonstrating that the Germans were realistic, practical and had high sense of responsibility. Upon hearing this, Mr. Kedelis slowly sat down and finally ceased to insist his offer.

The German company suggested another 2.1 million dollars offer after a while, but was rejected by China's 1.75 million. The two parties did not reach any agreement after a long dispute. But the China had succeeded in forcing the Germans to make a concession via their plan. So the Chinese personnel advised to have a rest and chose to negotiate later, hoping to further increase the likelihood of success. The German agreed.

Since negotiation about equipments and technique had reached an agreement and the lowest offer had been put forward, the Chinese party no longer assumed the passive position and even began to react more actively. Therefore, they determined to impose more pressure upon the other party by stopping asking for further negotiations. The Germans might assume that the Chinese had lost interest and planned to cooperate with other companies. So the Germans would initially ask for further negotiation with Chinese in order to consolidate their position. The Chinese, on the other hand, didn't ask for negotiation in the two days but simply planned themselves.

On the afternoon of the fourth day, the German could not wait any longer, so they paid the Chinese a visit and to continue the negotiation. The Chinese sincerely accented. In the negotiating room, Mr. Brawen finally stated, "we can cooperate and make certain efforts for the sake of the other party." Then he politely asked the Chinese personnel to suggest an offer. The Chinese party then put forward a fresh 1.85 million-dollar offer in accordance with their plan. After a while of discussion, no agreement was arrived at all. However, Mr. Kedelis then suggested a 2 million-dollar offer and asked the Chinese to consider. The Chinese personnel were surprised at this concession which fully displayed the characters of European and American enterprises. Such a concession was totally impossible in negotiations with Korean or Japanese enterprises. In the meantime, they noticed that the negotiation was coming to an end. There was only one last chance to bargain; otherwise the negotiation would come to a deadlock. Hence, after an immediate discussion, they decided to put forward the last offer and take the initiative. So the Chinese personnel clear implied: they cannot accept the 2 million-dollar offer and stressed that they had sincere intention of cooperation. The acceptable would be no more than 1.9 million-dollar, in addition, more easily-damaged spare parts should be provided, otherwise the negotiation was over.

Their resolution surely shocked the Germans who did not expect the Chinese company's rejection. The atmosphere in the room became a little bit tense. Then, Mr. Brawen, chief representative for the German company who had kept silent for a long while, straightened up (He was indeed an old hand in negotiation), laughed amiably, replied in a composed yet resolute fashion: "I have said that we can cooperate with each other, but in my opinion, 1.93 million is reasonable offer which is acceptable to us all. No more bargain and dispute, my distinguished guests, Ok?" Everyone knew quite well that his final offer was indisputable and this was indeed what the Chinese wanted, i.e. an ideal offer within 1.95 million dollars. The Chinese satisfactorily agreed.

Mr. Brawen was also very excited and he shook hands with every Chinese personnel to exchange congratulations to each other. He dexterously intermediated between their 2 million-dollar offer and the 1.85 million-dollar offer of the Chinese company in the final round. On the other hand, the Chinese personnel were no less satisfied than them, for they had successfully reduced 250,000 dollars from the initial offer 2.18 million dollars through their concerted efforts. It was reported that price of similar equipments and technique of this company had always floated within 10,000 dollars. Therefore the Chinese were pretty contented with this negotiating result. It was a win-win cooperation for the two companies.

Then the two companies had a friendly negotiation about supply of the spare parts and reached an agreement in terms of transportation, insurance as well as issues about the installing. A cooperation contract was eventually produced.

(*Excerpts from* Teaching Cases for Business Negotiation *by Ding Jianzhong*)

Questions for Case-analysis：

1. What are the reasons of Chinese company's success in the negotiation?

2. Whether the German company should ask for a further negotiation and the relevant negotiating agenda?

3. How long can the Chinese company wait provided the German company does not ask for the further negotiation first? Then what can the Chinese do?

4. The final offer of the German company was 1.93 million dollars, and will 1.95 million be acceptable as well?

Reference

1. Adair, W., Weingart, L., and Brett, J. "The Timing and Function of Offers in the U.S. and Japanese Negotiations." Journal of Applied Psychology, 2007, 92, 1056-1068.

2. Alon, I., and Brett, J. "Perceptions of Time and Their Impact on Negotiations in the Arab-Speaking Islamic World." Negotiation Journal, 2007, 23(1), 55-74.

3. Bai, Yuan. International Business Negotiation—Theory, Cases and Practices. Beijing: Ren Min University Press, 2014.

4. Blackman, C. Negotiating China: Case Studies and Strategies. Sydney, Australia: Allen & Unwin, 1998.

5. Blaker, M. Japanese International Negotiation Style. New York: Columbia University Press, 1977a.

6. Blaker, M. "Probe, Push and Panic: The Japanese Tactical Style in International Negotiations." In R. Scalpino (ed.), The Foreign Policy of modern Japan. Berkeley: University of California Press, 1977b.

7. Cogan, C. French Negotiation Behavior: Dealing with La Grande Nation. Washington, D.C.: U. S. Institute of Peace Press, 2003.

8. Ding, Jianzhong. Teaching Cases for Business Negotiation, Beijing: Press of Renmin University of China, 2005. Page 173-176.

9. Dou, Ran International Business Negotiation. Shanghai: Fudan University Press, 2011.

10. Etzioni, A. "The Gradualist Way to Peace." Presentation at the Fortieth Annual Meeting, American Orthopsychiatric Association, Washington, D.C., 1963.

11. Fisher. R., and Ury, W. Getting to Yes. New York: Penguin, 1981.

12. Gladwell, M. Blink: The Power of Thinking about Thinking. New York: Little Brown, 2005.

13. Graham, J. L. "The influence of culture on the process of business negotiations: An exploratory study." Journal of International Business Studies, 16(1), 1985, 81-96.

14. Gulliver, P. H. Disputes and Negotiations: A Cross-Cultural Perspective. New York: Academic Press, 1979.

15. Hodgson. J., Sano, Y., and Graham, J. Doing Business with the New Japan. (3rd Ed.)

Lanham, Md.: Rowan & Littlefield, 2000.

16. Huang, Wei, Qian, Li. International Business Negotiation, Metallurgical Industry Press, 2012.

17. Kapuscisnski, R. The Shadow of the Sun. New York: Vintage, 2002.

18. Lewicki, Roy J., Hiam, Alexander. Mastering Business Negotiation. Jossey-Bass, A Wiley Imprint, 2006.

19. Lincoln, W. F. "Presenting Initial Positions." Unpublished manuscript, National Center for Collaborative Planning and Community Services, Watertown, Mass., 1981.

20. Marano, Hara Estroff. "Polite Company: Interview with Miss Manners (Judith Martin)," Psychology Today, Mar.-Apr., 1998, p. 27.

21. Menger, R. "Japanese and American negotiators: Overcoming cultural barriers to understanding." Academy of Management Executive, 12(4), 1999, 100-101.

22. Moore, C. 1. In Other Words: A Language Lover's Guide to the Most Intriguing Words around the World. New York: Levinger Press, 2004.

23. Moore. C. The Mediation Process: Practical Strategies for Resolving Conflict. (3rd Ed.) San Francisco: Jossey-Bass, 2003.

24. Richmond, Y. From Nyet to Da: Understanding the Russians. Yarmouth, Me.: Intercultural Press, 1992.

25. Rinehart, L. M., & Page, T J.. Jr. (1992). "The development and test of a model of transaction negotiation." Journal of Marketing, 56, 18-32.

26. Sampson, A. Mandela: The Authorized Biography. New York: HarperCollins, 1999.

27. Sanger, J. "Tales of the Bazaar: Interest-Based Negotiation across Cultures." Negotiation Journal, 2002, 18(3), 233-250.

28. Schecter, J. Russian Negotiating Behavior: Continuity and Transition. Washington, D.C.: U.S. Institute for Peace Press, 1998.

29. Shapiro, D. L., & Rognes, J. "Can a dominating orientation enhance the integrativeness of negotiated agreements?". Negotiation Journal, 1996, 81-90.

30. Smith, R. Negotiating with the Soviets. Bloomington: Indiana University Press, 1989.

31. Smyser, W. R. How Germans Negotiate: Logical Goals, Practical Solutions. Washington, D.C.: U.S. Institute of Peace Press, 2003.

32. Solomon, R. Chinese Negotiating Behavior: Pursuing Interests through Old Friends. Washington, D.C.: U.S. Institute of Peace, 1999.

33. Tauroa, H., and Tauroa, P. Te Marae: A Guide to Customs and Protocol. Auckland: Heinemann Reed, 1986.

34. Weiss, J. "Trajectories toward Peace: Mediator Sequencing Strategies in Intractable Communal Conflicts". Negotiation Journal, 2003, 19(2), 109-115.

35. Yenson, H., Hague, K., McCreanor, T., with Kelsey, J., Nairn, M., and Williama, D. (Eds.). Honoring the Treaty: An Introduction for Pakeha to the Treaty of Waitangi.

Auckland, N.Z.: Penguin, 1989.

36. Young, O. "Intermediaries: Additional Thoughts on Third Parties." Journal of Conflict Resolution, 1972, 16(1), 51-65.

37. Zartman, I. W., and Berman, M. The Practical Negotiator. New Haven, Conn.: Yale University Press, 1982.

38. Zhao, J. J. The Chinese approach to international business negotiation. Journal of Business Communication, 37(3), 2000, 209-237.

Chapter IV Strategies and Tactics in International Business Negotiation

Learning Objectives

After studying this chapter, you will be able to

- Describe standard negotiation strategies.

- Use strategies countering negative negotiation tactics.

- Apply the methods to develop your negotiation strategies.

The Panama Canal Negotiations

The completion of the Panama Canal is one of the world's great engineering feats. The negotiations to complete and build this vital connector between two oceans spans decades. The cost in human lives, suffering, and capital staggers the imagination. It all began in 1847 when the United States entered in a treaty with New Grannada (later to be know as Colombia), and which allowed the U.S. a transit passage over the Isthmus of Panama. The treaty guaranteed Panama's neutrality and recognized that Colombia would have sovereignty over the region.

Nothing really occurred with this development and ultimately, a French company called the Compagnie Nouvelle de Panama acquired the contract to build the canal in 1881. By 1889, the Compagnie had gone bankrupt and had lost roughly around $ 287 million U. S. along with approximately 20,000 lives in the process. It is also in 1889 that the U.S. has become convinced that the canal passage was absolutely vital to their interests. They appointed Rear Admiral John Walker to head the Commission and to choose the most viable route.

Naturally, the U.S. was interested in the Panama route already started by the French. The French company, which had been heading for bankruptcy, and seeing the writing on the wall before their bankruptcy in 1889, had entered into negotiations with the U.S. The French company was eager to *extricate* themselves from the project. At the time, their holdings were extensive and included land, the Panama Railroad, 2,000 buildings, and an extensive amount of equipment. They felt their total holdings should be valued around 109 million dollars, but Rear Admiral Walker estimated them to be not greater than about 40 million dollars, a significant difference.

As negotiations progressed, the Americans began to hint that they were also interested in the possibility of building an alternative canal in Nicaragua. The French countered with the *poly* by claiming that both Great Britain and Russia were looking at picking up the financing to complete the canal's construction. It was subsequently leaked to the U. S. press, much to the French company's *pique*, that the Walker Commission concluded that the cost to buy out the French company was too excessive and recommended the Nicaraguan route.

A couple of days later after this news, the president of Compagnie Nouvelle resigned. The resulting *furor* caused the stockholders to demand that the company be sold to the U.S. at any price they could get. The Americans became aware that they could now pick up all the French holdings for 40 million dollars. However, the Walker Commission had not just been a ploy by the Americans because the Nicaraguan route was actually a serious proposal that had a lot of *bacing* in the U.S. Senate. President Roosevelt had to engage in some serious political maneuverings to get everybody on board of the Panama passage. The Walker Commission changed its recommendation to favor Panama as the Canal route.

But the story doesn't end there. Next, the U.S. signed a new treaty with Colombia's charge d'affairs which gave the U. S. a six mile area across the Isthmus and agreed its financial *remuneration* that was to be paid to Colombia. The Colombian charge d'affair had signed the treaty without communicating with his government. The treaty was rejected by Colombia. In the meantime, revolution against Colombia authority was afoot in Panama. Since they believed they had signed a legitimate treaty, Roosevelt sent warships to the area to negate the Colombians, and thus secured U.S. interests, and offered aid to the Panamanians in their quest to separate from Colombia. Panama succeeded in their revolt and became a republic. In 1914, the Panama Canal was opened.

(Adapted from The Chinese Negotiator *by Dr. Bob March)*

This case reveals how different negotiation strategies can be employed to negotiate and concludes a better international agreement. Negotiation strategies are established in order to achieve the negotiation objectives. They are acting guidelines and policies of the whole negotiation process and are subject to modification with the progress of the negotiation. Since different organizations work in different ways, and each has a characteristics style of negotiation, negotiators need training and experience before they can successfully handle the different styles of other parties. This chapter discusses several basic strategies that are used to achieve negotiation goals.

1   Standard Negotiation Strategies

Negotiators use a number of different approaches to achieve their goals. Knowing how to both use and cope with these strategies is essential for success at the bargaining table. Of course, proper preparation is the starting point, and achieving your negotiation objectives is the ultimate destination. However, the tools for getting there consist of the strategies employed at the bargaining table. And while the wrong strategy can hamper your progress, using the right tactics can speed things along to a successful outcome.

Here, we must make clear that strategy is the game plan you use to achieve your objectives, while tactics are the individual elements of your game plan.

Consequently, whether or not you personally employ a particular strategy, it's necessary to recognize each and everyone that may be used against you. Then, and only then, will you be able to avoid any obstacles that may be strewn in your path.

⇨ 1.1   Win-Win Strategy: Its Pluses and Minuses

Case 2

Shanghai Links operates a large International Golf and Country Club, located in San Jia Gang, Pudong District, Shanghai. Surrounded by its gulf course is a luxurious community of villas.

The only American school in Shanghai—Shanghai American School—is also located there. In order to ensure the students' safety, enclosing walls, financially backed by U. S. Department of Homeland Security, were going to be built around the campus. Therefore, the school signed an agreement with the Shanghai Links Golf and Country Club regarding the wall construction: the club agreed to provide the school with facilities for the construction of the walls—allowing vehicles carrying earth and stones and other building materials to come in and out of the course, on the condition that the building work does not affect the routine operation of the club and the normal way of life of the adjacent residents. To finish the construction before the new semester, the school representative in charge of the project asked the workers to work day and night. As such, lorries entered the golf course at night. When the club manager got to know it, he realized that it would seriously affect the night life of the residents in the nearby villas. Thus, the manager presented a note to the authorities of the Shanghai American School, reiterating that the agreement clearly indicated that the club should be informed before the lorries carrying earth and stones entered the golf course .In fact the school project manager did know it, so he made an immediate apology, and guaranteed that it would not happen again, but hoped that the club allowed them in to unload the lorries for that very night only. In order to avoid conflict, 'the club agreed after they had informed a resident in the villas, expressing their sincere apology. It was settled smoothly: the lorries were unloaded before midnight and the follow-up construction was never arranged to be done at night.

(Adapted from International Business Negotiation *by Dou Ran)*

This case is a typical win-win negotiation, in which the two sides not only kept their good cooperative relationship but also achieved their respective desired goals.

General negotiation strategy is usually classified as being a win-win joint problem-solving approach, or a strict adversarial proceeding. Win-win strategy asserts that the two parties are best served by working together to identify and solve the problems that hinder reaching agreement. On the other hand, the adversarial approach mandates that each party look out for its own self-interest, leaving the other party to represent its own cause.

However, as with a lot of other things in life, it's not quite so easy to put negotiating strategy into neat little boxes. It certainly sounds a lot nicer to be able to negotiate in an atmosphere where both parties lay their cards on the table and work amicably toward agreement. Nevertheless, there are some roadblocks to this sort of scenario. The first impediment is the necessity for both parties to be open and honest about what they want. Needless to say, if one party lays their cards on the table, and the other side doesn't show their hand, the straight-shooter is left without ammunition for the forthcoming battle.

Furthermore, in many negotiations, there are no sticky problems to be solved. The only real differences of opinion are in reaching a meeting of the minds on what constitutes a reasonable deal.

That, absent some unusual circumstance, is just a part of the negotiation process. Often, especially where price is involved, it's merely a matter of reaching agreement on a dollar figure that's acceptable to both parties.

In addition, there's no magic price that's the right one. One person may feel he paid top dollar by buying a business for $10,000,000. Yet, someone else may readily decide that paying $15,000,000 would be a bargain. And aside from personal judgments, there may be valid reasons for the difference. For example, perhaps the higher priced buyer is eliminating a competitor, which justifies the extra premium. Whatever the reason, the fact remains that rarely is there any objective criterion for establishing the right price and/or right terms that best serve the needs of both parties.

In reality, everyone wants the best deal they can get, which leads to another impediment to a joint problem-solving negotiation strategy—which is self-interest. Most people enter into negotiations with their own self-interest in mind. There's nothing wrong with that, since the end result will be an exchange of mutual benefit, not a charitable endeavor. As a result, maximizing your self-interest isn't necessarily furthered by worrying about solving the other guy's problems. Anyway, in most cases, his only problem is how to get you to give him the best deal he can get.

Of course, there are negotiating conditions where it's clearly beneficial for both parties to work in harmony at resolving some underlying problem which is posing an obstacle to agreement. Under these circumstances, if both parties are willing to work together with mutual trust, then a win/win, problem-solving strategy is the best approach to take. However, most run-of-the-mill business negotiations won't fall into that category.

Compounding the confusion is the implied assumption that an adversarial negotiating strategy is one where both parties are at each other's throats. This perception has been reinforced in the past by well-publicized negotiations that have been exceedingly hostile. Some labor disputes certainly have fit in this category. Nevertheless, most negotiations are conducted in a business-like manner without animosity or anger entering into the picture. So, implications that not using a joint-problem solving approach to negotiations, presumably leads to hostile negotiations is naive at best.

Furthermore, even though you approach negotiations from a point of view that emphasizes your own self-interest, that doesn't mean you won't look for ways to overcome obstacles that hinder reaching agreement. If during negotiations, the other party indicates that a particular hurdle must be overcome to reach agreement, then it's certainly in your interest to seek ways to resolve the problem.

The bottom line as to the proper approach to take toward negotiations is to first and foremost protect your own interests. If, within that context, it's feasible to work closely with the other party to reach agreement, then by all means do so. On the other hand, if it is quite evident that the other party to the negotiation is solely interested in getting the best possible deal, then it behooves you to proceed accordingly. This will be further elaborated in this Chapter.

⇨ 1.2　Stonewalling

1.2.1　How to Avoid the Frustrations

One of the most frustrating experiences you can encounter at the negotiating table is having the misfortune of going up against an adversary who lakes a position and simply stonewalls every attempt to reach agreement. No matter what your offer, and no matter how many concessions you make, stonewallers will respond with nothing but a "No".

There are several reasons why people will use stonewalling tactics. These include:

- They have no intention of reaching agreement unless they can get an irresistible bargain.
- They intend to make a deal, but hope that by stonewalling you will make repetitive offers—each one better than the last.
- They are stonewalling to force you into losing your poise and making mistakes.
- They are trying to send a message that they are hard to deal with in the hope that you will lower your expectations.
- They don't know what constitutes a reasonable agreement, but figure it will be somewhere around the last offer you make before threatening to scuttle the deal completely.
- They are stalling because of some known deadline which will force you to increase your offer.

Although it's disappointing when you're confronted by stonewalling tactics, it's a hazard you must challenge head on. Otherwise, the stonewaller will play out this ploy to exact every conceivable concession you can make, meanwhile surrendering nothing in return. The end result will be either a bad deal for you, or no deal at all. Therefore, once you detect an unwillingness to negotiate, you have to decide how best to counter this tactic. However, under any circumstances, don't lose control of your emotions—unless you are, of course, faking it to force the other side to end their stonewalling tactics.

However, before you employ any strategy to counter a stonewaller, try to assess the reason for their behavior, since it may be something other than just a tactic to get you to make concessions. For example, perhaps negotiations may have been proceeding fairly smoothly, when you suddenly hit the wall in getting any movement on one particular issue. It may well be that there are reasons why the other side doesn't want to point out their reluctance to discuss and/or yield on a particular topic. If you give it a little thought, you may be able to make a reasonably intelligent guess as to what the unknown stumbling block is. If so, you may be able to negotiate around it.

CAUTION: Stonewalling may be used as a tactic right from the start, or be brought into play at some point during the negotiations. It's a lot easier to recognize stonewalling if it's done initially. The danger is that if someone starts to stonewall during negotiations that have been proceeding smoothly, you may be less likely to recognize the tactic. That could lull you into making unwarranted concessions. Therefore, if you make a reasonable offer which the other side dismisses out-of-hand, while continuing to stick stubbornly to a totally unreasonable position, don't make further concessions. This is merely playing into their hands, and you will never get them off of their stonewalling kick.

1.2.2   Whittling away at Stonewalling Tactics

The key to stonewalling success can be summed-up in one word, and that's doubt. A stonewaller wants to plant doubt in your mind that he will accept anything other than the best deal you can give him. If successful, this leads you to accept the worst possible deal you can get, since your alternative would be no deal at all. From a practical standpoint, if you have done your homework before starting to negotiate, you know whether or not your offer is reasonable. Of course, there may be something you overlooked, and/or justification for the other side not agreeing with you. However, if that's the case, your adversary will be quick to point this out. So, if they fail to do this, and stubbornly refuse to discuss the matter, then it's obvious they are just stonewalling.

If you want to succeed at overcoming stonewalling tactics, first of all, resist any self-imposed doubts that you are the one being unreasonable. Having done that, there are several approaches to take in dealing with a stonewalling adversary.

- Set a deadline.

One countermeasure that can be taken once you realize the other side is stonewalling is to set a deadline for completing negotiations. If you do this, simply state it because the other side isn't negotiating in good faith. This has the advantage of letting them know you aren't going to put up with their nonsense.

The downside of this approach is that your adversary may well assume that you're just bluffing, and will continue to stonewall right up until the deadline expires. In other words, they will call your bluff. If that happens, then you have to be prepared to break off negotiations, perhaps by saying something such as, "We're getting nowhere, so as of now any possibility of a deal is dead. However, if you decide that you are willing to negotiate, give me a call."

NOTE: Whenever, you break off negotiations for any reason, always do so in a way that leaves it up to the other side to contact you. This gives you a tactical advantage if they do call you at a later date.

Case 3

Once, a company from Italy negotiated business with a Chinese company. When the negotiation went on not smoothly after a week, the representative Ronny from Italy told the representative Mr. Li from China that he only left two days to negotiate and hoped the Chinese company to take out a new scheme the next day. The next morning Mr. Li made a concession that they quoted a decrease of 35% instead of 40%, but Ronny insisted on the decrease of 15%.

Disagreeing with each other, they adjourned the meeting until afternoon. At last, Ronny said that his lowest decrease is 20% and if the Chinese company couldn't accept his terms before 12:00 the next day, he would leave at 2:30 by plane. The Chinese company was not satisfied with the price Ronny referred and after the meeting they checked out that there were not any plane fly to Italy 2:30 the next day. Therefore, they called Ronny 10:00 the next day and expressed that on the consideration of the concession Italy had made, they would like to decrease to 25%. Although Ronny didn't think the price was what he really wanted, he stayed to negotiate instead of living.

(*Adapted from* International Business Negotiations *by Huang Wei and Qian Li*)

- Ignore stonewalling tactics and keep on talking.

Another alternative is to ignore stonewalling tactics and just keep talking. Go on to other aspects of the negotiation if that's feasible. If the other side is negotiating seriously, then they're listening to what you're saying even though they give no indication of budging from their extreme position. Of course, if no headway is made by doing this, try making an outrageous offer of your own. Sometimes a party will start getting serious when they see that you're going to be just as unreasonable as they are.

- Lay it right on the line.

If all else fails, lay it right on the line that if they aren't going to be reasonable in their approach to negotiations, then there's no point in continuing the discussions. It may be tough to consider walking away without a deal, but no deal is better than a bad one. One reason that stonewalling succeeds is that the more time and effort people invest in a negotiation, the more reluctant they become to call it quits. So, no matter what approach you take to counter act stonewalling tactics, don't let it go on indefinitely. If your adversary won't move ***off-the-mark*** within a reasonable period of time, get up and walk away.

⇨ 1.3 The Good Samaritan Approach

In sharp contrast to a stonewaller who can quickly get your blood boiling, is the "good samaritan" who sets about to prove that he's doing you a favor if you accept his terms and conditions. Although your initial reaction to this approach may be bemusement, before negotiations are concluded a "good samaritan" negotiator can also succeed in driving you up the wall. The "good samaritan" negotiator operates on a premise of what's good for him is good for you, and takes advantage of every opportunity to convince you of that. A "good samaritan's" key to success is in lulling you to sleep with his apparent willingness to discuss anything and everything. This type of negotiator will never attack your position, or even disagree with it, but will ever so subtly simply ignore every fact and figure you put on the table.

The only way to deal with a "best deal in town" type of negotiator is to force them to focus on the facts. Cut them short once you realize what they're up to by saying something such as, "Look Charlie, I'm sure you have the greatest product in the world, but it isn't priceless. I'm offering you 'X' dollars which is quite reasonable. Let's concentrate on the figures I've presented and not the superlatives." Admittedly, it may take a while to get your point across, but eventually you will, and by no means, fall prey to pleas such as, "I'm trying to be fair, and you're taking advantage of me," or similar drivel. A died-in-the-wool "good samaritan" will forever swear— even long after the deal is done—that you got the best deal in the world. In the end, the key to coping with this sort of bargainer is to beware of accepting favors at the negotiating table, since they'll come back to bite your butt.

⇨ 1.4 **How to Halt the Good Cop/Bad Cop Caper**

Case 4

American entrepreneur Howard Hughes looked very serious. Once, Hughes had a negotiation with the aircraft manufacturer personally so as to purchase the planes in bulk. Hughes's character, appearance and his social status developed a unique negotiating style which could hardly be adapted by his opponents. And that time was no exception. Hughes had intended to purchase 34 aircraft, including 11 ones which had to be obtained in any case.

However, it was his tough stance that brought about a deadlock into the negotiation and it was less likely to make a compromise between them. The aircraft manufacturers were extremely disgusted and angry. Although their attitude was not as bad as Mr. Hughes', they could not tolerate his negotiating style. So a fierce argument resulted, and even a slight profit could be taken as an advantage. The negotiation was filled with the unfriendly atmosphere of severe conflicts and no one wanted to give in. Hughes' tough attitude and his strong way of speaking annoyed the manufacturers very much. Eventually, Hughes was kicked out of the negotiations, and the two sides broke up in disagreement.

But, in fact, such consequence was made by Hughes intentionally. Obviously, he could not take further negotiations with the manufacturers himself any more. Therefore, he appointed his deputy to deal with the following negotiations on his behalf. Before the commencement of the second-round negotiations, Hughes told his personal assistant that it was not necessary to win 34 aircraft, and those 11 would be sufficient. Then the assistant took the negotiations with his real purpose. Quite different from Hughes' overbearing attitude, his assistant acted as a nice guy, and exchanged his ideas with his rivals sincerely. Consequently, the negotiations went back to friendly and harmonious atmosphere and Hughes's personal assistant quickly tackled it very well.

Eventually, after a series of fierce but friendly negotiations, Hughes's personal assistant made a deal of 30 aircrafts, including those 11 ones requested by his boss. And Hughes was very surprised by what had happened. Overexcited and delighted, he asked his personal assistant how he could achieve such a big victory. Then he got the reply: "It is very simple. Every time when we failed to reach an agreement, I would ask them with whom they'd prefer to discuss the problems. Mr. Howard Hughes or me? Surprisingly, they accepted my request very happily. That's it."

One common technique you may be subjected to during negotiations is the tried and true good cop/bad cop ploy. This is nothing more than a little role playing, where one person acts the part of a hard-nosed bargainer, while a second individual seeks to gain your confidence by being mild mannered and considerate. Needless to say they are both working together to undermine your negotiation stance.

As business negotiations aren't conducted under klieg lights in an interrogation room, the negotiation equivalent of the good cop/bad cop caper doesn't have interrogators alternating between bullying and back stroking. The most frequent method for pulling off this ploy consists of using a hard-nosed negotiator who won't yield on anything. His or her boss then enters the picture as the understanding conciliator.

What generally happens is that the "good guy" will listen attentively to your plight, and then calmly explain why his side can only settle for what they're proposing. All of this is, of course, **interlaced** with **syrupy pleas** for your understanding. Naturally, if you fall for this trap, you end up pretty much giving the other side what they want. Of course, if the "good guy" negotiator encounters reluctance on your part, some minor concession may be offered to nudge you toward agreement.

At first glance, this type of tactic seems to be both silly and simplistic. However, it feeds upon basic emotional needs such as sympathy and understanding. Furthermore, you have likely been subjected to an extended period of negotiations with a most unreasonable person as your opponent. Having made no headway, and seeing the prospects of any agreement fading faster than the sun on a cold winter day, you are primed to be receptive to anyone who represents a voice of reason. Unfortunately, while the hard-nose was doing nothing more harmful than testing your temper, Mr. Good Guy's objective is to wallow in your wallet.

There are two extreme positions you can take to counteract this ploy.

- Play the game yourself.

The minute you are subjected to hard-nosed tactics, do a little browbeating of your own. You are now creating a tactical nightmare for the other side. Where they expected to be able to wheel Mr. Good Guy into action to extract concessions from a beleaguered and frustrated patsy, they now face a formidable foe.

It's likely that when they rethink their strategy, the discussion will focus on whether you're really a tough nut to crack, or are just playing the same game as them. Naturally, the only way to find out is by testing you. That should bring on an appearance by Mr. Good Guy, replete with his snake charmer's personality.

- Turn the tables.

Now, more than ever, is the time to turn the tables. Instead of settling down and being reasonable, maintain your hard line posture. With luck, that will convince the other side that while they were only playing a game, you are a true-to-life example of a difficult person to deal with.

At this point, you can subtly introduce your own version of Mr. Nice Guy into the game—in the form of your boss or other conspirator. He can then go about finalizing negotiations on terms favorable to your side. All of this may appear to be a little unseemly, but when it comes to negotiations you have to take your foes as you find them. And if they want to play games, it's to your advantage to teach them how to score.

Of course, if you're not partial to doing a little role playing, you can use more direct means to deal with the good cop/bad cop tactic. After subjecting yourself to a lengthy enough harangue to indicate you're your opposite is unwilling to discuss matters in any logical manner, insist on negotiating with someone else.

If the other party refuses, simply say something such as, "It's apparent you are unwilling to work toward an amicable agreement. If you change your mind, let me know." Then, get up and leave. The odds are you will be hearing from someone from the other side within a short period of time.

NOTE: One reason that people accept bad deals is because they are extremely reluctant to break off negotiations. This is unwise, since once the other side knows that an adversary isn't going to walk, it's a better sign than a smoke signal that they can press hard for a favorable agreement. What inexperienced negotiators fail to realize is that negotiations ebb and flow, often with interludes in between where there is little or no communication between the parties. Therefore, it's important to keep in mind that just because negotiations break off doesn't mean they have been scuttled for good. And although it's preferable for the other party to contact you to resume talks, the worst that can happen is that you may have to initiate the call.

⇨ 1.5   Using Surprise as a Negotiation Tool

The element of surprise can be an extremely effective weapon in your arsenal of negotiating tools if it's properly employed. But it can only be used once, otherwise, it isn't believable. Therefore, it's wise to be prudent about its use, which means saving it for when you really need it.

Some of the ways you can change the course of a negotiation session by catching your opponent off-guard include:

1) Introduce a completely new element into the negotiation. ("We've decided to close Plant 14 if we don't have a labor agreement by the end of the month.")

2) Adding competition. ("We have received an unexpected offer from the "x" Corp., which is significantly lower than what you're proposing.")

3) To undermine the other side's position. ("By the way, Jack Arnold will be coming in shortly. Since he used to work for you guys, I'm sure he's familiar with what you're proposing.")

4) Bringing in an expert to contradict the other side's position. ("I'd like you folks to meet Sammy Smart. As you know, he's the foremost authority on the subject of land valuation.")

5) To signal a shift in your thinking. ("I know you folks here in Swill City have said you can't make any further concessions if we locate our regional headquarters here. However, it's only fair to tell you that the folks down in Sunshine County have offered us a much more attractive package.")

6) To escalate the level of negotiations. ("Ernie Urgent, our president, plans to call your president, if agreement can't be reached by Friday.")

7) To create a sense of urgency. ("We're leaving for the Far East in two days, so if we can't wrap this up, it will just have to go on the back burner.")

As you can see, the possibilities for the use of surprise are endless. Nevertheless, there are two caveats that should be kept in mind.

- One, only use the element of surprise when there's a stalemate, and the prospects are bleak for making further progress.
- Second and paramount in importance, don't make an assertion that you can't back-up. Any negotiator worth their salt will always call a bluff. So, if you're just winging it/when you try to catch the other side offguard, you better have other negotiation alternatives waiting in the wings.

⇨ 1.6 Making a Weak Negotiation Position an Advantage

Knowing your own negotiation limits, and having the self-confidence to stick with them is the prime requisite for not being short-changed when your negotiation position is weak. However, if conditions are right, you can use a weak negotiating position to gain concessions you might not otherwise receive.

The biggest handicap you face when you're in a weak bargaining position is a lack of confidence which surfaces in an attitude of. "I'll take whatever deal they offer me." This is a typical attitude when a small business enters into negotiations with a large, well-financed enterprise. It's natural to assume that if the dictated terms aren't accepted, the larger company will take their business to someone more pliable.

Therefore, anytime you're in this sort of position, you have to ask yourself why the other party is negotiating with you in the first place. Is it just because they can dictate price and other terms to you, or are there other substantive reasons which work in your favor? For instance, perhaps you are geographically accessible, or furnish a higher quality product. The possibilities are endless in any given situation. However, if you are offering something of real value apart from being a weak negotiating opponent, then you have a valid basis for holding your own during negotiations.

It pays to be realistic when you make this sort of assessment. After all, you may be dreaming about taking a lousy deal now, with visions of profiting from the future business this relationship will bring. However, it may well be that the other party is thinking about a one-shot, low priced contract, with no intention of giving you any future work. Perhaps you are being used as a pawn to force down the price of the other guy's long-term supplier. In any event, it's beneficial to objectively weigh the merits of why the other side is dealing with you. At least then, if you choose to take the risks, you do so recognizing the possibilities.

The *flip* side of the coin is to weigh your own interests in entering into negotiations. Is it because you need the work at any price? If so, you better recognize that "any price" can be costly, which some businesses don't discover until they go bankrupt. All in all, the less desperate you are for the work, the better positioned you are to extract the most reasonable contract terms Possible-despite any apparent weakness in your bargaining position.

Another factor that shouldn't be overlooked when you are in a weak bargaining position is the integrity of the party you are dealing with. Sound business relationships—and reputations—aren't built upon driving unreasonable bargains with people who are in a weak negotiating position.

For instance, a company that wants to develop a long-term supplier relationship may drive a hard bargain—but it will be a reasonable one. Therefore don't ignore the track record of the other party, because if you do, it will be at your peril.

Once you have determined that you're doing business with a reputable firm, then you are in a position to ask for—and get—concessions at the bargaining table. Surprisingly enough, these can be concessions that some-one in a stronger bargaining position might not be able to negotiate. For example, a small business might not have the capability to finance a project internally. However, by presenting valid arguments in that regard, the other side may well be amenable to negotiating financial terms that they wouldn't grant to a better financed adversary. Let's look at how this might work.

Case 5

The LCO Company, a small, thirty-five employee manufacturer has been approached by Megacorp Inc., a large manufacturer of industrial products, for supplying 10,000 gizmos for use in one of Megacorp's products. Megacorp wants to develop LCO as a source, since the company needs a high quality responsive supplier. LCO, for their part, is drooling at the prospect of getting this business, since it will effectively double the company's size.

The negotiations move along smoothly until payment terms are raised. Arthur Able, LCO's president points out to Ralph Realistic, the Megacorp negotiator, that LCO would need progress payments in order to finance such a large order. They jointly explore financing alternatives and determine that there are no other reasonable alternatives. It is then agreed that Megacorp will provide progress payments under the contract based on 75% of costs incurred to be liquidated against deliveries when they are made. This helps LCO finance material purchases and work-in-progress costs without having to wait until delivery to be paid.

Megacorp knows that LCO does not have the financial capability to incur the labor and material costs to build the units if they receive no money until delivery begins, which is four months from the start date. Although Megacorp would probably not agree'to progress payments with a company that had the financial resources, it was considered a sound business judgment to do so in this case. Furthermore, Megacorp knows that once the stream of deliveries starts, LCO's financing picture will improve, so that progress pay moments won't be needed on future orders.

Although it's possible to gain concessions by virtue of being in a weak negotiating position, it pays to be realistic in terms of your expectations. After all, the other party isn't engaged in a charitable endeavor. Therefore, any concessions they make will be based upon (1) how good a case you can present, and (2) the advantage to them. Consequently, you have to know when to ask, and when to accept "No" for an answer.

(*Adapted from* The Negotiator's handbook *by George Fuller*)

⇨ 1.7 Coping with Hardball Tactics

Sometimes, there's a fine line between hardball negotiating tactics based on the issues. Actions such as threats—real or implied—or attempts at intimidation, are used.

The core of a hardball approach is coercion designed to extract concessions. Consequently, the proper formula for defeating this strategy is to resist the pressures that are applied. Like a lot of other things, it's easier said than done. For example, how willing would you be to say, "Buzz-off!" if you were sitting on the other side of the table when these threats were made?

- "If you don't agree to pay $28,000,000 by three o'clock tomorrow, we're taking the building off the market."
- "If an agreement isn't reached by Friday, we're taking a strike vote."
- "If our lease payments aren't reduced, we're signing an agreement to move our store into the 'Spiff City Mall'".
- "Either you accept a price of $280 a unit, or we'll put this sole-source contract out for competitive bids."
- "There's $2,000,000 budgeted for this contract. Either accepts that now, or we'll cancel the procurement."

Everyone's gut reaction when presented with threats of this nature is to say, "Screw you, go ahead." Of course, that's an open invitation for the other side to follow through with their threat. And even if they really don't want to, a blunt challenge forces them to act. Otherwise, they would be in the position of admitting that the threat is merely a bluff, which then leaves you holding the upper hand. As a result, directly defying the other party to act is foolish unless you like living dangerously.

The best practice for dealing with a threat is to analyze it. Of course, you may need a little time to do this. However, it's best to avoid stating that you would like to recess for that purpose, because that puts you in the position of having to come back with an answer. Therefore, casually suggest a brief break for refreshments, or for that matter, any purpose unrelated to the threat.

What you want to do is to assess the threat, both from your standpoint and the impact upon the other side if it's carried out. From your viewpoint, ask yourself what you will lose if the negotiation falls through. To a large degree, your answer goes back to the alternatives that you established when you prepared your pre-negotiation position. If you have pretty good alternatives in the event negotiations fail, then your worry index shouldn't be too high. Nevertheless, that still doesn't mean you should directly invite the other side to proceed with implementing their saber-rattling scheme. That's because until they actually carry out their threat, you are still in position to negotiate a favorable agreement.

Perhaps the key to your risk assessment is the potential harm to the other side if they follow through with their threat. You may discover that their threat isn't quite as ominous as it appears to be. In conducting your assessment ask yourself these types of questions:

1) Is their threat feasible? For instance, threatening to take one's business elsewhere isn't very practical if there's no viable competition.

2) What are the potential costs to the other side even if they can implement their threat? These costs can be tangible, such as having to pay a higher price, or intangible, such as the chance of getting a lower quality product elsewhere.

3) Are the potential risks greater than the possible rewards? For example, a union going on strike where workers can be readily replaced runs a higher risk than where substitute workers can't be quickly hired and trained.

4) Are there behind-the-scene factors that mitigate the threat? Perhaps a buyer can't afford the time delays involved in going to another supplier, or maybe the seller of a building is financially strapped and can't afford to look for another purchaser.

Once you have established to your satisfaction how real the threat is, you are in position to respond. Unless you are fairly secure about your alternatives and/or that the threat is just a bluff, it's best not to challenge it. In fact, even if your position is sound, a direct challenge isn't wise. It backs the other side to the wall, so they may feel compelled to break off negotiations even if they don't want to.

The best method for dealing with an ultimatum is to ignore it. Obviously, if the other side insists on a reply, then you have little recourse other than to say something such as, "Be my guest." However, unless they are on secure footing, that's not likely to happen. Therefore, just keep the discussions rolling as if no ultimatum was issued. The more time that passes after a threat is made, the less chance there is of it being carried out. In fact, if the other side continues to negotiate after making a threat, the tactical advantage will shift to you. This is so, since the ultimate negotiation weapon is threatening not to negotiate. Once that danger goes by the boards, it's more than likely a signal that the other side will remain sitting until an agreement is reached.

2　Countering Negative Negotiation Tactics

⇨ 2.1　How to Contend with Bullying Tactics

You may find bullying tactics being employed against you by an opposing negotiator. If it's of a continuing nature from the opening bell of a negotiation meeting, and involves outright hostility, you may have to respond with feigned anger, or a refusal to negotiate unless the behavior ceases. However, for the most part, the type of bullying you face will be sporadic, and deliberately pursued by a perfectly rational person in an attempt to gain a negotiating edge.

It helps to counteract attempts to bully you by trying to pinpoint the other negotiator's purpose, and then responding accordingly. Some fairly common reasons for the use of bullying tactics, along with appropriate ways to respond, are as follows:

1) It may be an attempt to steer you away from an area that the other negotiator doesn't want to discuss. This is often the case when you zero in on a weak point in the other side's negotiating position. A sure-fire signal this is happening is when you ask a valid question and, instead of an answer, get an angry and/or sarcastic retort. When this happens, ignore the non-reply and ask your question again. As an alternative, say something such as, "Perhaps my question wasn't clear enough. What I want to know is …" If you don't get a satisfactory response the second time around, be emphatic about getting an answer before going on to discuss anything else.

2) Bullying tactics may be employed at the beginning of a negotiation session to test your tenacity. What the other negotiator is looking for is your reaction. If you act submissive in the face of bullying at the outset, you can expect this sort of behavior to continue throughout the course of the negotiations. Therefore, draw your line in the sand right away to let your counterpart know that you won't be shoved around. You might say, "Look, we've got a lot to accomplish here, and it's not going to get done unless we both cooperate. If that's not going to be the case, then we might as well not even get started."

3) Under certain limited conditions, bullying may be used in a deliberate attempt to get you to break off negotiations. This happens when your opponent doesn't want to continue the negotiations at the present time, but prefers that the onus for ending the talks be placed upon you. For instance, when a labor negotiation is in the public spotlight, neither side wants to be viewed as the party responsible for breaking off the talks. In situations such as this, when you are forewarned that the other side is attempting to gain some sort of advantage by coercing you into ending negotiations, it pays to hang in there, and force them to play their hand. It may not be pleasant to do so, but then again, the alternatives may be even less desirable.

4) Bullying may be employed near the close of negotiations in an attempt to gain last minute concessions. It pays to be extra cautious when you're nearing agreement after a difficult negotiation. You may not only be tired, but also frustrated at the difficulties encountered along the

way. This can leave you particularly vulnerable to the use of anger by the other side. So don't let your guard down until an agreement is reached. Otherwise, you may give away in minutes what you fought long and hard for over the course of the negotiations.

⇨ 2.2   Counterattacking Intimidating Behavior

Aside from bullying tactics, other kinds of intimidating behavior may be directed toward you during the negotiation process. As a general rule, you should ignore intimidating behavior, if that's at all possible. However, always analyze the threat in terms of the probability it will be carried out as well as the implications for you if it is. Let's look at a few forms of intimidation and the means of neutralizing such threats.

1) Deadlines may be used in a variety of ways as a means of intimidation. One of the most hackneyed customs is to spring some sort of deadline requirement when there is an apparent deadlock in resolving differences in the respective negotiating positions. The scheme is to force you to be the one to make the final concession. This type of gambit usually takes the form of an ultimatum such as, "If we don't wrap this up today, then the deal is dead."

When confronted with such an ultimatum, anyone who resists the urge to panic and give the other side what they're looking for will win this challenge hands down. In the first place, these deadlines are usually shallow to begin with. Who, in their right mind, is going to throw away a deal they want by walking away at the last minute? Furthermore, if there were genuine reasons for a deadline, you would have heard about them before the negotiations even began.

Therefore, the best approach for coping with this tactic is to play right along with it. In fact, if you use a little bit of finesse, you might have your opponent wishing the subject hadn't been raised. To do this, when the deadline ultimatum is issued, give a response that's as close to glee as you can get without looking foolish. By doing this, you're sending a message that you're not that anxious to do business, which is just the opposite of the panicky plea that your adversary is looking for.

This kind of response signals that your last offer was it, and therefore, the other side had better move toward your position if they want a deal. To be extra convincing, take some action that indicates you are leaving. For instance, ask your counterpart if someone can make plane reservations for you. Here, as with other forms of intimidation, the one who generally wins is the one who cares the least—or at least is able to convey that impression to the other side. There's no room for timidity when it comes to countering intimidation attempts. In fact, the minute the other negotiating party sees that you won't be stampeded is the point when intimidation attempts will cease.

2) A garden-variety intimidation *gimmick* is for a negotiator to threaten to do business with the competition. This is frequently used to coerce someone into agreeing with what would otherwise be unacceptable terms. A variation of this theme is to threaten to perform the work in-house. Here

again is what generally constitutes an oversold threat. If they were going to do business with the competition, or do the work themselves, they wouldn't be wasting time and money negotiating with you.

For the most part, these are idle threats made to squeeze a better deal out of you. The best response is a simple, "Suit yourself". If you express any indication of concern, you're inviting the other negotiator to press you harder for concessions. Having the confidence to resist these threats is part of the process of getting the deal you want—not the deal the other side wants you to accept.

3) A somewhat trickier type of intimidation to deal with is the *assertion* by your counterpart that some people within his organization are opposed to the deal being negotiated. This problem takes the form of statements such as, "Our product engineering people are working against this deal." It's by no means uncommon for factions within an organization to have opposing viewpoints. However, if a project has gone as far as the negotiation stage, it's obvious that the opposing faction lost the power struggle. Hence, it's highly unlikely that the deal would be canceled at the last moment. So this sort of claim is merely useful fodder for negotiators to use in trying to secure better terms at the bargaining table. Therefore, don't be panicked into cutting a bad deal, because of a fear of the project being scuttled. Actually, if there is an internal power struggle, the proponents of the project will be anxious to see the deal go through, which works to strengthen—not weaken—your negotiating position.

Besides the more common intimidation practices typically associated with business transactions, are those utilized in specialized negotiation situations. These can range from strike threats during labor negotiations, to saber rattling on the international negotiation front. In fact, the possibilities for intimidation are limited only by the imagination of negotiators intent on finding ways to intimidate the opposition. Nevertheless, whatever the subject matter may be, the best protection against these practices is simply a steadfast refusal to be intimidated.

⇨ 2.3　Knowing When to Pounce on an Opponent

When your opponent engages in intimidation and other negative tactics, it's important to cut this behavior short early on in the negotiation process. Otherwise, it becomes more difficult to control. In fact, any type of ploy should be challenged promptly, since even if you don't fully succeed in halting such practices, your adversary will know you're not an easy mark.

Nevertheless, you shouldn't overreact to every tactic that doesn't meet with your approval. If you tactfully suggest that your counterpart's actions aren't likely to lead to an early and amicable agreement, and the response is simply denial, along with a continuation of the objectionable practices, don't provoke further confrontation. That is, unless the behavior is outrageous and irresponsible to the extent that it can't be tolerated.

First of all, what you're seeing may represent the personality traits and/or standard negotiating style of your opponent. Consequently, your objections—no matter how vehement—may have little or no impact. Furthermore, as long as you recognize the tactics being employed for what they are, you can success fully work around them. In addition, persistently *admonishing* your opponent about a negotiation table tactic you consider to be unreasonable, may have unforeseen results. For instance, the objectionable practice may cease, but your adversary may then resort to one or more retaliatory practices, such as:

- Nitpicking everything you say or do.
- Reverting to other undesirable tactics which aren't as easy to recognize.
- Being vague or reticent about answering your questions.
- Accusing you of using unfair tactics.
- Becoming generally more difficult to deal with.

Therefore, in dealing with objectionable negotiation tactics, although it's useful to register your displeasure, it's equally important to refrain from transforming them into the dominant issue under discussion. You can't choose your negotiating foes, so although you may find certain practices distasteful, don't let your objections deter you from reaching your negotiation objectives.

⇨ 2.4   Turning Threats to Your Advantage

You may encounter threats of one sort or another during the negotiation process. They can range from the relatively insignificant, to the ultimate scare tactic, which is breaking off negotiations without any deal being struck. However, despite the menacing posture that threats pose, they aren't always as intimidating as they seem.

To begin with, it's a *quantum* leap from making a threat to carrying it out. For example, following through with a threat and ending negotiations involves a lost deal for both parties—not just the party being threatened. That is, of course, unless the negotiation is so one-sided that the threatening party never had anything much to lose. And if that's the case, the recipient of the threat shouldn't have been negotiating in the first place.

Furthermore, the possibility of unsuccessful negotiations should have been factored into your pre-negotiation planning. Therefore, although they may be less desirable, you should have other alternatives available if the negotiation is unsuccessful. As a result, a threat of "no deal" shouldn't propel you into pushing the panic button, and accepting unreasonable terms and conditions.

In fact, the best method for disarming such a threat is to be cavalier about it. An obvious lack of concern about a threat to break off negotiations forces the other party to either back off, or follow through with the threat and end negotiations. Since the latter entails far greater risks than continuing to negotiate, in most instances it's not likely to happen. Instead, the other negotiator will just keep on negotiating, perhaps still huffing and puffing about ending discussions right down to the satisfactory conclusion of an agreement. However, once the initial threat hasn't been carried out, the tactical advantage switches to you, since the other side has tacitly acknowledged its reluctance to let the deal go down the drain.

As far as the specifics of dealing with a threat when it's first made, you can either (1) ignore it, and continue the discussions, (2) respond by acknowledging it as the other negotiator's prerogative, or (3) counterattack with a veiled threat of your own. Let's look at each of these possibilities individually.

- When someone threatens to break off negotiations, you can simply continue on with the discussions as if the threat wasn't even made. This forces your opponent to repeat the threat, but this may not happen. The reason is that by ignoring the threat you're sending a signal that you either don't take it seriously, and/or don't care whether or not the negotiations come to an end. This may give the other negotiator pause about repeating the threat if it's just a ploy that's not intended to be carried out. Your nonchalance shows the threat isn't likely to work, while continuing the discussions lets your counterpart avoid the embarrassment of having to back off if the threat is repeated and rebuffed.

- You can choose to force the other negotiator to bite the bullet by responding with resignation when the threat is made. For instance, say something such as, "Look Ms. Marple, if you want to call it quits, that's your choice. I have no intention of accepting unreasonable terms just to complete this deal." Your opponents then have the option of ending the negotiation, or continuing the discussions, but in any event, if they were bluffing, they now know you have called them on it.

- Yet another alternative for coping with a negotiation-ending threat is to reply with a little intimidation of your own. The specific course it takes will be based upon the facts of the negotiation you're participating in. However, from a general standpoint, it's useful to respond with escalating demands related to the alleged reason why the other negotiator is threatening to walk out. For instance, if your counterpart is threatening to scuttle everything because you won't agree to accept certain delivery dates, offer to do so, but increase your costs to a level that would either compensate you accordingly, or make it impractical for your opponent to accept.

Any threat made at the negotiation table is usually designed to exact some form of concession from you. It essentially is a last resort ploy to win with intimidation what couldn't be won with reasoned arguments. The ability to overcome this tactic is commensurate with your willingness to run the risk that the threat will be carried out. Of course, your opponent is banking upon your inability to resist the pressure.

In point of fact, people don't always stand their ground, and instead capitulate to the demands of a negotiating opponent. Depending upon the circumstances, this "less may be more" approach to negotiating can't be arbitrarily condemned. In the final analysis, if you can live with the end result, and it's the best available alternative, then that may be the appropriate way to go. That decision can only be made by the negotiator—not by armchair critics who delight in telling you how they could have gotten a better deal.

⇨ 2.5   How to Deal with Lies

Lying in negotiations is common practice. Do you always tell the truth, the whole truth and nothing but the truth? Of course not—you are trying to put the information across in a way in which it benefits you, and the other party is doing the same. It is a matter of degree, ranging from sins of omission, through selective truth telling to never, ever, telling the truth on principle. Famously, Disraeli quoted that there are "three kinds of lies: lies, damned lies, and statistics". Figures can prove anything and "facts" can be manipulated to suit the cause. Is this lying? Your answer to this question will depend on your values and whether or not you are on the receiving end.

When presenting facts everybody uses ones that suit their own position, and they will emphasize those points in their favor and play down (or ignore) the downsides. The salesperson wants to maximize the price, the buyer wants to lessen the price, and they will use tactics that help them to achieve that. Both sides need to be aware of this and act accordingly.

We can do something to counter it.

- Check your assumptions and facts. Know the market. Always look for objective data not opinion, and if an opinion is *proffered*— "Property in this area is selling at 20 per cent above the market at present"—and it is significant to the negotiation, this should prompt you to probe for the facts.

- Confronting suspected liars directly is usually a bad idea and can often end relationships on the spot, particularly if the liar feels trapped in their own deceit. A better approach is to ask to recheck the figures, or ask to know on what assumptions they are based, "My market data seems to be different to yours. I am only seeing a 10 per cent premium. Can we pool our sources?"

⇨ 2.6   Lacking Authority

A common delaying tactic is to claim limited authority in the hope that you will settle for what is on offer rather than wait for higher authority to be sought: "Your proposal is interesting but I will have to take it back to my boss for final approval."

In this case, check out who has the authority to agree in the opening phase, and if necessary negotiate with the other party to have that person present in the negotiation so that an agreement can be reached.

However, it is particularly important when negotiating internationally to recognize that there are some cultures where you can only speak to someone of the same status as yourself. So, if the decision maker is of higher status, then you would need to bring someone in from your side of similar status to ensure they can be present. To do otherwise would be seen to be rude and a loss of face.

⇨ 2.7　Countering Nibbling

This is a common tactic in sales negotiations. Just at the point of closing the deal, the negotiator asks for further small concession: "I think we're very close to a deal if we can just agree on this last item." The danger is that if you give way on this concession you will most likely be asked for another. The negotiator nibbles away at your side of the deal.

Once again, the rule is to never give a concession without getting something in return. If you can give the concession, then trade for it. If you can't give the concession, say so and refuse. It is also an opportunity to use a presumptive close: "So, you'll sign the contract if we agree to this?"

⇨ 2.8　Dealing with Stressful Environment

Places that are difficult and hard for you to get to; not being offered food or drinks; being kept waiting without any apology or explanation; uncomfortable seating; looking into a glare or strong light. These are all signs that the other party might be trying to gain an advantage by putting you under stress.

Of course, it might not be a tactic or dirty trick—it may just be that the other party has innocently put you in this position. Treating it an innocent mistake in your mind means that you don't attribute malicious tactics to the other party and blurt out a negative comment. So identify what is happening to you, and if you can live with it, then ignore it and you will not be under stress, whether intended or not. If you can't live with it, then politely ask for what you want: "Could I have a glass of water, please?", "Would it be alright to draw the blinds, the sun is in my eyes". Alternatively, move your chair or ask for a time out in order to regain your composure.

⇨ 2.9　How to Deal with Unreasonable Demands and Offers

Understanding someone's offer or demand is not the same as accepting it. You should seek to understand the other party's offers and demands, but once they are on the table, they gain validity unless you challenge them. This tactic may reveal itself in what the Americans call "high-balling" or "low-balling"—the negotiator starts with an extremely high or low offer. The hope is that this will affect the bargaining range in their favor.

Always question and challenge so that you do not leave an unreasonable or outrageous offer or demand "on the table". Knowing what is "unreasonable" or "outrageous" is another reason for doing your preparation well so that you know the market. You can then use the same counter as for lying: "My information seems to be different to yours… Can we check our assumptions and sources?"

3 Developing Your Negotiation Strategies

Planning your overall strategy is an important part of preparing for a negotiation. Because of different cultures, backgrounds, educations and other elements, everyone has his or her own characteristic negotiation approach, or style, when it comes to managing conflict. According to Thomas and Kilmann (1974), these different approaches can be grouped into five distinct categories as follows.

The five main negotiation strategies are: Competitive, Accommodation, Compromising, Collaborating and Avoidance. Competitive Strategy involves an "I win, you lose" attitude. Accommodation is "I will let you win in exchange for some other benefit I hope to gain now or later." Compromising is "I don't care who wins, I just want to get this over with quickly." Collaboration is "We can both win by expanding the pie before we cut it." and Avoidance is "I don't really want to play at all."

⇨ 3.1 The Competitive Strategy

The Competitive Strategy of "I win, you lose" is one most often used in settlement negotiation. It involves the use of intimidation, distraction, and diversion tactics to gain leverage.

You can choose a Competitive Strategy regardless of your bargaining position. If you have greater leverage, you can use competitive tactics to realize your advantage. But if your case is weaker, competitive tactics can themselves create value.

Most negotiations of every type begin with a Competitive Strategy. The parties need to test each other's wills before they begin bargaining seriously. The parties then continue their competitive bargaining of shift their approach to one of the four other tactics.

Following are examples of some competitive tactics:

1) Alternatives to settlement

Emphasize you have better choices than settlement. The side that cares more about settling is weaker. If you have the better BATNA (Best Alternative to a Negotiated Agreement), you have more "chips." Make that clear to your adversary.

One example is the threat to "beat your adversary in the marketplace." This threatens the lawful use of market power to make a legal victory Pyrrhic. Properly used, this tactic is effective.

2) "Anything but that"

Claiming your adversary's offer is not enough. Pick up other concessions before he "wrenches" your agreement from you.

3) Bluffing

Bluffing is at negotiation's core because each side has limited information. A good bluff uses your adversary's uncertainty to create even more doubts. And doubt translates into risk, and risk into money. Look for signs of uncertainty on his or her face or in his or her body language. But a bluff is not a lie—never expressly mislead.

A standard "bluff" is "to take it or leave it." Meet this bluff (and most others) by calling it. You won't know your adversary's limit unless you push for it.

4) Bringing in the media

Threaten to report some action or behavior to the media to induce concessions. Plaintiffs will use this tactic in media-sensitive industries, such as the entertainment industry. Recognize that parties in such industries have fair resistance to this tactic and will combat your disclosure press release of their own.

5) Creating deadlock

Creating deadlock is to force your adversary into concessions to move the negotiation along. But distinguish this tactic, as a tactic, from a legitimate impasse. Even reasonable people can disagree.

6) Diversion/Distraction

If you feel you are losing an important issue, shift the discussions to a different issue before you concede. Even change the subject altogether or use some other technique to distract your adversary from completing the current discussion.

7) Done deal

Take some unilateral action and present it to other side as a "done deal." Your adversary is thus forced to acquiesce or walk out. An example is when a co-party shows up at the negotiation only to discover that the other co-party has already settled.

8) Irrational behavior

Sometimes act irrationally, not only to distract and unnerve, but also to undermine your adversary's confidence. Lawyers tend toward rational argument. The irrational can throw off even an experienced negotiator.

9) Limited authority

Claim to lack authority to settle at some amount and ask your adversary to reduce the offer to your authority limits. To prevent your adversary from using this tactic, determine his or her authority in advance. If he or she lacks full authority, do not proceed.

10) Limited time

Constrain the time limits of the negotiation. Counter this tactic by clarifying time constrains in advance.

11) "Poor me"

Act like you have no background or training in negotiation and ask your adversary's help. He or she may sympathize with you and be more reasonable than he intended. This tactic can be especially effective for younger advocates.

12) Silence

Very few people can endure silence. Silence can impel your adversary to give you more information or concede more than he intended.

If your adversary's silence discomforts you, say something like, "I see you are thinking about my offer. I'm going to leave the room for a bit. Please let me know when you are ready to respond." And begin to leave. The silence will end before you reach the door.

13) Straw man

Demand agreement on Issue 1, which your adversary cares about most. Create deadlock and then "reluctantly" concede Issue 1 to gain agreement on Issue 2 (the one you care about most)— and maybe Issue 3 and 4 as well.

14) Turnabout

After you have conceded an issue or otherwise acted defensively, "gain space" by coming out strong on the next issue. But choose that issue wisely. It must be important, and you must win it.

15) Use of power

Threaten to use your power and sometimes actually use it. But heed this chess axiom: "The threat is more powerful than its execution." The threat creates doubt and, hence, concessions; but once implemented, you limit your adversary's choices, and he or she will do what he or she must respond to.

⇨ 3.2 **The Accommodation Strategy**

An accommodating party will sublimate its concerns to satisfy the other parties, at least for the present. You choose an accommodation strategy if you have done wrong and want to get the matter over with quickly and less expensively (airplane crashes and oil spills are two examples where quick settlements will save money). And there are less dramatic examples where a desire to limit personal or business disruption will encourage you to end the matter quickly. Or maybe you wish to gain some goodwill or other benefit now or later through a quick resolution.

Some accommodation tactics:

1) Face-saving

Prioritize the other parties dignity. Use every opportunity to give "face" and respect to the other side. Allow the other side to make tactful retreats to avoid embarrassment.

2) Identification

Align your interests with your adversary's, see the facts from his or her perspective, and agree with his or her arguments. But don't concede unnecessary issues.

3) Take the lead oar

Move the negotiation forward regardless of who created the difficulty. Suggest solutions, offer to prepare the documents, and be flexible about timing.

4) Take reasonable actions

Always be the party of reason, whether setting realistic deadlines or other conditions of the negotiation. Rarely if ever use a competitive tactic to move the other side.

⇨ 3.3　The Compromising Strategy

Compromisers look for an expedient, partially satisfactory middle ground. Their primary interest is haste and "rough justice." Thus, compromisers are willing to trade concessions, sometimes despite the merits, simply to make a deal. One example is a dispute involving an ongoing business relationship. You may choose to give a little to preserve the relationship.

Following are the compromiser's tactics.

1) Bit-by-bit

Gain your concessions "bit-by-bit" rather than all at once. As the direction of the incremental movement becomes clear, suggest meeting at the mid-point.

2) Conditional proposals

Make a proposal conditioned upon your adversary's acceptance of issues which need to be favorably resolved.

3) "Log-rolling"

Concede on an unimportant issue to you (but important to your adversary) in exchange for your adversary's concession on an issue that does matter to you.

4) "Splitting the baby"

At some point offer to split the difference with the other side, whether through an exchange of remaining issues or halving the dollar amount still in issue.

5) Tit-for-tat

Never make a concession without obtaining one in return. This rule underlies all bargaining (I won't negotiate against myself!"). But you must adhere to it when compromising or you will "compromise" away all your value simply for expediency's sake.

⇨ 3.4　The Collaborative Strategy

The collaborative strategy ("win-win") seeks to create value for both sides. Its focus is on each side's underlying interests, not their positions. You give the other side something it wants in exchange for something you want. You both gain in the process.

Business negotiators use the collaborative strategy. Business negotiations involve many different components of value and risk allocation, all of which can be traded against one another for an ultimately satisfactory outcome. The lesser opportunity for value and risk allocation in litigation settlement talks explains why most litigants begin with a competitive strategy.

The following are some collaborative tactics.

1) Be flexible.

Be flexible—the hallmark of a skilled collaborator. Know when to mount a tactical retreat and when to press for an important point. Be willing to reexamine decided issues, but don't feel obligated to make further concessions unless you also gain something.

2) Focus on process.

Process often translates into improved substance. Rearrange the mechanical steps of the negotiation to overcome impasse and deadlock and enhance problem-solving prospects. Typical examples: take a break in the negotiation; change the physical setting of the negotiation; or return the negotiation to the fact-finding stage.

3) Identify with others in similar circumstances.

This tactic might be termed the "transitive rule" of negotiation: argue that the other side has already treated similarly-situated X in a particular way, and they should treat you the same way. Defendants in multi-defendant suits often use this tactic when the plaintiff has settled favorably with one of them.

⇨ 3.5 The Avoidance Strategy

Try to ignore the entire dispute, or some specific issues, for at least some period of time. The avoider uses tactics to sidestep or postpone an issue or withdraw altogether from what the avoider perceives as a threatening situation.

The following are some avoidance tactics.

1) Negotiate money issue first.

If you prioritize money, insist that money be negotiated first. By fixing the money component of the settlement, you avoid discounts for the cash-worth of any non-money concessions.

2) Negotiate non-money issues first.

But if you wish to avoid paying money, address the non-money issues first. You can then value your non-money concessions and use those values to reduce the amount of money you will pay your adversary.

3) Refuse to combine negotiation of related disputes.

If you are litigating multiple related actions, refuse to negotiate the actions together if you determine that you are stronger in one case than another. You can thus avoid offsetting your strong cases with the other cases' weaknesses.

4) Walk out of negotiation.

If you become engaged in negotiations you are not ready for, walk out. You may state dissatisfaction with your adversary's proposals, but your goal is to defer discussions to a later time.

5) Withdraw an issue.

If you are not yet ready to address an issue, perhaps because it is too painful or simply not ripe for discussion, remove that issue from the negotiation, for at least some period of time.

6) Switch strategies.

You may decide to switch strategies if you feel you are making insufficient progress. As negotiations move forward and you want to encourage continued progress, you may abandon a competitive strategy for one of the cooperative strategies (accommodation, compromising, or collaborative). Or you may instead move to a more competitive strategy in response to the other side's competitive behavior.

In a word, the game of negotiation requires specific strategies and the fright tactics to implement that strategy. Your case and bargaining position will determine which negotiation strategy will work best for you: Competitive, when you must have what you want; Accommodation, when you have done wrong and want to settle quickly; Compromising, when expedience matters most; Collaborative, when you want to create a bigger pie; and Avoidance, when you are not yet ready to bargain.

Vocabulary

admonish/əd'mɔnɪʃ/v.

—to tell someone that they have done something wrong

e.g. His mother admonished him for eating too quickly.

—to advise someone to do something

e.g. Her teacher admonished her to work harder for her exams.

assertion/ə'sɜːʃən/n. [C]

—a statement saying that you strongly believe something to be true

e.g. I certainly don't agree with his assertion that men are better drivers than women.

v. assert

flip/flɪp/v.

—If you flip something, you turn it over quickly one or more times, and if something flips, it turns over quickly.

e.g. When one side is done, flip the pancake (over) to cook the other side.

I lost my place in my book when the pages flipped over in the wind.

You turn the television on by flipping the switch at the side.

furor/'fjʊrɔː(r)/n.

—a sudden excited or angry reaction to something by a lot of people

e.g. The government's decision to raise taxes has caused a great furor.

the furor over his latest film

extricate/'ekstrɪkeɪt/v.

—to remove or set free something with difficulty

e.g. It took hours to extricate the car from the sand.

I tried to extricate myself from the situation.

interlace/ˌɪntə'leɪs/v.

—to join different parts together to make a whole, especially by crossing one thing over another or fitting one part into another

e.g. In her latest book, she interlaces historical events with her own childhood memories.

nibble/'nɪbl/*v.*

—to eat something by taking a lot of small bites

e.g. Do you have some peanuts for us to nibble while the party warms up?

A mouse has nibbled through the computer cables.

Jenny's hamster's nibbled a hole in the sofa.

off-the-mark

—If something someone says or writes is off the mark, it is not correct.

e.g. His criticisms are way off the mark.

Bedini and Curzi were probably not far off the mark in their analysis.

pique/piːk/*n.* [U]

—a feeling of anger, especially caused by damage to your feeling of being proud of yourself

e.g. He stormed from the room in a fit of pique, shouting that he had been misunderstood.

poly

(*informal* for polytechnic)

proffer/'prɔfər/*v.*

—to offer something by holding it out, or to offer advice or an opinion

e.g. He shook the warmly proffered hand.

I didn't think it wise to proffer an opinion.

quantum/'kwɔntəm/*n.* [C]

— the smallest amount or unit of something, especially energy.

remuneration/rɪˌmjuːnərˈeɪʃən/*n.*

—(*formal*) payment for work or services

e.g. They demanded adequate remuneration for their work.

In return for some caretaking duties, we are offering a free flat and a small remuneration.

a remuneration package

syrupy/'sɪrəpi/*adj.*

—thick and sweet

—(*disapproving*) too good or kind or expressing feelings of love in a way that is not sincere

e.g. syrupy love songs

plea/pliː/*n.* [C]

—(*formal*) an urgent and emotional request

e.g. He made a plea for help/mercy.

whittle/'wɪtl/*v.*

—to form a piece of wood, etc. into a particular shape by cutting small pieces from it

e.g. An old sailor sat on the dockside, whittling a toy boat.

Exercises

1 Multiple Choice

1) Why do people choose stonewalling as a negotiation strategy?

A. Your counterparts use this strategy to force you into losing your poise.

B. The other side wants to get an irresistible bargain.

C. The other side wants to send a message that they are hard to deal with.

D. The other side doesn't have a reasonable agreement.

2) What is **TRUE** of dealing with stonewallers?

A. To make a deadline of signing the agreement.

B. To set a borderline between what's to do and not to.

C. To make your own offer.

D. To stop the negotiation right away.

3) Which of the following are negotiation tactics?

A. Stonewalling   B. Bullying

C. Intimidating   D. A good cop caper

4) How do you deal with lies in a negotiation?

A. Always look for objective data not subjective opinions.

B. Confront the lies directly.

C. Ask TOS for the figures on which their assumption is based on.

D. Present the facts yourself.

5) Which is **NOT** one of the negotiation strategies?

A. Accommodating strategy

B. Hardball strategy

C. Collaborating strategy

D. Compromising Agreement

6) Which of the following is an avoidance strategy?

A. Not to talk about disputes.

B. Put money as the priority.

C. Switch a strategy when you're in disadvantage.

D. Stop negotiating issues you're not ready for.

7) Which of the following is **NOT** true in international negotiation?

A. A collaborating strategy is a win-win strategy.

B. Never make a concession without obtaining one in return.

C. Gain your concessions "bit-by-bit" rather than all at once.

D. In a negotiation, always focus on the process not the disputes.

8) What is **TRUE** of individualist culture?

    A. Individualist culture rewards accomplishment.

    B. Individualist culture encourages autonomy of individuals.

    C. Individualist culture promotes interdependency of relationship between individuals.

    D. Individualist culture focus on relationship between a person and his community.

9) What is **TRUE** of negotiation strategies?

    A. Threaten to use your power but never actually use it.

    B. Prioritize the other party's dignity and don't make them lose face.

    C. Keep silent sometimes when you feel the negotiation is heading the direction to your disadvantage.

    D. Align your interests with your adversary's, see the facts from his or her perspective, and agree with his or her arguments.

10) What is **NOT** true of the following statements?

    A. If you feel you are losing an important issue, shift the discussions to a different issue before you concede.

    B. Always act like you have no background or training in negotiation and ask your adversary's help.

    C. Always understand the offer or demand of TOS, but be cautious to actually accept it.

    D. Emphasize you have better choices than settlement.

2 Interpretation of Terms

1) Negotiation Strategy

2) The "Good Samaritan" Negotiator

3) Stonewaller

4) Collaborating Strategy

5) Avoidance Strategy

6) High-context culture

_____

_____

7) Competitive Strategy

_____

_____

8) Accommodating Strategy

_____

_____

9) Compromising Strategy

_____

_____

10) Hardball Tactics

_____

_____

3 Case Analysis

Three companies, Australia company A, German company B and Chinese company C, are negotiating relevant issues about the talc investment among them. Company C, which wants to control the expert goods, cannot contribute cash to the cooperation, but wants to contribute human resource and intangible assets. Then company B and company C send their representatives to China to inspect the mines. And company C has its relevant personnel to keep their company. The whole agenda is considerately planned and well-prepared and meets the other two companies' demands in a limited period of time. All the three partners have discussed about the modes of cooperated investment on the initial preparation meeting and summary meeting.

A: Our company is one of the major companies specializing in talc production. Our talc goods have been enjoying a large market share in the global market, especially in terms of refined talc goods.

B: Company A has once invested in Chinese market but eventually failed. And now they are still dealing with some disputes. But they think China is pretty rich in natural resources and has great potential. And company A wants to find a partner to restart the business.

C: Well, you've made the right decision. And thanks for your company's appreciation of us. Then what is your idea about our cooperating pattern?

A: We'd like to find out a big company of good reputation and competence in China to jointly invest in the mines.

C: Our company is a talc-exporting company. No investment is permitted without assessment. But this industry is not the investment priority in line with our recent developing plans.

B: We understand your conditions, and company indeed has the intention of investing in Chinese market. But they haven't made their minds because of the last failure.

C: There is indeed certain imbalance in the investment of China. Developed regions and less developed regions coexist here. Once the capital is secured, things will change, especially the mining investment, which is closely connected with geological conditions. When mineral deposits stride over many villages and towns, issues concerning ownership will emerge. We've encountered such kind of problems in the past. And the foreign investors also need to handle problems in the following respects: earth-probing, investing partners, state policies, issues of humanities, business law and market, which will have certain influences upon both the cost and success of the investment.

A: What you have mentioned is exactly what we are worrying about. So we hope such a company like yours can solve these problems.

C: Our company is an cosmopolitan company and we will conduct business in accordance with international rules and regulations. As Chinese, we hold that the investment with foreign investors in line with international rules is of vital importance for China's economic development.

B: Your participation in the investment will be significant.

C: We've mentioned the problems your company may meet in such an investment, but we speak highly of your courage of this investment in China. As a Chinese partner, we'd like to help you as possible as we could. However, we will not contribute capital to it.

A: Such a contribution is significant for us all the same.

C: If you agree with the cooperating pattern we've put forward, please provide the work programs and define the cooperating relationship between us so as to pave the way for further cooperation.

B: We'll reply you in written form after we going back and having the whole discussion reported. Representatives of company A and B take company C's suggestion. Then company C has finally succeeded in the negotiation aiming at securing the control of export goods and avoiding capital input.

Questions for Case-analysis:

1. What strategies did company C employ in the negotiation?

2. How about the application of strategies of company A and B?

3. How do you judge the negotiation results of the three companies?

Reference

1. Fuller, George. The Negotiator's handbook, 1991.

2. Huang, Wei and Qian, Li. International Business Negotiations, Metallurgical Industry Press, 2012.

3. March, Bob. The Chinese Negotiator.

4. Ran, Dou. International Business Negotiation, Shanghai: Fu Dan University Press, 2007.

Chapter V　Ways of Breaking an Impasse in Negotiation

learning Objectives

After studying this chapter, you should be able to

- Identify the causes of an impasse in negotiation.

- Understand the strategies of breaking an impasse.

- Apply the strategies in negotiation simulation.

Case 1

In the middle of 1980s, Thailand, Denmark and the United States continually demanded to export raw chicken and cooked chicken products to Australia, and the Australian **Quarantine** & Inspection Service (AQIS) started to consider it in 1990. But the **Veterinarian** Association of Australia and the local livestock farmers were all worried that the imported meat would bring in Newcastle Disease and Infectious Brusal Disease (IBD), which might be a threat to Australian poultry industry and people's health. For the sake of safety, the AQIS started to make risk evaluation to the imported cooked chicken, but at the same time they put off the risk evaluation to the uncooked.

In the middle of 1995, the government allowed the importation of cooked chicken on principle, but the chicken must have been cooked at a particular temperature and for a certain length of time to make sure that the possible viruses have lost vitality. A series of experiments and researches were conducted by AQIS to determine these **parameters**. The outcome indicated that these two viruses were no longer active at 70 degrees centigrade for 190 minutes or at 80 degrees centigrade for 144 minutes. AQIS decided to adopt these criteria as a basis on which the "safe" cooking time and temperatures were determined. This decision was confronted with the opposition from Thailand. They complained that it would increase the cost and decrease the alimentation value of Thai cooked chicken so that they would be in a disadvantageous position in international competition.

To solve this dispute, AQIS entrusted the Central Veterinary Laboratory (CVL) of the UK with a test to examine the effect of IBD thermal treatment.

In 1997, the test was finished. It proved that temperature and time parameters did help reduce the vitality of Newcastle Disease virus, but it also revealed that these two parameters were not able to kill the two viruses completely. Then in November, 1997, Australia declared that cooked chicken was allowed to be imported from Thailand, Denmark and the US as long as it was treated in accordance with the criteria ranging from 70 degrees centigrade for 143 minutes to 89 degrees centigrade for 114 minutes. This decision again was met with opposition from Thai chicken exporters and Australian chicken industry. AQIS asked the British Central Veterinary Laboratory to conduct a second test.

The final results were submitted to AQIS in the middle of 1998. Base on these results, the lowest temperature and time parameters for killing the viruses were revised again to be cooked at a temperature ranging from 74 degrees centigrade to 80 degrees centigrade for 125 minutes.

(*Adapted from* International Business Negotiation *by Dou Ran*)

From this case we can see that, in the bargaining process, the two parties may keep their own point of view with strong attitude, and neither will intend to concede. What's more, their focuses of attention are on different things. If the Australian side had insisted on its own viewpoint and not try to make a new test, the negotiation about the imported chicken would have fallen into a deadlock at the very beginning; If the Australian side had held its own ground about the cooking time, or asked Thai side to change its cooking method, the negotiation would also have been quite likely to fall into an *impasse*.

In an international business negotiation, each side will stick to its own interests with strong attitude and not care whether the other side will understand or acknowledge its own intensions. If this occurs, the negotiation will fall into a dilemma. This kind of situation is the so-called "negotiation impasse". This doesn't necessarily mean there are unsolvable contradictions between the two parties or the negotiation will break down. It's usually due to both parties' subjective elements.

So at the time when the negotiators maintain their own benefits, they should also try to avoid the impasse resulting from some unimportant problems by sticking to a hard stance. That is to say, it's better not to fall into impasse. But once this happens, there is no need to fear about. The two parties should try to find the underlying causes of the conflict and actively search for ways out. Never give up a negotiation for a sudden impasse.

1   Causes of an Impasse

A negotiation might either make progress or stall depending on the choices the negotiators make. No matter how much planning and training has been undertaken, a negotiation rarely follows a prescribed path (negotiation is 'messy') and often reaches a point of deadlock. Why do negotiations stall? When they do, can they be turned around?

An impasse or stalemate can rise for a number of reasons, mainly including the following:

⇨ 1.1   Both parties are with widely divergent objectives.

In the above case, the reason why the two sides reached a final agreement was that although Australia was an importing country of chicken, it was not a major exporting country of Thailand's chicken. Australia noticed this point. Therefore, to avoid an impasse, the negotiating parties should find issues of common interests and then start with them to narrow the difference between the objectives of the two sides.

⇨ 1.2   One party mistakes firmness for rigidity and will not make concession.

In the previewed case, if the buyer had insisted on the opinion that "the cooking time was not in accordance with the requirement" or the seller had kept stressing the taste of the exported products, ignoring the quarantine and inspection, they might have led the negotiation to a deadlock.

⇨ 1.3 One party uses impasse as a deliberate tactic during a negotiation to force the other party to reconsider its position and make concessions.

Sometimes, in order to achieve the objective of a final success, negotiators may adopt the negotiation strategy of making trouble on purpose to throw the other party into confusion and forcing the other party to change its position and make concession.

However, if the other party recognizes this trick, it will drive the party using the trick into an embarrassing passive situation.

2 Strategies of Breaking an Impasse

There are many different methods you can use to keep the talks rolling when they start to stall. Sometimes it involves a bit of creativity in coming up with a different approach to skirt an impasse. On other occasions, you may be forced to take a hard line if your negotiating opponent does some last minute maneuvering in an attempt to extract additional concessions. The following sections discuss a variety of tactics that you can use to overcome some of the more common obstacles that frequently threaten to derail the negotiating process.

⇨ 2.1 Inventing Options When You Don't Have Any

You may participate in negotiations where both you and your opponent use up the slack in your respective negotiation positions, leaving no further room to *maneuver*. This is frequently the point where most unsuccessful deals go down the drain. However, when this sort of impasse occurs, it's worthwhile to stand back and explore other alternatives that can resolve and/or circumvent the impasse-creating problem.

It's always best if the two parties can work together in coming up with a solution. However, even if your adversary is reluctant to consider such a joint approach, it's worthwhile to put your own creativity to the test. On certain occasions, a relatively simple solution may come quickly to mind. At other times, the negotiations may actually break off when an impasse is reached, and will have to be resumed if (and when) you can come up with a satisfactory alternative.

The biggest drawback in exploring alternatives is often nothing more than the fact that both parties have been proceeding on one course without anticipating that an impasse would be reached. Consequently, neither party has given any thought as to how the conflict can be resolved. This is quite natural, since no matter how carefully you plan before negotiations *commence*, it's impossible to foresee all of the potential problems that may arise.

More often than not, the final hang-up is a seemingly *irreconcilable* difference of opinion on price. When this occurs look for compensating factors that would make an otherwise unreasonable price acceptable. For example:

- Stretching out delivery dates.
- Relaxing product and/or packaging *specifications*.
- Increasing or decreasing the quantity of items bought.
- The inclusion of an option provision for additional quantities.
- The inclusion of performance, cost, and/or delivery incentives.
- More favorable payment terms.

Sometimes the solution to the stalemate may involve a substantial restructuring in terms of the subject matter of the negotiation. In fact, what's finally agreed to may have little or no relationship to what's originally being negotiated.

On other occasions an added incentive that brings about agreement may be of little substantive value to you, but for one reason or another it has appeal to your counterpart. Therefore, it's useful to listen carefully for clues as to what's important to the other party while negotiations are taking place. Something said may have little significance at the time, but it may help later if an impasse does take place.

For instance, as negotiations are underway for the sale of a retail outlet, the present owner frequently *reminisces* about how he manages the business. When negotiations reach an impasse, the potential buyer, remembering this, offers to hire the owner as the manager of the business. This turns out to be the necessary ingredient that persuades the owner to go through with the transaction. In essence, when you hit an impasse, a solution may be at hand if you can come up with some form of creative compromise.

⇨ 2.2 Making Last-minute Concessions to Get Agreement

On occasion, negotiations may proceed to the point where the positions are relatively close, but your opponent still refuses to agree to a deal. More often than not, the other side is just holding out to see what sort of final concessions you will make. The purpose of this is for its use as a last minute deal *clincher*.

Nevertheless, you shouldn't just toss this concession on the table. You want the other side to think they have squeezed you dry, and have nothing left to concede. By doing that, the concession will appear to be a last ditch give-away in a final attempt to reach an agreement. Consequently, when you offer this final deal sweetener, emphasize that there will be no further concessions.

In fact, to add an air of finality, you may not want to make this final concession until after the negotiations have broken off because of a failure to reach agreement. This has the added advantage of the possibility the other side will contact you in the interim and accept your last offer, making the final concession unnecessary. However, you don't want to wait too long before contacting the other party, since they may reconcile themselves to the fact that the deal is dead and proceed with other alternatives. Whether or not you choose to let the talks be suspended temporarily is an evaluation you have to make based on your assessment of the risks involved.

In any event, when you do make a last-minute concession, combine it with an appeal to the ego of your counterpart. No one likes failure, and therefore if it's possible to reach an agreement, most people will do so, rather than walk away with nothing for their efforts. Let's look at how such a pitch can be made.

Case 2

Hank, a buyer for a large home improvement outlet, and Herb, a salesman for a building materials wholesaler, are negotiating a purchase order for building materials. After bargaining back and forth, they are $3,000 apart, with Hank a $98,500 and Herb at $101,500. The latter figure, is within Hank's upper limit of $105,000, while Herb will settle for an even $100,000. Of course, neither party knows the other still has room to move, and both negotiators have positioned themselves as having made their best offer.

The last minute concession

Hank: "Well, Herb, 1 guess that's it. It's too bad we got this close without making a deal."

Herb: "Hank. I've made you the best offer I can. You won't do any better elsewhere. "

Hank: "I think we can. It's a pretty competitive market. Frankly, I don't understand how you can walk away from a sale of this size. I'd hate to have to explain that to my boss. " (Hank is playing on Herb's emotions)

Herb: "It's all in a day's work. You win some and lose some. (He's sweating the deal, but projecting an image that he couldn't care less.) "

Hank: "I'll tell you what, Herb. I can't do it alone, but I'm willing to call Al (the outlet owner) to see if I can go to $100,000. However, there's no guarantee he'll go along with it, and I need your agreement that we have a deal before I call him."

Herb: "I'd like to, Hank, but I told you that I was stretching my limit when I offered you a price of $101,500."

Rank: "We're down to peanuts now, Herb. You don't want to throw a $100,000 sale down the drain for the sake of a lousy $1,500, do you? Not only that, but what about future business? You know how fast we're growing. "

Herb: "Grimacing says, 'Go ahead and make your call, but I'm telling you right now, if you can't get approval we won't be doing any more business."

Hank leaves the room and calls his wife to check what time they are meeting for dinner, returns and says, "We're in luck, Herb. I talked to Al and convinced him to approve the deal for $100,000."

(Adapted from The Negotiator's handbook *by George Fuller)*

Of course, you never know how these scenarios will play out. The important angle is to make your last minute concession appear as a last resort to *salvage* the agreement. If you do that, unless the other side truly finds your offer to be unacceptable, the odds are that an agreement can be reached.

⇨ 2.3   Shifting Gears to Reach Final Agreement

There are a number of factors that can stall a negotiation, all of which are controllable if you take necessary actions to counteract them. How you go about doing this is primarily determined by the type of bottleneck you face.

Sometimes a negotiation becomes bogged down when the parties are unable to agree on how to resolve a particular topic. When this happens, rather than senselessly arguing over the controversial issue, it helps to completely change the subject and talk about some other aspect of the deal. Frequently, as all of the other issues are ironed out one-by-one, it becomes easier to reconcile the differences on the previously insolvable item.

On other occasions, the problem is one or more members of the other negotiating team who are seemingly opposed to every position you take. When you're faced with this sort of dilemma, take the other negotiation team leader aside, and agree on the critical issues in private meetings. Sometimes this situation arises solely because too many people are participating on both sides on the table. Another alternative, if the circumstances are appropriate, is to break the meeting down into smaller fact-finding groups. Of course, if it's politically feasible, simply reduce the number of attendees at future sessions.

Once in a while you may encounter a situation where the other negotiator appears to be stalling for no apparent reason. Once this becomes obvious, diplomatically inquire as to what the holdup is. Actually, the problem may just be indecision on the part of the other person.

This can result from a reluctance to take the terms of the agreement to higher levels for approval. Perhaps the negotiator has a second-guessing boss, or maybe certain provisions are known to be objectionable to one or more people in the approval loop. In any event, if you can't establish the cause, get the negotiator's superiors involved. Whatever the reason and whenever negotiations start to stall, try to find a way to shift the focus toward more productive areas that will keep the discussion moving along toward a conclusion.

Case 3

In the 1980s, Yuan Geng, head of China Merchants in Shekou, Shenzhen, had a negotiation with the PPC Group from the U.S. about the establishment of a joint-venture for float glass production. During the negotiation, the two sides had a great disagreement over the issue that what percentage of the gross sales should be paid to the American side as royalty of patent right. The American side asked for 6% while Shekou countered 4%.

After a few rounds of bargaining, the price the American asked was lowered to 5% and Shekou dropped its price to 4.5%. Then, the two sides all refused to make concession any further. The negotiation reached an impasse.

During the adjournment, Yuan Geng attended the Luncheon held by the American side. When he was invited to deliver a speech, Yuan Geng deliberately diverted the topic and started talking about Chinese culture, "As early as thousands of years ago, our ancestors gave the Four Great Inventions—compass, papermaking, printing and gunpowder to the whole humanity without any condition. The later generation of these inventors have never complained that it was foolish not to ask for royalty payment. On the contrary, they highly praise their forefathers' great generosity and vision." His speech, bold, unrestrained but full of lofty sentiments, activated the atmosphere at the gathering. Then, he switched his speech, "In our cooperation with the PPC group, China Merchants did not intend to ask you to give your patent unconditionally, no, we only ask you to charge a reasonable price—as long as the price is reasonable, we won't pay you a penny less!"

This speech, though said out of the negotiation table, deeply moved the negotiators from PPC. After resuming the negotiation, PPC made a quick concession and agreed to close the deal with a 4.75% royalty payment for ten-year cooperation. The closing price of Shekou agreement was much lower than the similar agreements of other cities. From the agreement reached, compared with the initial asked price, the American side made a concession of 1.25% while the Chinese side only 0.75%.

(*Adapted from* International Business Negotiation *by Dou Ran*)

⇨ 2.4 Overcoming the Last-minute Offer Withdrawal

A not-so-pleasant event may sometimes occur as you reach what you think is the satisfactory conclusion of a negotiating session. It may be your misfortune to experience an unexpected withdrawal of an offer. This can take a variety of forms, but most of the time it happens when higher authority must approve an agreement. The buyer comes back to say something, such as, "I'm sorry, but I'll have to pull my offer of $500,000 off the table. I couldn't get approval topside." When this happens, it's easy to get irate, and respond with a "It's that or nothing" reply. However, that's not always either practical, or reasonable. From a practical standpoint, you may not have very satisfactory alternatives if the deal falls through. Therefore, a "take it or leave it" attitude can be a pretty risky position to avow. In addition, even in the absence of it being expressly stated, some form of review and/or approval is the norm rather than the exception with most agreements of any magnitude. Even where the person negotiating has the authority to make a commitment, this is often tempered by the need for a legal or administrative review of some kind.

Of course, before negotiations begin, the authority of your counterpart should be established. Nonetheless, the authority of the negotiator isn't always determined, and even when it is, it doesn't preclude someone from coming up with an argument such as, "We've agreed to a couple of provisions that run counter to our accounting system, so I'm forced to get this reviewed by top management."

In any event, your reaction shouldn't be reflexive anger at being **rebuked**, but instead should be based upon where your rejected offer was in relation to your negotiation objective. For instance, if you prepared a pre-negotiation position based on a most desirable selling price of $600,000, and a minimum price you would accept of $400,000, the withdrawal of a $500,000 offer by the other side still leaves you with room to maneuver.

Of course, any refusal of an offer should be challenged by insisting that the objecting party advise you directly as to why the offer is unacceptable. If the other negotiator won't comply, then refuse to negotiate further. This will force the other negotiator to get the objecting party involved, to break off negotiations, to back off and accept your offer. This is, of course, a general rule which will prevent you from being snookered by the old ploy of extracting additional concession by asserting that some higher level wouldn't approve the agreement. In fact, if the turned down offer was the maximum you would make, you usually have little recourse but to follow this approach.

However, there may be extenuating circumstances which don't justify forcing the issue to the point where negotiations break off. For instance, perhaps the objecting officials are at too high a level to expect their appearance at a working level negotiating session. Alternatively, perhaps you didn't really expect your offer to pass scrutiny at higher levels, and since you have plenty of room left to maneuver, and don't want to push things too far.

In any event, whether you force the issue to the extreme of threatening to walk away, or merely register mild disapproval, insist that the other negotiator make the next move. Generally, it will be some form of counteroffer and negotiations can continue from there. However, make it clear that whatever is finally agreed to will be subject to approval of higher authority on your side of the table, after—and only after—your counterpart has secured approval on his end. This gives you an advantage which can't logically be objected to, since it's only doing what the other side has already done.

⇨ 2.5 Taking Adjournment

As difficulties emerge between the parties, negotiators might feel the need to take an adjournment. This is often the first sign that a deadlock might occur and it needs careful handling. Prior preparation is important. A negotiator should think through what he might do if an adjournment is needed, perhaps determine to restate his main point to give himself time to regroup his thoughts. If negotiating as a team, they should establish clear signals on whether an adjournment should be called.

It is important that calling an adjournment does not give an impression of weakness. A negotiator should first foreshadow that she thinks an adjournment might be useful for both sides. If, for example, the negotiations have been getting heated, foreshadowing an adjournment may be all that is necessary to draw everyone's attention to what has been going on. When an adjournment occurs it is important to make sure that the other side has something to do during the break. Otherwise they will simply think you have adjourned to rethink your position and so will expect you to return with a concession. "I think it's getting near the time for an adjournment but before we do that, can we just summarize the areas of difference we still need to address…" or "we'll take time out to think about what options we might have on the price structure, but can you give some thought to the pattern of deliveries, because that's really important to us…" When the negotiations resume there would then be two items for discussion, not just one.

3   Six Approaches for Getting through to the Decision Maker

Occasionally, you may find yourself facing a negotiator who isn't being very cooperative in moving the negotiations along. The reasons for this can vary from a deliberate attempt to slow things down, as when your counterpart knows you're facing a deadline, to the simple misfortune of dealing with an indecisive person. Whatever the cause, you may inevitably have to take some form of action to keep things moving along. If so, one or more of the following tactics may be helpful in this regard.

- The simplest action you can take is to tactfully suggest that since the discussions appear to be going nowhere, perhaps they should be moved to a higher level for resolution. Naturally, before doing this, make certain that your superiors are thoroughly briefed on the negotiations that have taken place. This tactic will work well when you are dealing with an indecisive individual, who may be more than happy to be taken off the decision making hook.

- If you think the other negotiator may not be receptive to a suggestion on getting superiors involved, look for a justifiable reason during negotiations. For example, if the other negotiator insists that a boss won't buy a certain provision you're advocating, at that point insist that the boss be brought into the *loop*.

- Bring your own boss into the negotiation meetings. The other negotiator may feel compelled to bring someone at an equivalent level to the talks.

- Have your boss contact the other negotiator's superiors on an informal basis such as, "Just wanted to let you know how things are going."

- Force the issue from the very top of your organization to the highest level on the other side. This can be done by expressing a need for urgency such as, "I certainly hope this can be wrapped up tomorrow." In this way pressure will immediately flow through the chain of command on the other side. As a result, either your previously indecisive counterpart will start making some fast decisions, or someone who can will appear on the scene.

- Go over the other negotiator's head yourself. This can create tension, so try to do it in such a way that it doesn't appear to be deliberate. Any form of excuse that will get you talking to the other person's boss will do the trick.

4 Establishing Deadlines to Move a Deal Along

One obvious way to force the issue when negotiations start to stall out is to impose a deadline for the deal to be concluded. Naturally, if you're just bluffing, and your opponent calls the bluff, you either have to break off negotiations, or telegraph that it was a ploy by continuing to negotiate past your stated deadline. For this reason, there's often some reluctance to use this as a tactic.

Of course, if a deadline passes, and you don't follow through by breaking off negotiations, your credibility is weakened. Therefore, if you throw down this sort of a gauntlet, it's generally preferable to carry out your threat assuming that's the best available course of action at the time. However, if for one reason or another you continue to negotiate, that doesn't mean you can't carry out your threat at some future point in time.

In fact, if you're involved in a series of deadline threats that pass, when you ultimately carry one out, it can have a significant impact. For example, when a deadline threat is made, the other side will often make some sort of promise to keep you from acting on your threat. Then, once the deadline has passed, they will quickly backtrack from this commitment. This type of maneuvering can happen several times before you find yourself forced to take drastic action.

Whenever you find yourself in a position where carrying out some form of deadline threat is necessary, try to do it in such a way that the door is left ajar for the other side to contact you. For instance, saying, "Call me by nine tonight if you want to meet tomorrow." is a relatively mild alternative compared with stating, "This deal is dead, if we don't wrap it up today." The former also presents an opportunity for you to reestablish contact if you don't hear from your counterpart.

Vocabulary

clincher/ˈklɪntʃə(r)/n. (*usually singular*)

—something which helps someone make a decision

e.g. It was the offer of a large discount on the TV that was the real clincher.

commence/kəˈmens/v.

—(*formal*) to begin something

e.g. We will commence building work in August of next year.

Unfortunately, he commenced speaking before all the guests had finished eating.

impasse/ˈæmpɑːs/n.

—a situation in which further development is impossible

e.g. The dispute had reached an impasse, as neither side would compromise.

irreconcilable/ˌɪrekənˈsaɪləbl/adj.

—impossible to find agreement between or with; to deal with:

e.g. irreconcilable differences of opinion

They have become irreconcilable, with both sides refusing to compromise any further.

maneuver/məˈnuːvə(r)/*n.*

—a movement or set of movements performed with skill and care

e.g. Reversing round a corner is one of the maneuvers you are required to perform in a driving test.

loop/luːp/*n.*

—the curved shape made when something long and thin, such as a piece of string, bends until one part of it nearly touches or crosses another part of it

e.g. belt loops

a loop of string

the loop of the river

in/on a loop

e.g. If something runs in a loop, or is on a loop, it runs continuously, so that the same things are repeated again and again.

e.g. The tape ran in a continuous loop, repeating the same songs over and over.

parameter /pəˈræmɪtə(r)/*n.* (*usually plural*)

—a set of facts or a fixed limit which establishes or limits a fixed limit which establishes or limits how something can or must happen or be done

e.g. The researchers must keep within the parameters of the experiment.

quarantine /ˈkwɒrəntiːn/*n.*

—a period of time during which an animal or a person that might have a disease is kept away from other animals or people so that the disease cannot spread

e.g. The horse had to spend several months in quarantine when it reached Britain.specification

rebuke/rɪˈbjuːk/*v.*

—(*formal*) to speak angrily to someone because you disapprove of what they have said or done

e.g. I was rebuked by my manager for being late.

n.

e.g. He received a stern rebuke from the manager.

salvage/ˈsælvɪdʒ/*v.*

—to save goods from damage or destruction, especially from a ship that has sunk or been damaged or a building that has been damaged by a fire or a flood

e.g. gold coins salvaged from a shipwreck

After the fire, there wasn't much furniture left worth salvaging.

—to try to make a bad situation better

e.g. It was a desperate attempt to salvage the situation.

After the fraud scandal he had to make great efforts to salvage his reputation.

n.

e.g. They mounted a salvage operation after the fire.

salvageable /ˈsælvɪdʒəbl/ *adj.*

e.g. There is nothing that is salvageable in the building—we have lost everything.

veterinarian/ˌvetərɪˈneərɪən/ *n.*

—(*formal*) for vet

vet *n.*

—a person with a medical degree trained to take care of the health of animals

vicious/ˈvɪʃəs/ *adj.*

—violent and cruel (describing people or actions that show an intention or wish to hurt someone or something very badly)

e.g. a vicious thug

The police said that this was one of the most vicious attacks they'd ever seen.

—full of hatred and anger (describing an object, condition or remark that causes great physical or emotional pain)

e.g. a collection of vicious medieval torture instruments

viciously *adv.* viciousness *n.*

Exercises

1 Multiple Choice

1) What is **NOT** the reason for an impasse in a negotiation?

    A. One party will not make any concession.

    B. The objectives of two parties are widely divergent.

    C. One party uses the impasse as a negotiation strategy.

    D. Two parties have no intention of reaching an agreement.

2) What is the strategy to break off an impasse?

    A. Being creative in making solutions.

    B. Offering more favorable payment terms.

    C. Making concessions.

    D. Setting different objectives.

3) What is **NOT** true of Characteristics of Negotiation?

    A. Negotiation is a process.

    B. One negotiation needs at least two parties.

    C. Negotiation involves divergence in interests and goals for participants.

    D. Negotiation will result in an agreement.

2 Interpretation of Terms

1) Impasse

_____

_____

2) Approaches to reach the decision

_____

_____

3) Last-minute Concession

_____

_____

3 Case Analysis

Case 1

From the first half year of 1984, representatives of China and SLA, a Tunis company, have been negotiating on the setup of a fertilizer factory in China. After several rounds, the two sides decide to locate the factory on Qin Huang Dao Harbor which can provide preferential conditions. In October, hearing the business, Kuwait Petrol Co. intends to participate into the project. The negotiation becomes the tripart round. In one of the negotiation rounds with three parties together, Kuwait sends out their president as their lead representative. The president, hearing the preparation work having been done by China and Tunis, definitely says that all the previous work is meaningless and the construction work must be done from the very beginning.

Hearing the statement, not only China, but Tunis feels confused and surprised. It should be noted that China and Tunis have used 20 chemical industrial specialists and invested more than 300 thousand USD on the feasibility research report during 3 months. It would make no sense to make complete negation on previous work. Even though, China and Tunis dare not to confute the president. It turns out that the president is of high esteem in the industry and of great importance only next to the minister of petrol in Kuwait. Besides, the president is the chairman of International Organization of Chemical Fertilizer Industry. His holding companies own a large amount of shares in many companies in Tunis. For these reasons, China and Tunis cannot directly make any negative comments.

The local mayor, a member of China's negotiation team, is considering breaking the deadlock made by the Kuwait president. The requirements of the president cannot be accepted by China and Tunis. Even though the president is an authority, the mayor still exceeds his endurance. The mayor stands up and declares: "I, on behalf of the local government, declare here: we have arranged for the project a place with a lot of geographical preferences near the harbor. In order to show our sincerity on the friendship with you, we denied many other joint ventures' application for the place. If, according to the proposal of the president, the project will be delayed, then we will give this place to others! Excuse me. I should now leave the negotiation for other matters. I am waiting for your negotiation results in the afternoon!"

Then this local governmental representative walks out of the room. A local government official runs after the mayor and tries to persuade the mayor to come back. The mayor smiles and whispers to the official: "I will not leave here, I am now taking a rest in another room. I can promise that there must be something interesting next." Half an hour later, a department director excitedly finds the mayor: "You make a smart deal. The situation changes abruptly. That president now is looking forward to seeing you in the negotiation table and strongly requires taking that place." When the mayor again sits back to the table, the negotiation goes smoothly. The president makes no more negation, and the three sides reach the agreement.

Questions for Case-analysis:

1. What kind of negotiation strategies does the Chinese mayor use?
2. What risks are involved in this strategy?

Case 2

Konosuke Matsushita, former president of the Japanese Panasonic Corporation (Matsushita Electric Industrial Co., Ltd), was a businessman full of great wisdom. Under his leadership, Panasonic has gradually developed into a world famous electric manufacturer. Once, Mr. Matsushita negotiated with a company in Europe. As the counter party was a well-known local company, they could not help but put on airs. To maintain one's own interests, neither of the two companies was willing to make concessions. As the negotiation proceeded, they bargained intensely and loudly with each other, and even slapped on the table and stamped their feet. The atmosphere was unusually tense. Mr. Matsushita had to propose to adjourn the negotiation for a while and resume it after lunch. After the rest and reorganization at noon, Mr. Matsushita thought over the morning's confrontation carefully, and found that it was unwise to bargain in such a manner and instead of gaining more he would lose the deal. Thus, he thought about changing his negotiation strategy while the other side was not ready to make any concession at all relying on the fact that they had ideal opportunity, favorable terrain and friendly people. When the negotiation was restarted, Mr. Matsushita spoke first. The negotiators from the counter party had no expression on the face, showing no sign of reaction. Mr. Matsushita did not talk about the deal, and instead, he talked about the relationship between science and humankind. He said:" Just now, I went to the Science Museum in your city at noon break. There, I saw a quantum model. Human's pioneering endeavor in scientific research does deserve our admiration! It is said that your rocket Apollo III will fly to the moon again. Such level of man's wisdom and science development should be contributed to the great humankind." The counter party thought that Mr. Matsushita was *chitchatting*, drifting away from the negotiation point. They looked less nervous and more relaxed. Mr. Matsushita went on: "However, the relationship between human beings has not progressed as much as science. People often do not have a sense of confidence in each other. They hate each other and have quarrels with each other. *Vicious* incidents like wars and riots frequently happened in the streets, in all parts of the world. Crowds of people rub shoulders with each other, which appears to be a peaceful image. In reality, people have hideous fights with each other in their innermost world." He paused for a while and found that more and more members of the counter party paid attention to his words. Then, he said: "Well, why couldn't the relationship between human beings become more civilized and more progressive? I think that there should be trust between people and attacks on each other for the mistakes and shortcomings should be avoided. People should have mutual understanding and strive hand in hand for the common cause of the humankind. The rapid development of science and the backwardness of human spiritual civilization may lead to greater disasters. For example, people may kill each other with the bullets they make. During the World War II, Japan suffered from the disaster caused by the atomic bombardment, did she?"

At that very moment, people's attention has been attracted by Konosuke Matsushita's speech. Silence overwhelmed the negotiation room. Every one was in deep thought. Then Matsushita switched the topic to the major issues of negotiation. The atmosphere has changed, totally different from that in the morning, and the two sides became close partners, who would "cooperate for the common cause of human being." At last, the European company accepted the conditions proposed by Matsushita. The two parties reached an agreement quickly. So it is evident that when the negotiating parties face a deadlock, it is a good solution for them to change the topic.

(*Adapted from* International Business Negotiation *by Dou Ran*)

Questions for Case-analysis:

1. What's the purpose of using adjournment in the negotiation?
2. Please summarize the ways to break an impasse applied in this case.

Reference

Ran, Dou. International Business Negotiation, Shanghai: Fu Dan University Press, 2007.

Chapter VI   Communication Skills in International

Business Negotiation

Learning Objectives

After studying this chapter, you should be able to

• Identify the four styles of communication.

• Develop your communication style.

• Master non-verbal communication skills.

• Know cultural differences in Style Preferences.

1 Introduction

Case 1

During the CEBIT (Center for Office and Information Technology) exhibition held in Hannover, an American importer in the line of electronics wanted to purchase 3,000 sets of pocket control monitors of high resolution that can be used in office buildings and hotels. After making comparisons, he took a fancy to the color control monitors manufactured by the Korean G Company. This veteran American businessman did not express his purchase intention directly, but inquired about the prices of other products and then he asked casually, "How much is this control monitor?" The representative from G Company did not answer his question directly, but said with a smile, "It depends on how many sets you will purchase! This kind of control monitor is a newly-developed product of our company. It not only handles color pictures, but also has the highest resolution among all the control monitors." "If I buy 300 sets, how much is it per set?" asked the American businessman. The representative of G Company said it would be $4,990. The American businessman then asked, "What if I buy 3,000 sets?" The representative of G Company said, maintaining his composure, "You can enjoy a discount if you buy a large number of our products, and the lowest discount should be 10% off." 'What if I buy 10,000 or 20,000 sets?" the representative answered, "15% off at the most." The American representative shook his head with disappointment, got up and intended to move to another exhibition stand. Suddenly he turned round and asked, "What about 30% off?" The representative of G Company said calmly and meaningfully, "15% off is the largest discount I can give you! But I can give a price list to look at." The American businessman studied the price list printed out from the computer and found that the prices decreased with the increase of the purchase quantity, but for any quantity over 10,000 sets the discount was set at 15%. From this, the American businessman estimated the production cost, the distribution of the equipment and R&D cost, production capacity and profit margin, and finally he decided to buy 3,000 sets of control monitors from G Company. Through measured and skillful questioning, answering and persuasion, a deal was finally made.

(*Adapted from* International Business Negotiation *by Dou Ran*)

If preparation is one of the keys to ensuring success in a negotiation, then another equally important key is the ability to communicate effectively, not just to understand and influence the other party in the negotiation, but also to communicate effectively with all of the other stakeholders who have an interest in the outcome of the negotiation. In this chapter, the communication styles that are essential to the successful completion of the interaction phase of a negotiation are outlined.

The definition of a win-win negotiation—"an interactive process where two or more parties with common and conflicting interests come together to exchange ideas and propositions in order to reach an agreement where they all leave with a desirable result, after fully taking into account each other's interests"—confirms the importance of communication in a negotiation. Some negotiations may take place remotely and via technology where there is no face-to-face interaction and sometimes no real time communication, but there are still interaction and communication—and it could be argued that these remote environments are fraught with more communication difficulties, so require greater skill and ability.

2　Four Styles of Communication

If you observe how people interact with you and with each other, you will notice different styles of communication. There are four styles of communication.

⇨ 2.1　Direct Communication

Some people are very direct, to the point and positive in asserting their wishes and requirements. They let others know what is wanted from them and are quick to tell others when they are pleased or dissatisfied. They use their authority to get others to do what is wanted, getting people to agree with their plans and proposals and then follow up to make sure that people carry out their agreements. They have strength in bargaining and doing deals with others all the time to get things done.

⇨ 2.2　Measured and Systematic Communication

Other people follow a more measured and systematic approach. They produce detailed and comprehensive proposals for dealing with problems, presenting the logic behind ideas and using facts, arguments and opinions to support their position. They are quick to grasp the strengths and weaknesses in an argument and to see and articulate the logical connections between different aspects of a complex situation. They are unemotional and follow a very logical and rational approach in their communication.

⇨ 2.3　Open Communication

Then there are the people who openly and readily admit to not having all of the answers. They will spend time and listen attentively to the ideas and feelings of others, actively showing interest in others' contributions and trying to understand different points of view. They are willing to be influenced by others whilst also pursuing their own objectives. They appreciate and support others' ideas and accomplishments and they make sure everyone is heard before a decision is made. This group of people are renowned for building powerful and strong relationships by showing trust in others and helping to bring out the best in them.

➪ 2.4 **Emotional Communication**

Finally, you will see the group of people who appeal to the emotions and ideals of others through the use of forceful and colorful words and images. They demonstrate an enthusiasm for the future which is contagious. They bring people together by articulating a vision of future possibilities. They see the exciting potential in an idea or situation and can communicate that excitement to others. They are adept at getting others to see the values, hopes and aspirations which they have in common and build these common values into a shared sense of loyalty and commitment.

That is not to say that people only use one of these communication styles. Most of us use a mix of these styles, though we tend to have a preference for using one or two of them more than others. These are styles that we find easy to use; styles that get us results most of the time; styles that we have been taught to use through school and training; styles that fit the cultures we live and work in; and styles that fit our values and beliefs.

So someone who has learned to think and act in a logical and rational way and is working in an organization that is practical and systematic in its approach is likely to use a rational approach to communicate, basing their interactions on facts, rules, procedures and logical argument. By contrast, someone who has learned to value and care about people and works in an organization that is based on teamwork, self development and respect for the worth of the individual is likely to use a more people-oriented approach, interacting more with feelings and emotions and seeking to understand.

If someone has strong tendencies in these directions, they will find it difficult to communicate effectively with someone from an opposite preference and therefore influence them. On the other hand, they will work effectively with people who share their mindset. In a tight line management structure, different groups may exhibit similar characteristics—they have similar cultures and will have recruited people with traits that tend to fit. However, modern organizations and matrix/project structures encourage more cross-functional dialogues and the opportunity for different preferences and cultures to clash.

So the more we can develop flexibility and adapt our style to meet the preference of the other party, the greater will be our capacity to communicate effectively and exert influence.

In the negotiation arena, the effective use of all the four communication styles is essential in order to successfully complete a negotiation. So negotiators need to build the competence and confidence to use all the styles and to become adept at moving flexibly between them.

There are two main dimensions of behaviors in communication: the degree to which we are directive, and the degree to which we are responsive. People who are directive tend to be seen as more forceful and assertive, taking control, making quick decisions and taking more risks. People who are responsive will be sensitive to, and willing to share emotions and feelings, appear more friendly and are concerned about relationships. There are no absolutes in these two dimensions, as we are all directive and responsive to some extent, but we all have preferences. Our influence patterns can thus be broken down into four styles (see Figure 6.1).

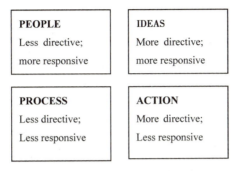

PEOPLE
Less directive;
more responsive

IDEAS
More directive;
more responsive

PROCESS
Less directive;
Less responsive

ACTION
More directive;
Less responsive

Figure 6.1   **The Four Communication Styles**

(Source: *Negotiations: How To Achieve Win-win Outcome*, by Geof Cox, FT Publications, 2012)

A note on the names of the four communication styles

The name of the style is used to describe a way of communicating. Do not take the names too literally. For instance, using the word "idea" in conversation does not mean the person is using the ideas style. You can present an "idea" in any of the four styles. Similarly, a low preference for the people style does not mean you dislike people, just that you use the people style less.

3   Developing Your Communication Style

Knowing your own preferred style and that of others helps you to know your strengths and areas for development. Take notice of how you communicate with others and how they communicate with you.

What style do they typically adopt? What style do you typically apply? What style do others employ? Which styles have a positive impact on you? Which style do you find more challenging when others use them? Which styles do you find easy? Which styles do you find difficult?

In a negotiation each of the styles is needed, so we need to develop flexibility to use each style, and also to respond positively to each one. We need to identify those areas where working in partnership with other people in a negotiation team, and where the strengths and weaknesses of each member complement the others. That would be particularly beneficial.

The four communication styles, their behaviors and outcomes are summarized and discussed in detail below.

⇨ 3.1 Action style

Table 6.1

Description	People talk about:	People are
Action-oriented mind-set is fundamentally geared to changing things, improving existing situations, translating ideas into actions, being effective, getting things down, moving ahead and achieving good results. Preferred type of Agreement: deal. Preferred style of Discourse: bargaining.	Results Objectives Performance Deals Challenges Moving ahead Responsibility Achievements Change Decisions	Pragmatic Direct Impatient Decisive Quick Energetic Challenging

Action people are task-oriented, keen to get things done, and decisive and direct (more directive and less responsive). They use energy that is moving against others, and can therefore be seen as forceful, pushy and aggressive if they overuse or misuse the approach.

Underuse of this style means that you will not be able to get things done quickly and may miss deadlines. The people you negotiate with may not have the clarity about what precisely you want from them and by when. So agreements will not be clear and may be open to misinter-pretation. Overusing the style, or not using both of the actions, can be perceived as arrogant, aggressive and dictatorial—you are only interested in getting what you want and not giving anything in return.

Effective use of the style comes from balancing the two behaviors—demanding and exch-anging. The outcome is a deal.

"If you agree to do X for me, I will do Y for you."

"In return for the car, I will give you the money."

Action style depends on the exchange you can make to influence someone to do something for you. The exchange can be obvious and material, based on the resources, position or information you have: a tip, promotion, contract, salary increase, gifts, information that the other party needs. Exchanges can also be less obvious and not material, based more on personal power: approval, status, attention, praise, inclusion, time. These latters and psychological exchanges are often more powerful and longer lasting than material ones.

The exchange backs up the demand that we are making. It has to be something that the giver has to offer, something that the receiver desires and considers of sufficient value to balance the demand made. The critical point for the influencer is that it is the perception of value and balance in the eyes of the receiver which is important, not the giver's idea of what is appropriate. Thus something of low cost to the giver, like praise, can be viewed as of immense value by the receiver.

In a negotiation, you need to pull together the elements of the agreement that have been discussed and make a clear statement of the exchanges and demands from both sides that make the deal. You may also need to make consequences very clear during the negotiation when the action style could be usefully applied.

⇨ 3.2   Process Style

Table 6.2

Description	People talk about	People are
The process-oriented mindset is characterized by the need to know, be factual, understand, organize, structure, set up strategies, tactics, establish rules, regulations , systems and manage. Preferred type of agreement: logical solution. Preferred style of discourse: debate.	Facts Details Observations Procedures Planning Proof Organizing Controlling Testing Analysis	Systematic Logical Factual Verbose Unemotional Cautious Patient

Process-style people also use a pushing type of energy, but are less directive and forceful, relying more on the logical and rational nature of their argument, moving at the other party in order to reach a solution. Overuse or misuse of this style results in inflexible sets of rules and procedures, bureaucracy and verbosity. It is a favorite style of communication for many people and for business, especially as the first resort.

The process style uses logical reasoning and debate in order to create structure in data and facts, and by analysis finds the best solution to the problem or situation being faced. It is an essential style in a negotiation to set out the facts and details involved from both sides, and to put together potential propositions for logically solving the issue.

Overuse or an imbalance of the two actions in this style can lead to bureaucracy, long and boring meetings, and slavish following of procedure and rules—even when it is clear that the procedure is not effective. That makes negotiations tiresome for both sides. It is a favorite style of many organizations as it allows some degree of participation in decision-making but it is not an appropriate style to use if a quick decision is needed or where you are not open to other options.

The effective use of the style comes from balancing the two behaviors—proposing and reasoning. The outcome is a solution.

"The conclusion from the analysis of the data suggests that we take this course of action."

"Weighing up the arguments on both sides, there is nothing to be gained from taking immediate action as the decision deadline is not until the end of the financial year, and there is no penalty for delaying the decision. Delaying the decision and gathering more data seem to be the best solution."

The reasoning backing up the proposal needs to be valid and based on facts and logic. It is the weight of argument which influences, not in quantity but in quality. Reasoning that is geared towards the receiver, not the influencer has the most impact. A strong reason for doing something from one perspective may hold no weight for the other person. So thinking in terms of benefits and what is important to the receiver is vital for success.

Quantity of argument is attractive, but ineffective. It is often perceived as trying to wear down the other party into submission through the sheer weight of data and argument. It also tends toward the verbose, so you need to control the urge to continue talking or writing so that you don't find yourself snatching defeat from the jaws of victory by having to defend a poorly researched piece of data or rationale which was not necessary. With proper preparation, a good proposal should not need more than two or three reasons to back it up.

➪ 3.3 People Style

Table 6.3

Description	People talk about	People are
The people-oriented mindset is characterized by men and women who care about people, have a strong drive towards people's needs, rights, communication, understanding each other, team work, ethics, synergy, feelings and emotions. Preferred type of agreement: empathy. Preferred style of discourse: understanding.	People Needs Self-development Sensitivity Relationships Motivations Beliefs Values Awareness Cooperation Communications Feelings Team spirit Understanding	Spontaneous Empathetic Warm Emotional Perceptive Subjective Sensitive

The people style adopts listening and sharing to help people to build understanding. The energy used is moving with, using the energy of the other person in a positive way to develop a relationship, not to manipulate or dominate. The mindset of people orientation is characterized by a strong desire towards teamwork, synergy, communication and the needs of others. It is empathetic and sensitive.

People style is the only style that gathers information, so it is very useful to help find out what values and desires the other party has which can then be used as possible exchanges, reasons or connections. It therefore has a strong strategic use. It also builds relationships with others through developing deeper understanding of each other. It is therefore a key style to be used for a negotiation where relationship and trust are critical.

This style does take up more time than any of the other styles, both to build rapport and to listen effectively. But if deeper insight into the thinking of the other person is important, then it is time and effort that are well spent.

The effective use of the people style, as with all of the other styles, comes from balancing the two behaviors—sharing and listening. The outcome is understanding.

"I'm confused by the aims of this project and I need your help to understand what 1 need to focus on (sharing) ... If I hear you correctly, your priority is that we must keep to the time deadlines at all cost. Could you expand on the importance of keeping to time so I can understand why it is more important than keeping to the specification (listening)?"

Sharing allows you to open up to the other party and show that you are willing to disclose information and feelings. This builds trust and gives the other party the confidence to reciprocate. Sharing too much will tend to have the opposite effect and erode trust as people will fell "dumped" upon. Listening too much, or listening selectively, will also build mistrust and the feeling of being manipulated, so it is important to balance sharing with listening, *Empathetic* listening is listening with the intent to understand. It is the highest level of listening, the others being:

- ignoring: staying quiet but not paying any attention to what the person is saying;
- pretending: using verbal or non-verbal clues but not really listening;
- selective: hearing only certain parts of what the person is saying—usually those parts we agree with;
- attentive: actively paying attention and focusing on understanding what is being said.

Empathetic listening is listening to really understand the other person's frame of reference—to see and feel the world as they do. (Covey, 1989)

Tips for listening empathetically:

- Be quiet: Stop talking to yourself in your head (e.g. rehearsing your next question) as well. If the other person stops talking, count to three before saying anything. If they continue talking, keep quiet.
- Be attentive: Focus all your attention on the other person. Use your voice tone, postures and eye contact to let the other know that you are paying attention.
- Suspend judgment: Clear your mind of your own thoughts. Do not make judgments based on your own views or perceptions. Seek to understand the other person's views and perceptions before expressing your own.
- Understanding is not necessarily agreeing: The objective is to understand, not to agree. Understanding the other person does not mean you are forced to agree with them. You can still hold your own opinion. You don't need to defend your ideas or position in order to understand the other person's.
- Paraphrase and summarize frequently: Summarize the message in your own words. Check with the other person that you have heard what they meant to say—that you have got the right message. Doing this much more frequently than you think is necessary—it keeps you on track and demonstrates your interest and understanding. Always paraphrase before asking a question—it should flow naturally. If the question you were planning does not

flow, then don't ask it!

- Listen to feelings: Share your own feelings. Pay attention to the signals (both verbal and non-verbal) that indicate what the other person might be feeling. Summarize these and check to see if you have guessed correctly.
- Encourage possibilities: Use open questions to encourage the other person to consider other possibilities. Do not give advice or state your own opinions.

⇨ 3.4 Idea Style

Table 6.4

Description	People talk about:	People are
Ideas-oriented people handle the world in terms of concepts, abstractions, theories and models. They value imagination, innovation and creativity very much. They are future oriented. Preferred type of agreement: shared vision. Preferred style of discourse: inspire.	Concepts Innovation Creativity Potential Opportunities Possibilities Grand designs Improving Interdependence What's new in the field Alternatives New methods	Imaginative Charismatic Difficult to understand Ego centered Unrealistic Creative Full of ideas Provocative

Idea-oriented people use their responsiveness to connect with other people's values and beliefs and build exciting possibilities for the future. Outcomes of cooperation are achieved through moving together with the people they are trying to influence. This style is dependent on your personal ability to take the lead in putting forward your vision in an inspiring way. It is a style that does not try to influence by pushing people into action, but by attracting or pulling them.

The idea style combines high responsiveness with high direction. It bases its influence on building strong connections with people and then directing that latent energy into a direction—a vision. It relies on generating enthusiasm and attracting people with common ground to a common vision of what might be. In that sense it is quite idealistic, so the more far-sighted the vision, the deeper the connection has to be with the other party(ies) to make sure that they come with you. It is not worth having a great vision if people are not attracted to it and don't "buy in". Equally, having a great connection with people is a wasted opportunity if that energy is not directed into a positive direction.

In a negotiation arena, the idea style is useful to create a positive climate of cooperation, a vision of successful outcomes and a sense of common ground and connection. The idea style builds cooperation.

4   Non-verbal Communication

Consider this scene in a typical Singapore office: an American expatriate concludes his presentation of the coming year's sales program with a typical American expression of gung-ho enthusiasm—perhaps making a fist and hitting it against the open palm of his other hand. Initially, his staff is excited by his line-up of concepts and acknowledges this by continuously nodding their heads during his presentation, a signal, he supposes, that he has effected a coup. But shortly after he hits his fist in his other palm, he notices how the faces of his team members fall, and this is accompanied by a mysterious silence. Then they simply walk out of the conference room. (Craig, 1979)

Scenes like this, typical for workers and executives, thrust them into an intercultural setting without preparation. If the American executive had been briefed beforehand, he would have been spared the embarrassment he has brought upon himself by simply not knowing that he has just made an insulting gesture before his entire staff. Miscommunication can be extremely costly; narrow-minded ethnocentric minds are unforgiving; and an untimely faux pas is difficult to recover.

Non-verbal communication is simply communication without words. At the extreme, a mime artist or ballet dancer is conveying the whole meaning through non-verbal communication. But in most situations, non-verbal communication is an amplifier of—or detractor from— the spoken word.

The whole *gambit* of non-verbal communication includes gestures and touches, facial expressions, eye contact, body language, posture, dress, clothing, spatial distance, physical appearance, and the rhythm, intonation, stress and tone of voice.

The international communication is complex especially when it's nonverbal. Here we explore in depth "international body language"—i.e., the social rules governing nonverbal communication in different societies. We'll look at faces, eyes, touching and hand and other body gestures; office layouts; how to tell when TOS(the other side) is lying to you; and how to influence TOS with your body language. Then we give some guidelines on how to make you a better judge of what is actually on TOS's mind, with them not knowing that you've had this valuable information.

Maybe you have already known most of the fundamentals, for if you're an experienced negotiator, you do have some knowledge of body language, and you can sense already if TOS is accepting or rejecting you. You might even be able to figure out when TOS is lying to you. But when at abroad or talking to a foreigner in your own country, you may not necessarily have this facility. More often than not, you are unfamiliar with the body language of foreigners, even if many gestures mean the same in most countries. In the absence of this familiarity, you find yourself relying heavily—perhaps more than is justified—on what the foreigners are saying. But if you are unfamiliar with the language, you will fumble over patches of data and information and proceed blindly.

There are a few areas in which people of different cultures overlap in their understanding and use of nonverbal communication. Many researchers have found that most people understand the expressions we have on our faces when we're sad, happy, angry, surprised or afraid; the basic emotions aroused by situations that result in these facial expressions are pretty much universal. Cultures, though, vary in the rules their societies impose regarding the manner in which emotions are displayed in public.(Ames, 1986) For example, Filipinos, Thais and Malaysians are quite *effusive* about their smiles as they try to maintain smooth interpersonal relations. The Americans, British and Japanese, though, aren't as generous with such positive signals and are much more restrained in their facial expressions. Yet there are differences even among the second group of countries: the Japanese are considerably more restrained than the Americans, for instance. An expert once said that if you observed a group of Japanese watching a highly stressful movie without their knowledge, you would see many emotional facial expressions—much as the Americans would. But should an authority figure steps into the room, you'll see those facial expressions instantly disappear. The social rules in Japan prohibit the public display of emotions. (Ekman, 1985)

Here we cover six specific peculiarities of body language in many countries: face, eye and touch behaviors; movements of the entire body; space management and office layout; and lying gestures.

⇨ 4.1 Facial Behavior

North Americans and Europeans, who are used to formal and restrained behavior, might find the smiles that come so readily to Filipinos, Thais and Malaysians a bit disconcerting. These Asians value keeping smooth and harmonious interpersonal relationships, which they think their smiles facilitate. The French also use their faces a great deal in person-to-person interaction, but in a different way. Basically, they practice restraint in their expressions. However, they won't hesitate to use facial movements to help emphasize what they're saying. (SRI, 1987) Meanwhile, North Americans, and to a greater extent the British and Japanese, tend to exert a greater control over their facial expressions of emotions than most other cultures: Indonesians smile or *giggle* while giving bad or tragic news to a friend to assuage the hurt that the message may evoke (Draine and Hall, 1986); Japanese may laugh not so much to respond to something funny, but to give way to emotions of confusion, embarrassment and dismay.(Chesanow, 1985)

Casual movements like blinking and winking are taboo motions in some countries and regions. Blinking in Taiwan and winking (especially at women) in Australia are considered impolite. What might appears to you as an obscene gesture, such as using your index finger to make a screwing motion into the centre of your cheek, is in fact a gesture of praise in Italy! A somewhat similar gesture, the "head screw", using the screwing motion of your index finger this time to your temple means "You're crazy!" in Germany. A circular motion of your finger around your ear means "crazy" in most European and some Latin American countries. You will observe many interesting facial motions in business meetings: pulling the end of the eyelids tells you that a person is on the alert or that he or she wants you to be alert in Europe and some Latin American countries. To show that highly confidential information is being discussed, a British business executive may tap his or her nose; the same motion will indicate a friendly warning to Italians. Brazilians and Paraguayans flick their chins to tell you they don't know something; Italians use the same motion to tell you they're not interested in what you're saying or to get you out of their sight! Argentineans tap their heads to show that they're thinking. Paraguayans tilt their heads backwards to show that they've forgotten something. (Axtell, 1985) While Yugoslavians and South Indians shake their heads to mean "yes". (Copeland and Griggs, 1985)

⇨ 4.2   Eye Behavior

Case 2

In Spring Canton Fair in 1993, a Chinese young man was negotiating about a chemical product export with an American young woman in her 20s. After one-hour fierce discussion, all the other terms and conditions of the contract were fixed except the price. After some silence, the young man offered the young woman the lowest price: USD 2,100 per ton FOB Qingdao, China. "Is it the lowest price?" the American young woman asked, looking at the young man directly. No woman looked at him like this before, especially a young beautiful golden-haired woman. The young man felt a little bit shy and looked away while he said "Yes, it is." To his surprise, the American young business woman left the table and never returned.

One month later, he met a Canadian customer delegation and told the story to his customer. "You made a big mistake." The Canadian customer said and told him the secret.

Fortunately, in Autumn Canton Fair in the same year, the young man met another American business woman in her 30s. This time he was confident with the lesson learned. When the bargaining part came, the young man said: "USD 2,300 per ton FOB Qingdao, China, the lowest price!" with his eyes firmly looking back at the American woman. Surprisingly, with $200 higher than last time, the American woman did not bargain and accepted it pleasantly. The contract was signed.

(*Adapted from* International Business Negotiation *by Liu Baiyu, Wang Meiling and Zhang Yanling*)

Americans think that keeping direct eye contact is a sign of openness, honesty and assertiveness. (DeVito, 1986) Other cultures that appreciate consistent eye contact are Saudi Arabia, South Korea, Thailand and Scandinavia. In business meetings, South Koreans maintain eye contact as a sign of courtesy, attention and a means of keeping one's relationship with another. Saudi Arabians are even more intense in their involvement with eye contact: they look closely "behind a person's eye" to search into the soul and evaluate TOS's inner qualities. The Arabs know that dilated pupils are an indication of interest, and so they observe the person they're dealing with for such signs. Conversely and cleverly, they're fond of wearing tinted eyeglasses even indoors to conceal the extent of their interest, just in case the party they're dealing with is as shrewd as they are. Meanwhile the Thais use eye contact in order to facilitate their daily activities: if you're taking a bus ride in Bangkok and have inadvertently been skipped by the conductor who collects tickets, all you'll have to do is catch his or her eye and raise you eyebrows to be attended to. (Chesanow, 1986)

Scandinavians appreciate eye contact, which they consider to be a sign of sincerity. (SRI International, 1978) There are differences, though, in the way they express eye contact. Swedes, in particular, look less frequently at their partners in conversation than do the Americans and British, but they hold their look for longer periods of time.(Vargas, 1978) Pursuing this a little further, the British and Americans also differ in their manner of eye contact. The British tend to look away from you as they talk, while the Americans keep their full attention on your eyes and words. The British turn-yielding signal is when they look back at you—this indicates they are through with what they have to say. Furthermore, the British give the appearance of looking directly at your eye without really doing so—they try to look at an angle rather than directly. This is quite unlike the Americans, who look directly but alternately between your left and right eye. People in Mexico, Japan and Puerto Rico consider direct eye contact an aggressive gesture. A Japanese boss who looks a subordinate in the eye is considered punitive, while a subordinate who looks the boss in the eye is seen as hostile or somewhat insane.(Winston, 1978)

The several examples of the nuances of eye behaviors only underscore the delicateness of intercultural interaction.

Chances for even more extreme misunderstandings occur when two people's interpretations are diametrically opposed. A North American would be offended by the behavior of the Vietnamese who are taught to look at a person directly in the eye while keeping their arms folded across their chest. This sign of humility and respect to the Vietnamese suggests arrogance to the North American. Taking another situation, this time a Puerto Rican is involved.

An American high school principal in New York City misconstrued the eye behavior of a Puerto Rican girl. She was accused of wrongdoing, and he called her into his office. Because she was unable to look at the principal directly in the eye, he suspended her. The principal was ignorant of Puerto Rican culture, so he concluded she showed signs of guilt. He didn't know that Puerto Ricans do not look at their superiors in the eye out of respect. (Vargas, 1978) Koreans' approach to eye behavior is embodied in the concept of nuichee. This approach actually helps them save face. Highly conscious of status differences, Koreans look at your eyes for answers to their questions instead of directly asking for an answer. This saves both parties some embarrassment. (Malandro and Barker, 1983)

⇨ 4.3　Touch Behavior

There is a whole spectrum of touch behavior around the world. "High-contact" cultures include the French, Brazilians, Spanish (among those of the same class), Russians, Indonesians, Filipinos, Mexicans and other Latin Americans, Saudi Arabians and the Thais. (Copeland and Griggs, 1985) Friendly touch behavior is a sign of warmth and acceptance in Indonesia, the Philippines and Thailand—but only among locals and not with foreigners they don't know very well. Touch behavior is acceptable even in business situations for Saudi Arabians, Mexicans and Thais. Arabs shake their hands with business colleagues and visitors frequently, using both hands. Among themselves, Arab men don't hesitate to walk hand in hand, arm in arm in public. During discussions they may tap another person gently or rest their hand or arm on the other person's arm or shoulder to express a feeling or emphasize a point. Similarly, Mexicans, who are close business colleagues, express mutual support and friendship through the abrazo, or embrace. This is frequently used as a greeting. (SRI International, 1987)

The Thais may not be as demonstrative as the Mexicans, but they will occasionally move close to and touch each other to emphasize a point. (SRI International, 1987) In business encounters the French are ordinarily a "non-touch" culture. However, on social calls and at gatherings, the French, just like the Brazilians, will publicly kiss enthusiastically. (Copeland and Griggs, 1985) Spaniards of one social class keep their distance from people of other social classes; however, when with members of their own class, they may be uninhibited in touching each other during animated conversations. Touching is essential in Latin America. Friends don't just greet each other or wave their hands. They shake each other's hand then hug with both arms, or squeeze each other's upper arm. When conversing, they tend to tap the other person's lapel with their fingers or tap their shoulders, or squeeze their arm to bridge the emotional gap or to stress what they're saying. (Mehrabian, 1971)

Non-contact cultures include the British, Americans, Scandinavians and certain Asian groups, especially the Japanese, Indians, mainland Chinese, Singaporeans and Koreans. Physical contact between the sexes in public is especially taboo in these Asian countries. There physical contact, such as holding each other's hand or arm, or holding on the waist and shoulder, is usually interpreted in amorous or sexual terms. Although there is a great deal of physical crowding in larger cities in Asian countries, the people don't seem to mind huddling together in buses and don't feel this crowding is a violation of their personal space. A peculiar taboo in Thailand, Malaysia, Singapore and China is touching the top of TOS's head. This is a violation, because the top of the head is a sacred spot of wisdom and spirituality. (SRI International, 1978)

Scandinavians are unique in having seemingly widely contradictory inclinations. Although they are basically a no-touch culture, the physical privacy that they staunchly protect is abandoned once a social gathering takes place in a sauna. Here Scandinavians unabashedly go naked and invite their guests to do likewise. Being invited to the sauna is a sure sign that the road to friendship has been taken. Americans are also basically a non-tactile culture, and their personal "buffer zone" is a distance of about six to ten feet. They sit that far apart when seated during negotiations. However, don't be surprised to find them touching one another sometimes when they wish to emphasize a point.(SRI International, 1978)

➩ 4.4 Hand and Other Body Movements

Be careful when you move your hands in foreign countries! Be especially careful when you point your finger, pass food or articles with your left hand, gesture, beckon and put your hands in your pockets or on your hips. These movements are of special concern because of the wide variety of intercultural sensitivities regarding their meanings. Pointing at people and things with your fingers, particularly your index finder, is considered rude in the Philippines, Korea, Singapore, Indonesia and the Middle East. Malaysians and Indonesians will tolerate finger pointing if you use your thumb with your other fingers folded into your palm. The rules are somewhat more complicated in Thailand, where pointing with your finger isn't as rude as pointing with your foot. The Thais' tolerance is also greater if you point at objects (but not sacred objects) rather than at people. If it is really necessary to point at somebody because you can't identify him or her verbally, then move your chin slightly upward towards the person you're identifying. Filipinos like to point at persons, objects or locations by pursing their lips; You will notice that this happens quite often in casual conversations.

Don't use your left hand to pass objects or food in Singapore, Malaysia, South Korea, Saudi Arabia, Indonesia and India. People in these countries generally consider the left hand unclean because it is the one used to clean oneself after going to the bathroom.(Craig, 1979) This is a very important rule, and don't break it, even if you're left-handed!

Italians, Saudi Arabians and Latin Americans use their hands a great deal. They make lively gestures to emphasize or support what they're saying. Male Italian speakers will use both arms, making broad and sweeping symmetrical movements. Arabs use their hands and heads when expressing themselves. If their message is "yes", they will shake their heads from side to side; and if it is "no", they will tilt their head upward and lightly click their tongue. The Arabs are largely uninhibited, so they think the more exaggerated is the gesture, the more effective they will be.(Vargas, 1986)

The hand-beckoning gesture is another source of confusion. When you beckon by hand, you hold all four fingers close together, with your palm facing upward or downward: hand *beckoning* with the palm up is acceptable in England, Holland, the USA France, and many other places; however, the opposite is true in Japan, Singapore, Thai land, Portugal, Spain, Latin America, Italy, Sardinia, Malta, and Tunisia—and it is considered rude to beckon with your palm facing upward.(Morris, 1982)

Don't put your hands on your hips: many people will think you're challenging them. This holds true in such widely dispersed countries as Mexico, Saudi Arabia, Singapore and the Scandinavian region. Don't show the soles of your shoes or feet to Indians, Arabs, Chinese, Malaysians and Thais. Feet and shoes are considered unclean, and keeping them out of sight is a matter of social courtesy. Indians even apologize to one another when the accidentally touch with their shoes. (SRI International, 1978)

Watch your postures too. Koreans, Indonesians and Taiwanese are sensitive about the crossing of legs. Generally they think that it is rude because they regard that whoever does it is presuming a premature familiarity. Indonesians consider sitting erect with feet flat on the floor as a proper behavior in the presence of elders. This posture also impresses the Japanese and Koreans. These Asians and northern Europeans share this bias for the "proper" posture, which is both upright and more formal. Americans are the complete opposite, in that they prefer to be relaxed at meetings and naturally slouch in their chairs. Sometimes this leaves the impression that they are rude and arrogant, but they don't mean to appear that way. They don't know any better! (Copeland and Griggs, 1985)

The next point is touchy: when you can't control your bodily functions, you may tarnish the pleasant relations you are trying to establish. For example, be careful with Koreans and Saudi Arabians, they are sensitive about guests who sneeze, blow their nose, cough, cluck, hiccup, and so forth. You may be more relaxed with Americans, who are more at home with such exigencies. But don't fart loudly in public anywhere! Burping is also taboo in most countries. (SRI International, 1978)

Expressions of salutation with hand gestures is also important to know about. The ceremonial formalism of Asians is reflected in a variety of greeting behaviors with a bow. Thais are extremely elaborate in their use of the *wai*, a way of distinguishing between those who belong to the higher and lower echelons of society. People of both the higher and lower levels incline their heads until they meet the thumbs of both hands, the palms being held up together, with fingers pointing upwards. The person in the inferior social position initiates the *wai* when meeting with a person of superior level, and then the superior person reciprocates. Historically the *wai* was used by weaker men to prove that they were unarmed; in addition, they lowered their eyes and heads to emphasize that they were harmless. A person in a very superior position, such as the king or queen, does not have to perform the *wai* in return, but most people in a superior position will return the gesture to show courteousness. Thais also offer the *wai* to monks and sacred objects and places like temples and the elephant god. Male visitors unfamiliar with the social rules covering the *wai* should merely shake hands with male Thais and offer female Thais a courteous half-smile. If you want to use the *wai*, here are a few rules you should know about: do not use the *wai* on lower-status people such as servants, laborers or children; if the high *wai* is offered to you, respond with the low *wai*. It would be safe for you to offer the *wai* to monks and older Thais. The proper way of showing respect is to lower your head and body rather than raise your hands. (Cooper, 2008)

Malays in Singapore and Malaysia practice the salaam ritual, which is performed with a member of the same sex. It is similar to hand-shaking. Usually Malay men and women do not shake hands with one another, but Malay women greet Malay men with a salaam only if the man's hand is covered with a cloth—a sign that he has ritually cleansed himself before praying. You execute the salaam by offering both hands to your friend, lightly touching the friend's outstretched hands and then bringing your own up to your breast. This translates as: "I greet you from my heart." The procedure is slightly more elaborate among women in the rural areas.(Craig, 1979)

You should not hazard an encounter with the Japanese without some briefing beforehand on how the bow is correctly done. Greater respect, gratitude, sincerity and humility are indicated by a bow that is lower and held for a longer period of time. Usually the Japanese use three kinds of bow. The "informal" bow is used for casual occasions or when people of equal rank are dealing with one another. Here you bend you body at a 15-degree angle while keeping your hands at your sides. With the "formal" bow, you bend your body at a 30-degree angle and hold your hands together, palms down, touching your knees. Normally you keep this position for about two to three seconds, and then once again stretch to your upright position. Bows are usually repeated several times, and a practical problem arises when you don't know when to terminate the constant reciprocation of bowing. It would be safe for you to bow about three times only, making your first bow the deepest and gradually raising your head to the last bow. You probably won't ever use the third or "deep" bow; more properly called the *saikeirei*, it is the traditional form of bowing as commonly used by the elderly who wish to preserve their heritage.(Boye de Mente, 1981)

Less ceremonial forms of bowing are practiced in India and China. Indians exchange greetings with the namaste gesture. You hold your hands together, palms touching, and fingers pointing upwards; this is accompanied by a nod of your head. The Taiwanese appreciate a simple and slight bow to indicate politeness during business meetings. (Axtell, 1985)

Other than the bow, enthusiastic handshaking and kissing of the cheeks are also used for greeting in many parts of the world. Saudi Arabians extend their left hand to the visitor's right shoulder and kiss both the cheeks, after which they hold the visitor's hands for a long period of time to show friendliness. Latin Americans enthusiastically offer double handshakes and warm hugs, together with a light buzz on both cheeks, even among mere acquaintances: the hugs are known as *abrazos*. North Americans, incidentally, feel that using both hands in a handshake is a phony gesture.(Axtell, 1985)

Most Europeans and North Americans shake hands lightly as a form of greeting. They don't quite take as long, nor are they so frequent, as the handshakes given by Latin Americans, but nevertheless they are friendly. An exception is the West German who shakes hands vigorously and frequently; one study showed the average West German employee spent 20 percent of the time shaking hands. When meeting a group, it is customary to shake the hands of the most senior in position or the oldest member first. In addition, you should shake hands with everyone at a gathering; if you miss somebody, this is considered rude. (Chesanow, 1985)

⇨ 4.5　Space Management and Office Layout

International differences are very apparent in the use of the environmental space within which people work and live. Here our main interest, of course, is the workplace, so we won't talk about what people's homes are like.

Americans associate higher status with larger spaces. The person with the most power in a company is the president, and his or her office is usually the largest and most private; it is often in a corner of the building, high up, with a nice view. This office is followed in size by that of the vice-president, then the division managers and finally departmental managers. Countries such as China, Singapore, Thailand and the Philippines also associate larger office space with higher rank and status. Americans, though, seem to appreciate space and privacy the most. This is probably because of the country's enormous territory. Businesses there have traditionally used incredible amounts of space to construct their offices and buildings. You will also notice that Americans like to place their desks near walls. The center of the room is usually left open for traffic and human interaction. (Vargas, 1986)

Europeans arrange their offices quite differently. Authority flows from the middle of the room outwards, not from the corners inwards, as in the USA. Usually desks are placed in the middle of the room. Top executives and managers in France, Latin America and Mediterranean Europe have their desks situated amid open departmental areas. They feel it is easier to exert control from the middle. Following their traditional management rules, these managers prefer to keep an eye physically on their subordinates. Britons and Germans, though, are highly protective of their office space. Often they keep their office doors shut, and entering without a previous appointment is considered very rude. (Vargas, 1986)

Higher-level Japanese executives have office suites of their own. The size of the office space is usually in direct proportion to the power the executive holds. At the departmental level senior managers are usually located near windows, if there are any, but they will also have full view of the entire department. Junior personnel are usually situated in the middle of the department's office. (Mente, 1981)

Offices of the most senior Saudi Arabian officials are enormous and luxurious, but they are also crowded with official guests, friends and relatives. The crowding becomes acute in the smaller, cramped offices of lower-level officials and executives of smaller firms. This may be confusing if you are not used to seeing a crowd of people over which the receptionists exercise little control. The *majiles* system in Saudi Arabia allows friends, relatives and countrymen of the top official to enter at almost any time. These people have higher priority, and Saudis will interrupt ongoing business meetings just to attend to the needs of their nearer kin; guests already in the office simply have to be patient. Those waiting outside will have to be even more patient—and be prepared for people walking in ahead of them. (Chesanow, 1985)

⇨ 4.6   Differentiating Lies through Reading Body Language

A higher-level body language skill is that of the ability to detect lies. Paul Ekman and his colleagues compiled concrete guidelines for detecting lies in their recommendable book, *Telling Lies*. Detecting lies is a somewhat elusive task, complicated by the fact that there may be really no signs of deceit. You must be able to select and piece together clues from a barrage of information revealed by the different parts of TOS's body simultaneously. Your knowledge of TOS and the context of the situation within which the lie or truth fits will help you reach the correct conclusion. A good way to begin is to look at the face, listen to the words and look at the body movements (emblems, illustrators and manipulators) of TOS.

4.6.1 The Face

Most people are unskilled in the art of detecting lies. We pay more attention to people's words and faces, but both of them are highly manipulable.(Littlepage, Maddox and Pineault, 1985) And words are easier to falsify than the face. It's confusing to interpret the face because it expresses both voluntary and involuntary movements. Unlike words, the face is connected with parts of the brain directly involved with emotions.(Meihlke, 1973) For instance, facial movements for the emotions of sadness, sorrow and grief are very hard to act out. To express these emotions, you have to pull the corners of your lips downwards without moving a chin muscle.(Ekman, 1985) Try it in front of your mirror—you will find that this is hard to do. Here we discuss six facial "leakages" that will help you to detect lies.

A. Smiles

Smiles are one of the most unreliable signals to interpret because people use them so often to mask their true emotions. What is more, there are more than 50 different kinds of smile, and dozens of other expressions for one particular motion can accompany a smile.(Hall, 1984) These expressions are hard to detect because they don't last very long; they are referred to as "micro expressions". These facial movements, then, reveal the true and concealed emotions, but they flash on and off in less than one quarter of a second; it's easy for an untrained observer to miss such expressions. One hour's training, though, will sensitize you to them. Ekman tells the story of a psychiatric patient who told her doctors that she was no longer depressed and then requested a weekend pass to enable her to visit her family, The truth in fact was that she wished to get away in order to commit suicide. How did the psychiatrist find this out? She was filmed when talking to her doctor, the film was played in slow motion and a micro-expression of complete sadness manifested itself for a fleeting instant, with a quick smile following this micro-expression. They didn't give her the pass.

B. Squelched Expression

The second facial leakage is the "squelched expression". This happens when you become aware of an expression emerging on your face that you do not want to show, so you quickly interrupt it and cover it with another expression or mask, such as a smile; the squelched expression is usually an incomplete expression, but it lasts longer than the micro-expression and is consequently easier to spot.(Harper, Wiens and Matarazzo, 1978)

C. Asymmetrical or Crooked Facial Expression

The third facial leakage is an asymmetrical, or crooked, facial expression. This happens when you try to fake an emotion and you're not very good at it. When you do this, it appears on both sides of your face, but it's much stronger on one side of your face than the other. These asymmetrical or crooked facial expressions indicate that you aren't genuinely feeling the emotion that you are attempting to represent.(Ekman, 1985) One study asked one group of people to smile deliberately to express happiness. A second group smiled spontaneously and genuinely. There were many more crooked or asymmetrical smiles in the spurious group than in the genuine one; and right-handed fakers had stronger expressions on the left sides of their faces, and vice versa. (Ekman, Hager and Friesen, 1981)

D. How Long the Facial Expression Lasts

The fourth facial leakage has to do with how long the facial expression lasts—i.e. both the time it takes to appear and to disappear. Most facial expressions that last longer than four to five seconds are phony ones. However, extreme emotions last on the face for much longer—ten seconds or more. Expression of less extreme emotions won't last that long. You can be almost certain that your subordinates are feigning amusement at one of your jokes if they continue laughing long after the punch line is over.(Knapp, 1980) Look out for smiles that are dropped too abruptly—they are almost always false.(Ekman, 1985)

E. Signals in Relation to Body Movements, Voice Changes and Flow of Speech

The fifth facial signal of falsehood appears in relation to body movements, voice changes and flow of speech: it is really easy to tell when you're falsifying anger. If the angry expression appears on the face only after saying: "I'm fed up with your behavior", or after the fist is banged on the table, there's a reasonable basis to suspect faking. When telling the truth, they appear simultaneously.(Morris, 1982)

F. Movement of the Eyes

The sixth signal of facial deceit concerns movement of the eyes. Ordinarily, the eyes can be easily used to deceive. Watch out for blinking and pupil dilation. Both of these occur involuntarily when you are emotionally aroused. Here the only difficulty is that these two movements don't tell you which particular emotions are being felt—just that they are being experienced strongly. Watch out also for tears. They are hard to fake, even for experienced actors and actresses. Our autonomic nervous system produces them involuntarily whenever we're distressed or sad or relieved or laugh uncontrollably.(Hess, 1975)

4.6.2   Words

You can tell if a person is lying to you with words by looking out for slips of the tongue, tirades and the voice itself. Freud believed that the ordinary errors we make in our daily life, such as slips of the tongue, forgetting of familiar names and mistakes in reading and writing are symptoms of internal conflict within us. (Strachey, 1976) Speech errors and pauses occur when you're caught in a situation where you feel compelled to lie but are unprepared to do so. It happens, for instance, when somebody asks you a question that you didn't anticipate, and you didn't rehearse your lines ahead of time. Or even when you've prepared amply, for just the simple fear of being found out will produce such errors. (Mehrabian, 1972) A tirade is an outpouring of information that takes place when you're carried away by some emotion; in the process you may well unknowingly reveal damaging information. (Weisman, 1977) Watch for tirades: they are valuable sources of honest information. The voice is also a rich source of clues to deception. Listen to the pitch of the voice. It increases whenever you lie. But a high-pitched voice by itself is not a reliable sign because it also accompanies genuine expressions of fear, anger and excitement. (Scherer and Ekman, 1982)

4.6.3　Body Movements—Emblems

You must also closely watch body movements for clues. Pay attention to "emblems". These are movements that have specific meanings within a particular culture. Examples are the shrug when Americans want to say "I don't know", "I'm helpless" or "What does it matter?"; the head nod indicating "yes"; the "come-here" beckoning gesture; the hitchhiker's thumb and so forth.

An *emblematic* slip is an excellent sign of the concealment of information. There are two ways to detect this slip. First, look out for a fragment of an emblem—for instance, a complete shrug is usually performed by (1) raising both shoulders; (2) by raising the eyebrows, drooping the upper eyelids and shaping the mouth into a horseshoe; (3) by turning up both palms: or (4) by tilting the head sideways. Any combination of these emblems may also occur. When you show only a fragment of an emblem, you are usually lying. For example, you only turn up one of your palms; you push up only your lower lip; or you only raise one shoulder; and so on. (Poyatos, 1976) The second way to detect a lie is to look for an emblem that is performed outside the ordinary position—for instance, when medical students were subjected to stressful interviews, one of them gave the interviewing professor the finger from her knee instead of thrusting her finger right in front of her face, which is the usual spot from which this obscene gesture is done. (Knapp, 1980)

The second group of body movements that you should keep an eye open for are known as "illustrators" because people make these movements to illustrate what they are saying—examples include tracing in the air your flow of thought or drawing a picture in space to emphasize what you are saying. The clue to deceit is simple here: look for a significant decrease in the number of illustrators that TOS would usually use (obviously, you must already know TOS's usual body movements to use this clue effectively). Here is why a decrease in the number of illustrators usually means that TOS is lying: (1) the decrease shows a lack of emotional investment in what TOS is saying—e.g. people tend to be less animated when they are bored, disinterested, depressed or saddened; and (2) people don't use the same number of illustrators when they aren't quite sure what to say, and deceit may or may not be involved in this case—e.g. the sales rep making a pitch for the first time before an unfamiliar and hostile audience may be so cautious about the verbal content of his/her canned presentation that he/she leaves out all hand gestures, in other words, this is not lying, but caution.(DeVito, 1986)

4.6.4   Body Movements: Manipulators

"Manipulators" are those movements where one part of the body touches, rubs, picks, scratches or seeks some other kind of contact with another part of the body. Pay very close attention to them, too. Here we talk about them not so much because they indicate deception in themselves, but rather because it is all too easy to impute deception when these movements are made. Remember, you may be wrong. People use many manipulators both when they are relaxed and when they are tense. Therefore manipulators are unreliable clues to deceit. One such manipulator gesture that almost always indicates lying, though, is talking with your hand in front of your mouth. (DeVito, 1986)

4.6.5   Lying: Eight Guidelines

Detecting lies is the hardest part of interpreting TOS's body language. If, however, you follow these eight general pointers, and practice a lot, you will eventually get better at it. (Ekman, 1985) But you'll never become an expert at detecting lies unless you make it your life-study. Start with these guidelines, but don't stop there.

1) First, analyze your reasons for suspecting that TOS may be lying. This will help you weed out unsound preconceptions and biases that you may have.

2) Secondly, be open to the possibility of committing the two most common errors in lie detection—not believing the truth and believing the lie.

3) Thirdly, the absence of clues to deceit in TOS's body movements does not mean they are truthful. Conversely, the presence of some of these signs is no guarantee that TOS is lying. In the early 1970s, John Dean, a former aide to US President Richard Nixon, gave a remarkable performance during the Watergate hearings held by the US Senate. This was due, in part, to the absence of emotion in his voice. Dean was a gifted actor, and his own words let us know this: "It would be easy to overdramatize, or to seem too flip about my testimony... I would, I decided, read evenly, unemotionally, as coldly as possible, and answer questions the same way... People tend to think that somebody telling the truth will be calm about it. (Mehrabian, 1972)

4) Fourthly, re-examine yourself and see if there are any other factors that may cloud your judgment. Are you jealous of, or angry at TOS? If you are, it's going to be easy for you to have an overemotional reaction to whatever TOS does.

5) Fifthly, keep an open mind about TOS's signs of emotion. These may not actually be clues for reading deceit, but rather the reactions of TOS to being suspected of lying. Make sure you're certain TOS knows you suspect him or her in order for you to make a valid judgment.

6) Sixthly, if you have good reason to believe that TOS is lying, you may want to use Lykken's Guilty Knowledge Technique, together with a polygraph test. (You can't do this with a business partner; often you can't do it even with an employee, for the law may not allow it.) The polygraph is a machine, which shows if a person is under stress; it does not indicate a lie per se, but people are usually under more stress when they lie than when they tell the truth. The Guilty Knowledge Technique uses a battery of questions. It assumes the person who takes the test is covering up a lie, and it investigates further into the person's knowledge of the details of the situation that it is supposed is being lied about. The psychologist who devised this technique found that changes occur in the autonomic nervous system of persons who are lying and are confronted with the cine correct alternative to the question they are answering at that moment. (Ekman, 1985)

7) Seventhly, never consider as final the conclusion you reach about whether TOS is lying or telling the truth, based on the behavioral or body clues you notice. Always look for further information because you may have missed some important clues. Put all the clues you gather into clusters to see if they all point in the same direction. Some clues may contradict others. Look at all the clues within the context of the situation in which they were detected in the first place.

8) Eighthly, it is hard enough to tell if somebody within your own country and from your own culture is lying to you. As we have said; this is the hardest part of body language. But imagine how much harder it will be to tell if somebody from a different country and culture is lying to you, or telling you the truth. In short, you must watch TOS even more closely if they are from other parts of the world.

➡️ 4.7　Guidelines for Increasing Your Sensitivity to Body Language

In order to help sharpen your ability to read body language across cultures, remember the following seven guidelines about body language in general:

A. First of all, strive for self-understanding at all times.

Although this does not absolutely guarantee that you'll interpret TOS's body language accurately, it will at least establish an attitude of maintaining mental openness and patience when observing others. This attitude is most important to develop your skills.

B. Persevere in your efforts to be more and more observant of details when you analyze body language.

You'll often be confronted by a barrage of data, and it will be hard to sift the relevant information from all of that.

C. Always interpret TOS's body language from their own cultural perspective.

Learn the body language code of the particular culture you're dealing with. Don't assume from what you may have read in popular literature that body language is universal. There are many differences and we've pointed out only a very few in this chapter.

D. Always look for a cluster of gestures, and consider them within the situational context in which they take place.

Do not try to read the body language clues you observe as you would a dictionary, that is for looking up the meaning for one word or gesture at a time. It doesn't work that way! Interrelate the gestures as you observe them; and observe a person's gesture clusters over a certain period of time to make sure you interpret them accurately. The following is an example of what I mean.

Look at this distinguished-looking female executive. She is apparently chairing a department meeting. She appears to conduct herself professionally—she is sitting erect, nods at her subordinates' suggestions, echoes some of their mannerisms and smiles sparingly to give the impression that she's in command. So far, all her gestures indicate that she's a competent and credible boss. However, she occasionally covers her mouth with her hand, especially when the group breaks out in laughter. Occasionally she does this when she speaks. If you took a "cook-book" approach in interpreting her movements, you would think she was trying to cover up something or isn't completely trustworthy. (Remember covering you mouth when you speak is a manipulator gesture.) If you stopped there, though, you'd be wrong about this executive. Watch her more closely, talk to her a little, and you'll discover that she's candid enough to admit that she recently had orthodontic work done on her teeth. The dental wiring, she explains, prevents her from laughing freely and once in a while she feels the need to cover her mouth when she talks. With this new piece of information, your interpretation changes completely. Thus a more accurate and fairer picture of her performance in the department meeting emerges. All her gestures in the meeting, save the minor detail of occasionally covering her mouth, indicate that a professional executive is in charge. Knowing the context—the fact that she had just recently had orthodontic treatment means that your initial suspicion that she may be lying or covering up something was wrong.

E. Our own cultural biases color and complicate the way we perceive and interpret the actions of people from other cultures.

We also often project our own qualities on to the people we're observing, especially when we lack a frame of reference from which to interpret what they are saying or doing. Thus you should consult someone from the culture you're observing; compare notes and clarify your first interpretations.

F. Be greedy for knowledge about TOS.

The more you know about them, the more powerful you are when you negotiate; the less you know about them, the less powerful you are. Knowledge is power. Get your knowledge by observing TOS. Knowing how to interpret body language is a skill, and as with any skill, you must practice it often to stay skillful. Practice by watching people all the time, even when you're not negotiating. Try to guess what's on their mind. If you watch people often enough, you will eventually become skilled in accurately reading body language.

G. Never let TOS know that you know how to read body language successfully.

It will frighten TOS so much that they will "freeze up" whenever you are around. This promotes dishonesty, not honesty. And honesty, on both sides, is crucial for the success of any negotiation.

5　Cultural Differences in Style Preferences

Style preferences are affected by a number of influences—education, upbringing, role models, parents, profession, gender, age, nationality—all combining to build a strong identity of "how you do things". Cluster people together who have similar identities, and you have a culture, whether that be a national culture; a professional culture such as sales, engineering or accountancy; an organization culture (this is the way we do things around here); or one that is age or generation related. These different cultures have often developed a way of communicating and influencing that suits them, and this then has an impact in your influencing arena whenever you cross a barrier and try to work with someone from a different culture.

Crossing these frontiers or barriers is commonplace now with a global workforce that spans national boundaries and project working where cross-functional teams are the norm. Understanding different cultures will help you to communicate better by enabling you to adapt to the needs and preferences of the different cultures.

5.1　A Preference for Action-oriented Communication

A preference for action-oriented communication can be identified in the USA, Canada, Australia and other nationalities where action and speed are of the essence. Organizations that rely on short-term decision making—fast moving consumer goods, sales, retail—will probably have a preference towards the action style. Many senior managers in organizations also prefer this style as they are rewarded for getting results.

5.2　A Preference for Process-oriented Communication

Process-oriented communication is preferred in cultures where structure and logical decision making are paramount. Countries such as Austria, Germany, Denmark and Sweden immediately come to mind. It appeals to professions such as technology, engineering and accountancy where there is a strong reliance on a scientific and systematic methodology. Process-driven organizations—oil and chemicals, pharmaceuticals, engineering, manufacturing, government—rely on solid, data-driven problem solving, and have strong process style tendencies. Process style communication is also predominant in the way children are taught in schools, so it has a comfortable feel, even if it is not an individual preference.

⇨ 5.3　A Preference for People-oriented Communication

People-oriented communication is the cultural norm in countries where consensus and respect for people and their ideas are important (e.g. Asia, Japan). In this culture, the relationship is more significant than the task, so it can also be identified in social science-driven professions like social work, human resources, health and education (primarily at the delivery point rather than in the management, which accounts for some of the difficult relationships in these professions between practitioners and managers).

⇨ 5.4　A Preference for Idea-oriented Communication

Ideas-oriented communication is typical of cultures where it is the norm to ask questions like, "What are the arguments for doing it this way? Why? Why not?", where people must be convinced of the substance in the message being conveyed. This is common in countries like France and in research and development and project leadership. It is a style that is attractive to some of the younger generation who want to believe in what they are doing and the purpose behind the organization, not just to do a job.

Vocabulary

beckon /ˈbekən/ *v.*

—to move your hand or head in a way that tells someone to come nearer

e.g. The customs official beckoned the woman to his counter.

He beckoned to me, as if he wanted to speak to me.

—If something beckons, it attracts people.

e.g. For many young people, the bright lights of London beckon, though a lot of them end up sleeping on the streets.

—If an event or achievement beckons, it is likely to happen.

e.g. She's an excellent student, for whom a wonderful future beckons.

effusive /ɪˈfjuːsɪv/ *adj.*

—(*formal*) expressing welcome, approval or pleasure in a way that shows every strong feelings

e.g. They gave us such an effusive welcome it was quite embarrassing.

emblematic /ˌembləˈmætɪk/ adj.

—representing a particular person, group, or idea:

e.g. A sword is emblematic of power gained by violence.

empathetic /empəˈθetɪk/ *v.*

—to be able to understand how someone else feels

e.g. Now, we've known for a long time that empathetic feeling is not logically linked to morality.

gambit /ˈgæmbɪt/ n.

—a clever action in a game or other situation which is intended to achieve an advantage and usually involves taking a risk

e.g. Her clever opening gambit gave her an early advantage.

Their promise to lower taxes is clearly an election-year gambit.

giggle /ˈgɪgl/ v.

—to laugh repeatedly in a quiet but uncontrolled way, often at something silly or rude or when you are nervous

e.g. Stop that giggling at the back!

squelch /skweltʃ/ v.

—to make a sucking sound like the one produced when you are walking on soft wet ground

e.g. He got out of the car and squelched through the mud to open the gate.

Exercises

1 True or False

_____ 1) The reasoning backing up the proposal in a negotiation needs to be valid and based on facts and logic.

_____ 2) Process-style people also use a pushing type of energy, but are less directive and forceful.

_____ 3) The international business negotiation is often a process to deal with disputes arising from different practices in trade, payment, transportation and insurance.

_____ 4) Action style depends on the exchange you can make to influence someone to do something for you.

_____ 5) People style is not the only style that gathers information, so it is very useful to help find out what values and desires the other party has like some other communication styles.

_____ 6) Empathetic listening requires you to stop talking to others and yourself in your head as well.

_____ 7) Idea-oriented people use their responsiveness to connect with other people's values and beliefs and build exciting possibilities for the future.

_____ 8) Most people are unskilled in the art of detecting lies no matter how hard they try. So it is not possible for them to deal with lies in a negotiation.

_____ 9) An asymmetrical facial expression happens when you try to fake an emotion and you're not very good at it.

_____ 10) It is not verified yet whether you can tell if a person is lying to you with words by looking out for slips of the tongue, tirades and the voice itself.

2 Interpretation of Terms

1) Verbal Communication

_____

_____

2）Non-verbal Communication

3）Direct Communication

4）Idea Style Communication

5）People Style Communication

6）Process Style Communication

7）Action Style Communication

3 Case Analysis

Mr. Herb Cohen is a world-famous negotiator and once held the position of negotiation adviser for the former American presidents Carter and Regan. He was often invited by some transnational companies or governmental agencies to negotiate with other parties on their behalf as well as to make speeches all over the world. The fee for his presence is usually extremely high—always hundreds of thousands or millions of dollars—an astronomical number.

One day, a clerk in Mr. Cohen's office received a telephone call from a large information technology company in California's Silicon Valley. The caller was a female executive who wanted to know the fee for a speech by Mr. Cohen at a public conference in San Francisco. According to the routine practice, the telephone conversation began with the usual formulas, such as how long the speech would be, who would be in the audience and finally a question like "What is the fee for the speech?" The office clerk would make a quotation of "astronomical numbers" as usual even though it might scare 10% of the inquirers away. However, this time, what the female executive said on the other end of the phone was so extraordinarily brilliant that it made Mr. Cohen treated her with more respect. She did not ask directly, "How much does Mr. Cohen want to charge for his speech?" or "How much do we have to pay?" Instead, she asked with discreet gentility, "Well, what is an appropriate gift to Mr. Cohen in token of gratitude?" A gift in token of gratitude? What did it mean? The office clerk got muddled (even though he knew such brilliant words apparently and simply implied that she intended to pay a little symbolic fee), but he still quoted a standard charge of an astronomical figure.

To his surprise, his counterpart did not sound a bit surprised or dissatisfied at all in her response—she did not say, "Who does he think he is? Whoever he is, he is not entitled to charge such a high price!" On the contrary, she said with delight, "I know he is completely entitled to charge such a high price. In addition, our vice CEO heard a speech by Mr. Cohen, and he said that Mr. Cohen is worth more than twice as that fee. If we had had that much money, we would have felt fortunate, happy and lucky to give that sum to Mr. Cohen!" Then she said with a little shame, "But unfortunately our budget allow only this sum of money." Can you guess whether her words would work?

Six months later, Mr. Cohen appeared on the platform of the Sheraton Hotel in San Francisco.

Questions for Case-analysis:

What kinds of persuasion tactics and techniques were used by the female executive in the IT company so that the world famous negotiator Mr. Cohen abandoned his extremely high standard quotation and accepted the speech fee she could afford?

Reference

1. Axtell, Roger E. Aguide to International Behavior: Dos and Taboos around the World, New York: Benjamin Co. Inc, 1985.

2. Bull, Peter. Body Movement and Interpersonal Communication, New York: Wiley, 1983.

3. Chesanow, Neil. The World-Class Executive: How to Do Business Like a Pro around the World, New York: Rawson Associates. 1985.

4. Cooper, Robert. Culture Shock! Thailand, New York: Marshall Cavendish Corporation, 2008.

5. Copeland, Lennie and Griggs, Lewis. Going International: How to Make Friends and Deal Effectively in the Global Marketplace, New York: Random House. 1985.

6. Covey, Steven. The Seven Habits of Highly Effective People, New York: Simon & Schuster, 1989.

7. Cox, Geof. The Financial Times Essential Guide to Negotiations, Pearson Education Limited, 2012.

8. Craig. Joann. Culture Shock! What Not to Do in Malaysia and Singapore. How and Why NOI to Do It. Singapore: Times Books International, 1979.

9. Dean, John. Blind Ambition, New York: Simon and Schuster, 1976.

10. DeVito, Joseph A. The Interpersonal Communication Book, New York: Harper and Row, 1986.

11. Draine, Cathie and Hall, Barbara. Culture Shock! Indonesia, Singapore: Times Books International. 1986.

12. Ekman, Paul. "Facial signs, fantasies and possibilities": in Thomas A Sebeok (ed.), Sight, Sound, and Sense, Bloomington, Ind.: Indiana University Press, 1978.

13. Ekman, Paul. Telling Lies: Clues to Deceit in the Marketplace. Politics. And Marriage, New York: WW. Norton, 1985.

14. Ekman, Paul. "Movements with precise meanings". Journal of Communication. 26. 1976.

15. Ekman, Paul and Friesen, W.V. "Measuring facial movement", Environmental Psychology and Nonverbal Behavior, 1976. 56-75.

16. Ekman, Paul, Friesen, W.V. and Tomkins, S.S. "Facial affect scoring technique: a first validity study". Semiotica. 3. 1971. 37-58.

17. Ekman, Paul and Friesen, W.V., Wallace V. "Nonverbal behavior and psychopathology". in R.1. Friedman and M.N. Katz (eds). The Psychology of Depression: Contemporary Theory and Research, Washington. DC: J. Winston, 1974.

18. Ekman, Paul, Friesen, Wallace V. and Scherer, Klaus. "Body movement and voice pitch in deceptive interaction", Semiotica. 16. 1976.

19. Ekman, Paul, Roper, Gowen and Hager, Joseph C. "Deliberate facial movement". Child Development. 51. 1980.

20. Fernando Poyatos. Man Beyond Words: Theory and Methodology of Nonverbal Communication, New York: NYSEC Monographs. 1976.

21. Fuller, George. The Negotiator's Handbook by published, New Jersey: Prentice Hall, Englewood Cliffs, 1991.

22. Haggard, E.A. and Isaacs, F.S. "Micromomentary facial expressions as indicators of ego mechanisms in psychotherapy". in L.A. Gottschalk and AH. Auerbach (eds). Methods of Research in Psychotherapy, New York: Appleton-Century-Crofts. 1966.

23. Hall, Judith A. Nonverbal Sex Differences, Baltimore: Johns Hopkins University Press, 1984.

24. Harper, Robert G., Wiens, Arthur N. and Matarazzo, Joseph D. Nonverbal Communication: The State of the Art, New York: Wiley, 1978.

25. Hendon, Donald W. and Hendon, Rebecca Angeles. World-class negotiating—Dealmaking in the global marketplace, John Wiley & Sons Inc., 1990.

26. Hess, E.H.. The Tell-Tale Eye, New York: Van Nostrand Reinhold. 1975.

27. Janisse ,M.P. and Peavler, W.S. "Pupillary research today: emotion in the eye". Psychology Today. 7. 1974.

28. Johnson, Harold G., Ekman, Paul and Friesen, Wallace V. "Communicative body movements: American emblems". Semiotica. 15. 1975.

29. Kasl, S.V. and Mahl, G.F. . "The relationship of disturbances and hesitations in spontaneous speech to anxiety". Journal of Personality and Social Psychology. I. 1965.

30. Kendon, Adam, Harris, Richard M. and Ritchiekey, Mary (eds). Origin of Behavior in Face-to-Face Interaction, Chicago: Mouton, 1975.

31. Knapp, Mark L. Essentials of Nonverbal Communication, New York: Holt. Rinehart and Winston, 1980.

32. Knapp, Mark L. Nonverbal Communication in Human Interaction, New York: Holt. Rinehart

and Winston, 1978.

33. Littlepage, Glenn and Pineault, Martin A. "Detection of deception of planned and spontaneous communication", Journal of Social Psychology. 125 (2). April 1985.

34. Malandro, Loretta A. and Barker, Larry L. Nonverbal Communication, New York: Newberry Award Records Inc., 1983.

35. Mente, Boye de. The Japanese Way of Doing Business: The Psychology of Management in Japan, NJ: Prentice-Hall. 1981.

36. Mehrabian, Albert. Nonverbal Communication, New York: Aldine Atherton, 1972.

37. Mehrabian, Albert. Silent Messages, New York: Aldine-Atherton. 1972.

38. Moore, Christopher W. and Woodrow, Peter J. Handbook of Global and Multicultural Negotiation, Jossey-Bass A Wiley Imprint, 2010.

39. Morris, Desmond. The Pocket Guide to Manwatching. London: Triad & Granada, 1982.

40. Liu, Baiyu, Wang, Meiling, Zhang, Yanling. International Business Negotiation. Beijing: Renmin University Press, 2011.

41. Pease, Allan. Body Language: How to Read Others' Thoughts by Their Gestures, Australia: Camel, 1981.

42. Poyatos, Fernando. Man Beyond Words: Theory and Methodology of Nonverbal Communication, New York: NYSEC Monographs. 1976.

43. Ramsey, Sheila J. "Nonverbal behavior: an intercultural perspective". in Molefi Kete Asante, Eileen Newmark and Cecil A Blake (eds). Handbook of Intercultural Communication, Califorlia: Sage, 1975.

44. Rice, B. "Rattlesnakes, French fries and pupillometric oversell". Psychology Today. 7. 1974.

45. Rosenthal, Robert, Hall, Judith A., DiMatteo, M. Robin, Rogers, Peter L. and Archer, Dan. Sensitivity to Nonverbal Communication: The PONS Test, Baltimore: Johns Hopkins University Press, 1979.

46. Scherer, Klaus. "Methods of research on vocal communication: paradigms and parameters". in Klaus Scherer and Paul Ekman (eds), Handbook of Methods in Nonverbal Behavior Research, New York: Cambridge University Press, 1982.

47. Sirica, John. To Set the Record Straight, New York: WW. Norton. 1979.

48. Stem, D.N. and Bender, E.P. "An ethological study of children approaching a strange adult: sex differences". in RC. Friedman. RM. Richart and RL. Vande Wiele (eds). Sex Differences in Behavior, New York: Wiley, 1974. 233-258.

49. Strachey, James(ed). The Complete Psychological Works, New York: W.W. Norton, 1976.

50. Vargas, Marjorie Fink. Louder than Words: An Introduction to Nonverbal Communication, Iowa: Iowa State University Press. 1986.

51. Weisman, John. "The truth will out". TV Guide. 3 September. 1977.

Chapter VII Styles of International Business Negotiation

Learning Objectives

After studying this chapter, you will be able to

- Identify the priorities of business negotiation in different countries and regions.

- Describe the characteristics of business negotiation styles in different countries and regions.

- Exemplify influences of cultural differences in international business negotiation.

- Analyze how the cultural factors decide the negotiation.

1 Introduction

The concern for negotiating effectively across cultures is hardly a new phenomenon (Imai, Gelfand, 2010). The dramatically increasing need for intercultural business negotiation has put negotiators in a global scene. According to the research of culture and negotiation scholars, negotiators tend to achieve more profits with better cross-cultural awareness in international negotiations. So how to handle the cultural factor in a negotiation is a big lesson on negotiators' table.

The great diversity of the world's culture makes it impossible for any negotiator, no matter how skilled and experienced, to fully understand all the cultures that he or she may encounter. How then should an executive prepare to cope with the culture in making deals in Singapore this week and in San Hose next week? One approach is to identify important areas where cultural differences may arise during the negotiation process. Knowledge of those factors may help an international business negotiator to understand a counterpart and to anticipate possible misunderstandings.

Hence, the influence of national culture on business negotiations has been the subject of extensive researches (Agndal, 2007; Salacuse, 2003).

In 1954, American sociologist Alex Inkeles and psychologist Daniel Levinson suggested that the following qualities as common basic problems worldwide with consequences for the functions of societies:

1) Relation to authority
2) Conception of self, in particular:
   a. The relationship between individual and society, and
   b. The individual's concept of masculinity and femininity
3) Ways of dealing with conflicts, including the control of aggression and the expression of feelings. (Inkeles and Levinson, 1969)

Twenty years later, Greet Hofstede did a survey of over 50,000 workers from more than 50 countries who worked in the local subsidiaries of a large multinational corporation—IBM. He did a statistical analysis of the answers on questions about the values of these workers in the following areas:

1) Social inequality, including the relationship with authority;
2) The relationship between the individual and the group;
3) Concepts of masculinity and femininity: the social implications of having been born as a boy or a girl;
4) Ways of dealing with uncertainty, relating to the control of aggression and the expression of emotions.

"The empirical results covered amazingly well the areas predicted by Inkeles and Levinson 20 years ago". (Hofstede, 1991) Hofstede hence named four dimensions of culture and later added one as the fifth:

1) power distance (from small to large)

Power distance is the extent to which the less powerful members of institutions and organizations within a country expect and accept that power is distributed unequally.

2) collectivism vs. individualism

Individualism pertains to societies in which the ties between individuals are loose: everyone is expected to look after himself or herself and his or her immediate family. Collectivism pertains to societies in which people from birth onwards are integrated into strong, cohesive in-groups, which throughout people's lifetime continue to protect them in exchange for unquestioning loyalty.

3) femininity vs. masculinity

Masculinity pertains to societies in which social gender roles are clearly distinct (i.e., men are supposed to be assertive, tough, and focused on material success whereas women are supposed to be more modest, tender, and concerned with the quality of life); femininity pertains to societies in which social gender roles overlap i. e., both men and women are supposed to be modest, tender, and concerned with the quality of life).

4) uncertainty avoidance (from weak to strong)

Uncertainty avoidance can be defined as the extent to which the members of a culture feel threatened by uncertain or unknown situations. This feeling is, among other things, expressed through nervous stress and in a need for predictability: a need for written and unwritten rules.

5) long-term vs. short-term orientation

It refers to a long-term versus a short-term orientation in life. It deals with two different poles of values: the values on one pole are more oriented towards the future (especially perseverance and thrift); they are more dynamic. And values on the opposite pole are more oriented towards the past and the present; they are more static. Michael Bond called it "Confucian Dynamism", referring to the teachings of Confucius.

The fifth dimension was because of Michael Harris Bond, a Canadian living in the Far East for many years, who studies people's values around the world using questionnaire composed by 'Eastern', in this case Chinese. Hofstede then realized "even the minds of the researchers studying it are programmed according to their own particular cultural framework". (Hofstede, 1991)

On the other hand, based on a review of the literature as well as interviews with practitioners, the scholar Salacuse identified 10 factors, in his book *Making Global Deal—Negotiating in the International Market Place*, which seemed to be the most problematical in negotiation process. These 10 factors, each of which consisted of two poles, were (1) negotiating goals (contract or relationship?); (2) attitudes to the negotiating process (win/win or win/lose); (3) personal styles (formal or informal); (4) styles of communication (direct or indirect?); (5) time sensitivity (high or low); (6) emotionalism (high or low); (7) agreement form (specific or general); (8) agreement-building process (bottom-up or top-down); (9) negotiating team organization (one leader or consensus); (10) risk taking (high or low).

And as to the agent itself in negotiation process, here agent being negotiators, there are five factors to consider in the negotiation process according to Brett and Gelfand (2005):

1) Judgment and concession making: Do the negotiators aim to persuade using rationality or emotionality?

2) Motivation: Is the motivation to achieve economic capital or social capital?

3) Attributions: What are the traits of the negotiators: dispositional attribution vs. situational attribution?

4) Communication: Do the negotiators use direct information or indirect information sharing?

5) Confrontation: Are the negotiators using direct voice and talk or avoidance and indirectness?

In this chapter, the major cultural factors which are considered to influence the process of international business negotiations will be discussed with a combination of cultural dimensions proposed by Hofsted and negotiation factors by Brett and Gelfand. The styles will be approached geographically. In each geographically separated area, concept of time, collectivism vs. individualism, communication patterns as well as power distance and decision-making process will be the major factors to be discussed, while a part of diversity of the cultures in the related area will be added due to the complex and dynamics of cultures. Besides the major factors, some unique cultural primers will be following diversity as to provide a more comprehensive picture for negotiators from cultures other than the area discussed.

Though the cultural factors influencing negotiation styles in this chapter are geographically located, it is vital to remember "the world has a staggering diversity of cultures". (Lewicki, Sanders, Minton&Barry, 2002) Within the same area, while certain observers speak of "Latin American culture" as if it was a homogeneous set of values, norms and beliefs followed universally by the people in Latin America. In reality, however, the negotiating style of Agentinanies is different from that of Brazilians. Costa Rica is described as "most firmly rooted democracy in Latin America". "There is ample evidence that Costa Ricans have felt a stronger bond to their countrymen than Nicaraguans." (Harrison, 1985) Individualism prevails more in Costa Rica than its Latin American peers which usually considered as more collective. So pre-negotiation preparation discussed in Chapter Four is of vital importance in this regard.

2　Negotiating in Asia

Case 1

A well-known US candy company Planned to sell its products overseas, and it found a possible partner based in Tokyo. The Tokyo company seemed to be perfect for the deal. After many phone calls between the two parties, a decision was made to meet in Tokyo. The US company chose one of their businessmen, Mike Waller, to represent it. He was the company's most persuasive negotiator.

Before Waller left the United States, he and the company lawyer worked together to write a detailed contract for the deal. The contract was fifty pages long. The deal would be advantageous for both firms. It promised big profits. Waller left for Japan with the contract. He was pleased with his careful preparation. He thought his future partners would be satisfied with his work and would be ready to bargain about the details of the contract. He had studied their company interests and was sure they would want to change a few conditions in the contract. He planned to agree to those changes as concessions. He was certain the meetings would result in good negotiations and a quick final agreement.

On the day of the meeting in Tokyo, Waller entered the boardroom with copies of the contract for the Japanese businessmen at the meeting. He handed them each a copy and began discussing the details. The representatives of the Tokyo firm did not open the contract. They didn't discuss the contract at all, but instead spoke about general business issues. They spoke about the proposed cooperation between the two companies but they didn't make any promises.

Waller then went back to the United States. He felt extremely surprised and disappointed. The Japanese had never asked him one question about the contract. No agreements or commitments had been made. He wasn't even sure if there would be another round of negotiations.

Questions for Case-analysis:

1. How did the two companies first communicate with each other?

2. How did the American representative prepare for the first meeting?

3. How did the Japanese businessmen respond to the contract?

4. Why do you think Mike Waller brought a contract to the first meeting?

5. Why do you think the Japanese representatives didn't look at the contract during the first meeting? What did they expect from that meeting?

6. Why do you think the two parties failed to reach an agreement?

⇨ 2.1 Asia Overview

Asia is the largest and most densely-populated area on earth. Though it covers only 8.7% of the Earth's total surface area (4.427 million), it comprises 30% of earth's land area, and has historically been home to the bulk of the planet's human population (currently roughly 60%). Asia has witnessed the most dynamic economy and fastest economic growth (particularly East Asia) as well as robust population growth during the 20th and 21st century. Given its size and diversity, the concept of Asia—a name dating back to classical antiquity—may actually have more to do with humane geography than physical geography. Asia varies greatly across and within its regions with regard to ethnic groups, cultures, environments, economics, historical ties and government systems.

Whether you are buying or selling, Asian countries should be a critical part of almost any company's global strategy. The vast potential is certainly being realized with the emergence of China as a major economic player, surpassing Japan for the first time in history as the second largest economy with its national GDP in 2009. Japan's economy is third only to that of the United States and China. According to World Bank report, East Asia and Pacific remained the world's growth engine in 2013, accounting for over 40% of the increase in global output. In the short term, the region's developing countries navigated the global economic crisis successfully, maintaining high growth. In the mid-term, ensuring sustainable and inclusive growth is a major challenge for the region that will require raising productivity and addressing wide-ranging vulnerabilities. The business climate can be characterized as creative and aggressive cooperation, where there are close alliances between government and industry and between banks and manufacturers. There are also strong, interlocked groups of companies such as the *keiretsu* of Japan and the *chaebol* of South Korea.

Though a lot of countries in Asia are influenced by Confucianism, there are diversities in these cultures. For example, Singaporeans focus on building good relationships, as do Chinese people. But the way they build relationship is different. A great number of Chinese negotiators have had embarrassing experiences when negotiating with Singaporean counterparts. For example, it is common in China for people to exchange gifts before or after the negotiation. This is to express a wish to establish good relationships. But when the Chinese offered gifts to Singaporean negotiators, the gifts were refused. Because Singaporean government has very strict rules towards gift exchanging, such a gift might be considered a bribe. So try not to violate such a sensitive rule.

The Republic of Singapore is unique in the world marketplace. Its economic success is due to many factors, including hard work, frugality, effective government etc. Those of us who have worked for years under conditions of tropical heat and humidity can appreciate the impact of climate on productivity and the work ethic. (Dou, 2012)

➩ 2.2　Business Style in Asia

In negotiating with Asians, who place great importance on preserving smooth interpersonal relations and the appearance of harmony, they observe society's standards of what is right and wrong, acceptable and unacceptable, rather than their own internalized system of values. In that society making the appearance of conforming to society's standards is very much the basis of their personal worth. Asians, then, invest a lot more personally in preserving acceptable appearances than do Westerners. In addition, they judge persons more on the basis of their actions rather than their words.

2.2.1 Concept of Time

You can expect extreme patience from your Asian counterpart. Each stage of the negotiation process is likely to be slower than in North American and some European countries.

This protracted process is due to three main reasons: (1) Emphasis is put more on the long-term relationship than on the task of negotiating the deal; (2) The custom is to have several people on each negotiating team; and (3) The decisions tend to be made by the entire group.

Negotiations in Singapore and Hong Kong are likely to move more rapidly than in other parts of the region.

Negotiators in Asian countries, like Japan and China, view the goal of a negotiation not as a single contract, but more as a start of a long-term relationship. That's why normally they spend more time in building pre-negotiation relationship compared to negotiators from west Europe and North America.

2.2.2 Communication Styles

Case 2

A U.S. airplane manufacturer and a Japanese airline company were negotiating the price of some airplanes. The American negotiating team suggested a price. In response, the Japanese were quiet. The American team then lowered the price. The Japanese team again were quiet. The American team lowered the price again. The Japanese team continued to keep silent. In the end, the Japanese team came away from the negotiation with a price lower than they ever expected. The Americans were disappointed because they sold the planes at a very low price.

Questions for Case-analysis:

1. Why do you think the Americans kept lowering the price?
2. Why do you think the Japanese kept silent?

A. Verbal Communication

There are strong elements of Confucianism, Buddhism, and Taoism in these cultures, creating such communication values as humility, silence, modesty, and mistrust of words. Verbal communication in Pacific Rim cultures is generally quite indirect. In high-context cultures such as Japan or China, people expect the person to whom they are talking to know what is on their mind. They give the other person all the necessary information except the crucial piece. This can be illustrated in the way negotiators say no. Instead of saying it directly, as would be the case with most American negotiators, this message may be conveyed by saying, "We will study the matter." or "We want to get more opinions on your idea." This communication pattern makes it imperative that you listen carefully.

If one negotiator from North America responses to a proposal: "That's difficult." The response would be interpreted by his American colleague as there could further discussion and possibly the proposal needs improvement. While on the contrast, when the same response is made by a Japanese or Chinese to a proposal, the message is a No to this proposal even it's a very indirect No. So the different communication style can often lead to misunderstandings when this is the case in a cross-cultural negotiation.

Another typical example is silence in conversations. Compared to cultures that value verbal agility, the Japanese usually take longer to respond. For them, it is a normal period to reflect on the question and figure out a proper response. But for their North American counterparts, silence can mean "rudeness, lack of understanding and a cunning tactic to get the Americans to reveal themselves" (Lewicki, Sanders, Minton&Barry, 2002), as is shown in case two in this chapter. When Americans sometimes find it confusing to understand the period of silence in conversation with Japanese, they may find it equally agitated to negotiate with Brazilians even though Brazil is a country that values verbal agility. That's because some Latin American countries have a tendency to respond quickly. "Indeed, they may answer a point once they have understood it even though the other side has not finished speaking." (Lewicki, Sanders, Minton&Barry, 2002) So it may mean interruptions to negotiators from North America or west Europe.

B. Nonverbal Communication

Body language is generally more reserved than in a lot of other regions. Expressive gestures are seldom seen, and eye contact is almost always brief. Personal space is a little closer than in the United States, but touching in business setting is generally restrained. Brief handshakes or bows, rather than hugs and other forms of touching, are typical.

2.2.3 Decision-making Process

The need for role orderliness and conformity helps explain why it is so important for those in the Asian cultures to build a relationship with their negotiating counterpart. Getting to know one's negotiating counterpart is a way to bring orderliness and certainty to one's world. Social stratification over the centuries and the influence of the Confucian ethic make proper social relationships extremely important. These relationships form the basis for such social traditions as rituals of courtesy, formality in behavior, excessive politeness, loyalty to and identification with the group, deference to the elderly, avoidance of direct conflicts, and extreme modesty when speaking of one's status, accomplishments, and family.

2.2.4 Diversity

Turner and Trompenaars did a research among thousands of executives from all over the world on the influence of different cultural values on their basic business management, such as decision-making process. For example:

What is a better way to choose a person to represent a group?

1. All members of the group should meet and discuss candidates until almost everybody agrees on the same person; or

2. The group members should meet, nominate persons, vote, and choose the person with a majority of the votes even if several people are against the person.

In this question, according to the author, the values of adversarial democracy and consensual democracy were in tension. While 84.4 percent of the Japanese opted for Answer one (consensual democracy), only 37.7 percent of the Americans did so. It is interesting to note that there were differences among Asians on this question. For example, unlike the Japanese, only 39.4 percent of the Singaporeans chose Answer One, exhibiting an aversion to consensual democracy that is perhaps reflected in Singapore's authoritarian political system.

Case 3

A Japanese American, whose firm conducted business in Japan, told once how he averted a near disaster in United States-Japanese relations. His company selected and addressed 500 Christmas cards to its Japanese joint-venture partner. The cards were red (in Japan funeral notices are red). The Japanese American manager stopped the mail in time. He said, "We almost sent 500 funeral cards to our Japanese partner."

(*Adapted from* International Business Negotiation *by Liu Ting*)

Questions for Case-analysis:

1. Would you guess the consequence of sending these Christmas cards?

2. Name some colors and explain their cultural implications in different countries.

3　Negotiating in Europe

⇨ 3.1　Europe Overview

Europe is the world's second smallest continent by surface area, covering about 10,180,000 square kilometres (3,930,000 sq mi) or 2% of the Earth's surface and about 6.8% of its land area. Of Europe's approximately 50 countries, Russia is by far the largest in both area and population, taking up 40% of the continent (although the country has territory in both Europe and Asia), while Vatican City is the smallest. Europe is the third-most populous continent after Asia and Africa, with a population of 739-743 million or about 11% of the world's population.

Europe, particular ancient Greece, is the birthplace of Western culture. The fall of the

Western Roman Empire marked the end of ancient history and the beginning of an era known as the "**Middle Ages**". The Renaissance humanism, exploration, art, and science led the "**Old Continent**", and eventually the rest of the world, to the modern era. From this period onwards, Europe played a predominant role in global affairs. Between the 16th and 20th centuries, European nations controlled at various times the Americas, most of Africa, Oceania, and the majority of Asia.

The Economy of Europe comprises more than 731 million people in 48 different countries. Like other continents, the wealth of Europe's states varies, although the poorest are well above the poorest states of other continents in terms of GDP and living standards. The difference in wealth across Europe can be seen roughly in former Cold War divide, with some countries breaching the divide (Greece, Portugal, Slovenia and the Czech Republic). Most European states have GDP per capita higher than the world's average and are very highly developed. Some European economies are still catching up with European leading countries.

Based on the environment, culture, and economic similarities, Europe is divided into four different regions.

Eastern Europe is territorially the largest region, consisting of, the Czech Republic, Estonia, Latvia, Lithuania, Poland, and the Slovak Republic. The southern half of Eastern Europe is referred to as the Balkans or Balkan Peninsula after the mountain range in Bulgaria. This includes the countries Albania, Bosnia-Herzegovina, Bulgaria, Croatia, Hungary, Romania, Slovenia, and Serbia-Montenegro.

Western Europe, is the industrial heartland of Europe and the core of its economic power, with a total population around 187 million. This area covers Belgium, France, Germany, Luxembourg, the Netherlands, the Republic of Ireland, and the United Kingdom, with Alpine Europe and the British Isles included as well.

England, Scotland, Wales, Northern Ireland, and the Republic of Ireland, make up the British Isles. Austria and Switzerland make up Alpine Europe. Northern Europe includes Denmark, Finland, Greenland, Iceland, Norway, and Sweden. This area is known for harsher environments. It is generally cold, with poorly developed soils and limited mineral resources. This region has a population of over 25 million people.

Southern Europe, also known as Mediterranean Europe, is located on the south side of Europe's center, and consists of Greece, Italy, Portugal, and Spain. The culture among these countries goes back to Greco-Roman times.

The major industrial core extends from the southeastern corner of England, down to Belgium, the Netherlands, and Luxembourg, into the eastern part of France, the western section of Germany, all of Switzerland, the western tip of Austria, and into northern Italy.

3.1.1　Eastern Europe

Though definitions vary in the fast-changing European political and economic landscape,

Eastern Europe consists of countries such as the Czech Republic, Hungary, Poland, Romania, and Turkey, as well as Russia, Kazakhstan, Ukraine, and other countries that formerly constituted the Soviet Union. Russia is the world's largest nation, spanning eleven time zones.

"Eastern Europe can be a very tough part of the world for a negotiator." (Acuff, 2008) Eastern Europe witnessed profound political changes in the last few decades. Hence, the business environment is strongly influenced by the fundamental changes in economic and political structures. However, opportunities always arise by changes. "An emphasis is likely to be put on the creation of an auto industry in Hungary, Poland, and the Czech Republic to meet projected domestic and international demand. Feeder industries will involve the mechanical engineering, electronics, electro-technical, chemicals, glass, and sheet metal subsectors." (Acuff, 2008)

Considering investing in Eastern Europe will give priority to auto industry, consumer goods, processed food, health, telecommunications, or computers. Investment viability will be enhanced by improvements in business conditions. From the view of a global procurement strategy, Eastern Europe offers major cost advantages, mainly because of inexpensive labor. The attractiveness of Eastern Europe is also enhanced by active involvement of the World Bank, United Nations, International Monetary Fund, and New European Bank for Reconstruction and Development.

The business arrangements favored in Eastern Europe in the twenty-first century by many multinational companies are joint ventures, direct investment, or start-ups. Joint ventures are popular because of their export and hard currency potential.

There are key obstacles to overcome in much of this part of the world. First, the concept of "profit" is still not fully understood in some parts of Eastern Europe. Another obstacle is currency. As a rule, Eastern currencies are considered of less value in other parts of the world. Alternative financial arrangements must therefore be found to circumvent this problem. Certainly, entrance into the European Union by the Czech Republic, Hungary, Poland, and other Eastern European countries should aid this process.

3.1.2 Western Europe

The nations of Western Europe have completely recovered from the World War Ⅱ era and transitioned past the Cold War into the European decade. France (the geographically largest Western European nation) and Germany (the most populous and largest economy) are the two powerhouses. With vast resources, strong infrastructure and large industries, Western Europe plays a central role in the world's economic and political systems.

Western Europe is responsible for over half of Europe's GNP, and 16% of the global economy. It is not surprising that both France and Germany have been attracting tens of thousands of migrant workers. It is also not surprising these nations are attempting to modernize and globalize their economies further while maintaining their significant social infrastructure. Although some industries have been privatized, most governments retain significant stakes in leading firms and use government regulation to reduce the gaps between rich and poor and provide for health and welfare.

The entire Western Europe will come to grips with an aging workforce, which will present problems in medical care and pensions.

The governments are stable. Belgium faces some ethnic tensions, but generally no government in this region is likely to fall any time soon. Western Europe is a key player in the European Union.

3.1.3　Southern Europe

The countries of Southern Europe were once great empires, but most have lost the glories of past positions and struggle to advance into the modern global economy. The individual countries are fairly small and many are landlocked. Although resources like timber, water and metals are abundant, small amount of oil and rare metals can be found. Many of these countries sit on key trade routes between Europe and Asia. Most have suffered from air and water pollution. Nearly all have experienced severe earthquakes and continue to be at risk.

Although most of the governments are stable, many are barely so. Albania and the states of the former Yugoslavia have recently endured sharp wars and are still trying to rebuild. Spain is still dealing with the Basque separatist movement. Greece, Italy, Portugal and Spain are older countries trying to come to grips with new economic and political realities. Crime and corruption are present everywhere. Albania is struggling with the drug trade. Economically, all of these nations have seen better days. Southern Europe's GNP is just slightly greater than Northern Europe's, even though it has half as many people. Poverty and unemployment are widespread, with up to one quarter of some countries living below the poverty line. Most of the countries are, to some degree, dependent on tourism. The former members of Yugoslavia are still rebuilding after war. Aid from the European Union forms a small but significant minority of national budgets. Sporadic violence still causes many investors to be skittish.

3.1.4　Northern Europe

The ten nations (and three smaller island chains) of Northern Europe may be small, but their contributions to global politics, economics and missions are substantial. They are far enough north that ice can impede maritime traffic. Rare and precious metals can be found in the region, as can fish, timber and arable land. Petroleum and natural gas are found in small quantities, but these will likely be depleted in the near future.

This is the least populated region in Europe, and one of the least populated in the world. It is also one of the slowest growing. At a growth of only 300,000 people per year, it will likely increase from 94 million in AD 2000 to only 101 million in 2025. It is heavily urbanized and over 83% of the population live in cities. Over 180 cities have a population of one million or more. Northern Europe has the third highest concentration of elderly in the world: 20% of the people are 65 or older.

Although they have many rich resources, most of the nations are dependent on trade with other nearby countries for certain key items. And they have been successful. The people of Northern Europe are very wealthy (as usual, some more so than others). The region accounts for one-fifth of Europe's total Gross National Product (GNP), with economies that are a modernized mix of capitalism and extensive welfare systems. All have benefited from globalization and low defense requirements. While Norway, Sweden and Finland are among the best economies in the world, Latvia, Lithuania and Estonia lag behind. Iceland is pursuing hydrogen energy, and Sweden and Finland have highly advanced telecommunications companies. All have stable governments. Estonia, Latvia and Lithuania have ongoing thorny issues with ethnic minorities (particularly Russians). Britain and Ireland have cemented a peace agreement which is being implemented, though slowly and not without difficulty.

⇨ 3.2   Introduction to EU

Negotiating in Europe can sometimes be quite challenging since the negotiating styles differ from country to country. The most important business development in Western Europe in the last few decades is the emergence of the European Union (EU). The EU is a unique economic and political partnership between 28 European countries that together cover much of the continent. The EU was created in the aftermath of the Second World War. The first steps were to foster economic cooperation: the idea being that countries that trade with one another become economically interdependent and so more likely to avoid conflict. The result was the European Economic Community (EEC), created in 1958, and initially increasing economic cooperation between six countries: Belgium, Germany, France, Italy, Luxembourg and the Netherlands. Since then, a huge single market has been created and continues to develop towards its full potential. What began as a purely economic union has evolved into an organization spanning policy areas, from development aid to environment. A name change from the EEC to the European Union (EU) in 1993 reflected this.

The EU is based on the rule of law: everything that it does is founded on treaties, voluntarily and democratically agreed by all member countries. These binding agreements set out the EU's goals in its many areas of activity. Now the EU is a powerful economic and political force, whose goals are to regulate Europe, that is a single market to become Europe without frontiers, where there will be an unrestricted movement of money, products, services, and people. It is likely that other countries will join the EU, mainly from Eastern Europe. Europeans see the EU as a critical step in regaining their competitive position with the United States, Japan, China, and other parts of the world. The biggest opportunity for its member countries may lie in the ability to exploit economies that are available in the widely expanded "home" market. The most likely impact of the EU on your business activities is in the area of common standards, deregulation, economic research and development, fiscal harmony, open government procurement, and taxation and tariff reforms.

What all this means in practical terms is that, among many other things, workers from member countries will be able to work anywhere in the EU, sales taxes and value-added taxes (VATs) will be made more uniform, foreign exchange controls will be discontinued, and property laws will be standardized. Products will be sold anywhere in the EU as long as they meet home-country standards. Flexible manufacturing will produce standard products (regarding packages and sizes) that will cater to local markets. But, again, realize that member countries will almost certainly retain key national differences when it comes to negotiations.

Case 4

Volkswagen, a German company, was once involved in a titanic struggle with several other major auto manufactures to secure a partnership with Shanghai Automotive Industrial to make cars in China. Volkswagen spared no expense, hiring local consultants and Chinese-speaking American employees to make sure the company did "everything right" to impress the Chinese with their cultural sensitivity and understanding of Chinese business customs. When Volkswagen gave Chinese officials expensive gifts from the New York jewelers, Tiffany's, the company had them wrapped in red ribbons (all items from Tiffany's are originally wrapped with white ribbon, which has been one of Tiffany's features and traditions). The reason for doing so is clear: In China, red means good luck and white signifies sorrow and death. The Chinese were obviously impressed with the cultural sensitivity of Volkswagen. Through the thoughtfulness of the ribbon switch, Volkswagen presented itself as an internationally savvy company prepared to work in the framework of local cultural and business sensitivities. It came across as a class act and, who knows for sure, maybe white ribbons would have been a deal killer. So with this auspicious beginning, the negotiation went smoothly and resulted in a win-win agreement.

(*Adapted from* International Business Negotiation *by Dou Ran*)

Questions for Case-analysis:

1. What's the difference between this case and the previous Christmas case?

2. Can you summarize the importance of knowing other cultural traditions in international business?

⇨ 3.3　Business Style in Europe

3.3.1　*Concept of Time*

Due to historical reasons, the Western Europeans share common views of time with North Americans more than any other area in the world. Business life is generally quite fast-paced. Punctuality is much appreciated and meetings almost always start and end on time.

3.3.2 Communication Style

A. Verbal Communication

Eastern Europeans are generally direct in their communication, making straightforward, firm requests and demands. Once past any language barrier, there is little guesswork regarding their point of view. Though they are very gracious as hosts, the communication styles of Eastern Europeans may sometimes seem abrupt and aggressive, even to Western Europeans and North Americans.

Articulation is highly valued in Western European business situations and ambiguity is generally considered as improper business behavior. The communication style is formal and understated. Face-to-face communication is expected in the start-up contacts. Emotional behavior should be avoided in business situations, especially in negotiations.

B. Nonverbal Communication

"Western Europeans are typically more reserved in their body language than North Americans and much more so than Latin Americans or Middle Easterners." (Acuff, 2008) Big body movements are almost always inappropriate in either a business or social setting. "Expect most Western Europeans to have about the same personal space as do North Americans in business settings—usually about three feet." (Acuff, 2008) Physical contact is usually limited to a brief handshake in business situations.

Personal space in Eastern Europe is generally closer than in North America or most of Western Europe. Hand and arm gestures are usually quite expressive. Handshakes are firm and brief. An exception is handshakes between men and women, which can be quite lengthy in countries such as Poland or the Czech Republic, with the man kissing the woman's hand.

3.3.3 Decision-making Process

"Order, discipline, and responsibility are highly valued in the family and at work. The path to the corporate world is a mixture of education and connections." (Acuff, 2008)

Responsibility for one's family is highly valued in Western Europe. Working overtime can be accepted but not viewed as a general practice for employees. To enjoy leisure time with family is a long kept tradition, and various kinds of month-long holidays and leave are typical. For example, it is rare to see two-or-three-year-long parental leave in Asian or middle-east societies. In contrast, is is not uncommon in many Western European countries. For example, in Sweden, working parents are entitled with 13 months paid leave per child at 77.6% of the employee's monthly salary. UK provides female employees 52 weeks of maternity (or adoption) leave, "39 weeks of which are paid, planned to rise to 52 weeks paid, with the first six weeks paid at 90% of full pay and the remainder at a fixed rate (£ 136.78/week as of 2014)."

Power in organizations flows from the top down, and the hierarchy is important. Top managers usually have a great deal of technical expertise and tend to dislike power sharing and delegation of responsibility. In addition, top managers do not communicate regularly with lower managers. Consequently, lower-level managers may not have much information about the corporate goals or mission. An exception is Scandinavia, where top managers communicate regularly with middle managers, and substantial power is delegated for key decisions. Though Western Europeans have high occupational mobility, long tenures exist within the same organization. Job hopping tends to be viewed with disfavor, and loyalty and hard work are rewarded.

In Eastern Europe, there is, on one hand, predictability as to one's place and strict rules and regulations surrounding organizational behavior. On the other hand, it is not always clear who exactly is in charge. This is probably the result, in large part, of the cumbersome bureaucracies that generate duplication of effort and occasionally blurred lines of authority. Decisions generally flow from the top down.

4　Negotiating in North America

Case 5

In the earlier years of China's reform and opening to the outside world, many American businesses came to China to do business with Chinese firms. When Chinese people first came into contact with Americans, they always felt a little uncomfortable and awkward. They just could not get used to the "American style"—American always addressed others by their first names, and enjoyed coming directly to the point and being more than straightforward. American behavior seemed to be too open and expressive. They never considered saving face for others, and sometimes even made others lose face. It took a long time for Chinese people to understand that this is just cultural. Finally, both sides did spend time getting to know each other and adjusting to their cultural differences.

(Adapted from International Business Negotiation *by Dou Ran)*

Questions for Case-analysis:

1. What's the essential preparation concerning cultural traditions of the other party?
2. Can proper preparation about the cultural traditions of TOS solve the cultural problems arising in the negotiation?

⇨ 4.1　North America Overview

North America is a continent wholly within the Northern Hemisphere and almost wholly within the Western Hemisphere. North America covers an area of about 24,709,000 square kilometers (9,540,000 square miles), about 16.5% of the earth's land area and about 4.8% of its total surface. North America is the third largest continent by area, following Asia andAfrica, and the fourth by population after Asia, Africa, and Europe. In 2013, its population was estimated at nearly 565 million people in 23 independent states, or about 7.5% of the world's population, if nearby islands (most notably the Caribbean) are included.

Present-day cultural and ethnic patterns reflect different kinds of interactions between European colonists, indigenous peoples, African slaves and their descendants. European influences are strongest in the northern parts of the continent while indigenous and African influences are relatively stronger in the south. Due to the history of colonialism, most North Americans speak English, Spanish or French and societies and states commonly reflect Western traditions.

Canada, Mexico and the United States have significant and multifaceted economic systems. The United States has the largest economy in North America, and in the world. In 2014, the US had an estimated per capita gross domestic product (PPP) of $54,980, and is the most technologically developed economy in North America. The United States' services sector comprises 76.7% of the country's GDP (estimated in 2010), industry comprises 22.2% and agriculture comprises 1.2%. Canada's economic trends are similar to that of the United States, with significant growth in the sectors of services, mining and manufacturing. Canada's per capita GDP (PPP) was estimated at $44,656 and it had the 11th largest GDP (nominal) in 2014. Canada's services sector comprises 78% of the country's GDP (estimated in 2010), industry comprises 20% and agriculture comprises 2%. Mexico has a per capita GDP (PPP) of $16,111 and as of 2014 is the 15th largest GDP (nominal) in the world. Being a newly industrialized country, Mexico maintains both modern and outdated industrial and agricultural facilities and operations. Its main sources of income are oil, industrial exports, manufactured goods, electronics, heavy industry, automobiles, construction, food, banking and financial services.

The North American economy is well defined and structured in three main economic areas. These areas are the **North American Free Trade Agreement** (**NAFTA**), *Caribbean Community and Common Market* (**CARICOM**), and the **Central American Common Market** (**CACM**). Of these trade blocs, the United States takes part in two. In addition to the larger trade blocs there is the **Canada-Costa Rica Free Trade Agreement** among numerous other free trade relations, often between the larger, more developed countries and Central American and Caribbean countries.

The economy of North America (the United States and Canada) is the largest in the world. There is a climate of free enterprise where most laws are designed to promote competition rather than restrict it. Big corporations dominate the business environment, particularly in the manufacturing and oil sectors. Small and medium-sized businesses are prevalent in the service, retail, and construction industries. U.S. and Canadian businessmen try to keep up to date on the latest management techniques and ideas. Anyone planning to do business with North Americans should be aware of such management trends as Six Sigma, customer relationship management, strategic thinking, and participative management (giving nonsupervisory employees more power to participate in decision making).

4.2 Business Style in North America

4.2.1 Concept of Time

The pace of business is vigorous in North America, particularly in the United States. Whether a negotiation takes place over the telephone, in an office, or over a business meal, emphasis is put on getting through the content of the negotiation as efficiently as possible. Don't be surprised, however, if final decisions are occasionally bogged down in detailed analysis by financial, strategic planning, legal, or other managers. This slow, exhaustive review is sometimes irreverently referred to as a paralysis of analysis. Financial analysis of one-to-five-year returns on investment are typical. There is often more of an emphasis on short-term profits than on long-term growth, although this is more the case in the United States than Canada. Many shareholders demand quick results.

4.2.2 Communication Style

Shake hands firmly and briefly with both men and women upon meeting and leaving, and smile. American greetings are informal. A peck on the cheek or a hug may be given between women or between men and women who have been acquaintances for a long time. "Hello" is a common greeting for English-speaking people. In the French parts of Quebec, the handshake should be a little bit less firm, and "Bonjour" is appropriate; exchanging light kisses on each cheek is typical.

In Canada, first names are not typically used in business situations, except by close friends. First names are used in most business situations. In US, possible exceptions would be to use "Mr"., "Mrs"., or "Miss" for a very senior person in age and rank, or in formal situations. Business cards are routinely exchanged in a business setting, though not in social settings. In Canada, use business cards printed in both French and English for French speaking clients.

A. Verbal Communication

North American verbal communication is direct and open. This means that a U.S. or Canadian negotiator is likely to tell you directly, "I'm sorry, but we can't accept your offer." If your North American counterpart is unwilling to make further concessions, she may tell you, "This is our bottom line—our final offer." The English language as used by North Americans has many slang expressions that make understanding difficult. Each region of the United States and Canada has its own forms of expression. Be sure to ask for clarification if you do not understand what is being said. Silence is avoided in conversation, and interruptions are common. Don't be surprised or take it personally if a North American negotiator, particularly one from the United States, finishes your sentence for you if you hesitate when you are speaking.

B. Nonverbal Communication

North Americans like more space in their organizational lives than individuals in most other regions of the world. A distance of three feet is typical between people in business situations. Very little touching takes place. Handshakes, for example, are usually firm and brief. You rarely see two North American business-people hugging each other upon greeting or leaving (an exception is in French-speaking Canada). Some North American executives are known to be "back slappers"—those who give others a light slap on the back to show camaraderie or encouragement. Even this gesture is brief and often not appreciated by others.

4.2.3　Decision-making Process

There is a low need for role orderliness and conformity in North American organizations compared with those in other regions of the world. More emphasis is put on the content than on the form of the negotiation. How business is done tends to get less emphasis than getting it done efficiently. U.S. negotiators sometimes say, for example, "Let's not stand on ceremony—let's just get on with it." North Americans are generally quite informal in their business dealings; although in French speaking Canada there is a bit more formality than elsewhere in North America. The use of first names in business characterizes North American informality.

An exception to this informality is the significant role that attorneys often play in finalizing negotiations, particularly in the United States. This sometimes leads to the feeling that U.S. negotiators have a "home field advantage" because of the unpredictable nature of what might be decided in a U.S. court of law. U.S. contracts tend to be lengthy and are reviewed in detail by attorneys. This is largely because U.S. organizations tend to be very concerned about potentially costly lawsuits.

4.2.4　Diversity

In the United States, management gurus such as Jim Collins, Peter Drucker, W. Edwards Deming, Daniel Goleman, Joe Juran, John Maxwell, Tom Peters, and Michael E. Porter strongly influence management thinking. Fixed ideas about the behavior of North American negotiators are particularly dangerous because of the enormous heterogeneity in the backgrounds of the negotiators themselves. How one might behave in Manhattan may be quite different from one's behavior in Jackson, Mississippi, or Calgary, Alberta, or Montreal, Quebec. The gender, racial, and ethnic mixes of the U.S. and Canadian workforces are going through unprecedented demographic changes.

For example, in the United States, women are now almost half the workforce. There are vast increases in the Hispanic and Asian populations, and large numbers of immigrants are entering the country. Caucasian males, who once dominated the U.S. workforce, are now a minority and are expected to be increasingly so in the future.

Although the United States and Canada have strong civil rights laws, employees can be routinely dismissed individually or in large groups for economic or performance reasons. For example, a scene feared by a U.S. employee is being called into the boss's office on a Friday afternoon, being terminated, and then being asked to clear out his or her desk immediately before being escorted out of the building. North American organizations would generally find their employee protection laws less stringent than in Europe. U.S. businesses are organized by state rather than at the federal level, but once a business is established in one state, it can operate in any of the other states. It is generally advisable to organize in the state where you do the most business. However, liberal incorporation laws, tax breaks, and other considerations make states such as New York and (especially) Delaware favorite incorporation sites. In Delaware there is no need for any one of the incorporators to be a U.S. citizen.

Usually, foreign investors face few problems in North America (unless there are security-related reasons, such as in the defense, communications, and airline industries). In fact, a French company has the same status as a Delaware company incorporated in the state of Ohio.

An American's Report Card

How do American negotiators stack up in their global negotiating skills? Let's look at their report card. It itemizes the criteria that will make you a masterful negotiator. This assessment is based on discussions with hundreds of Americans who negotiate internationally as well as with their international counterparts in other countries.

The Seven SINs

There are many challenges in keeping a firm footing on the international negotiating terrain. There are, however, seven main areas where U.S. negotiators tend to stumble. They are what I call the seven SINs (Slips in International Negotiating). These SINs are areas where American negotiators tend to score a C or lower in terms of key international negotiating skills.

Individualism vs. Collectivism

Individualism is prized in North America. With no aristocracy in either Canada or the United States, one earns social status largely through individual competitiveness that leads to business success. Although family commitments and outside interests are extremely common and deeply held, a preoccupation with business success is usual, particularly in the United States. The fierce competition of New York City executives typifies this preoccupation. However, executives in the midwestern, southern, and western parts of the United States, and most of Canada, do not stress individualism to the same degree. Team negotiations with, say, seven or more individuals are very unlikely unless the negotiation is very complex and critical to the company's future. Even with several team members present, there are normally only one or two key decision makers on whom you should focus most of your attention. These one or two key players usually "call the shots"—that is, they have the authority to make decisions that can consummate a business deal, or consummate the deal subject to the review of various financial, legal, and other technical experts in the company. Be aware that while many U.S. and Canadian companies are trying to find ways to involve workers in key decisions through participative management techniques, and any such involvement normally impacts operational decisions rather than business negotiations.

5   Negotiating in Latin America

Case 6

In the 1960's Kennecott, a U.S. company was about to enter into renegotiation over its contract with the government of Chile concerning its El Teniente copper mine. At the time, Chile's BATNA appeared overwhelmingly strong as the government was possessed of a strong pro-sovereignty stance towards foreign management of its natural resources. "Can we take some lessons for our mortgage renegotiations?" The government of Chile was politically positioned to establish their own tough financial terms or had the option of declining to renegotiate by simply ejecting Kennecott from their involvement altogether by expropriating the mine. Chile had its own experts who could manage and operate the mine, perform the processing, and could readily market this very useful natural resource. Simply put, Kennecott found itself in the position of either acceding to the contract renegotiation terms dictated by the Chilean government or have the mine snatched out from under them.

Realizing that their own BATNA was weak, Kennecott executives came up with a very creative solution which ultimately weakened Chile's position while leveraging their own BATNA more favorably by creating value for both sides.

The proposal made by Kennecott entailed the following six strategies thereby changing the rules of the game:

1. The deal consisted of Kennecott offering to sell a majority equity interest in the mining operation to the Chilean government.
2. Realizing that Chile would not particularly care to divest the funds of the sale into U.S. banks, Kennecott offered to use the funds, combined with an outside loan, to finance the mine's expansion. This allowed Chile to preserve its nationalistic interests and have greater financial gain from future profits. They were able to re-negotiate and establish a partnership which was mutually acceptable to both parties.
3. Next, Kennecott then persuaded the Chilean government to guarantee the loan and have this guarantee subject to the law of the state of New York.

4. Then, as many of the company's mining assets as possible were insured with U.S. backed guarantees, against the potential expropriation threat.

5. Kennecott then negotiated that the copper output derived from the expansion would be sold exclusively to clients in Europe and North America.

6. Lastly, the rights to collect from these new contracts would be sold to a consortium of financial institutions based in Japan, the United States and Europe.

This allowed for a greater diversity in the customer base and additional partners. In future contract renegotiations, this would result in a much larger multi-party negotiation then just Kennecott having to renegotiate on its own. Many of these outside interests would also be engaged in other unrelated negotiations with the Chilean government, thereby reducing Chile's leverage in any future contract renegotiations. Mortgage re-negotiators won't have as much flexibility to change the negotiation game when they re-negotiate their contracts.

Lastly, because of the insurance guarantees obtained by Kennecott, even if the renegotiations collapsed, Kennecott had succeeded in protecting a good portion of its interests should Chile opt to go ahead and appropriate the copper mine. Additionally, the company could also call in its other partners to act as allies.

In the end, some years later, the mine was eventually expropriated by Chile, but Kennecott was in a far much better position than it had initially been before it initially started to renegotiate the contract. Kennecott enhanced its BATNA by making an offer the Chileans couldn't refuse, while taking steps to protect their interests should negotiations collapse.

Questions for Case-analysis:

1. What were the initial positions in the negotiation?

2. What was the creative steps Kennecott take?

⇨ 5.1　Latin America Overview

Latin America is a region of the Americas that comprises countries where primarily Spanish and Portuguese are predominant. Latin America generally refers to Mexico, Central and South America, and the Spanish-speaking Caribbean. Although Mexico is geographically part of North America, culturally it is usually considered part of Latin America. It consists of twenty sovereign states which cover an area that stretches from the southern border of the United States to the southern tip of South America, including the Caribbean. Latin America has an area of approximately $19,197,000$ km^2($7,412,000$ sq mi), almost 13% of the earth's land surface area. As of 2013, its population was estimated at more than 604 million and in 2014, Latin America has a combined nominal GDP of $5,573,397$ million USD and a GDP PPP of $7,531,585$ million USD. The term "Latin America" was first used in 1861 in La revue des races Latines, a magazine "dedicated to the cause of Pan-Latinism". The inhabitants of Latin America are of a variety of ancestries, ethnic groups, and races, making the region one of the most diverse in the world.

Business practices differ in the many different cultures collectively referred to as Latin. With over 400 million people, a large market exists in Latin America. In addition, vast natural resources make Latin America a potentially strong economic force in the world. Political and economic policies have here to fore hampered progress.

⇨ 5.2 Business Style in Latin America

5.2.1 Concept of Time

The typical Latin American sees time as abstract—more a series of events than in terms of hours or minutes. There is no sense of urgency in the traditional way of life, rooted in the seasons of agriculture. It is natural in Latin America to consider a 10:00 a.m. appointment as meaning roughly 10:30 a.m. or 11:00 a.m.; in fact, that is considered prompt. Latin Americans are more present-oriented than future-oriented. They accept many things as "just happening" rather than applying logical or technical analysis and planning.

5.2.2 Communication Styles

A. Verbal Communication

Latin negotiators are likely to have a lot of voice inflection, gestures, and emotion. While individuals from North America tend to consider softer tones, fewer gestures, and less emotion as the sign of a poised individual, in Latin America expressiveness and emotion in talking are tied to the Latin concepts of individualism and machismo. Expect to get interrupted frequently. This is not seen as being impolite so much as eagerness to share points of view with you.

B. Nonverbal Communication

You can expect the physical space to be quite close among Latin Americans compared to the United States and Canada. People in the United States and Canada stand at an arm's length when conducting business face-to-face, but Latin Americans stand much closer.

Latins often complain that North Americans are impersonal and don't want to get close to them—personally or figuratively. Embracing is common among men who have established business acquaintances; similarly, women may briefly kiss the other's cheek. You will probably shake hands unless you get to know your counterpart quite well. Handshaking is softer than in North America; firm handshakes may be perceived as hostile. North American negotiators sometimes mistakenly think that the soft Latin handshake is an indication that the Latin negotiating counterpart is unassertive and will not negotiate a very effective agreement on his or her own behalf. Only later does the North American negotiator learn that the Latin American negotiator was in fact very effective. There is no general rule on eye contact. On one hand, some Latin Americans are taught that it is respectful to look down when with someone in a position of authority. This can sometimes look shifty to a North American who does not know the cultural influence at work. On the other hand, sustaining eye contact is considered important in Argentina. Latin America is a good place to be expressive in your hand, arm, and facial gestures. Smiles are valued in Latin America.

For example, in Brazil, the use of significant amounts of exaggerated body language (by the standards of less tactile cultures) plays a significant role in normal communication. Brazilians are very tactile—even across the sexes—and work at very close proximity. They also exhibit strong levels of eye contact when speaking to people. This combination of tactility, proximity and a steady gaze can be intimidating in some cultures (many Asian cultures for example), but it is important that you adapt to these issues as quickly as possible, otherwise your own conservativeness could be misinterpreted as unfriendliness.

5.2.3　Decision-making Process

The decision-making process in Argentina is centralized and top management will most likely need to provide final approval. Understand who is at the table, how much authority they have and who needs to approve the agreements—and when they need to be approved. Argentines tend not to bargain. They would rather build a relationship as part of the business agreement than exact the last penny from a deal.

In general, the negotiations will be held in a meeting room. Subordinates will arrive early and higher-status executives will arrive later, usually with a personal secretary and an interpreter. Knowing this can help you identify the key negotiators.

5.2.4　Establishing Personal Rapport

Latin Americans generally prefer to conduct business negotiations face to face. The personal aspects of business—developing and maintaining relationships—are very important here, and the hard, direct approach frequently associated with the U.S. negotiating style does not work well in any country in Latin America.

Most Latin American business people prefer to work with those they consider friends, rather than individuals with whom they have not established rapport—even if the strangers have a good offer. Negotiating in Latin American countries generally takes longer and will have many more discussions and meetings.

For example, Brazilians view a negotiation as a relationship and a long-term agreement, so you need to spend time building rapport with your colleagues. While the negotiation process will take longer in Brazil than in the United States, it will be somewhat faster in the major city of Sao Paulo.

Mexico is a relationship-oriented culture in which family is a primary concern. A fair amount of socialization is expected before proceeding into business, and your colleagues may want to discuss their family and inquire about yours. Plan to spend more time at meetings than you are accustomed to.

There is probably no more decisive factor in the success or failure of government-to-government relations or business dealings with Latin Americans than the extent to which you are able to establish trusting interpersonal rapport. Latins give great importance to being able to trust people with whom they work. People in the United States seem to have less of a need. We tend to put our trust in governments or particular companies, while Latins tend to distrust impersonal institutions and put much greater reliance on personal relationships.

To succeed with Latin Americans, you must work actively to gain their confidence and trust. No matter how prestigious your agency or firm is, if you cannot convince your Latin American associates that you are personally reliable, you will probably fail in your dealings with them. And that trustworthiness must be sincere, not simply playing a role. The U.S. government and most firms now give much higher priority to picking representatives who can develop such rapport. But not all people can. And those government and business representatives who do not—or cannot—develop trusting personal relations with their Latin American associates are doomed to failure or mediocre performance at best, usually at considerable cost to the government or firm they represent.

5.2.5 *Language and Respect*

Nothing pleases Latin Americans more than sincere expressions of respect for their culture and national achievements in which they take great pride. It means that learning as much as you can about their country and culture is necessary, especially proper social and business protocol within that culture. It also means showing enough respect to learn at least basic communication skills in their language is necessary. No one expects language fluency or even facility, but just demonstrating that you want to speak their language says a great deal about your respect for them. On the other hand, showing a lack of interest in even trying to learn basic expressions also says a great deal about your respect for them. Most U.S. Government agencies and global companies normally give high priority to having their representatives learn to communicate well in the language of the country where they will serve as representatives. Yet, there are still many U.S. officials and businessmen who do not bother to learn much about the country or culture of the Latin Americans with whom they are working, much less attempt to learn their language. That's an immediate mark against that person when he or she is trying to create a favorable impression—and first impressions are extremely important to Latin Americans.

If your work involves close and frequent association with Latin Americans, you would benefit greatly from reading extensively about their country and culture and from taking out some tapes on Spanish or Portuguese—or taking a short language immersion course in the particular language. It doesn't take that much to show respect and the benefits are immeasurable.

Today's internet allows smaller sellers to reach global audiences once reserved for large multinationals. But you must adapt your existing Web site. In addition to the obvious need to translate text into Spanish and/or Portuguese, you may have to adjust the visual appearance of your site, such as photos, logos, and graphics, to conform to the local culture. Being able to respond quickly with online technical assistance in the customer's language will go far to alleviate Latins' fears of dealing across international borders.

➩ 5.3　Diversity

Latin Americans share many values and perspectives stemming from the continuing powerful influence of their common Iberian heritage. And Latins themselves recognize that they share much more in common with each other than they do with people from the United States or Canada. But each country has its own culture and historical experiences which make it unique, and stereotyping "Latin Americans" is not only wrong, it creates resentment. Latin Americans take great pride in their own country of origin and see themselves as Mexicans or Colombians or Chileans or Brazilians. And more particularly, they see themselves as individuals deserving respect for their uniqueness. They dislike being lumped together as "Latin Americans."

To work successfully with Latin Americans, you need to avoid over-generalizing and make it a point to emphasize and show respect for the values and sources of pride of the particular Latin American country which you are dealing with.

Successful personal relationships with Latin Americans must be cultivated and nourished over the long term, especially since Latins tend to see agreements and even contracts and treaties as personal arrangements which may need adjustment as conditions change or problems arise. The common U.S. view that "a contract is a contract" to be fulfilled under threat of litigation clashes with Latin American values and can severely damage the underlying trust that enabled the agreement in the first place. Moreover, the lingering Latin American mistrust of the U. S. government and business as interested only in their own benefits needs to be handled with great care.

This means careful nourishment of relationships, with frequent personal contact and consultations maintained with Latin American associates and ensuring that you seek and respect their insight on matters involving their country. And decisions must be based on mutual benefits for all parties concerned. As long as you can keep your eye on the long-term relationship of trust and confidence—and as long as you treat your Latin American associates with the same respect, fairness and consideration with which you expect others to treat you—you will achieve enormous success in your relations with Latin Americans.

There's another special factor for negotiators to consider which could not even be considered as a problem in major developed and developing countries. Transportation accounts for 10 to 20 percent of the cost of imported products in most of Latin America, and, whereas transportation cost has generally fallen in the rest of the world, it has generally climbed in Latin America.

To put a fine point on the competitive disadvantage created by a substandard logistics system, consider the case of El Salvador. The average Salvadorian exporter suffers a delay of 43 days to make an overseas shipment, whereas a German exporter can ship merchandise out of the country in only 6 days. Having its inventory held up over seven times longer in port and terminal handling, customs and inspection, and export and pre-arrival documentation, the Salvadorian exporter must tie up a proportionately greater amount of working capital. Adding to the competitive burden of a seven-times disadvantage in the amount of working capital required is the Salvadorian exporter's cost of that capital, perhaps paying interest rates two or three times greater than the German. As a result, the Salvadorian exporter may be competitively handicapped by financial costs that are 15 to 20 times larger than those of the German. Brazil provides a macroeconomic perspective on Latin America's desperate demand for infrastructure improvements. Brazil registered a 2008 GDP of $2 trillion. Given that transportation accounts for 12.63 percent of GDP, hauling goods amounts to about $252 billion. If Brazil were to enjoy transportation costs proportionate to those of the United States of 8.19 percent,39 the savings of $89 billion would enable Brazil to more than double the amount it spends annually on education.40 The Salvadorian and Brazilian examples help explain research results showing that, as a country's transportation cost doubles, its trade falls by 80 percent, and that each additional day of delay in shipping a product out of a country reduces trade by at least one percent.

6   Negotiating in the Middle East

Case 7

A businessman negotiating with Saudi Arabia recalled how his choice of a bright green tie drew favorable remarks and helped him a lot in negotiation. Green is the color of Islam. However, the businessman had not intended to honor that religion, rather he had chosen a green tie because it was St. Patrick's Day and he wished to display his Irish roots. Initially, he simply couldn't figure out why Saudi Arabians would care so much about an Irish holiday. Only after he became more familiar with the religion did he discover the real reason—his green tie earned him compliments.

(Adapted from International Business Negotiation *by Dou Ran)*

Questions for Case-analysis：

1. What do you know about Islam and St. Patrick's Day?

2. The businessman has earned him compliments from his counterparts for wearing the tie. Is it necessary do you think to make some little friendly gestures (i.e., to learn their language, to wear their costumes, etc.) to honor your counterparts?

Case 8

A medium-sized Swedish high-technology corporation was approached by a compatriot, a businessman with good contacts in Saudi Arabia. The company sent one of their engineers, Johannesson to Riyadh, where he was introduced to a small Saudi engineering firm, run by two brothers in their mid-thirties, both with British university degrees. Johannesson was to assist in a development project on behalf of the Saudi government, however, after six visits over a period o f two years, nothing seemed to happen. Johansson's meetings with the Saudi brothers were always held in the presence of the Swedish businessman who had established the first contact. This annoyed Johannesson and his superiors, because they were not at all sure that this businessman did not have contacts with their competitors as well—but the Saudis wanted the intermediary to be there. Discussions often dwelt on issues having little to do with the business—like Shakespeare, of whom both brothers were fans.

Just when Johannesson's superiors started to doubt the wisdom of the corporation's investment in these expensive trips, a telex arrived from Riyadh inviting him back for an urgent visit. A contract worth several millions of dollars was ready to be signed. From one day to the next, the Saudis' attitude changed：the presence of the businessman-intermediary was no longer necessary, and for the first time Johannesson saw the Saudis smile, and even make jokes.

So far, so good；but the story goes on. The remarkable order contributed to Johannesson being promoted to a management position in a different division. Thus, he was no longer in charge of the Saudi account. A successor was nominated, another engineer with considerable international experience, whom Johannesson personally introduced to the Saudi brothers. A few weeks later a telex arrived from Riyadh in which the Saudis threatened to cancel the contract over a detail in the delivery conditions. Johannesson's help was asked. When he came to Riyadh it appeared that the conflict was over a minor issue and could easily be resolved—but only, the Saudis felt, with Johannesson as the corporation's representative. So the corporation twisted its structure to allow Johannesson to handle the Saudi account although his main responsibilities were now in a completely different field.

(Adapted from Cultures and Organizations：Software of the Mind *by Geert Hofstede)*

Questions for Case-analysis:

1. Why was an intermediate involved in the first several visits of Johannesson to Riyadh?

2. What was the reason that Johannesson was asked to help with the contract after a successor was nominated?

⇨ 6.1   Overview of the Middle East

The Middle East (also called the Mid East) is a Eurocentric description of a region centered on Western Asia and Egypt. Traditionally included within the Middle East are Iran (Persia), Asia Minor, Mesopotamia, the Levant, the Arabian Peninsula, and Egypt. In terms of modern-day countries, these are: Bahrain, Cyprus, Egypt, Iran, Iraq, Israel, Jordan, Kuwait, Lebanon, Oman, Palestine, Qatar, Saudi Arabia, Syria, turkey, United Arab Emirates, Yemen. Arabs, Azeris, Kurds, Persians, and Turk constitute the largest ethnic groups in the region by population, while Armenians, Assyrians, Circassians, Copts, Druze, Jews, Maronites, Somalis, and other denominations form significant minorities.

The history of the Middle East dates back to ancient times, and the region has generally been a major center of world affairs. In modern times the Middle East remains a strategically, economically, politically, culturally and religiously sensitive region.

Middle Eastern economies range from being very poor (such as Gaza and Yemen) to extremely wealthy nations (such as Qatar and UAE). According to the World Bank's World Development Indicators database published on July 1, 2009, the three largest Middle Eastern economies in 2008 were Turkey ($794,228,000,000), Saudi Arabia ($467,601,000,000) and Iran ($385,143,000,000) in terms of nominal GDP. The economic structure of Middle Eastern nations are different in the sense that while some nations are heavily dependent on export of only oil and oil-related products (such as Saudi Arabia, the UAE and Kuwait), others have a highly diverse economic base (such as Cyprus, Israel, Turkey and Egypt). Industries of the Middle Eastern region include oil and oil-related products, agriculture, cotton, cattle, dairy, textiles, leather products, surgical instruments, defence equipment (guns, ammunition, tanks, submarines, fighter jets, UAVs, and missiles). Banking is also an important sector of the economies, especially in the case of UAE and Bahrain. Except for Cyprus, Turkey, Egypt, Lebanon and Israel, tourism has been a relatively undeveloped field of the economy, in part because of the socially conservative nature of the region as well as political turmoil in certain regions of the Middle East. In recent years, however, countries such as the UAE, Bahrain, and Jordan have begun attracting a greater number of tourists because of improving tourist facilities and the relaxing of tourism-related restrictive policies.

Unemployment is notably high in the Middle East and North Africa region, particularly among young people aged 15~29, a demographic representing 30% of the region's total population.

⇨ 6.2   Business Style in the Middle East

6.2.1   *Trust and Relationship*

In most countries, trust and relation are considered as the precondition to establish business cooperation. Arab negotiators tend to spend a considerable amount of time in the pre-negotiation stage to establish personal acquaintance with the negotiators from the other parties. This investment in relationship building is considered vital to the negotiation process, and can increase the amount of time required to complete the negotiations with Arab managers. Ghauri (2003) identifies the use of time and the emphasis on personal relationships as two key cultural factors that influence the negotiation process. The priority given to trust and relationship in Arab regions may lead to a more personalized approach to negotiation: creating more preliminary contacts prior to the negotiations, increasing face-to-face meetings during negotiating process, as well as social contacts, like dinners and gift-exchanging (Cramton & Dees, 1993). For example, if you are doing business in Egypt, one of the most important things to remember is that they value relationships very strongly. It is common to spend a significant amount of time developing a relationship before business is conducted.

According to Khakhar and Rammal, in the interview with 30 Lebanese managers, the words "trust" and "relations" were used frequently. While interestingly, trust is more associated with the size of a company. "Nearly all the managers interviewed stated that they would trust a large foreign multinational enterprise (MNE) as opposed to a new small to medium enterprise looking to enter the Arab region" (Khakhar, Rammal, 2013). This suggests that the larger the market power the foreign MNE held (Ghauri, 2003), the more they were trusted.

> "Recently we signed a major deal with a multinational based in France. Our other options included a new medium-sized enterprise based the United Kingdom; however they were discussing exit-strategies from the first day of our negotiations. The French party has a good reputation and [were] not interested in short-term work. We trust [them] and are happy with the relationship we have formed with the French." (Khakhar, Rammal, 2013)

This is quoted from one of the interviews conducted by Khakhar and Rammal. It suggests that the Arab managers tend to trust companies that have well-established market presence and power, and would feel comfortable negotiating with such companies. The interviews also revealed that in order to foster trust during the negotiations, the Arab managers spent a considerable amount of time during the pre-negotiation stage communicating information between the parties to create a somewhat informal 'atmosohere' before beginning the actual negotiations.

A number of the interviewees explained that in an attempt to create trust between the parties at some personal level and to foster long-term relationships, the Arab managers even invited foreign negotiators to their private residences for an informal dinner before the negotiations commenced. The managers believe that by creating a personal relationship, the parties would be able to negotiate in a cordial and trusting environment.

However the political uncertainty faced by many Middle Eastern nations has forced Arab managers to change their behavior and although they preferred to invest time in getting to know their counterparts, they practiced discipline and no longer make this the central purpose of the negotiation process. (Kakhar, Rammal, 2013)

6.2.2   Concept of Time

Time in the Middle East, as in most parts of the world, is not as precise as it is in some western countries. "That is, Middle Easterners will often arrive half an hour late for a meeting, but this is on time for this person." (Acuff, 2013) Nor are appointments held in the esteem that they are in North America. The fact that your negotiating partner does not show up at all should not necessarily be taken personally.

Middle Easterners and North Africans don't believe that schedules should rule their lives. Hurrying a Middle Easterner or North African through a negotiation is an insult. Similarly, it is believed to be unlucky or unwise to plan too far ahead. There is some feeling of awe about the future, that if you plan in detail you take on too much upon yourself and invite disaster.

Negotiations with Saudi Arabian negotiators were seen to be slow. However, the ability to work within deadlines was seen as essential for successful negotiations for managers from countries like Lebanon, although this was not necessarily the case in other Arab countries. Thus, unlike Hall's (1966, 1981) classification of Arab countries as poly-chronic societies, where deadlines were not adhered to, Lebanese managers tend to display monochromic attitudes in relation to meeting deadlines. Negotiators from the United States and United Kingdom demonstrated high sensitivity towards time and it was difficult for Arab managers to create a personal relationship with these negotiators. Thus, while the formal negotiations seemed to commence quickly, in reality the lack of a personal relationship and trust meant that real negotiation may proceed slowly.

The findings of Kakhar and Rammal reveal that Arab negotiators from Saudi Arabia, Kuwait and the UAE still follow the poly-chronic time systems, whereas managers from politically volatile countries such as Lebanon and Syria display behavior which is more commonly associated with mono-chronic cultures.

6.2.3   Communication Style

A. Verbal Communication

Due to the complicated religious and racial situation in Middle east, communication styles could be very diversified. Verbal communication in Israel is generally quite direct and open. Verbal communication in Arab countries, by contrast, is quite indirect, vague, and expressive. In such high-context cultures, the speaker does not feel obligated to be specific as long as the receiver of the message can infer the message. For example, Arabs will seldom give you a direct no, even if they disagree with your idea, plan, or suggestion. If you ask whether something is a good choice and the person hesitates, then agrees, the hesitation is a strong clue that he or she might actually disagree with it, just for the courtesies involved. So a white lie in the name of good manners and someone's feelings is considered better, just as it is to a lesser extent in North America. U.S. negotiators are very quick to say, "I don't know, but I'll find out." This is not a good idea in most Arab countries of the Middle East. A person of status is not expected to hesitate over an answer. If you don't know, try to stall. Then quickly and privately find the answer or risk losing respect and power. Don't be alarmed if Arabic-to-English translations sound very exaggerated. The Arab language is conducive to exaggeration. For example, there are common endings of words that are meant to be emphasized, along with numerous rhetorical devices to achieve even more exaggeration. Fantastic metaphors are common, and many adjectives are often used to modify the same word. Arabs generally have a strong feeling that information is critical, and they are therefore masters at incremental disclosures—slow at letting you know what is really on their minds. The truth is considered something that can be cruel, dangerous, and rude, as well as a matter of negotiation.

B. Non-verbal Communication

Gestures are quite expressive in Middle Eastern and North African countries, and negotiators generally maintain direct eye contact with their counterparts and have closer physical distance than in most Western countries. These combined behaviors are sometimes viewed as "coming on too strong" by some Western negotiators. Arab men tend to touch each other (but not Arab women, except in private). Embracing upon meeting and holding hands in public are typical in Arab countries. This touching is not sexual, but a display of friendship. If an Arab makes a short jerk upward with his head, he means no. Often it's accompanied by a task sound. If he tilts his head sideways, it means yes (yes, I heard you, not necessarily yes, I agree).

6.2.4 Decision-making Process

There is a relatively high need for role orderliness and conformity in most Middle Eastern and North African countries. Solid personal relationships are vital to the success of negotiations. Before the content of the negotiation is addressed, the parties spend a good amount of time chatting about things that have nothing to do with specific business issues. Middle Eastern and North African negotiations, particularly those in Arab countries, often seem chaotic to most Western negotiators: people coming in and out of the room when you are speaking, many telephone interruptions, or your counterpart stopping to talk about other matters when you are addressing a key point. You should expect such interruptions to take place. For the Arab, it is masculine to read poetry, use intuition, and be sensitive. It's feminine to be cool and practical. Therefore, when you are negotiating, it sometimes helps to be a little emotional, or your sincerity may be doubted.

6.2.5 Diversity

A. Impact of Political Environment

The Arab region has recently witnessed a period of substantial political change and instability. Lebanon has experienced instability since the civil war of 1975—1990 and more recently during the Lebanon-Israel war of 2006. Because of the political uncertainty, the region was considered to be in a state of constant "flux" (a term that was repeatedly used in the interviews), which has a profound impact on all aspects of business in the region. Ghauri (2003) in his model classifies this under the "environment" factor and states that influences such as the political and regulatory environments have a direct impact on the international business negotiation process. (Khakhar, Rammal, 2013).

It was generally acknowledged by the interviewees that Arab managers tend to refrain from communicating their views on politics during negotiations, regardless of whether the issues were local, regional or global. According to the interviewees, during times of political unrest, greater concessions are given by the Arab negotiators as compensation for the disadvantage faced by international firms due to the unfavourable country risk. While this behaviour would be expected from managers from countries with high levels of longterm political risk, in countries such as Lebanon, the history of civil wars can affect business deals even though the political event may only last for a short period. One manager explained:

> "During the 2006 war with Israel and … in 2008 when we had an internal civil war for around seven days … our foreign partners threatened to pull out of existing and future deals. As we were in a compromised position, we had to give into many demands that we may not (normally) have. Although these were tough decisions, long-term gains from their business meant more to us then short-term losses." (Khakhar, Rammal, 2013)

The interviews also revealed that the political risk also influenced the location of the negotiations. Recalling their experience during the political turmoil, the managers revealed that in many instances the negotiations were held in the non-Arab party's country. While negotiating in the other party's country does not allow the Arab manager to exploit the home country advantage, the interviewees explained that negotiating in a foreign country at least provided the opportunity to continue business activities.

B. Referent Power

Arab negotiators almost always imply future business with the foreign parties they were negotiating with, or made explicit their "connections" and local knowledge within the Arab countries that may be of use to foreign companies. The term that is specific to the region and used extensively in the interviews was "wasta", which translates loosely to nepotism or "a connected person" (Cunningham & Sarayah, 1993). Although this concept may be difficult for some to grasp, using networks and connections for favorable outcomes is an accepted business practice in the Arab world. It is widely acknowledged that dealings with government departments in Arab countries can be "very frustrating" for foreigners due to the highly bureaucratic management structure. Thus, during international business negotiations Arab managers tend to point out the personal connection within the various governmental agencies that could expedite the approval process and is seen as a strategy to secure a deal. With the long history of political turmoil in countries such as Lebanon, these networks are seen to be useful in ensuring that the business operations remain uninterrupted. As one manager explained, the connections he had in the Ministry of Economy and Trade helped him expedite the registration process for his foreign business partner, which would usually take several weeks:

> "I recently submitted standard registration paperwork to "Le Ministere Economique Libanais" (The Ministry of Economy and Trade) on behalf of a foreign partner we work with in Beirut. I had assured the partner during the negotiations that it would be done within a week. After a few phone calls (to my contact in the Ministry), the paperwork was delivered within the week and the foreign counterpart was impressed by this." (Khakhar, Rammal, 2013)

During the interviews it became clear that most of the Arab managers attempted to demonstrate that they have referent power or "wasta" as a bargaining chip during negotiations. For the non-Arab business negotiator it is important to separate genuine and non-genuine use of referent power. The interviewees explained that the referent power can sometimes be overstated or indirectly used in order to secure a deal when in reality the Arab manager may not have the required connections. One manager described such a situation when dealing with a Chinese supplier.

The two sides had reached a deadlock over the price of the supplies and the negotiations had stalled. At that point one of the negotiators from the Arab side began discussing trends and opportunities in the industry, and mentioned another local company was also seeking supplies for their business. By overstating the level of his friendship with the management of the other party, he was able to convince the Chinese side to lower their price in exchange for introducing them. The manager then spent the next few days working with the management of other Arab company and succeeded in convincing them that if they acted as allies, they could secure a better price from the Chinese supplier.

According to the managers, this high level of "wasta" often surprises Western managers who are not used to this unique use of referent power in negotiations, and can sometimes help the Arab manager get a better than expected outcome.

7　Negotiating in Africa

⇨ 7.1　Overview of Africa

The continent of Africa is the world's second largest continent after Asia, with a total surface area covers 6% of Earth's total surface area and 20.4% of its total land area, 30,313,000 square kilometers. It has 54 independent countries, nine territories and two de facto independent states with limited or no recognition. With 1.1 billion people as of 2013, it accounts for about 15% of the world's human population. Africa's population is the youngest among all the continents; 50% of Africans are 19 years old or younger. Africa hosts a large diversity of ethnicities, cultures and languages.

The economic powerhouse of Africa south of the Sahara Desert is South Africa. Through its well-developed infrastructure and deepwater ports, South Africa handles much of the trade for the whole southern African region. In 1970 its immediate neighbors, Botswana, Swaziland and Lesotho, and latterly Namibia, signed the *Southern African Customs Union* (*SACU*) enabling them to share in the customs revenue from their trade passing through South African ports.

In order to counter the economic dominance of South Africa in the southern African region, the countries to the north of it organized themselves into the *Southern African Development Conference* (*SADC*). Member states include those of the SACU as well as Angola, situated north of Namibia, and it's oil-rich enclave of Cabinda, and Mozambique on the east coast, and the countries of south-central Africa, Zimbabwe, Zambia and Malawi.

The eastern region of Africa is home to the great wildlife reserves of the Serengeti plains and the Rift Valley lake system which stretch across the countries of Kenya, Uganda, and Tanzania. These countries signed the Treaty for Enhanced East African Co-operation to allow for the free flow of goods and people.

Further north lie the countries of the Horn of Africa and the source of the longest river in the world, the Nile River, which flows northwards over 6,690 kilometres to end in the Mediterranean Sea. Somalia occupies much of the coastline, while Ethiopia and Sudan are large inland countries. On the coast of the Red Sea are the two independent republics of Djibouti and Eritrea.

The small landlocked central African countries of Rwanda and Burundi form part of an economic union of countries in the central African region. Other members of the Economic Community of Central African States are Cameroon, the Central African Republic, Chad, Equatorial Guinea, the oil-rich Congo and Gabon and the vast country of the Democratic Republic of Congo.

The *Economic Community of West African States* (*ECOWAS*) is a solid geographical bloc of 15 states from Nigeria in the east to Mauritania in the west. The countries of Mauritania, Mali and Niger are located in the southern stretch of the Sahara Desert while the remaining countries are splayed out along the coast line. As a result of their respective colonial histories, these countries are divided into French and English-speaking states. The francophone countries include the republics of Benin, Burkina Faso, Togo, the Ivory Coast (Côte d'Ivoire), Guinea and Senegal while the remaining states of Nigeria, Ghana, Liberia, Sierra Leone, and the Gambia have English as their official language. The Republic of Guinea Bissau is a Portuguese-speaking state to the south of Senegal.

North of the Sahara Desert lie five predominantly Muslim countries all bordering on the southern shores of the Mediterranean Sea. Moving from west to east are the three countries which form the Maghreb region, the Kingdom of Morocco which has laid claim to the state of Western Sahara (Sahrawi Republic), a former Spanish colony on its southern border, and the republics of Algeria, and Tunisia. The remaining countries are Libya and finally Egypt occupying the north-east corner of Africa and having an extension across the Gulf of Suez into the Sinai Peninsula through which runs the Suez Canal physically cutting off the continent of Africa from the Middle East. Both Algeria and Libya have vast oil and gas producing fields and are active members of the ***Organization of Oil Exporting Countries*** (***OPEC***).

There are six independent island states associated with the continent of Africa. Off its west coast are the Cape Verde Islands off the coast of Senegal. In the Gulf Guinea off the coast of Gabon is the small island state of Sao Tomé and Principé. Off the east coast of Africa is the island republic of the Comores, and Madagascar, the world's third largest island with an area of 587,041 square kilometres. Further east in the Indian Ocean are the island republics of Mauritius and the Seychelles. Lying close to Mauritius is the island of Reunion, a dependency of France although its economy is closely linked to that of the east African coast and Indian Ocean islands.

While many people mention Africa as the continent of despair, other enterprising individuals and organizations have recognized the huge, untapped potential of Africa and are actively pursuing business ventures across the continent.Africa's gross domestic product (GDP) growth is expected to strengthen to 4.5% in 2015 and 5% in 2016 after subdued expansion in 2013 (3.5%) and 2014 (3.9%). The 2014 growth was about 1% lower than predicted in last year's African Economic Outlook, as the global economy remained weaker and some African countries saw severe domestic problems of various natures. But the world economy is improving and if the AEO 2015 predictions are right, Africa will soon be closing in on the impressive growth levels seen before the 2008/09 global economic crisis.

Table 7.1 **Africa's Growth by Region**, 2013—2016

(Real GDP growth in percent)

	2013	2014 (o)	2015 (p)	2016 (p)
Africa	3.5	3.9	4.5	5.0
Central Africa	4.1	5.6	5.5	5.8
East Africa	4.7	7.1	5.6	6.7
North Africa	1.6	1.7	4.5	4.4
Southern Africa	3.6	2.7	3.1	3.5
West Africa	5.7	6.0	5.0	6.1
Memorandurn items:				
Africa excl Libya	4.0	4.3	4.3	5.0
Sub–Saharan Africa (SSA)	4.7	5.2	4.6	5.4
SSA excl. South Africa	5.4	6.2	5.2	6.2

Note: (e)estimates; (p) projections.

Source: Statistics Department, African Development Bank.

Africa's opportunities, which range in risk from investing in emerging market funds or one of the listed multinationals active in Africa to trading with African partners, include: 1) oil and gas

(Angola and Libya); 2) mining (West and Central Africa); 3) privatizations (South Africa and Nigeria); 4) international trade (oil producers and SADC); 5) infrastructure (pipelines, roads, telecommunications); 6) stock exchanges that are mushrooming in many countries; 7) using educated English and French speaking African nationals; 8) and leisure.

The biggest challenge of doing business in Africa is the lack of quality information about Africa. And there are some of the other challenges: 1) fluctuating currencies; 2) bureaucratic red tape, which is slowly getting easier to wade through; 3) graft and corruption, as much a fault of the non-Africans who pass the brown paper bags as the poor and often unpaid civil servant who accepts the bag; 4) nepotism; 5) wars and unrest, though the changes in South Africa are starting to create a ripple of peace and democracy throughout the region; 6) lack of local capital; 7) monopolies such as marketing boards, state trading firms, foreign exchange restrictions, trade taxes and quotas and concentration on limited commodities all place a disincentive on exports, thus delinking Africa from the world economy; 8) lack of infrastructure, though in areas such as telecommunications and energy, Africa is able to use new technologies to leapfrog more advanced economies.

➪ 7.2 Business Style in Africa

7.2.1 Concept of Time

Time in sub-Saharan Africa is generally quite precise, although it differs from country to country. Meetings are more likely to start on time, and negotiations move more briskly in South Africa and Zimbabwe than in Nigeria. Also, schedules and agendas are likely to be present in this region of the world, though adherence to them will differ from place to place.

There is a relatively high need for role orderliness and conformity in most sub-Saharan African countries. It would be difficult for negotiations to proceed without strong personal relationships. Doing business in person is essential for any important negotiation.

Formality and respect are key. Sending an older negotiator can be helpful, since wisdom is often connected with experience. Expect complicated governmental regulations in most sub-Saharan African countries.

7.2.2 Communication Style

A. Verbal Communication

Verbal communication is likely to be animated and friendly. Verbal exchanges are on occasion quite direct and openly critical, but avoid statements that would offend your negotiating counterpart's dignity.

B. Non-verbal Communication

Expect physical space to be quite close, though there will be less hugs or other sustained touching than found in Latin America or Eastern Europe. Direct eye contact is limited, particularly when addressing an older person or a person in a position of authority. Children are usually taught not to look at their elders directly in the eye because this is seen as disrespectful. Sub-Saharan Africa is a good place to be warm and friendly, yet maintain a refined image.

Exercises

Case Analysis

Case 1

Tom is a student who graduated from a business school with a major in marketing. He has been working in the marketing department of a famous Chinese company for several years. Recently, Tom's manager asked him to prepare for the negotiation with an American company about new product development. Tom made great efforts to make every aspect perfect. After several rounds of hard negotiation, both sides reached an agreement. But when Mr. White, the representative of the American company came into the meeting room ready to sign the contract, he suddenly turned around and left in a huff. No one knew what annoyed Mr. White, but it seemed that Mr. White would never again consent to sign the contract. It was a big loss to the company, and Tom was blamed for everything and was fired afterwards.

Questions for Case-analysis:

1. So what annoyed Mr. White?
2. Is there any solution you can think of to continue the business?

Case 2

The following case took place in Shanghai, China.

ABC Company, a smaller earing-aid manufacturer based in USA, found the Chinese market in the year 2000 very attractive. There were few competitors in this sector in China and people there had been to realize the importance of using hearing-aids to improve the quality of their lives. This presented them with a great opportunity. So ABC Company planned to launch its products first in Shanghai, a coastal cosmopolitan city in China. Since ABC Company was totally ignorant of the Chinese market, it wanted to find a single local distributor to market products for it. So it searched the Internet and found only two companies in Shanghai selling hearing-aids. Then, it decided to send emails and make phone calls to get further information.

To its great surprise, its phone calls were considered a big mistake. When the people on the other end of the line heard that ABC Company wanted to do business with them, they seemed to take it as a joke. And they even laughed at it for being so creative. The callers from ABC Company felt helpless to convince these two companies.

At that time, there happened to be an exhibition of products for the disabled in Shanghai and ABC Company quickly decided that this would be a good chance to go to Shanghai and negotiate with the two companies face to face.

So ABC sent a young marketing manager and his assistant, a young lady (Lily), who had profound knowledge of the hearing-aid market, to Shanghai.

After three weeks, they came back to the USA and reported to the company that they had failed completely in their attempts to reach an agreement with either of this two Chinese companies. "I still couldn't figure out why we failed, because it seemed that they wanted to do business with us. Maybe I am being a little over-sensitive but I think the Chinese don't like us." The young man looked depressed. "We made an appointment to meet the company's marketing manager, a man of 50 years old or more, whom we call "Li Xiaomo", the first day we arrived in Shanghai. He agreed to arrange a meeting for us and after that he never appeared again. Well, that was OK since we could discuss business with his colleagues. But can you imagine how inefficient the Chinese people are! They were late for the meeting, and then did nothing but sat around the table asking us some irrelevant questions! It lasted for an hour and then lunch time came. They then invited us for a luncheon and we were taken to a luxurious restaurant. After the luncheon, we two insisted on paying our own bills and the Chinese became a little embarrassed. And then, we went to the meeting room again and Lily quickly put forward our ideas and suggestions to avoid possible small talk. It lasted for an hour and then we asked for their ideas. The Chinese told us that they would think about it so we waited in hotel for two days. But when I called them two days later, the Chinese told me that they would not do business with us and they thought I knew that. But how on hell should I know? They only told me that they would think about it. Oh, my god, everything seemed to run in the wrong track."

Questions for Case-analysis:

1. Why did the two American fail to reach an agreement with their Chinese counterparts?

2. Can you imagine more possible mistakes the two might commit?

3. Would you please give the two Americans some suggestions about negotiating with Chinese?

4. In this case, if they still want to do business with the Chinese, what can they do?

Case 3

On June 26, 1994, Vitro and Corning, the Mexican and U.S. glass companies, decided to end joint ownership of their consumer glassware divisions, although continue an alliance through supply and distribution agreements. In the fall of 1991, in the midst of the NAFTA negotiations, Vitro Sociedad Anonima (Vitro), the $3 billion Mexican glass maker, had signed a tentative $800 million joint venture with Corning Inc. In the deal, each company took an equity stake in the other and agreed to a series of marketing, sales, and distribution relationships (LDC Debt Report, 1991). Just two years later, the joint venture was dissolved. According to company officials and external analysts, cultural differences were a principal cause of the alliance's failure.

Questions for Case-analysis:

Though not specified in the case, can you make a guess of the cultural differences between the two parties?

Case 4

TransOceanic is a worldwide logistic service company involved in freight forwarding and container consolidation, based in the United States. For almost six months it had been working hard to expand its network of local representatives throughout the Middle East. TO's number one regional priority was to conclude a representation agreement with Arabco, one of Saudi Arabia's largest and best-established logistics companies.

To achieve this goal, Regional Manager Ted Goodfellow of TransOceanic had been meeting once or twice a month with Arabco. By now the two companies had agreed on all the financial, legal and technical issues. Ted was now back in Riyadh to wrap up the final details and sign the contract. This visit was largely a formality—both sides clearly wanted this agreement.

During a pleasant meeting with the top Arabco executives, Goodfellow casually mentioned, "We at TransOceanic are really looking forward to working with you here in the Persian Gulf!" At that time there was a moment of shocked silence on the Arabco side of the conference table. Then the three senior executives arose and strode angrily out of the room, breaking off negotiations.

Bewildered, Ted looked at the two junior Saudis who had remained behind. He feared to see six months of hard work going up in smoke. "What happened here?" he asked the young Arabs across the table. "Did I say something wrong?"

After some hesitation one of the Arabco employees explained that in Saudi Arabia, the body of water in question is called the Arabian Gulf. By misnaming it Ted had unintentionally implied that the Gulf belong to Iran, a country which Saudi Arabia at that time considered hostile and threatening.

The bosses of Arabco were now too upset with Ted to listen to an apology from him. "Well, what should we do then to get these talks back on track?" asked Ted. At this the young Arabs shrugged, smiled faintly and ushered the American to the door. On the way back in his hotel Ted Goodfellow focused his mind on finding a way to repair the damaged relationship.

Questions for Case-analysis:

1. Do you have any suggestions for Ted?
2. How can he solve the problem?

Case 5

A Japanese buyer of a women's clothing-store chain phoned the Paris headquarters of a French clothing manufacturer to send a representative to Tokyo to present its autumn collection. The two companies had done business often over the past few years. The Paris firm sent designer

Christine Beaumont to Tokyo to make the presentation. She knew the Japanese firm invited representatives from its competitors, so she had a big selling job to do. She had never been to Japan before. Two days after she arrived, the company scheduled her presentation. Christine assumed she could get right down to business, considering her company's long-time relationship with this Japanese firm. And so Christine glossed over social pleasantries and immediately proceeded to her slide presentation. Then she discussed the pricing of the clothes and how they could be marketed. Christine met with a rather bland reaction to her presentation from the company president and representatives. After a long silence, the Japanese president took over and abruptly shifted the focus to Christine herself. He questioned her about her training in the fashion world, previous work experiences, the fashion schools she had attended, her hobbies, how long she's been with the Paris Company, and so on. At first, Christine was taken aback because of the sudden switch, but she quickly recovered and answered the questions. The president then talked about how successful his firm's relationship had been with the Paris Company, the profitable projects that both companies engaged in, using names of high-ranking executives who had visited Tokyo and their out-of-town trips together, and so forth. Christine was then told by the president to remember all that information because she would need it when meeting the other company executives. Later she made a phone call to her head office and told the boss how uncertain she felt about the results of her presentation.

Questions for Case-analysis:

What went wrong in this business meeting?

Case 6

Trevor Sutton, born and reared in London, has for the past five years been a top-ranking financial officer in the Hong Kong branch of the Standard Chartered Bank. One of his main responsibilities is to evaluate applicants for corporate loans. The bank has been a significant contributor to the development of Hong Kong, and it has supported a number of successful business ventures. One firm whose fate was turned around after the bank gave them a loan is owned by a prominent Kowloon family. It produces polyester-cotton and polyester-viscose yarn. It was January, and the time was drawing near for the Chinese New Year. In Hong Kong this is a time of great commercial activity and gift-giving. Trevor unexpectedly received a letter from the owner of this firm, expressing gratitude for the bank's support. Their annual report showed large profits. The letter said that as a token of the firm's gratitude, he had purchased a Jaguar motor car for Mr. Sutton, and he hoped he would accept the gift. The keys were enclosed in a separate envelope. Trevor thought this was an outstanding present, but to accept it would be outrageous. He quickly typed up a letter declining the gift, and called on his special assistant to handle the matter discretely.

Questions for discussion：

How would you interpret the motivations of the Chinese owner in offering the car as a present to Trevor?

Reference

1. Acuff, Frank L. "Negotiating in the Pacific Rim," The International Executive (May—June 1990): 20-21.

2. Acuff, Frank L. How to negotiate anything with anyone anywhere in the world. 2008.

3. Al-Khatib, Jamal A., Malshe, Avinash, & AbdulKader, Mazen. Perception of unethical negotiation tactics: A comparative study of US and Saudi managers. International Business Review 17 (2008), 78-102.

4. Becker, Thomas H. Doing Business in the New Latin America, Santa Barbara, Cali: ABC-CLIO, 2011.

5. Combs, Gwendolyn M., Nadkarni, Sucheta. "The tale of two cultures: Attitudes towards affirmative action in the United States and India", Journal of World Business 40 (2005) 158-171.

6. Cramton, P. C., & Dees, G. J. Promoting honesty in negotiation: An exercise in practical ethics. Business ethics quarterly (1993), 3(4), 359-394.

7. Cunningham, R. B., & Sarayah, Y. K. Wasta: The hidden force in Middle Eastern society. Westport and London: Praeger, 1993.

8. Fang, Tony, Worm, Verner, Tung, Rosalie L. "Changing success and failure factors in business negotiations with the PRC", International Business Review 17 (2008) 159-169.

9. French, J. R., & Raven, B. (1959). "The bases of social power". In D. Cartwright (Ed.), Studies in social power (pp. 150-167). Ann Arbor: Institute for Social Research, University of Michigan.

10. Ghauri, P. N. (2003). "A framework for international business negotiations". In P. N. Ghauri J.-C. Usunier (Eds.), International business negotiations (2nd ed., pp. 3-22). Oxford: Elsevier Ltd.

11. Hall, E. T. The Hidden Dimension. New York: Doubleday, 1966.

12. Hall, E. T. Beyond Culture. New York: Doubleday, 1981.

13. Haltiwanger, John, Jarmin, Ron and Miranda, Javier. "Business Formation and Dynamics By Business Age: Results from the New Business Dynamics Statistics," Center for Economic Studies, U.S. Census Bureau, 2008.

14. Hampden-Turner, Charles, Trompenaars, Fons. The Seven Cultures of Capitalism. New York: Doubleday, 1993.

15. Harris, Simon, Carr, Chriss. "National cultural values and the purpose of businesses", International Business Review 17(2008) 103-117.

16. Hosfstede, Geert. Cultures and Organizations: Software of the Mind, London: McGraw-Hill

International Limited, 1991.

17. Imai, Lynn, Gelfand, Michele J. "The Culturally Intelligent Negotiator: The Impact of Cultural Intelligence (CQ) on Negotiation Sequences and Outcomes," Organizational Behavior and Human Decision Processes, 112(2010) 83-98.

18. Khakhar, Priyan, Rammal, Hussain Gulzar. "Culture and business networks: International business negotiations with Arab managers", International Business Review 22 (2013) 578-590.

19. Luo Yadong, Shenkar, Oded. "Toward a perspective of cultural friction in international business", Journal of International Management 17 (2011)1-14.

20. Lewicki, Roy J., Saunders, Daivd M., Minton, John W., Barry, Bruce. Negotiation: Readings, Exercises, and Cases. P. R. Donnelly & Sons Company, 2002.

21. Metcalf, Lynn E., Bird, Allan, SShankarmahesh, Mehesh, Aycan, Zeynep, Larimo, Jorma, Valdelamar, Didimo Dewar. "Cultrual tendencies in negotiation: A comparison of Finland, India, Mexico, Turkey, and the United States", Journal of World Business 41 (2006), 382-394.

22. Salacuse, J. W. Making Global Deal—Negotiating in the International Market Place. Boston: Houghton Mifflin, 1991.

23. Shi, Xingping, Wright, Philip C. "The potential impacts of national feelings on international business negotiations: a study in the China context", International Business Review 12 (2003) 311-328.

24. Sternheimer, Karen. Everyday Sociology Reader. New York: W. W. Norton & Co Inc, 2010.

25. Volkema, Roger J. "Demographic, cultural, and economic predictors of perceived ethicality of negotiation behavior: A nine-country analysis," Journal of Business Research, 57(2004) 69-78.

26. Volkema, Roger J. "Ethicality in Negotiations: An Analysis of Perceptual Similaries and Differences Between Brazil and the United States. Journal of Business Research 45(1999), 59-67.

27. Wilken, Robert, Jacob, Frank, Prime, Natalie. "The ambiguous role of cultural moderators in international business negotiations", International Business Review 22(2013), 736-753.

Chapter VIII The Principles of Negotiation

Learning Objectives

After studying this chapter, you will be able to

- Identify the risks.

- Know the principle of pie.

- Analyze the negotiation.

In Chapter One, the basic principles of international business negotiation are explained. However, these are basic guiding rules to lead any negotiation without calculation of numbers. In this chapter, the principles will be explained more specifically, like how to analyze what's on the stake, how to offer and bargain and how to do the math problem—money in business negotiation.

1   The Definition of Pie

Example:

Abby and Bob spent two hours helping their neighbor to repair the pipe in the house. Their neighbor really appreciated their help and gave them an apple pie in return. So how to divide the pie?

Suppose, Abby said: "I want the whole pie." Bob said: "I want the whole pie."

Actually, both of them expressed their opinion, but this is not an argument. Because either Abby or Bob has the pie. The two claims are equally valid or invalid. And they won't be satisfied either way. Negotiators need more principled argument to achieve their goal—get their slice of the pie. Desiring the whole pie without sharing is unreasonable in a negotiation. Approaching the negotiation from a dispassionate way and understand what's on stake. Then it's wise for negotiators to allow others take a slice and so to get their slice.

For example, let's re-look at the previous example pie. If Abby and Bob think of the problem from a more dispassionate way, that is, think about what will happen if the negotiation fails, they will find if they stuck to the claim, they wouldn't be able to reach an agreement. No one will have the pie before an agreement. Maybe the choice left is a deadlock, to wait the pie to go sour. If they don't want that happen, they need a way out. Once understanding that no one will benefit if the negotiation fails, both party will sit and think about a real argument.

Bob then said: "How about equal split, half of the pie for each of us?" Abby didn't agree. She thought she's twice stronger, so she could finish the repair work within three hours and Bob probably needed six hours. So she wanted a bigger slice, two thirds of the pie. And Bob should take the rest.

If we think about the problem in a different way, from what Abby and Bob can get on their own. If Abby did the job on her own, she got two slices of the pie, and if Bob on his own, he got one slice. That made three slices in total. Now suppose the pie they got from their neighbor was bigger than the three slices together. The extra slices is the pie.

So, the pie is how much more two parties, A and B, can achieve by working together than they can get if they don't reach an agreement. In more technical terms, the pie equals net benefit from working together−(A's net benefit on its own + B's net benefit on its own) where net benefit is the benefit leftover after costs.

That is to say, if Abby works on her own, she can get one slice from the pie without the help of Bob. Bob gets one without the help of Abby. Now they work together and get more than two and one in total. Abby needs Bob as much as Bob needs Abby to get the extra slices. Abby could argue that she is stronger so she deserves twice or more times of that of Bob. Bob could say: "No, that doesn't work. If I walk away, the extra is lost." Abby could say the same thing as Bob. So maybe the best policy for splitting the real apple pie is to equally split the PIE, the extra slices they earned by working together.

The example here might be too simple, but it highlights any fundamental principle that underlines all business negotiation: what is the pie? In real business negotiation, people may not agree with what the pie is, or one party may try to hide part of the pie. The same principle, however, applys. Indeed, the more complicated the problem, the more important it is to have a principle.

In a real business world, nobody will go out and tell you what the pie is. Negotiators have to figure it out themselves. Another example: John, a well-known financial expert, lives in Los Angeles. He was invited to give a talk in New York and then another one in Houston.

He wanted to do a triangle trip instead of two round trips since the schedule is very close. That is, he can fly to Houston, then from Houston to New York, and then back to LA. So he told the two hosts about this plan. Then is the question: how should the two hosts divide the fare? The air ticket from Los Angeles to Houston was 420 dollars, from Houston to New York was 660 dollars, and New York back to LA is 930 dollars. The total would be \$2,010. The two hosts agreed to the fare, but they wanted to pay as little of the amount as possible. They began to negotiate.

The negotiator from New York might want the simple solution: each host shared half of the air ticket, \$1,005. The other came up with a simple one, too, paying only the ticket from LA to Houston, \$420. He might continue to point out that even the round trip from LA to Houston was only \$840, so why he had to pay more?

Then the New York host proposed that each party paid half of the air ticket from Houston to New York, that is \$420 plus \$330 for Houston host and \$330 plus \$930 for itself. Then Houston didn't agree, since even if New York paid \$930 plus \$660, it would still be cheaper than a round trip ticket from LA to New York of \$1,860.

Then the New York host proposed they shared the air ticket from Houston to New York based on their proportion of the fare. He should pay 31/45 of \$660, and Houston 14/45. Then some people would settle the problem with the last solution since it sounds like equal treatment. Or another common solution is to divide in terms of distance, to count how far is from New York and from Houston and use the ratio to divide the total air ticket.

But now with the concept of pie in mind, we should more seek a principled argument: what is the pie? The previous solutions attempting to make a settlement of the negotiation fail to take into consideration one focal point: why the two hosts were negotiating? If John wasn't flying the triangle trip, the Houston host had to pay \$840 and the New York had to pay \$1,860, which made \$2,700, \$690 more than \$2,010 which was the total of the triangle trip. So the \$690 is exactly what the pie is and what the negotiation is really about. Of course as negotiation goes, each party will try to get as much of the pie as possible. The two hosts could propose to have half of the pie since they were equally powerful. If any of them walked away from the triangle plan, they would pay more.

Case 1

Planet-Gazette Merger Negotiations

The New Haven Planet and the Hartford Gazette are contemplating a merger. Roughly speaking, newspapers are valued on a per-reader basis. The Planet has 100,000 subscribers, while the Gazette is twice as large with 200,000 readers. Currently, the Planet has a market cap of $10m, while the Gazette has a market cap of $22m.

The reasons for a merger are as follows:

By combining their joint purchasing, the two papers expect to reduce paper and printing costs by 2.3%. The present discounted value of this cost savings is $2m to the Planet and $4m to the Gazette.

The Gazette is starting from a position with lower production costs than the Planet. The cost advantages of the Gazette can all be transferred to the Planet's operation. The projected savings are $125k annually to the Planet, which adds $1 million to the current value (or market cap) of the company.

The merger will allow the two papers to cut overhead. The reduction in headcount is worth a total of $150k annually, or $1.2m in present discounted value.

It is believed that there is a possibility of expanding readership through joint subscription offers. It is thought that 5% of Planet readers will start subscribing to the Gazette and 5% of Gazette readers will start subscribing to the Planet. The value of the new 5,000 Gazette readers is worth $550k (at current market prices), and the value of the new 10,000 Planet readers is worth $1m (at current market prices). If we assume the Planet will have the same profitability as the Gazette post-merger, then the new Planet readers will be worth $1.1m.

In addition, there is a reduced need for working capital, synergies in selling ads, and in building the online paper. These synergies have not been quantified.

As a result of the merger discussions, both parties have all the information above. These two papers have agreed on how the editorial side of the business will combine operations. The major sticking point is the financial terms for the merger. The two sides agree the new combined entity will have a market cap of $41.85 million.

Based on the relatively small size of these two papers, you should assume that there are no other potential merger partners. No joint ventures are possible. Either the Planet and the Gazette reach a deal or they don't. If no deal is reached, then both sides continue with their business as usual and none of the synergies are achieved.

Questions for Analysis：

1. If your birthday is between January 1 & June 30 then：

You are representing the Hartford Gazette in the merger. Your job is to make the best case for paying a low price. What is the lowest purchase price you can justify, and how do you justify it? What do you think is the fair outcome?

2. If your birthday is between July 1 & December 31 then：

You are representing the New Haven Planet in the merger. Your job is to make the best case for getting a high price. What is the highest purchase price you can justify, and how do you justify it? What do you think is the fair outcome?

Case analysis：The merger one is a typical one of considering what the pie is. Before the merger, Hartfort Gazette is half the size of Haven Planet. With the merger, they could make a change together, like to share readers, transfer knowledge and purchase jointly. Prior to the theory of Pie, negotiators may think of the deal in the way how the deal will benefit them. Like Haven Planet has a large reader base, they would ask to benefit more since they bring more readers to the new company. On the other hand, Hartford Gazette would argue that they would enjoy the profit from the production of know-how since this is their exclusion knowledge. Either way, the other party won't agree and the negotiation will become a battle of getting more profits for themselves and end up with a deadlock. Now, with the concept of Pie, negotiators may think of the deal in the way how the deal will benefit them more than no deal at all.

Compare the two forms as follows：

	New Haven Planet	Hartford Gazette
Pre-merger readership	100,000	200,000
Pre-merger market cap	$10,000,000	$22,000,000
Merger synergies		
Joint purchasing	$2,000,000	$4,000,000
Production know-how		$1,000,000
Reduced overhead	$375,000	$825,000
New readers	10,000	5,000
Value of new readers	$550,000	$1,100,000
Total synergies	$2,925,000	$6,925,000
	New Haven Planet	Hartford Gazette
Pre-merger readership	100,000	200,000
Pre-merger market cap	$10,000,000	$22,000,000
Merger synergies		
Joint purchasing	$3,000,000	$3,000,000
Production kuow-how	$500,000	$500,000
Reduced overhead	$600,000	$600,000
New readers	10,000	5,000
Value of new readers — Planet	$550,000	$550,000
Value of new readers — Gazette	$275,000	$275,000
Total synergies	$4,925,000	$4,925,000

Fig 8.1

2   Reservation Value

Think about the following scene: You're traveling in a foreign craftsman market and thinking about buying a beautiful hand-made pottery vase. You ask for the price and the vender give you one, which you think is much overpriced. Then you give him a price in return, a very low one you don't expect him to accept. And of course he refuses and asks you to raise the price. Through several rounds of bargain, you get the vase with a price you're fairly satisfied with. This might not be uncommon to the readers since it can happen when one travels or every day. The key to the satisfactory result of the bargain is you already have a price in your mind when you walk in the bargain, even though it may not be the first price you offer. This price to the buyer is the most possible price he could pay before walking away and to the seller is the least price he could accept. The price is called the Best Alternative to a Negotiated Agreement, BATNA, according to Roger Fisher. And economists call this reservation value.

Thinking about the concept of pie, the pie equals to what combined reservation values of both parties is deducted from what both parties can get together. The purpose of any kind of negotiation is to get something better or more than your reservation value. So, getting into a negotiation means always knowing one's BATNA, or reservation value and try not to accept anything less than that as a seller and try not to pay anything more than that as a buyer. In a real negotiation, it is very crucial for negotiators to know their reservation value before they even get into a negotiation. As a buyer, the value is not the price that you start to have reservations if you are offered. It means you don't want to close the deal if any offer is lower than the price. For example, company A is offering the price of \$420,000 to sell the patent of company B. As the negotiator of company B, you are assigned in the negotiation group with the ideal price for your company as \$380,000. If the price is raised to \$390,000 through the negotiation, you start to have hesitations. Some people may take the price of \$390,000 as the reservation value. Actually it's not. Though you're told, before the negotiation, \$380,000 is the ideal price, you also have a price of \$400,000, which is given by your boss and no deal will be closed if the price go beyond it. So the reservation value is just high enough that you're ambivalent to walk away and just low enough that you're willing to proceed. So, to know the reservation value as a negotiator from the buyer helps you to get a deal with a price lower than it. And the reverse is also true for the seller.

Case 2

Zincit (pronounced Zinc-It)

Eli Hasan had always wanted to be an inventor. In high school, he was a runner-up in the Intel Science Talent Search. He went on to study chemistry at MIT, before earning an MD from Tufts. Dr. Hasan's day job was radiation oncology in private practice, but weekends were a chance to experiment. His latest experiment was highly personal. Hasan's father was suffering from acid reflux, a condition that is both extremely unpleasant and dangerous, as it can lead to esophageal cancer. Hasan experimented with traditional medicines along with minerals, and settled on a compound made up of turmeric, barley grass, and zinc salts. This compound was added to calcium carbonate, the main ingredient in Tums, and compressed into a tablet.

After seeing dramatic benefits for his father, Dr. Hasan did a pilot study and used the data to obtain a patent on the use of zinc salts for acid reflux. The results were published in the *American Journal of Gastroenterology*. After the article came out, Hasan started receiving inquiries from companies looking to obtain an exclusive license to the patent. One company had plans to use the tablet as a competitor to Tums. The "Zums" team was not going to apply for FDA approval; they would sell Hasan's invention as a dietary supplement. Dr. Hasan hired lawyer Sam Massey to help negotiate the deal. Hasan was more than a bit surprised (and pleased) when Massey came back with a $20 million all-cash offer.

While this was a great option, as a physician and scientist Hasan wanted the invention to have the credibility of a medicine, not a dietary supplement. That was not an option with Zums, who had no experience or interest in seeking FDA approval. However, Massey had been talking with a second potential buyer of the license. The "Zincit" team had experience with the FDA approval process and was willing to pursue that approach. After a long back-and-forth, the discussions with Zincit led to the following five packages being under mutual consideration:

Table 8.1

Package	Upfront	Bonus If FDA Approval
A	$25m	$0
B	$20m	$15m
C	$20m	5% royalty
D	$17m	7.5% royalty
E	$12m	10% royalty

Getting FDA approval would be a huge boost to sales, but it would likely cost $10 million to go through the process. Zincit was willing to commit to the expense. If succeeded, the company expected to earn $200 million in total revenue and $130 million in profits over the life of the drug (all numbers in present discounted value). Thus a 5% royalty was worth $10 million to Hasan. If the FDA did not grant approval, Zincit would settle for the dietary supplement route, where its estimated profits would be $30 million. Note: the $130 million and the $30 million do not include the $10 million FDA cost.

The Zincit team concluded Hasan's compound only had a 1 in 10 chance of winning approval. Even after hearing Zincit's estimates, Hasan still believed the efficacy of the drug was so great there was a 60% chance it would be approved.

Given the Zums offer, Zincit knew it couldn't buy the company for less than $20 million. At the other extreme, the 10% chance of earning an extra $100 million just offsets the regulatory costs, so Zincit couldn't afford to pay more than the $30 million it stands to profit from the supplement approach.

As Hasan's lawyer, Massey receives a fee of 5% of Hasan's upfront payment. His contract doesn't provide for any share of a bonus in the event of FDA approval. There is no potential to go back and renegotiate Zums'$20 million offer. And there are no other potential bidders.

Question for Case-analysis:

What's the best package for Hasan or Zincit?

Case Analysis: In the Zincit case, the first thing to do is to know the expected payoffs of the given five packages, to calculate not only your own payoffs but also the payoffs of the other side. For package A, the simple answer of that the payoffs is $25 millions. With option B, the payoffs is split with $20 million up front and a $15 million bonus. For Hasan, the chance is 60% and that equals $9 million. Therefore, package B is worth $29 million for him. For Zincit, the 10% chance to pay off is $1.5 million. So the expected cost to the buyer is $21.5 million. Doing the similar calculations down the list to package E. Then the payoffs are listed as follows:

Table 8.2

Package	Upfront	FDA Bonus	Value to Hasan	Cost ro Zincit
A	25	0	25	25
B	20	15	29	21.5
C	20	10	26	21
D	17	15	26	18.5
E	12	20	24	14

And then according to the theory of pie and the reservation value, the next step is to compare all the payoffs to the loss if they don't reach a deal. A simple calculation of the payoff, the original gain for the seller and the reserve prices from the buyer would help both parties know what the pie is and how to split it.

Gains over No Deal

Table 8.3

Package	Upfront	FDA Bonus	Gains: Hasan	Gains: Zincit
A	25	0	5	5
B	20	15	9	8.5
C	20	10	6	9
D	17	15	6	11.5
E	12	20	4	16

Then, the benefit for each party is quite clear.

Having the theory of pie in mind, a negotiator will always frame a negotiation with what the pie is, the gains over no deal, rather than the profit as a total of the deal. For example, Jack got a chance to star in a TV commercial with a daily pay. If he refused to take the job and find another office job, he got paid 300 dollars. So his reserve value is 300 dollars considering if he walks away from the first offer, he still got 300 from the second job. So when he talked to the agency about the pay of the role in the TV commercial, he thought about the 300 dollars as the reservation value, not only the price the agency liked to pay him, like $200 a day. So he argued about $500 a day or more. The gain over no deal is $200 rather than $500. So he would not take the job thinking about he would lose $500 a day and it's a big sum. $200 rather than $500 gave him a better position in the negotiation.

Case 3

Cade Hauber and his sister-in-law Helen Ganske are the founders of Outᴪder (Outpsider) Art magazine. This Brooklyn-based journal specializes in what is often referred to as "outsider art." The artists featured are typically self-taught and their work falls outside the traditional art scene. This includes everything from folk art to paintings and sculptures by children, inmates, and those with mental illnesses. The painting on the right was on a recent cover. The work is done by Ken Grimes, an artist in New Haven, CT, whose images typically involve extra-terrestrial visits. Outpsider's mission is to explore outsider art, contextualizing it within the larger cultural framework. The magazine has been up and running for ten years and has a loyal following. Issues are published bimonthly, and circulation is at 50,000. Surveys suggest there are 4.2 readers per issue, reflecting an overall reach of 210,000. The readers are highly desired by advertisers, as they tend to be high-income professionals. The median reader spends $10,000 a year on art, regularly attends theater and concerts, and buys over fifty books annually. The magazine does have a website, but, much like the art, it is quite primitive. Annual subscription revenue is just over $900k, and advertising revenue is just over $400k. But printing and mailing a high-quality glossy art magazine are expensive. Besides production costs, commissions to sales people, fees to freelance writers, and wages for the part-time office staff are all paid. Cade has been able to provide himself with a salary of $70,000. At this point, the company does not provide any other benefits, such as a 401(k) plan or health insurance. Helen lives in San Francisco and is not active in the day-to-day management of the business, but she shares control rights with Cade. She contributes a regular column as well as a few in-depth articles per year. Cade (and Helen if she is available) has a meeting scheduled with Pat Bennett from Iceberg Media. Iceberg is rapidly becoming the Bloomberg of the art world. Instead of financial data, it provides art data. If a collector wants to locate a piece of art, research its historical pricing, or be notified if it comes up for sale, Iceberg Media is the go-to source. Iceberg has acquired several high-profile art magazines and has expressed interest in purchasing Outpsider Art.

Negotiation simulation:

Students are grouped as the seller and the buyer. Read the case closely and simulate the negotiation. The teacher may give the following confidential information to each side.

Confidential Instructions for Cade and Helen (Sellers)

Outpsider

Summary: Cade Hauber is interested in selling the business, both for strategic reasons (company needs of capital and liquidity for investors) and personal reasons (surgery, new job opportunity). However, there is an unhappy investor that can block the deal unless the purchase price is at or above $2/share. Helen Ganske is happy to help Cade sell the company but also wants to look out for her own interests. Details are below.

Your magazine business has been going well, but it is clear that the future will be online. Indeed, you've seen the future in the form of Iceberg Media. Their website and award-winning mobile app provide a catalog of auction prices, allow galleries to show their inventories, and are a central clearinghouse for art. In addition, they own several online and print magazines focusing on trends in various parts of the art world. You are hoping they will want to include what you have built at Outpsider as part of their portfolio. You are meeting with Pat Bennett of Iceberg to discuss this possibility.

While you are happy with the current business, there are several factors leading you (Cade) to sell:

1. You have been running *Outpsider* for ten years. You are the editor-in-chief as well as the publisher. While the business is growing and provides you with a reasonable income ($70,000), the business cannot afford to provide health insurance to you and the other employees.

2. You would like to be able to provide some liquidity for your investors. Even better would be to provide them with a return. Your investors are family, friends, fraternity brothers, a few angels, and one shark. With the notable exception of the shark, they have been patient, but there is a limit to their patience. Thus far there have been no dividends.

3. The shark is your major, very unhappy investor: a venture capital firm called Artagis. You believe they are trying to steal your business and, as a result, you are not on speaking terms. You would love to no longer have to deal with them.

4. To be competitive in the business will require making a large investment in your website and digital content. This is not something you have expertise in, but you think it would cost around $300,000 to do a good job. You do not have access to this kind of cash, so it would require capital raising. This would be difficult in any case and even more so with Artagis as an investor. You don't want them to put in more cash and get control, and they do not want you to bring in new investors and thereby dilute their stake.

5. You have an old hip injury from your college days as a wrestler. It has become increasingly painful. As a result of the Affordable Care Act, you have been able to obtain health insurance without a pre-existing condition exemption. The orthopedic surgeon says you need a total hip replacement. You would like to have this surgery sooner than later, but with recovery and recuperation time this would be incompatible with keeping the magazine going. There is no one who can run the magazine in your absence.

6. With all these concerns, you haven't been sleeping well. The doctor has suggested Ambien, but you think there should be a better solution to reduce the stress in your life.

7. In the process of running the magazine, you have met and befriended many outsider artists. Several have asked if you would be willing to represent them. This would be an impossible conflict of interest while running the magazine, but this is something you would like to do. Indeed, others have seen this potential. You have a standing job offer from the leading outsider art gallery, Ricco Maresca in New York City, which is an easy commute from your current place in Williamsburg. The salary is about what you make today, but it includes health insurance and a 401(k). Plus it will be much less stressful.

What is your business worth? While the value is in the eye of the beholder, you think it is worth at least $500,000, and perhaps much more to Iceberg. Under the status quo, the business is generating $70,000, which pays your salary. But, with the resources of Iceberg, they could:

- Increase the number of subscribers
- Increase the number of advertisers
- Reduce printing costs
- Consolidate operations

There are also some cross-selling opportunities. Some of your readers might want to subscribe to Iceberg's other publications and some of your advertisers might want to run campaigns across multiple magazines.

A hidden benefit is that Iceberg will be able to use your magazine to provide low-cost ads for their other businesses. Iceberg runs conferences, art fairs, and sells premium subscription services with access to their art databases. A full-page ad in *Outpsider* is priced at $4,500, but the printing and mailing costs per page are only $500. Thus the owner of the magazine can give themselves a $4,000 discount. You are well aware of this because you are doing it today. Your co-founder Helen has been buying two full pages in each issue at cost ($500/page) to advertise her art gallery.

Perhaps the biggest benefit to Iceberg is the potential from developing *Outpsider*'s online business. Building the database and website will likely cost them less than $300,000. You firmly believe developing the site would be worth $600,000, so this would be a no brainer.

But this opportunity is also a problem. You worry that if Iceberg does not purchase *Outpsider*, they will create a competing website that will substantially reduce the potential value of your online business.

Information about your ownership:

Table 8.4

Capitalization Table**	
Shareholder	Shares
Artagis	100,000
Cade	50,000
Helen	50,000
Friends/Angels	50,000
Total	**250,000**

Artagis put in $100,000 at $1/share. In retrospect, you can't believe you sold a single investor 40% of your business, but you did. While they are minority investors, Artagis obtained some negative control rights as part of the investment, meaning they can block certain actions. In particular, they can veto any deal that does not provide them with a 100% return. Moreover, any such offer must be all-cash. Thus, in order to complete a sale without their approval you must obtain a $2/share, or $500,000, all-cash offer. You have argued with Artagis that this might not be feasible, but they are not persuaded. Actually, you think they would rather you not get such an offer. Artagis is interested in purchasing the company for itself and has made an offer of $400,000 ($1.60/share). This is as high as they are willing to go. They would prefer to veto any other offer, even those above $400,000, in order to acquire the company. As a result, you and Artagis are currently not on speaking terms. Absent providing Artagis with a $2/share cash offer, you will not be able to sell the company to any other bidder.

Even if you were tempted to pay off Artagis, you would open yourself up to a lawsuit if you treated one shareholder better than the others. Theoretically, you could treat yourself worse than everybody else, but that would be a last resort. You and your sister-in-law are on good terms, but if you gave her anything less than what Artagis is getting (on a per-share basis), that would be a problem for your family relationship.

In your negotiations with Iceberg, they have seen the overall ad revenue and ad pages, but not the breakdown. Thus they will likely have done the calculation that $402k of ad revenue and 100 pages of ads mean you are getting $4,020 per page. Looking deeper, you are getting $4,500/page on 88 pages and $500/page on 12 pages, but they don't know that. On the plus side, this means advertisers are willing to pay $4,500 per page; on the down side, there is less opportunity to raise rates than it may appear. If Iceberg asks for a breakdown of the advertiser revenue, you will, of course, provide this detail. But if they do not ask, you do not have any legal or other obligation to disclose this additional information.

Helen's perspective: You are happy to help Cade sell the company, but you also want to look out for your own interests. You have been buying two full pages in each issue at cost ($500/page) to advertise your art gallery. Given the size of your business, you would not be willing to pay the full price. You estimate the pages are each worth $3,000, which means this arrangement is worth $2,500×2 pages×6 issues = $30,000 a year to you. Even though you are a co-owner, it would not have been fair to the other investors to give you these ads at cost. However, you are not paid for your columns or features, so this has seemed like a reasonable deal to all parties. It is important that in any deal you do not receive favorable treatment relative to other investors. If the magazine is sold, you appreciate that the new owners would likely have little need or interest in having you write a column or features for them.

Note: If Helen is not available to be part of the negotiation, Cade should work to faithfully represent her interests.

Confidential Information for Pat Bennett (Buyer)

Outpsider

Summary: You are interested in purchasing *Outpsider* magazine to increase both the existing business and the online business. While the economics look very favorable, you have been authorized to spend no more than $470,000.

Your current job responsibility is selling advertising for the various Iceberg magazines. You have recently asked to join the strategic investment team and you think this move is likely. Indeed, they have given you a chance to negotiate the purchase of Outpsider Art magazine. Normally, someone from the regular M&A team would negotiate this deal, but they are currently in an all-hands-on-deck situation with a very large potential acquisition in Asia. Thus they have given you the chance to do this small deal on your own.

The value of the business comes in two parts.

1. The ongoing magazine business

- The ability to cross-sell other Iceberg media to the existing subscribers
- The ability to cross-sell Outpsider to your other readers
- The ability to raise ad prices
- The ability to sell advertisers ads across several publications
- The ability to advertise the Iceberg Art Fairs and other related businesses in Outpsider

2. The potential online business

- The ability to build a digital version of the magazine
- The ability to develop a database and app for outsider art

As a standalone, you think you could increase *Outpsider* circulation by 10%. That would increase both subscription revenue and ad revenue (as advertisers pay on a price-per-reader basis). Net of printing and postage costs, this represents an extra $100,000 in annual profits.

There might also be an opportunity to raise ad revenue even without increasing circulation. Last year, there were 100 pages of ads and $402,000 in revenue, which translates to just over $4,000 per page. Given Outpsider'sreadership, $4,500 per page would seem closer to the market price. If you make a conservative assumption that you could raise prices to $4,400/page, that would be worth $38,000 annually.

As an owner, you expect to place two new pages of ads per issue promoting other Iceberg properties. The printing and production cost for a page of the magazine is $500. While the normal market price of such a page is $4,500, a full-page ad is only worth $3,000 to you, so you would not normally buy such an ad on the open market. If you owned the magazine, however, you could give Iceberg a net gain of $2,500 ($3,000 value minus the $500 production cost) ×2 pages×6 issues = $30,000 annually.

You also think you can add one more ad page per issue and get existing *Outpsider Art* advertisers to buy some pages in your other publications, especially with a package discount. Even with a package discount price, this represents an annual gain of roughly $42,000. And, because

Iceberg publishes a large number of magazines, you are confident you can cut salary and overhead costs by at least $40,000 a year.

Therefore, you estimate that the total annual gain from the magazine business is $250,000. At a price of $470,000, this would provide a payback in under two years, which is above average for Iceberg's M&A transactions. Of course, there is some risk that the projections may not pan out. But they could also be conservative.

The ace in the hole is the website. To say it is primitive is an understatement. The homepage is little more than a placeholder with the subscription phone number. You anticipate an invesment of $200,000 to build it into a world-class site. (Here you are taking advantage of your other web assets and infrastructure. For someone doing this from scratch, it would cost double.) With the potential revenue from premium subscriptions, banner ads, and targeted ads, you estimate that the lifetime value of this site (net costs of the construction and maintenance) is $350,000.

Having the website linked to the existing *Outpsider Art* property is valuable, as is the *Outpsider Art* domain name, but you could also build a website and online magazine for outsider art under a different name. Building a website under a different name would be worth $200,000, so the extra value created by the *Outpsider Art* name and connection is $150,000.

Absent any cost savings or website, the current business has no value (it has been breaking even). Given the risk involved, the potential value of this deal is estimated to be $150k from the website plus $1m from the increased revenue and reduced costs or $1.150m in total pretax, $750k post-tax, minus what you have to pay.

The head of the M&A team has authorized you to spend up to, but absolutely no more than, $470,000 for this acquisition. Of course, it would be better if you purchased the magazine for less. Iceberg is doing a roll up and is very concerned about the price paid as this will be used as a comparable for subsequent acquisitions.

You expect this will be an all-cash deal. You were told any commitments you make to the seller cannot extend beyond three years. You hope you can reach an agreement at the meeting. If not, any negotiation will likely be postponed for at least two months till the M&A team returns from Asia.

Negotiation hints:

1. This is a hard case, and you have a limited amount of time to reach an agreement. You should not waste precious time trying to convince the sellers of things that are not true. As Mark Twain famously said: Never try to teach a pig to sing. It wastes your time and annoys the pig.

2. It is a good idea to start off the negotiation looking to better understand the interests and objectives of the other party. What are the sellers hoping to achieve with this sale? What are the sellers' hesitations and reservations? How can you help the sellers achieve their objectives? Of course, simply paying more is one way to do that, but that will drive you right into the conflict zone. You want to look for opportunities that are not zero-sum, e.g.,

things that cost you $1 but are worth more than $1 to the other parties.

3. Added value.

Case 4

Planet-Gazette-Sun

In the original version of the case, the New Haven Planet and the Hartford Gazette were contemplating a merger. The Planet has a market cap of $10m, while The Gazette has a market cap of $22m. Because of cost savings and expanded readership, the two firms together would have a market cap of $41.85 million, which is $9.85 million more than their individual valuations combined.

To keep things simple, we will think of the Gazette as the buyer and the Planet as the seller. Thus the Gazette is willing to pay as much as $19.85m and the Planet is willing to sell for anything above $10m. Absent any other bidders, we expect the two parties to settle on a price that splits the gains evenly.

In this new version of the case, we add a second potential buyer for the Planet. The new potential buyer is the Stamford Sun. The Sun is willing to pay up to $18 million for the Planet. (The Sun can create synergies, but not quite as much as the Gazette.)

Assume that all the three players in this negotiation are fully aware of all these numbers. Thus the Planet knows the Gazette is willing to pay up to $19.85m and the Sun is willing to pay up to $18m. Similarly, the Gazette and the Sun know each other's valuations as well as the Planet's current market value of $10m.

Based on the relatively small size of these papers, you should also assume there are no other potential merger partners. No joint ventures are possible. The Planet will reach a deal with either the Gazette or the Sun. If neither deal is reached, then all three parties continue with their business as usual and none of the synergies are achieved.

Note 1: The Sun has no interest in purchasing the Gazette (or vice versa), and there is no potential for all three papers to combine.

Note 2: In many contexts it is illegal to pay a firm not to compete. Thus, in this negotiation exercise, the Gazette may not pay or provide other type of compensation to the Sun for it not to compete.

Questions for Case-analysis:

1. What's the pie?

2. What has been changed in the game if the third party joined compared to the previous case?

Through closely reading and analyzing Case 4, one question may come to your mind: what if there are more than two parties in the negotiation and they do not have equal power in the game? That's an important question which discloses more about the real international business negotiation.

Compared to domestic negotiations, an international one usually involves more parties from different parts of the world and may also attract many potential participants who are not yet in the game. So understand your power in the negotiation and add your power if you are relatively powerless would essential to the outcome of the negotiation.

One crucial concept for the power distribution in a negotiation is called Added Value, which is equal to the size of the pie when one party is in the negotiation minus the size of the pie when you're not in the game. Some negotiators want the biggest slice of the pie disregarding the fact that they are the powerless participants in the game. Very unfortunately, it is highly unlikely for anyone to get more than their added value. For example, if you can bring 4 to the pie, the other two parties bring altogether 10 to the pie. If you ask for 5 of the pie, the other two parties will let you go away other than giving you 5. If you walk away, the pie only shrinks with 4. So they'd better play without you by taking back 5. So if you get more than your added value, you are in jeopardy that you may be kicked out of the game.

In this sense, the added value is the flip side of BATNA. You should always try to get more than an amount according to the concept of BATNA, but you can never get that amount based on added value. More importantly, it's not your real added value that determines the game but what other parties think about your added value that determine how much you can get from the pie.

One case dating back to 1986 in United States reveals the truth or power of added value. Back then, there was a company named Monsanto which sells aspartame under the brand NutraSweet. It was an incredibly profitable business, with over $700 million annual sales and growing still. The price was $80-90 a pound. And aspartame is 180 times sweeter than sugar. Aspartame is the patent, which was about to expire in Europe in 1988 and in US in 1992. Then a company named Holland Sweetener was thinking about getting into the market.

What is the added value for Holland Sweetener? First, they could expand the market. Would there be people who didn't use NutraSweet now would try Holland Sweetener's aspartame since they got into the market? But one feature of the product is that it's not heat stable and so it couldn't be used for bakery. The primary use of NutraSweet is in soft drinks, chewing gums and lozenges. The high profit gave Monsanto a strong incentive to find every potential user who would use NutraSweet. It was not clear whether there would be new applications or new users. Another possibility was to enter the market with lower cost. Consider the chance of building a new and better cost structure than Monsanto which were in this business for many years and managed to bring the cost to really low level. So neither new demand nor lower cost. And if Holland Sweetener wanted to get a better brand of aspartame to bead Monsanto's NutraSweet head on in the market, it was an incredibly big cost. So stop and think about the question: is it a good business decision to enter the American market for Holland Sweetener? The fact was that Holland Sweetener entered the market and spent $40 million but only got a grapefruit drink named Diet Squirt not Coke Cola or Pepsi.

If they rethought about their added value from a different angle, not from themselves, but from the other participants in the market, they would have a very different idea about what their added value was. What happened was Holland Sweetener changed the market. They could negotiate with Coke and Pepsi before they entered the market. They could argue, "We know you're happy with Monsanto and you just don't like the price for NutraSweet. Now that we're in the market, we can help you get a good price from Monsanto which doesn't benefit us much. If you want to lower the price you pay, you could offer us money for the plant, $40 million up front or a guaranteed contract with a price of $70 a pound, or give Holland Sweetener 10% of the cost savings we make possible from your new contract with Monsanto." So this is Holland Sweetener's really added value, a power to change the game, which enables them to pre-negotiate before others' negotiation.

Exercises

1. Barry is flying from New York → Baltimore → San Francisco → New York. The airfare for each leg is as listed on the chart below, and the cost of a round trip exactly doubles the one-way fare. The total airfare for the triangle route is $2,084.

$99

$742

+$1,243

$2,084

San Francisco and Baltimore must agree on how to split the cost in order to do the triangle route. How much of the $2,084 should Baltimore pay?

Note: Some of you may have noticed that it is less expensive to fly to San Francisco via Baltimore than to fly direct. However, due to flight schedules and connection times, it doesn't work to fly to San Francisco via Baltimore unless there is a reason to spend a day there. Thus the triangle route is the only option if the two parties hope to reach an agreement.

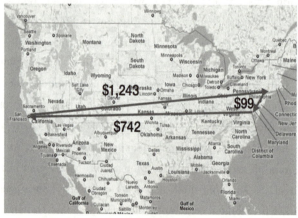

Fig 8.2

A. $1,042-Half of the total

B. $470-The full cost of New York → Baltimore plus half the fare from Baltimore → San Francisco

C. $154-Based on Baltimore's share of the total round trip ($198/(198 + 2,486)$)

D. -$102-San Francisco should pay Baltimore to do the deal.

E. $0-The stop in Baltimore doesn't cost extra, so Baltimore shouldn't have to pay anything.

2. In the original version of the case, the New Haven Planet and the Hartford Gazette were contemplating a merger. The Planet has a market cap of $10m, while the Gazette has a market cap of $22m. Because of the cost savings and expanded readership, the two firms together would have a market cap of $41.85 million, which is $9.85 million more than their individual valuations combined. To keep things simple, we will think of the Gazette as the buyer and the Planet the seller. Thus the Gazette is willing to pay as much as $19.85m and the Planet is willing to sell for anything above $10m. Absent any other bidders, we expect the two parties to settle on a price that splits the gains evenly (or splits the pie).

In this version of the case, we add a new player, the Stamford Sun, as a second potential buyer for the Planet. The Sun is willing to pay up to $18 million for the Planet. (The Sun can create synergies, but not quite as much as the Gazette.) Assume all the three players in this negotiation are fully aware of all these numbers. Thus the Planet knows the Gazette is willing to pay up to $19.85m and the Sun is willing to pay up to $18m. Similarly, the Gazette and the Sun know each other's valuations as well as the Planet's current market value of $10 m. Based on the relatively small size of these papers, you should also assume there are no other potential merger partners. No joint ventures are possible. The Planet will reach a deal with either the Gazette or the Sun. If neither deal is reached, then all the three parties continue with their business as usual and none of the synergies are achieved.

And to keep things simple, you should assume that the Sun has no interest in purchasing the Gazette (or vice versa), and there is no potential for all three papers to combine. Below is a recap of the relevant numbers:

Table 8.5

Planet alone	$10m
Gazette alone	$22m
Planet + Gazette	$41.85m
Total Synergy of Planet-Gazette merger	$9.85m
Most Gazette will pay for Planet	$19.85m
Total Synergy of Planet-Sun merger	$8m
Most Sun will pay for Planet	$18m

Given the presence of this additional bidder, what price do you expect the Planet will get?

A. $14.925m (the same as before)

B. $18.925m ($4m more)

C. $18m ($3.075m more)

D. $19.85m ($4.925m more)

3. Andrea and Beth are dining at a fine restaurant. There is a bottle of 2009 Grgich Hills

Chardonnay on the menu and the price is $100. To keep things simple, albeit unrealistic, assume that the restaurant only sells whole bottles and this is the only wine they carry.

A. Andrea would be willing to pay $110 to drink the whole bottle.

B. Andrea would be willing to pay $90 to drink half the bottle.

C. Beth would be willing to pay $80 to drink the whole bottle.

D. Beth would be willing to pay $50 to drink half the bottle.

They would like to share a bottle if it makes sense to do so (and if they can agree on how to divide the costs). To see if it makes sense, what is the pie, in dollars?

4. Consider a potential merger between two hypothetical beer companies. Prior to the merger, the first, Ann Hy, is worth $150 billion and the second, Czar Bosch, is worth $100 billion. If they merge, they will gain $30 billion in increased value from reduced costs and additional sales (in present discounted value). Thus the combined value of the new entity (called Ann Hy-Czar Bosch) would be $280 billion. How much more could Czar Bosch hope to get by using the theory of the pie instead of proportional division?

A. 0

B. $1.3 billion

C. $3 billion

D. $5 billion

E. $10 billion

F. $10.7

5. Abe and Bea have some money to invest in a CD (Certificate of Deposit). Abe has $5,000 and Bea has $20,000. Both are interested in making a 6-month investment in Synchrony Bank. The CD rates for Synchrony Bank (as of July 8, 2015) are as listed below.

Table 8.6

CD Rates and Terms					
Terms	$2,000– $14,999	$15,000– $24,999	$25,000– $49,999	$50,000– $99,999	$100,000+
	APY++	APY++	APY++	APY++	APY++
3 MONTH	0.27%	0.32%	0.32%	0.32%	0.32%
6 MONTH	0.41%	0.50%	0.60%	0.60%	0.60%
9 MONTH	0.45%	0.60%	0.65%	0.65%	0.65%
12 MONTH	1.25%	1.25%	1.25%	1.25%	1.25%
18 MONTH	1.25%	1.25%	1.25%	1.25%	1.25%
24 MONTH	1.45%	1.45%	1.45%	1.45%	1.45%
36 MONTH	1.50%	1.50%	1.50%	1.50%	1.60%
48 MONTH	1.70%	1.70%	1.75%	1.75%	1.75%
60 MONTH	2.20%	2.20%	2.25%	2.25%	2.25%

With 0.41% interest, Abe would get $5,010 in six months. With 0.50% interest, Bea would get $20,050 at the end of six months. If they pool their funds, they will be able to purchase a $25,000 CD, which pays a higher interest rate. The 0.60% interest will return $25,075 at the end of six months. Obviously, Abe gets back his $5,000 principle, and Bea gets back her $20,000 principle. How should the $75 interest be divided between the two of them?

    A. Divide up the interest according to the amount invested. Since Bea has 80% of the funds, she should get 80% of the interest, or $60 in total. This is the same as both parties getting 0.60% interest on their funds.

    B. Divide the interest in two, so each gets $37.50.

    C. Abe gets $17.50 and Bea gets $57.50.

6. Anya and Boris are planning to take a 7-day trip together. Anya would like to spend more time playing golf, and Boris would like to spend more time at the beach. The following four options are the only ones available to them.

Table 8.7

	Anya	Boris
1. All 7 Days playing Golf	10	2
2. 5 Days playing Golf / 2 at the Beach	12	3
3. 3 Days playing Golf / 4 at the Beach	9	6
4. All 7 days at the Beach	6	7

All the payoffs above are known to both parties. Anya knows that Boris does not like Option 1, so she proposes taking Option 1 off the table if Boris agrees to reciprocate. What should Boris do?

    A. Agree if Anya will take Option 3 off the table.

    B. Agree if Anya will take Option 4 off the table.

    C. Agree if Anya will take Options 3 and 4 off the table.

    D. Turn down Anya's offer and take nothing off the table.

7. You are negotiating a division of two assets, say beets and broccoli. You like broccoli more than beets, but both are good. The other side likes beets but dislikes broccoli. These preferences are known to all parties. What is your best course of action?

    A. Suggest the other side to give broccoli another try.

    B. Suggest that you divide the beets and broccoli equally between you two.

    C. Suggest that you divide the beets and broccoli equally between the two of you, and then propose to trade half your beets for all of the other side's share of broccoli.

    D. Suggest that you get all the broccoli and the other side gets all the beets.

    E. Suggest the other side to divide the broccoli and beets into two parts, and then you get to choose which part to take.

8. Anjay is selling his coffee company, and there are two potential buyers, Bert and Cecilia. Bert values the business at $40,000, while Cecilia values it at $50,000. Anjay is willing to sell for any amount over $20,000. All of these facts are known to all of the parties. If Bert has not read the book, how much do you expect **Bert** to make?

    A. $0   B. $5,000   C. $10,000   D. $15,000   E. $20,000

9. Anita and Bonita have been roommates for the past two years while they are in graduate school. Now that they're graduating, and planning to move to different cities. Their one joint asset is a rug, which both of them really like. They have agreed to play a Texas Shoot-Out to decide who gets the rug. Anita knows that Bonita values the rug somewhere between $400 and $600, and she thinks all values in this range are equally likely. Bonita knows that Anita values the rug at $300. Both sides are fully aware of all this. Furthermore, the roommates are on good terms, so you can assume neither side will act spitefully toward the other.

What offer should Anita expect to receive from Bonita?

---

10. Ai Ping is looking to buy Bao Wun's antique cabinet. Bao Wun isn't sure of the value. He has been asking for $10,000, but so far the most Ai has offered is $2,000. It looks like a deal isn't possible, so the two sides are ready to walk away. Before giving up completely, Ai suggests they try a settlement escrow and Bao agrees. Confidentially, Ai is willing to pay up to $8,000, and Bao is willing to sell for as little as $6,000. If they employ a settlement escrow, what do you expect will happen?

    A. The device will report that no deal is possible.

    B. The device will report that they should do a deal at $7,000.

    C. The device will report that there is a deal to be done.

    D. The device will report that Ai is willing to pay $8,000 and Bao is willing to sell for $6,000.

11. Brigitte has a gas station for sale, which Albert is interested in purchasing. Based on the financials, Albert firmly believes the station is worth more than $800k. However, he has been authorized to pay up to but no more than $520k. Brigitte has a firm offer for $500k but would like to get $600k. The negotiations break down. At this point, Albert has come up to $520k, and Brigitte has come down to $560k. Which of these is Albert's best course of action?

    A. Albert should come up to $530k. The station is still a great deal at that price.

    B. Albert should offer to meet halfway, at $540k.

    C. Albert should ask Brigitte for an option to buy the station for $560k if he can get approval.

    D. Albert should see if Brigitte will give him an option to buy the station at $560k if he can get approval; if she won't provide such an option, he should offer to buy the station at $540k outright.

    E. Albert should walk away.

12. Brigitte has a gas station for sale, which Albert wants to buy. If Brigitte can sell the

station for $600k, then she can take a two-year sailboat trip around the world. Brigitte shares her plans and the reason why she needs $600k. Albert honestly thinks this is the stupidest plan he's ever heard. And even if it were a good idea, this isn't a valid reason for him to pay more money. How should Albert reply?

A. Albert should explain why sailboat trips are not a cost-effective way to travel.

B. Albert should say: I appreciate that you want to take a round-the-world trip. I want to be 7 ft. tall and play for the Lakers. But that isn't going to happen either.

C. Albert should say: Why do I care how you spend your money? I'm prepared to pay what the station is worth, not what it costs you to travel around the world.

D. Albert should say: I can't just pay you more so you can travel around the world, but help me understand more about your plans so I can see how I might be able to help.

13. You get into a taxi and discover that the meter is "broken". It is late at night and taxis are hard to find. Which of these should you do?

A. Negotiate the fare at the start.

B. Start the negotiation when you arrive.

C. Start the negotiation when you arrive and have exited the taxi.

Reference

1. Fisher, Roger. Getting to Yes: Negotiating Agreement Without Giving in. Boston/New York: Houghton Mifflin Harcourt, 1991.

2. French, J. R., & Raven, B. (1959). "The bases of social power". In D. Cartwright (Ed.), Studies in social power (pp. 150-167). Ann Arbor: Institute for Social Research, University of Michigan.

3. Hall, E. T. The Hidden Dimension. New York: Doubleday, 1966.

4. Hosfstede, Geert. Cultures and Organizations: Software of the Mind, London: McGraw-Hill International Limited, 1991.

5. Lewicki, Roy J., Saunders, Daivd M., Minton, John W., Barry, Bruce. Negotiation: Readings, Exercises, and Cases. P. R. Donnelly & Sons Company, 2002.